JAVA NUMBER CRUNCHER

The Java Programmer's Guide to Numerical Computing

Ronald Mak

PRENTICE
HALL
PTR

Prentice Hall PTR
Upper Saddle River, New Jersey
www.phptr.com

ISBN 0-13-046041-9

95499

9 790130 460416

Library of Congress Cataloging-in-Publication Data

Mak, Ronald
   Java number cruncher: the Java programmer's guide to numerical computing / by
   Ronald Mak.
      p. cm.
   Includes bibliographical references and index.
   ISBN 0-13-046041-9 (pbk.)
     1. Java (Computer programming language) 2. Numerical analysis.--Data processing. I. Title.

QA76.73.J38 M335 2003
005.13'3--21   2002032956

Editorial/production supervision: *Tiffany Kuehn, Carlisle Publishers Services*
Cover design director: *Jerry Votta*
Cover design: *Talar A. Boorujy*
Art director: *Gail Cocker-Bogusz*
Interior design: *Meg Van Arsdale*
Manufacturing manager: *Alexis R. Heydt-Long*
Executive Editor: *Paul Petralia*
Editorial assistant: *Richard Winkler*
Marketing manager: *Debby vanDijk*
Full-service production manager: *Anne R. Garcia*

© 2003 by Pearson Education, Inc.
Publishing as Prentice Hall PTR
Upper Saddle River, New Jersey 07458

Prentice Hall books are widely used by corporations and government agencies for training, marketing, and resale.

For information regarding corporate and government bulk discounts please contact:
Corporate and Government Sales (800) 382-3419 or corpsales@pearsontechgroup.com

Printed in the United States of America
10 9 8 7 6 5 4 3 2 1

ISBN 0-13-046041-9

Pearson Education LTD.
Pearson Education Australia PTY, Limited
Pearson Education Singapore, Pte. Ltd.
Pearson Education North Asia Ltd.
Pearson Education Canada, Ltd.
Pearson Educación de Mexico, S.A. de C.V.
Pearson Education—Japan
Pearson Education Malaysia, Pte. Ltd.

To Java programmers with the curiosity to learn something new.

Contents

PART II   Iterative Computations   71

PART III   A Matrix Package   227

Preface

The last time I looked, the Java programming language still had $+$, $-$, $*$, $/$, and $\%$ operators to do operations with *numbers*. It may be hard to believe today, but programming is not only about Web pages, graphics, enterprise software, database systems, and computer games.

I wrote this book to remind today's programmers, especially Java programmers, that computers really are quite good at numerical computing, affectionately known as "number crunching." In fact, some numerical computing underlies most programs—for example, not too many graphics applications or interactive computer games would get very far without crunching at least a few numbers. Of course, scientific, mathematical, statistical, and financial programs rely heavily on numerical computing.

So it behooves the typical Java programmer, besides knowing the standard API alphabet soup—JFC, RMI, JSP, EJB, JDBC, and so on—to know something about how to do good numerical computing. You'll never know when a roundoff error will bite you, or why that "correct" formula you copied right out of your favorite physics textbook into your program somehow computes the wrong answer.

Another reason I wrote this book is that I'm fascinated by the dichotomies of pure mathematics and computer science. On one hand, you have mathematics, a rigorous, abstract world where it is possible to prove, absolutely, that a computation is correct. On the other hand, you have computers, where computations are, well, they're *fast*. And yet, mathematicians and computer scientists can work together to devise some very clever ways to enable computers to do mathematics and, in the great majority of cases, to compute the *right* answer.

This book is an introduction to numerical computing. It is not a textbook on numerical methods or numerical analysis, although it certainly shows how to program many key numerical algorithms in Java. We'll examine these algorithms, enough to get a feel for how they work and why they're useful, without formally proving why they work. Because Java is ideal for doing so, we'll also demonstrate many of the algorithms with interactive, graphical programs. After seeing how we can dodge some of the pitfalls of floating-point and integer computations, we'll explore programs that solve equations for x, do interpolation and integration, solve differential equations and systems of linear equations, and more.

Numerical computing is not all work, either. This book also contains several chapters on lighter (but not necessarily less useful) topics, including computing thousands of digits of π, using different ways to generate random numbers, looking for patterns in the prime numbers, and creating the intricately beautiful fractal images.

I tried hard to keep the math in this book at the freshman calculus level or below—knowledge of high school algebra should be enough for most of it.

All the interactive programs in this book can run either as applets or as stand-alone programs. My friends and I have tested them with the Netscape 4.7 browser running on Windows, Linux, and Solaris, with Microsoft Internet Explorer 6.0 running on the PC, and Microsoft Internet Explorer 5.1 running on the Macintosh. I've tested the stand-alone programs on my Windows 98 PC with JDK 1.2, 1.3, and 1.4. Of course, there's no guarantee they'll all work perfectly for you, but the source code for all the programs, along with instructions on how to compile and run them, are available for downloading.

I wrote all the programs strictly as illustrative examples for this book. You're free to use the source code anyway you like, but bear in mind that this is *not* fully tested, commercial-quality code. Neither Prentice Hall nor I can be responsible for anything bad that may happen if you use these programs.

Although creating this book was primarily a solitary activity, I must acknowledge the help I got from several longtime good friends. Steve Drach, Bob Nicholson, and Owen Densmore tried out my demo applets to let me know whether they were any good and whether they ran properly in different browsers on various machine platforms (PCs, Macintoshes, and Sun workstations). Steve and I had a couple days of fun seeing how fast I could get my π programs to run.

I give extra special thanks to my technical reviewer, Wes Mitchell, another longtime friend who is currently an enterprise architect extraordinaire and formerly a mathematics and computer science professor. Wes made many suggestions for improving the text and caught some really embarrassing misstatements. (Any remaining errors are intentional—I want to see if you're paying attention.)

My agent from Waterside Productions, Danielle Jatlow, and my editor at Prentice Hall, Paul Petralia, got this project underway and kept it going.

I had a lot of fun writing this book and its programs, and I hope that comes through in the text. If you're inspired to learn more about any of the topics, then I will be very happy. You can send me e-mail at *ron@apropos-logic.com* or write to me at

Apropos Logic
P.O. Box 20884
San Jose, CA 95160

How to Download the Source Code

You can download the source code for all the Java programs in this book, along with instructions on how to compile and run them, from Prentice Hall at *http://www.phptr.com/mak*.

You can also get the source code and instructions from the author's Web site at *http://www.apropos-logic.com/nc/,* where you can play with all the applets.

PART I

WHY GOOD COMPUTATIONS GO BAD

Simply copying formulas out of a math or statistics textbook to plug into a program will almost certainly lead to wrong results. The first part of this book covers the pitfalls of basic numerical computation.

Chapter 1 discusses floating-point numbers in general and how they're different from the real numbers of mathematics. Not understanding these differences, such as the occurrence of roundoff errors, and not obeying some basic laws of algebra can lead to computations that go bad.

Chapter 2 looks at the seemingly benign integer types. They don't behave entirely as the whole numbers of mathematics do. Arithmetic operations such as addition, subtraction, and multiplication take place not on a number line, but on a clock face.

Finally, in Chapter 3, we look at how Java implements its floating-point types. We examine the IEEE 754 floating-point standard and see how well Java meets its provisions.

CHAPTER 1

FLOATING-POINT NUMBERS ARE NOT REAL!

When the designers of the early programming languages FORTRAN and ALGOL named one of their numeric data types REAL, was it simply for convenience, or were they being optimistic?

Just how close is Java's float type to the real number system of mathematics? Or, for that matter, what about the int type and the mathematical set of integers (the whole numbers)? We know there are gremlins such as overflows and roundoff errors, but there may be more nasty stuff lurking. What other pitfalls are out there?

1.1 Roundoff Errors

Consider the common fractions $\frac{1}{2}, \frac{1}{3}, \frac{1}{4}, \frac{1}{5}, \frac{1}{6}$, and $\frac{1}{7}$. In the decimal, or base 10, number system, we can represent $\frac{1}{2}, \frac{1}{4}$, and $\frac{1}{5}$ exactly as 0.5, 0.25, and 0.2, respectively. In the decimal system, we can represent any fraction whose denominator divides evenly into a power of 10 exactly as a decimal fraction. But the denominator 3 doesn't divide evenly, and so $\frac{1}{3}$ repeats infinitely: 0.3333 . . . . Neither does the denominator 6, and $\frac{1}{6}$ is 0.16666 . . . . Neither does the denominator 7, and $\frac{1}{7}$ is 0.142857142857 . . ., where the last group of six digits repeats infinitely.

Like most modern computers, the Java virtual machine uses the binary, or base 2, number system. How well can we represent these fractions in base 2? Program 1–1 prints and sums some of their values. See Listing 1–1.

Listing 1–1 Fractions.

```java
package numbercruncher.program1_1;

/**
 * PROGRAM 1-1: Fractions
 *
 * Print and sum the values of the fractions 1/2, 1/3, 1/4, and 1/5
 * to look for any roundoff errors.
 */
public class Fractions
{
    private static final float HALF    = 1/2f;
    private static final float THIRD   = 1/3f;
    private static final float QUARTER = 1/4f;
    private static final float FIFTH   = 1/5f;
    private static final float SIXTH   = 1/6f;
    private static final float SEVENTH = 1/7f;

    private static final int FACTOR = 840;

    public static void main(String args[])
    {
        System.out.println("1/2 = " + HALF);
        System.out.println("1/3 = " + THIRD);
        System.out.println("1/4 = " + QUARTER);
        System.out.println("1/5 = " + FIFTH);
        System.out.println("1/6 = " + SIXTH);
        System.out.println("1/7 = " + SEVENTH);

        float sum = 0;
        System.out.println();

        for (int i = 0; i < FACTOR; ++i) sum += HALF;
        System.out.println("1/2 summed " + FACTOR + " times = " + sum +
                           " (should be " + FACTOR/2 + ")");

        sum = 0;
        for (int i = 0; i < FACTOR; ++i) sum += THIRD;
        System.out.println("1/3 summed " + FACTOR + " times = " + sum +
                           " (should be " + FACTOR/3 + ")");

        sum = 0;
        for (int i = 0; i < FACTOR; ++i) sum += QUARTER;
        System.out.println("1/4 summed " + FACTOR + " times = " + sum +
                           " (should be " + FACTOR/4 + ")");
```

```
        sum = 0;
        for (int i = 0; i < FACTOR; ++i) sum += FIFTH;
        System.out.println("1/5 summed " + FACTOR + " times = " + sum +
                           " (should be " + FACTOR/5 + ")");

        sum = 0;
        for (int i = 0; i < FACTOR; ++i) sum += SIXTH;
        System.out.println("1/6 summed " + FACTOR + " times = " + sum +
                           " (should be " + FACTOR/6 + ")");

        sum = 0;
        for (int i = 0; i < FACTOR; ++i) sum += SEVENTH;
        System.out.println("1/7 summed " + FACTOR + " times = " + sum +
                           " (should be " + FACTOR/7 + ")");
    }
}
```

Output:

```
1/2 = 0.5
1/3 = 0.33333334
1/4 = 0.25
1/5 = 0.2
1/6 = 0.16666667
1/7 = 0.14285715

1/2 summed 840 times = 420.0 (should be 420)
1/3 summed 840 times = 279.99915 (should be 280)
1/4 summed 840 times = 210.0 (should be 210)
1/5 summed 840 times = 167.99858 (should be 168)
1/6 summed 840 times = 139.99957 (should be 140)
1/7 summed 840 times = 120.001114 (should be 120)
```

We appended an f to some of the numeric literals in the program to make them single-precision float numbers. That way, 1/2f uses floating-point instead of integer arithmetic.

The first set of the program's output lines doesn't look too bad; $\frac{1}{2}$, $\frac{1}{4}$, and $\frac{1}{5}$ appear to be fine. There's a small roundoff error for $\frac{1}{3}$ — it's a bit odd that the rightmost digit got rounded *up*, but the error is quite small. There are similarly small roundoff errors for $\frac{1}{6}$ and $\frac{1}{7}$.

The second set of the output lines shows what happens when we let even small errors accumulate. Although there was a rounding *up* error in $\frac{1}{3}$, we now see that it accumulated a rounding *down* error! Evidently, there was initially a tiny hidden error in $\frac{1}{5}$ that accumulated a rounding down error. $\frac{1}{6}$ also accumulated a rounding down error, and $\frac{1}{7}$ accumulated a rounding up error. $\frac{1}{2}$ and $\frac{1}{4}$ apparently had no errors, but then, of course, they are exact powers of 2: $\frac{1}{2} = 2^{-1}$ and $\frac{1}{4} = 2^{-2}$.

1.2 Error Explosion

Before we look at a much more dramatic example of roundoff errors, one that does not involve any loops, let's define a few terms:

DEFINITION: **Absolute error** $= |\text{(computed value)} - \text{(correct value)}|$

DEFINITION: **Relative error** $= \dfrac{\text{(absolute error)}}{\text{(correct value)}}$

DEFINITION: **Percentage error** $= \text{(relative error)} \times 100\%$

Relative error is the ratio of the absolute error to the correct value. We can compare different errors meaningfully by comparing their relative errors. A percentage error expresses a relative error as a percentage.

For example, we saw how $\frac{1}{2}$ can be represented exactly. The fraction $\frac{10,000,001}{20,000,000}$ should be very close to $\frac{1}{2}$ — the difference is merely $\frac{1}{20,000,000}$. Now, if we invert this difference, we should get the value of the denominator—namely, 20,000,000. In equation form, we have

$$\frac{1}{\left(\dfrac{10,000,001}{20,000,000}\right) - \left(\dfrac{1}{2}\right)} = \frac{1}{\left(\dfrac{1}{20,000,000}\right)} = 20,000,000$$

If we assume that we're doing some computation whose correct result should be $\frac{1}{2}$, but we got $\frac{10,000,001}{20,000,000}$ instead, then our absolute error is $\frac{1}{20,000,000}$.

Program 1–2 performs these computations, where variable a equals $\frac{10,000,001}{20,000,000}$ and variable b equals $\frac{1}{2}$. See Listing 1–2.

Listing 1–2 Roundoff errors.

```
package numbercruncher.program1_2;

/**
 * PROGRAM 1-2: Roundoff Errors
 *
 * Demonstrate how a tiny roundoff error
 * can explode into a much larger one.
 */
public class RoundoffErrors
{
    public static void main(String args[])
    {
```

```
        float denominator = 20000000;
        float a           = 10000001/denominator;
        float b           = 1/2f;
        float diff1       = Math.abs(a - b);
        float pctError1   = 100*diff1/b;

        float inverse     = 1/diff1;
        float diff2       = Math.abs(inverse - denominator);
        float pctError2   = 100*diff2/denominator;

        System.out.println("       a = " + a);
        System.out.println("       b = " + b);
        System.out.println("   diff1 = " + diff1);
        System.out.println("pctError1 = " + pctError1 + "%");

        System.out.println();
        System.out.println(" inverse = " + inverse);
        System.out.println("   diff2 = " + diff2);
        System.out.println("pctError2 = " + pctError2 + "%");

        System.out.println();
        System.out.println("  factor = " + pctError2/pctError1);
    }
}
```

Output:

```
      a = 0.50000006
      b = 0.5
  diff1 = 5.9604645E-8
pctError1 = 1.1920929E-5%

 inverse = 1.6777216E7
  diff2 = 3222784.0
pctError2 = 16.11392%

 factor = 1351733.6
```

We see in Listing 1–2 that $diff1$, which should be $\frac{1}{20,000,000}$ $(= 5 \times 10^{-8})$, is computed to be nearly 6×10^{-8}, but the computed percentage error $pctError1$ is very small, less than 0.000012%. However, the computed inverse of $diff1$ is off from 20,000,000 $(= 2 \times 10^{7})$ by the large value of $diff2$, and now the percentage error $pctError2$ is over 16%. Thus, the very small original percentage error exploded by a factor of over 1.3 million! How can this happen with just a few lines of computations that have no loops?

Let's first examine the value of $diff1$. $\frac{10,000,000}{20,000,000}$ is 0.5 exactly, and $\frac{1}{20,000,000}$ is 0.00000005 exactly, so $\frac{10,000,001}{20,000,000}$ is 0.50000005 exactly. But due to roundoff errors, the displayed value of a is

0.50000006. That isn't too bad—of the eight digits after the decimal point, only the last one is wrong, and it's only off by 1. Now look what happens when we subtract 0.5:

$$
\begin{array}{r}
0.50000006 \\
-0.50000000 \\
\hline
0.00000006
\end{array}
$$

We lose all of the correct digits and end up with the incorrect one. The value of diff1 displays as 5.9604645E-8—only the first of its eight digits is correct, since the exact value is 0.00000005, or 5.0E-8 . The error in the value of diff1 comes from subtracting one value from another that is very close—in this case, $\frac{1}{2}$ from $\frac{10,000,001}{20,000,000}$. Such a subtraction causes the loss of most of the significant digits and leaves behind a difference consisting of mainly the incorrect digits from the right ends of the values.

> DEFINITION: A **cancellation error** occurs when most of the significant digits are lost during the subtraction of two very nearly equal values.

Then, we proceed to compound the error. We know that dividing a numerator by a very small denominator (one close to 0) produces a quotient whose value is much larger than the numerator. The value of inverse is 1 divided by the value of diff1 . The value of diff1 is very small, and it is mostly wrong, so the division greatly magnifies the first error we got from the subtraction.

Now, you may be thinking that this example is very contrived. Very true, but its point is to demonstrate that *it's very possible to generate very large computational errors with just a few statements, even when the operations are mathematically correct.*

So, what can we do about cancellation errors? First of all, just knowing that they can happen is a major step. We need to be very wary of the results from subsequent calculations. But often, with some forethought, we can perform some algebraic manipulations and rewrite our algorithms to lessen or even avoid cancellation errors altogether.

A classic example of how to do this is the hoary quadratic formula we learned in grade school to compute the two solutions to the equation $ax^2 + bx + c = 0$, where $a \neq 0$:

$$
x = \frac{-b \pm \sqrt{b^2 - 4ac}}{2a}
$$

If the value of $4ac$ is very small compared with the value of b, then the value of $\sqrt{b^2 - 4ac}$ is very close to $|b|$. In the case that b is positive, $-b + \sqrt{b^2 - 4ac}$ can cause a cancellation error, and the corresponding computed root would be wrong. So, we compute one root x_1 using $-b - \sqrt{b^2 - 4ac}$, which doesn't have the cancellation error. From the quadratic formula, we know that, if x_1 and x_2 are roots, then $x_1 x_2 = \frac{c}{a}$, and so $x_2 = \frac{c}{ax_1}$. In the case that b is negative, we compute x_1 using $-b + \sqrt{b^2 - 4ac}$ instead.

In general, many roundoff errors can be prevented, or at least lessened, if we try to be smarter about how to code formulas into our programs. Chapter 4 has more to say about techniques for dealing with roundoff errors.

1.3 Real Numbers versus Floating-Point Numbers

Roundoff errors do not occur with pure mathematics. They are a by-product of *computation,* whether by hand or by computer. Since we're working with computers, let's see what some of the differences are between pure math and computer math in order to understand why roundoff errors happen.

In pure math, the real numbers are infinite. There is neither a smallest number nor a largest number. Between any two numbers, no matter how close together their values are, there exists yet another number. In other words, the real numbers are continuous—there are no gaps. Our intuition also tells us that the numbers are all "evenly distributed" along the real number line. Each number is also infinitely precise—the digits after the decimal point go on and on, whether it's a single repeating digit (including 0), a repeating group of digits, or (in the case of an irrational number) just more and more digits without any apparent pattern.

Now let's consider the numbers of computer math—specifically, Java's floating-point numbers. Chapter 3 examines these numbers in detail, but we already know enough to point out some of their major differences with the real numbers.

First and foremost, the floating-point numbers are not infinite. There is a smallest one, and there is a largest one. There is only a fixed number of floating-point numbers, and so there are gaps between them. Single-precision floating-point numbers (type `float`) have about eight significant decimal digits, and double-precision floating-point numbers (type `double`) have about 17 significant decimal digits. We have to use the word *about* because, internally, the numbers are represented in base 2, not base 10, and the conversion between the internal binary form and the external decimal text form introduces some fuzziness.

How are the floating-point numbers distributed along the number line? Again, Chapter 3 goes into this with much greater detail, but it suffices to say for now that a floating-point number is stored internally in two parts, a *significand*[1] and an *exponent,* similar to scientific notation. Each part can be positive or negative. So, the number 0.012345 is stored as 1.2345 and –2, which together represent 1.2345×10^{-2}. (We'll stick to base 10 for these examples.) Unless the number is 0, the significand always has a single, nonzero digit to the left of the decimal point.

To answer the distribution question, let's simplify matters by assuming that the significand is limited to a single decimal digit and that the exponent is restricted to only the values -1, 0, and $+1$. Table 1–1 lists all the positive values we can represent.

In Table 1–1, note that most of the 0 row is empty. The special case is when the significand and the exponent are both 0—the value is 0 itself. A similar table with negative significand values along the left would list all of the negative values we can represent.

---

[1] Called the *mantissa* in older textbooks.

Table 1–1   All of the positive values (and 0) that we can represent when we limit the significand to a single decimal digit and we restrict the exponent to only the values -1, 0, and 1. The positive significand values are on the left at the head of each row, and the exponent values are on top at the head of each column. The representable values are in bold within the table.

	-1	0	$+1$
0		**0**	
1	$1\times10^{-1} = \mathbf{0.1}$	$1\times10^{0} = \mathbf{1}$	$1\times10^{1} = \mathbf{10}$
2	$2\times10^{-1} = \mathbf{0.2}$	$2\times10^{0} = \mathbf{2}$	$2\times10^{1} = \mathbf{20}$
3	$3\times10^{-1} = \mathbf{0.3}$	$3\times10^{0} = \mathbf{3}$	$3\times10^{1} = \mathbf{30}$
4	$4\times10^{-1} = \mathbf{0.4}$	$4\times10^{0} = \mathbf{4}$	$4\times10^{1} = \mathbf{40}$
5	$5\times10^{-1} = \mathbf{0.5}$	$5\times10^{0} = \mathbf{5}$	$5\times10^{1} = \mathbf{50}$
6	$6\times10^{-1} = \mathbf{0.6}$	$6\times10^{0} = \mathbf{6}$	$6\times10^{1} = \mathbf{60}$
7	$7\times10^{-1} = \mathbf{0.7}$	$7\times10^{0} = \mathbf{7}$	$7\times10^{1} = \mathbf{70}$
8	$8\times10^{-1} = \mathbf{0.8}$	$8\times10^{0} = \mathbf{8}$	$8\times10^{1} = \mathbf{80}$
9	$9\times10^{-1} = \mathbf{0.9}$	$9\times10^{0} = \mathbf{9}$	$9\times10^{1} = \mathbf{90}$

Figure 1–1 plots the represented positive values on the number line. In (a), we see the numbers from 0 through 1; in (b), we see the numbers from 0 through 10; in (c), we see the numbers from 0 through 90. Thus, it is apparent that the numbers are not evenly distributed—the gaps between numbers widen by a factor of 10 with each increase in the exponent value. There are infinitely many numbers we *cannot* represent, such as 0.25 or 48.

Of course, we would be able to represent more numbers if we allowed more digits in the significand, and their range would be wider if we allowed more exponent values. But the key facts remain—there will be only a finite number of representable numbers, and they will not be evenly distributed.

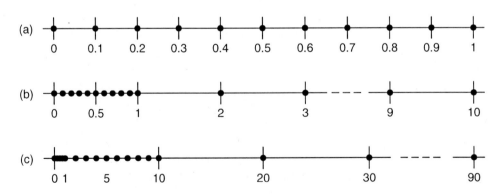

Figure 1–1   The representable floating-point numbers plotted on the number line. (a) From 0 through 1, (b) from 0 through 10, and (c) from 0 through 90.

So let's return to our original question of where roundoff errors come from. Whenever a computed value lies between two representable values (and, more likely, it will not land right *on* a representable value), the computed value is replaced by the nearest representable value. The resulting roundoff error is the difference between the computed value and the representable value.

> DEFINITION: **Roundoff error** is the difference between an exact value and its representable value.

1.4 Precision and Accuracy

We often use the words *precision* and *accuracy* when we discuss floating-point computation.

> DEFINITION: The **precision** of a floating-point value is a measure of the number of significant digits it has in its significand. The more significant digits a floating-point value has, the more precise it is.

Double-precision `double` values are more precise than single-precision `float` values. The `double` literal 0.3333333333333333 is a more precise representation of the exact value $\frac{1}{3}$ than the `float` literal 0.3333333f.

We mentioned in the previous section that having more significant digits in the significand allows us to represent more values, thus making the set of representable values more "finely grained." With higher precision values, we can have a representable value that is closer to an exact value than is possible with lesser precision values. We saw this in the previous paragraph—0.3333333333333333 is closer to $\frac{1}{3}$ than is 0.3333333f.

> DEFINITION: The **accuracy** of a floating-point value is its *correctness,* or closeness to a true exact value.

If the true value is exactly $\frac{1}{3}$, but the computed `double` value is 0.3444444444444444, then we can say that the `double` value is inaccurate, despite its precision, because most of its significant digits are wrong. On the other hand, the `float` literal 0.3333333f is more accurate because its value is closer to the true value. *Computational errors, such as roundoff and cancellation, affect a floating-point value's accuracy.* Increasing the precision from single to double gives us the *potential* for increased accuracy, but it doesn't guarantee it.

1.5 Disobeying the Laws of Algebra

The real numbers of pure math always obey the laws of algebra. For example, the associative law of addition states that, for any real numbers a, b, and c,

$$(a + b) + c = a + (b + c)$$

Similarly, the associative law of multiplication states that

$$(ab)c = a(bc)$$

So how do the floating-point numbers behave? Program 1–3 indicates that floating-point addition and multiplication are *not* always associative. See Listing 1–3.

Listing 1-3 Failures of the associative laws for floating-point addition and multiplication.

```
package numbercruncher.program1_3;

/**
 * PROGRAM 1-3: Not Associative
 *
 * Demonstrate that floating-point addition and multiplication
 * are not associative operations.
 */
public class NotAssociative
{
    public static void main(String args[])
    {
        // Addition: Insufficient precision

        float a = 1;
        float b = 3.0E-8f;
        float c = 4.0E-8f;

        System.out.println("a = " + a);
        System.out.println("b = " + b);
        System.out.println("c = " + c);

        float s1 = (a+b)+c;
        float s2 = a+(b+c);

        System.out.println();
        System.out.println("(a+b)+c = " + s1);
        System.out.println("a+(b+c) = " + s2);

        // Addition: Roundoff error
        float d   = 0.54385f;
        float e   = 0.9599806f;
        float f   = 0.2252711f;
```

```
        System.out.println();
        System.out.println("d = " + d);
        System.out.println("e = " + e);
        System.out.println("f = " + f);

        s1 = (d+e)+f;
        s2 = d+(e+f);

        System.out.println();
        System.out.println("(d+e)+f = " + s1);
        System.out.println("d+(e+f) = " + s2);

        // Multipication: Underflow

        float u = 0.5f;
        float v = 1.0E-45f;
        float w = 3.0E38f;

        System.out.println();
        System.out.println("u = " + u);
        System.out.println("v = " + v);
        System.out.println("w = " + w);

        float p1 = (u*v)*w;
        float p2 = u*(v*w);

        System.out.println();
        System.out.println("(u*v)*w = " + p1);
        System.out.println("u*(v*w) = " + p2);

        // Multiplication: Roundoff error

        float x = 0.9091322f;
        float y = 0.8606576f;
        float z = 0.5684686f;

        System.out.println();
        System.out.println("x = " + x);
        System.out.println("y = " + y);
        System.out.println("z = " + z);

        p1 = (x*y)*z;
        p2 = x*(y*z);

        System.out.println();
        System.out.println("(x*y)*z = " + p1);
        System.out.println("x*(y*z) = " + p2);
    }
}
```

Output:

```
a = 1.0
b = 3.0E-8
c = 4.0E-8

(a+b)+c = 1.0
a+(b+c) = 1.0000001

d = 0.54385
e = 0.9599806
f = 0.2252711

(d+e)+f = 1.7291018
d+(e+f) = 1.7291017

u = 0.5
v = 1.4E-45
w = 3.0E38

(u*v)*w = 0.0
u*(v*w) = 2.1019477E-7

x = 0.9091322
y = 0.8606576
z = 0.5684686

(x*y)*z = 0.4447991
x*(y*z) = 0.44479907
```

We can analyze Program 1–3's output. In the first addition example, the exact value of (a+b) is 1.00000003, but single-precision float has insufficient precision to represent that sum, and so it is rounded down to 1. Adding the value of c to that sum also results in the rounded down value of 1 for the same reason. However, the exact value of (b+c) is 0.00000007, and 1 plus that sum is exactly 1.00000007, which, to be a float value, is rounded up to 1.0000001.

In the second addition example, the exact sum of (d+e)+f and d+(e+f) falls between two representable float values. Adding one way rounds up, and adding the other way rounds down.

In the first multiplication example, (u*v) underflows because the value of v is so small, causing the product to be set to 0, and so (u*v)*w is also 0. However the product of (v*w) is a valid float value greater than 0, and then so is u*(v*w) .

The second multiplication example is similar to the second addition example. The product of (x*y)*z and x*(y*z) falls between two representable float values. Multiplying one way rounds up, and multiplying the other way rounds down.

How often do the floating-point addition and multiplication operations fail their associative laws? Do the failures occur so rarely that we can safely ignore them? Program 1–4 repeatedly generates sets of three random floating-point values to test addition and multiplication. See Listing 1–4.

Listing 1–4 The percentage of failures of the associative laws for floating-point addition and multiplication.

```
package numbercruncher.program1_4;

import java.util.Random;

/**
 * PROGRAM 1-4: Not Associative Percentage
 *
 * Figure out what percentage of floating-point additions
 * and multiplications fail their associative laws.
 */
public class NotAssocPercentage
{
    private static final int TRIALS = 1000000;  // one million

    public static void main(String args[])
    {
        Random random = new Random();

        int addCount  = 0;
        int multCount = 0;

        // Loop to perform trials.
        for (int i = 0; i < TRIALS; ++i) {

            // Generate three random floating-point values.
            float a = random.nextFloat();
            float b = random.nextFloat();
            float c = random.nextFloat();

            // Add both ways.
            float s1 = (a+b)+c;
            float s2 = a+(b+c);

            // Multiply both ways.
            float p1 = (a*b)*c;
            float p2 = a*(b*c);

            // Compare sums and products and count the failures.
            if (s1 != s2) ++addCount;
            if (p1 != p2) ++multCount;

        }
        System.out.println((100*addCount)/TRIALS + "% failures of the " +
                        "associative law of addition.");
        System.out.println((100*multCount)/TRIALS + "% failures of the " +
                        "associative law of multiplication.");
```

```
    }
}
```

Output:

```
17% failures of the associative law of addition.
34% failures of the associative law of multiplication.
```

Well, it's probably not a good idea to ignore the failures!

Floating-point arithmetic also fails the distributive law, which states that, for any real values *a, b,* and *c,*

$$a(b + c) = ab + ac$$

and the cancellation law (not to be confused with the cancellation error, defined earlier), which states that, for any real values *a, b,* and *c,*

If $ac = bc$ and $c \neq 0$, then $a = b$

Program 1–5, shown in Listing 1–5, demonstrates that we cannot count on the multiplicative inverse law, which states that, for any real value *a,*

$$\text{If } a \neq 0, \text{ then } a\left(\frac{1}{a}\right) = \left(\frac{1}{a}\right)a = 1$$

Listing 1–5 The percentage failures of the inverse law for floating-point multiplication.

```
package numbercruncher.program1_5;

import java.util.Random;

/**
 * PROGRAM 1-5: No Multiplicative Inverse
 *
 * Figure out what percentage of floating-point
 * multiplicative inverses fail.
 */
public class NoMultInverse
{
    private static final int TRIALS = 1000000;  // one million

    public static void main(String args[])
    {
        Random random = new Random();
```

```
       int failCount = 0;

       // Loop to perform trials.
       for (int i = 0; i < TRIALS; ++i) {

           // Generate a random floating-point value.
           float a = random.nextFloat();

           // Multiply both ways.

           float p1 = a*(1f/a);
           float p2 = (1f/a)*a;

           // Compare products and count the failures.
           if ((p1 != 1) || (p2 != 1)) ++failCount;
       }

       System.out.println((100*failCount)/TRIALS + "% failures of the " +
                           "multiplicative inverse law.");
   }
}
```

Output:

```
15% failures of the multiplicative inverse law.
```

If it's any consolation, floating-point addition and multiplication *do* obey the commutative laws, which state that, for any real values *a* and *b*,

$$a + b = b + a$$

and

$$ab = bc$$

Whew!

1.6 And What about Those Integers?

We've seen how the floating-point numbers can get us into trouble if we're not careful. We may reasonably conclude that, at best, the floating-point numbers are only a crude simulation of the real number system. It's quite amazing that we can make them work as well as they do, as we'll see in the following chapters. But what about the integer numbers?

Java represents the whole numbers with integer types. Integer numbers are certainly simpler and generally faster than floating-point numbers in computations, but are they absolutely safe to use? Of course they're not. After all, we are dealing with computers here. We'll examine the integer types in detail in the next chapter before we return to floating-point numbers in Chapter 3.

References

Chapra, Steven C., and Raymond P. Canale, *Numerical Methods for Engineers,* 3rd edition, New York: WCB/McGraw-Hill, 1998.

Chapra uses a clever illustration to explain the differences between accuracy and precision on pages 59–60.

Hamming, Richard W., *Numerical Methods for Scientists and Engineers,* 2nd edition, New York: Dover, 1986.

This text discusses the quadratic formula and how to rearrange formulas in general in Sections 3-1 through 3-5.

Sterbenz, Pat H., *Floating-Point Computation,* Englewood Cliffs, NJ: Prentice-Hall, 1974.

This entire book is on floating-point arithmetic. It proves that floating-point arithmetic fails certain laws of algebra in Section 1.6.

CHAPTER 2

HOW WHOLESOME ARE THE INTEGERS?

Compared with what we saw of the floating-point types in Chapter 1, the integer types must seem pretty tame and safe! We'll see how valid that assumption is in this chapter.

Java has five integer types named by the keywords `byte`, `short`, `char`, `int`, and `long`. The values of these types represent the whole numbers of pure mathematics, which we use for counting and for doing arithmetic that doesn't involve fractions. We must use the word *represent* because Java's integers, unlike the whole numbers, are not infinite.

2.1 The Integer Types and Operations

Table 2–1 shows the bit size, the minimum value, and the maximum value of each of Java's integer types.

Except for type `char`, which does not have negative values, the absolute value of the minimum value of each type is one greater than the maximum value of that type. (We'll see in Section 2.2

Table 2–1   Java's integer types.

Integer Type	Size (Bits)	Minimum Value	Maximum Value
byte	8	-128	127
short	16	$-32,768$	32,767
char	16	0	65,535
int	32	$-2,147,483,648$	2,147,483,647
long	64	$-9,223,372,036,854,775,808$	9,223,372,036,854,775,807

Table 2–2   The type of the result depends on the types of the operands when performing the integer addition, subtraction, multiplication, division, and remainder arithmetic operations.

Operand 1	Operand 2	Result
int	int	int
int	long	long
long	int	long
long	long	long

why this is so.) Except for `char`, exactly one half of each type's values are negative, and the other half consists of 0 and the positive values.

Java supports various arithmetic operations on `int` and `long` values. At run time, it automatically converts `byte`, `short`, and `char` values to `int` before it performs an operation. The *additive operations* are addition and subtraction, and the *multiplicative operations* are multiplication, division, and remainder. The *postfix operations* are postincrement and postdecrement, and the *unary operations* include negation, pre-increment, and predecrement.

The result type of a postfix or a unary operation is the same as the type of its single operand. Table 2–2 shows how the result type of an additive or a multiplicative operation depends on the types of its two operands.

The result is type `int` only if both operands are type `int`. Even if we multiply two `int` values, the product is an `int`, not a `long`. Integer arithmetic never throws an exception if an overflow occurs. (We'll see in Section 2.3 what really happens during an overflow.) The only exception that it does throw is an `ArithmeticException` if we attempt to divide by zero during a division or a remainder operation.

2.2 Signed Magnitude versus Two's-Complement

How does the Java virtual machine encode integer values internally in binary?

Positive values are straightforward. If we imagine that Java has a primitive integer type "nybble" (half a byte) of 4-bit integer values, then the bit patterns for the values 0 through 7 are

```
0   0000
1   0001
2   0010
3   0011
4   0100
5   0101
6   0110
7   0111
```

We reserve the leftmost bit to represent the sign: 0 for positive and 1 for negative.

Now, what about the negative numbers? One encoding format, *signed magnitude,* simply sets the sign bit to 1:

```
-0   1000
-1   1001
-2   1010
-3   1011
-4   1100
-5   1101
-6   1110
-7   1111
```

But signed magnitude has two undesirable features. First, there are two zeros, positive (bit pattern 0000) and negative (bit pattern 1000). Second, we can't use the normal binary addition logic when we have negative values—for example,

```
 6   0110          -3   1011
-3   1011          -2   1010
 1   0001           5   0101
```

Clearly, the preceding sums are wrong. Special negative number logic would be required to get the correct answers.

Another encoding format is *two's-complement.* It encodes the positive values the same way as signed magnitude, with the leftmost bit as the sign. However, it forms each negative value by complementing each bit of the positive value and then adding 1. So, for example, to form the two's-complement representation of −6,

```
    Start with positive 6:   0110
    Complement each bit:     1001
                  Add 1:        1
       Gives negative 6:      1010
```

All of the negative values are encoded as follows:

```
-1   1111
-2   1110
-3   1101
-4   1100
-5   1011
-6   1010
-7   1001
-8   1000
```

There is only a single 0, and there is room for another negative value, -8. Now, we can also use the normal binary addition logic when we have negative values and still get the correct answers:

```
 6  0110        -3  1101
-3  1101        -2  1110
 3  0011        -5  1011
```

The Java virtual machine uses the two's-complement format for its `byte`, `short`, `int`, and `long` values. A value of the `char` type does not have a sign bit—all 16 bits encode zero or a positive value.

2.3 Whole Numbers versus Integer Numbers

In Chapter 1, we emphasized how floating-point numbers are not the same as the real numbers of pure mathematics. So far, we've conceded that Java's integer numbers differ from pure math's whole numbers in a major way—the integer numbers are not infinite. Well, at least we don't have to worry about roundoff errors! But how does the finiteness of the integer types affect integer arithmetic?

We first learned how to add and subtract in grade school by using a number line. For example, Figure 2–1 shows that $2 + 3 = 5$.

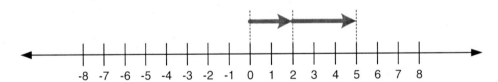

Figure 2–1 $2 + 3 = 5$ on the number line.

Figure 2–2 shows that $6 - 4 = 2$.

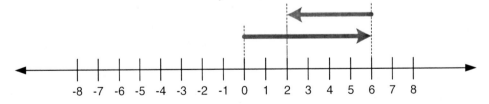

Figure 2–2 $6 - 4 = 2$ on the number line.

The number line extends infinitely in both the positive and negative directions.

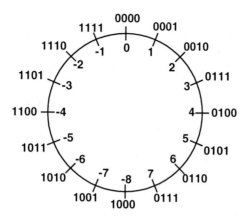

Figure 2–3 Type nybble's values arranged on a clock face.

But Java's integers are not infinite. When we add 1 to the maximum, or most positive, value of an integer type, the sum "wraps around" to the minimum, or most negative, value of that type. So, instead of an infinite linear number line, we should use a circular arrangement, like a clock face.

Figure 2–3 shows how we arrange the values of our pretend nybble integer type. The negative values are in the two's-complement format. Note how the binary values simply increment by 1, from 0000 through 1111 (decimal 0 through –1), as we move clockwise around the face. In particular, when we add 1 to 7 (binary 0111), the most positive value, the sum wraps around to –8 (binary 1000), the most negative value.

Figure 2–4 shows 2 + 3 = 5 on the clock face. Compare this with Figure 2–1.

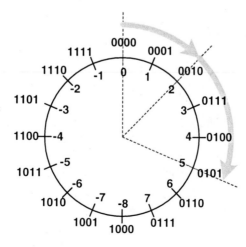

Figure 2–4 2 + 3 = 5 on the clock face.

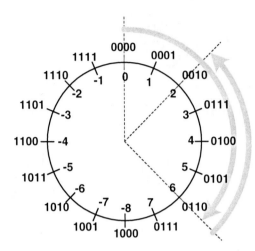

Figure 2–5   6 − 4 = 2 on the clock face.

Figure 2–5 shows 6 − 4 = 2. Compare this with Figure 2–2.

The virtual machine doesn't consider crossing a boundary between the positive and the negative numbers to be an error, so in nybble arithmetic, 5 + 4 really is −7, as shown in Figure 2–6. Therefore, *integer arithmetic does not throw overflow exceptions.*

Adding two large positive values of an integer type can give a negative sum. Multiplying large positive values means going around the clock face several times. The product can be either positive or negative.

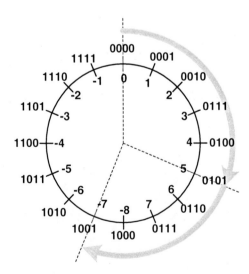

Figure 2–6   5 + 4 = −7 on the clock face.

Overflows can be silent killers of integer arithmetic! Program 2–1 shows the effects of overflow and of division by zero with `int` values. See Listing 2–1.

Listing 2-1 The effects of integer overflow and division by zero.

```
package numbercruncher.program2_1;

/**
 * PROGRAM 2-1: Integer Overflow
 *
 * Show the effects of integer overflow and of division by zero.
 */
public class IntegerOverflow
{
    public static void main(String args[])
    {
        int big = 2147483645;

        for (int i = 1; i <= 4; ++i) {
            System.out.println(big + " + " + i + " = " + (big + i));
        }
        System.out.println();

        for (int i = 1; i <= 4; ++i) {
            System.out.println(big + " * " + i + " = " + (big*i));
        }
        System.out.println();

        int dze = big/0;
    }
}
```

Output:

```
2147483645 + 1 = 2147483646
2147483645 + 2 = 2147483647
2147483645 + 3 = -2147483648
2147483645 + 4 = -2147483647

2147483645 * 1 = 2147483645
2147483645 * 2 = -6
2147483645 * 3 = 2147483639
2147483645 * 4 = -12

java.lang.ArithmeticException: / by zero
        at
numbercruncher.program2_1.IntegerOverflow.main(IntegerOverflow.java:24)
Exception in thread "main"
```

2.4 Wrapper Classes

Java's integer types are called *primitive types* because their values are not objects. A primitive value does not have fields that maintain its state, nor does it have methods that manipulate the value. On the other hand, a *reference type* can be a class or an array type. Its values are objects, which are instances of the class or array type. In a Java program, a variable whose type is a primitive type represents a value of that type. A variable whose type is a reference type represents a pointer to an object of that type.

Java provides a wrapper class for each of the primitive integer types, named `Byte`, `Short`, `Character`, `Integer`, and `Long`. These are class names, not keywords.

A wrapper class's constructor creates a wrapper object for a primitive type's value. For example, new `Integer(3)` wraps the `int` value 3 in an object.

The wrapper classes contain useful methods and constant fields. Each one has a `MIN_VALUE` and a `MAX_VALUE` constant, which represents the minimum value and the maximum value, respectively, of the corresponding primitive type. Classes `Integer` and `Long` have a `toBinary-String()` method and a `toHexString()` method, which return string representations of an integer value as an unsigned binary and an unsigned hexadecimal number, respectively.

Program 2–2 demonstrates some of the features of the wrapper classes. See Listing 2–2.

Listing 2–2 The integer wrapper classes.

```
package numbercruncher.program2_2;

/**
 * PROGRAM 2-2: Integer Wrapper Classes
 *
 * Print the values of some of the constants
 * defined in the integer wrapper classes.
 */
public class IntegerWrapperClasses
{
    public static void main(String args[])
    {
        // Byte
        System.out.println("Byte.MIN_VALUE = " + Byte.MIN_VALUE);
        System.out.println("Byte.MAX_VALUE = " + Byte.MAX_VALUE);
        System.out.println();

        // Short
        System.out.println("Short.MIN_VALUE = " + Short.MIN_VALUE);
        System.out.println("Short.MAX_VALUE = " + Short.MAX_VALUE);
        System.out.println();

        // Character
        System.out.println("Character.MIN_VALUE = " +
                           (int) Character.MIN_VALUE);
```

```java
            System.out.println("Character.MAX_VALUE = " +
                              (int) Character.MAX_VALUE);
            System.out.println();

            // Integer
            System.out.println("Integer.MIN_VALUE = " + Integer.MIN_VALUE);
            System.out.println("Binary: " +
                              Integer.toBinaryString(Integer.MIN_VALUE));
            System.out.println("   Hex: " +
                              Integer.toHexString(Integer.MIN_VALUE));
            System.out.println();
            System.out.println("Integer.MAX_VALUE = " + Integer.MAX_VALUE);
            System.out.println("Binary: " +
                              Integer.toBinaryString(Integer.MAX_VALUE));
            System.out.println("   Hex: " +
                              Integer.toHexString(Integer.MAX_VALUE));
            System.out.println();

            // Long
            System.out.println("Long.MIN_VALUE = " + Long.MIN_VALUE);
            System.out.println("Binary: " +
                              Long.toBinaryString(Long.MIN_VALUE));
            System.out.println("   Hex: " +
                              Long.toHexString(Long.MIN_VALUE));
            System.out.println();
            System.out.println("Long.MAX_VALUE = " + Long.MAX_VALUE);
            System.out.println("Binary: " +
                              Long.toBinaryString(Long.MAX_VALUE));
            System.out.println("   Hex: " +
                              Long.toHexString(Long.MAX_VALUE));
    }
}
```

Output:

```
Byte.MIN_VALUE = -128
Byte.MAX_VALUE = 127

Short.MIN_VALUE = -32768
Short.MAX_VALUE = 32767

Character.MIN_VALUE = 0
Character.MAX_VALUE = 65535

Integer.MIN_VALUE = -2147483648
Binary: 10000000000000000000000000000000
   Hex: 80000000
```

```
Integer.MAX_VALUE = 2147483647
Binary: 1111111111111111111111111111111
   Hex: 7fffffff

Long.MIN_VALUE = -9223372036854775808
Binary: 1000000000000000000000000000000000000000000000000000000000000000
   Hex: 8000000000000000

Long.MAX_VALUE = 9223372036854775807
Binary: 111111111111111111111111111111111111111111111111111111111111111
   Hex: 7fffffffffffffff
```

2.5 Integer Division and Remainder

If both operands of the division operator / are of an integer type, then Java performs integer division. Integer division always results in an integer value—any fraction in the quotient is simply *truncated,* or chopped off. We can think of this as rounding down the quotient to the next integer closer to zero, if the quotient isn't already an integer.

The remainder operator % gives the remainder of performing an integer division of its two operands. Given any two integer values *m* and *n,*

$$(m/n)*n + (m\%n)$$

always equals *m*. From that, we can deduce the sign of the result of the remainder operation, as shown in Table 2–3 . The sign of the first operand determines the sign of the remainder.

As we mentioned in Section 2.1, the division and remainder operations will throw the ArithmeticException if we attempt to divide by zero.

2.6 Integer Exponentiation

Unlike such languages as FORTRAN, Java does not have an exponentiation operator. We conclude this chapter with a static method that returns the double value of x^n, where *x* is any double value, and *n* is an int value. If the value of *n* is 0, the method returns 1. It does not check for overflow.

Table 2–3   The sign of the remainder operation's result.

Operand 1	Operand 2	% Result
+	+	+
−	+	−
+	−	+
−	−	−

Suppose the value of n is 13. A straightforward computation would be to multiply the value of x 12 times:

$$x \cdot x \cdot x \cdot x \cdot x \cdot x \cdot x \cdot x \cdot x \cdot x \cdot x \cdot x \cdot x$$

But that involves 12 multiplications. This is not an efficient algorithm whenever the value of n is large.

We can partition 13 into the sum of powers of 2. Because $13 = 8 + 4 + 1$,

$$x^{13} = x^8 \, x^4 \, x^1$$

If we look at 1101, the binary encoding of 13, we can devise a more efficient algorithm. For each bit in the binary encoding of n, we repeatedly square the value of x, and so we compute x^1, $(x^1)^2$ $= x^2$, $(x^2)^2 = x^4$, and $(x^4)^2 = x^8$. We then multiply together the power of x corresponding to each 1 bit to give us $x^8 x^4 x^1$. This involves a total of five multiplications. The savings in multiplications is greater with larger values of n.

Listing 2–3a shows class IntPower with a static method raise() that computes and returns the value of x^n. It is the first of several useful classes that we'll define in the numbercruncher.mathutils package.

Listing 2–3a Class IntPower for doing integer exponentiation.

```
package numbercruncher.mathutils;

/**
 * Raise a double value to an integer power.
 */
public final class IntPower
{
    /**
     * Compute and return x^power.
     * @param x
     * @param power the integer power
     * @return x^power
     */
    public static double raise(double x, int exponent)
    {
        if (exponent < 0) return 1/raise(x, -exponent);

        double power = 1;

        // Loop to compute x^exponent.
        while (exponent > 0) {

            // Is the rightmost exponent bit a 1?
            if ((exponent & 1) == 1) power *= x;
```

```
        // Square x and shift the exponent 1 bit to the right.
        x *= x;
        exponent >>= 1;
    }

    return power;
    }
}
```

Program 2–3 is a short program that tests class `IntPower` by comparing its `raise()` method to `java.lang.Math.pow()`. See Listing 2–3b.

Listing 2-3b A test program for class `IntPower`.

```
package numbercruncher.program2_3;

import numbercruncher.mathutils.IntPower;

/**
 * PROGRAM 2-3: Test Class IntPower
 *
 * Test the IntPower class.
 */
public class TestIntPower
{
    public static .void main(String args[])
    {
        System.out.println(IntPower.raise(2, 5)   + " " +
                           Math.pow(2, 5));
        System.out.println(IntPower.raise(2, -5)  + " " +
                           Math.pow(2, -5));
        System.out.println(IntPower.raise(2, 0)   + " " +
                           Math.pow(2, 0));
        System.out.println(IntPower.raise(2.5, 5) + " " +
                           Math.pow(2.5, 5));
        System.out.println();
        System.out.println(IntPower.raise(-2, 5)   + " " +
                           Math.pow(-2, 5));
        System.out.println(IntPower.raise(-2, -5)  + " " +
                           Math.pow(-2, -5));
        System.out.println(IntPower.raise(-2, 0)   + " " +
                           Math.pow(-2, 0));
        System.out.println(IntPower.raise(-2.5, 5) + " " +
                           Math.pow(-2.5, 5));
    }
}
```

Output:

```
32.0 32.0
0.03125 0.03125
1.0 1.0
97.65625 97.65625

-32.0 -32.0
-0.03125 -0.03125
1.0 1.0
-97.65625 -97.65625
```

References

Arnold, Ken, James Gosling, and David Holmes, *The Java Progamming Language,* 3rd edition, New York: Addison-Wesley, 2000.

This text discusses integer arithmetic in Section 6.6.1.

Gosling, James, Bill Joy, Guy Steele, and Gilad Bracha, *The Java Language Specification,* 2nd edition, New York: Addison-Wesley, 2000.

This text describes Java's integer types and how Java does integer arithmetic in Section 4.2.2. Sections 15.17 and 15.18.2 specify the multiplicative and additive operators, respectively.

THE FLOATING-POINT STANDARD

Chapter 1 covered floating-point numbers and floating-point arithmetic in general. This chapter gets into the details of how Java implements floating point and how well it adheres to the IEEE 754 floating-point standard.[1] We'll begin to understand the behavior of Java's `float` and `double` types.

3.1 The Floating-Point Formats

Before the IEEE 754 standard was published in 1985, there were many different floating-point formats which the computer manufacturers implemented in hardware and software. It was difficult to port programs that did numerical computations from one machine platform to another— the computed results would vary. Most computer hardware manufacturers today adhere to the IEEE 754 standard, and to various degrees software, such as language compilers, supports the standard's features.

The standard specifies number formats, operations, conversions, and exceptions. *Number formats* refer to how the numbers are encoded in memory.

Java's two primitive types `float` and `double` conform to the standard's 32-bit single-precision format and the standard's 64-bit double-precision format, respectively. Each format breaks a number into three parts: a sign bit, an exponent, and a fraction. The two formats differ in the number of bits allocated to the exponent and fraction parts. Figure 3–1 shows the layouts of the single-precision and double-precision formats, with the bit sizes of each part. In both formats, the most significant bits of the exponent and of the fraction are at their left ends.

---

[1] Pronounced "I triple E," IEEE is the Institute of Electrical and Electronics Engineers, a professional organization under whose auspices the standard was published in 1985 after a historic cooperation between computer scientists and microprocessor chip designers.

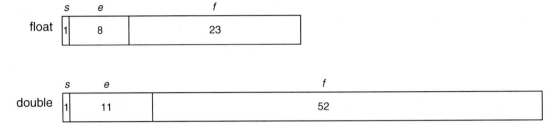

Figure 3–1   The layouts of the single-precision `float` and double-precision `double` number formats. The numbers are the bit sizes of each of the parts.

The sign bit represents the sign of the number value: 0 for positive and 1 for negative.

The exponent is unsigned, and so it is always positive. To allow it to represent negative exponent values, the standard adds a positive bias. We call this a *biased exponent*. To get the *unbiased* (true) value of the exponent, we must subtract off the bias. In the single-precision format, the exponent is 8 bits. It can store the biased values 0 through 255, but 0 and 255 are reserved. The bias is 127, and so the unbiased exponent values are -126 through $+127$. In the double-precision format, the exponent is 11 bits. It can store the biased values 0 through 2047, but 0 and 2047 are reserved. The bias is 1023, and so the unbiased exponent values are -1022 through $+1023$.

We can use the fraction part to calculate the floating-point number's value v. Let s be the value of the sign bit, e be the biased exponent value, E be the unbiased exponent value, and f be the fraction value.

Normalized Number

If the e is not a reserved value (0 and 255 for `float`, or 0 and 2047 for `double`), then there is an implied 1 bit followed by an implied binary point just to the left of f's first bit. Move the implied point to the right or left E bit positions (depending on whether E is positive or negative, respectively) to get the number's absolute value, and s determines whether the value is positive or negative (0 for positive, 1 for negative):

$$v = (-1)^s \times 2^E \times (1.f)$$

This is a *normalized* number.

The implied bit, the implied point, and the fraction constitute a number's *significand,* so a single-precision number has 24 bits in its significand, and a double-precision number has 53 bits in its significand.

For a `float` example, let

$$s = 0$$

$$e = 125$$

$$f = \text{binary } 10000000000000000000000$$

Then

$$E = 125 - 127 = -2$$

and the significand is binary 1.10000000000000000000000 after we append the implied 1 bit and the implied binary point. If we move the binary point two places left, the value in binary is 0.011, which is

$$2^{-2} + 2^{-3} = \frac{1}{4} + \frac{1}{8} = 0.375$$

The maximum positive `float` value has

$$s = 0$$
$$e = 254$$
$$f = \text{binary } 11111111111111111111111$$

Then

$$E = 254 - 127 = 127$$

and the significand is binary 1.11111111111111111111111. The value is

$$\left(2^{127} \times \sum_{i=0}^{23} 2^{-i} \right) \approx (2^{127} \times 2) \approx (3.4 \times 10^{38})$$

If we set $s = 1$, we get the most negative value, which is approximately -3.4×10^{38}.

Denormalized Number

If $e = 0$ (one of the reserved values) and $f \neq 0$, then we have a *denormalized* number (also known as a *subnormal* number). There is an implied binary point just to the left of f's first bit and an implied 0 bit just to the left of that point. For `float`, move the implied point to the left 126 bit positions to get the number's value; for `double`, move the implied point to the left 1022 bit positions to get the number's value. The variable s determines whether the value is positive or negative:

$$\text{float } v = (-1)^s \times 2^{-126} \times (0.f)$$

and

$$\text{double } v = (-1)^s \times 2^{-1022} \times (0.f)$$

For a `float` example, let

$$s = 0$$

$$e = 0$$

$$f = \text{binary } 00101000000000000000000$$

and the significand is binary 0.00101000000000000000000 after we insert the implied 0 bit and the implied binary point. We move the binary point 126 to the left, and we get the value

$$(2^{-129} + 2^{-131}) \approx (1.84 \times 10^{-39})$$

The minimum positive `float` value has

$$s = 0$$

$$e = 0$$

$$f = \text{binary } 00000000000000000000001$$

and the significand is binary 0.00000000000000000000001. The value is

$$(2^{-126} \times 2^{-23}) = 2^{-149} \approx (1.4 \times 10^{-45})$$

If $s = 1$, the minimum negative `float` value is approximately -1.4×10^{-45}.

There are several special cases to implement some constant values:

Zero If both e and f are 0, then the number value is -0 or $+0$, depending on s:

$$v = (-1)^s \times 0$$

Infinity If e is 255 for `float` or 2047 for `double` (which are reserved values), and f is 0, then the number value is $-\text{Infinity}$ or $+\text{Infinity}$, depending on s:

$$v = (-1)^s \times \infty$$

NaN If e is 255 for `float` or 2047 for `double`, and f is nonzero, then we have NaN, or Not-a-Number. NaN is neither positive nor negative, so s is ignored:

$$v = \text{NaN}$$

For example, dividing 0 by 0 results in NaN.

Table 3–1   Summary of Java's `float` and `double` formats.

Type	Exponent Bias	Unbiased Exponent Range	Significand Size	Minimum Values	Maximum Values
`float`	127	-126 through 127	24 bits	$\pm 1.4 \times 10^{-45}$	$\pm 3.4028235 \times 10^{+38}$
`double`	1023	-1022 through 1023	53 bits	$\pm 4.9 \times 10^{-324}$	$\pm 1.7976931348623157 \times 10^{+308}$

This is all quite messy, but fortunately, the Java virtual machine takes care of all of it automatically. Table 3–1 summarizes the two formats.

3.2 Denormalized Numbers

Why do we need denormalized numbers?

Recall that, in Chapter 1, we observed that the floating-point numbers are not evenly distributed along the number line. They are densest near 0, and the size of the gaps between successive numbers increases exponentially as the exponent value increases. In the IEEE 754 standard, the base of the exponent is 2, and so the gaps double in size with each increment of the exponent value.

The smallest positive normalized `float` value has

$$s = 0$$

$$e = 1$$

$$f = \text{binary } 00000000000000000000000$$

Then

$$E = 1 - 127 = -126$$

and the significand is binary 1.00000000000000000000000. The value is

$$2^{-126} \approx (1.2 \times 10^{-38})$$

Without the denormalized numbers, the next smaller number is 0. When computing with extremely small numbers, this gap causes a "flush to zero."

The largest possible denormalized `float` value has

$$s = 0$$

$$e = 0$$

$$f = \text{binary } 11111111111111111111111$$

and the significand is binary 0.11111111111111111111111. Its value is

$$\left(2^{-126} \times \sum_{i=1}^{23} 2^{-i} \right) < (2^{-126} \times 1) \approx (1.2 \times 10^{-38})$$

So the largest possible denormalized `float` value is slightly less than the smallest positive normalized `float` value; since we already know that the smallest possible positive denormalized `float` value is approximately 1.4×10^{-45}, the denormalized values help fill in the gap between 0 and the smallest possible normalized `float` value.

Thus, Java supports the more elegant "gradual underflow." As computed values get smaller and smaller, they become denormalized. Thus, instead of having the values abruptly flush to zero, there is a smoother approach to 0.

3.3 Decomposing Floating-Point Numbers

Listing 3–0a shows interface `IEEE754Constants` in package `numbercruncher.` `mathutils`. The interface defines several constants related to the IEEE 754 standard.

Listing 3-0a Interface `IEEE754Constants` for constants related to the IEEE 754 standard.

```
package numbercruncher.mathutils;

/**
 * Constants related to the IEEE 754 standard.
 */
public interface IEEE754Constants
{
    static final int FLOAT_SIGN_INDEX          =    0;
    static final int FLOAT_SIGN_SIZE           =    1;
    static final int FLOAT_EXPONENT_INDEX      =    1;
    static final int FLOAT_EXPONENT_SIZE       =    8;
    static final int FLOAT_EXPONENT_RESERVED   =  255;
    static final int FLOAT_EXPONENT_BIAS       =  127;
    static final int FLOAT_FRACTION_INDEX      =    9;
    static final int FLOAT_FRACTION_SIZE       =   23;

    static final int DOUBLE_SIGN_INDEX         =    0;
    static final int DOUBLE_SIGN_SIZE          =    1;
    static final int DOUBLE_EXPONENT_INDEX     =    1;
    static final int DOUBLE_EXPONENT_SIZE      =   11;
    static final int DOUBLE_EXPONENT_RESERVED  = 2047;
    static final int DOUBLE_EXPONENT_BIAS      = 1023;
    static final int DOUBLE_FRACTION_INDEX     =   12;
    static final int DOUBLE_FRACTION_SIZE      =   52;
}
```

Listing 3–0b shows class `IEEE754` in the `numbercruncher.mathutils` package. This class has constructors that decompose a floating-point number into its constituent parts according to the IEEE 754 standard, as well as constructors to reconstitute a floating-point number from its parts. It also includes a `print()` method, which prints the parts of a floating-point number.

Listing 3–0b Class `IEEE754`, which decomposes and reconstitutes floating-point numbers according to the IEEE 754 standard.

```
package numbercruncher.mathutils;

/**
 * Decompose a floating-point value into its parts
 * according to the IEEE 754 standard.
 */
public class IEEE754 implements IEEE754Constants
{
    /** sign bit as a string */      private String signBit;
    /** exponent bits as a string */ private String exponentBits;
    /** fraction bits as a string */ private String fractionBits;
    /** implied bit as a string */   private String impliedBit;

    /** biased exponent value */     private int  biased;
    /** fraction value */            private long fraction;

    /** exponent bias */             private int bias;

    /** float number value */        private float  floatValue;
    /** double number value */       private double doubleValue;

    /** true if number
        value is zero */             private boolean isZero;
    /** true if reserved
        exponent value */            private boolean isReserved;
    /** true if number type
        is double */                 private boolean isDouble;
    /** true if denormalized
        number value */              private boolean isDenormalized;

    //--------------//
    // Constructors //
    //--------------//

    /**
     * Constructor. Decompose a float value.
     * @param value the float value to decompose
     */
    public IEEE754(float value)
    {
```

```java
        // Convert the value to a character array of '0' and '1'.
        char bits[] = toCharBitArray(Float.floatToIntBits(value), 32);

        floatValue = value;
        isDouble   = false;

        decompose(bits,
                    FLOAT_EXPONENT_BIAS,   FLOAT_EXPONENT_RESERVED,
                    FLOAT_SIGN_INDEX,      FLOAT_SIGN_SIZE,
                    FLOAT_EXPONENT_INDEX,  FLOAT_EXPONENT_SIZE,
                    FLOAT_FRACTION_INDEX,  FLOAT_FRACTION_SIZE);
    }

    /**
     * Constructor. Decompose a double value.
     * @param value the double-precision value to decompose
     */
    public IEEE754(double value)
    {
        // Convert the value to a character array of '0' and '1'.
        char bits[] = toCharBitArray(Double.doubleToLongBits(value), 64);

        doubleValue = value;
        isDouble    = true;

        decompose(bits,
                    DOUBLE_EXPONENT_BIAS,   DOUBLE_EXPONENT_RESERVED,
                    DOUBLE_SIGN_INDEX,      DOUBLE_SIGN_SIZE,
                    DOUBLE_EXPONENT_INDEX,  DOUBLE_EXPONENT_SIZE,
                    DOUBLE_FRACTION_INDEX,  DOUBLE_FRACTION_SIZE);
    }

    /**
     * Constructor. Reconstitute a float value.
     * @param sign the sign bit value, 0 or 1
     * @param biasedExponent the biased exponent value, 0..255
     * @param fraction the fraction bits
     * @throws numbercruncher.mathutils.IEEE754.Exception
     */
    public IEEE754(int sign, int biasedExponent, FloatFraction fraction)
        throws Exception
    {
        // Check the sign.
        if ((sign != 0) && (sign != 1)) {
            throw new Exception("Invalid sign bit.");
        }

        validateFloatBiasedExponent(biasedExponent);
```

```
        // Consolidate the parts.  First the sign ...
        int intBits = sign;

        // ... then the biased exponent value ...
        intBits <<= FLOAT_EXPONENT_SIZE;
        intBits += biasedExponent;

        // ... and finally the fraction value.
        intBits <<= FLOAT_FRACTION_SIZE;
        intBits += fraction.toInt();

        // Convert to the float value.
        floatValue = Float.intBitsToFloat(intBits);
        isDouble   = false;

        // Convert the value to a character array of '0' and '1'.
        char bits[] = toCharBitArray(intBits, 32);

        decompose(bits,
                  FLOAT_EXPONENT_BIAS,   FLOAT_EXPONENT_RESERVED,
                  FLOAT_SIGN_INDEX,      FLOAT_SIGN_SIZE,
                  FLOAT_EXPONENT_INDEX,  FLOAT_EXPONENT_SIZE,
                  FLOAT_FRACTION_INDEX,  FLOAT_FRACTION_SIZE);
    }

    /**
     * Constructor. Reconstitute a double value.
     * @param sign the sign bit value, 0 or 1
     * @param biasedExponent the biased exponent value, 0..2047
     * @param fraction the fraction bits
     * @throws numbercruncher.mathutils.IEEE754.Exception
     */
    public IEEE754(int sign, int biasedExponent, DoubleFraction fraction)
        throws Exception
    {
        // Check the sign.
        if ((sign != 0) && (sign != 1)) {
            throw new Exception("Invalid sign bit.");
        }

        validateDoubleBiasedExponent(biasedExponent);

        // Consolidate the parts.  First the sign ...
        long longBits = sign;

        // ... then the biased exponent value ...
        longBits <<= DOUBLE_EXPONENT_SIZE;
        longBits += biasedExponent;
```

```java
        // ... and finally the fraction value.
        longBits <<= DOUBLE_FRACTION_SIZE;
        longBits += fraction.toLong();

        // Convert to the double value.
        doubleValue = Double.longBitsToDouble(longBits);
        isDouble    = true;

        // Convert the value to a character array of '0' and '1'.
        char bits[] = toCharBitArray(longBits, 64);

        decompose(bits,
                  DOUBLE_EXPONENT_BIAS,    DOUBLE_EXPONENT_RESERVED,
                  DOUBLE_SIGN_INDEX,       DOUBLE_SIGN_SIZE,
                  DOUBLE_EXPONENT_INDEX,   DOUBLE_EXPONENT_SIZE,
                  DOUBLE_FRACTION_INDEX,   DOUBLE_FRACTION_SIZE);
    }

    //------------------------//
    // Methods to return parts //
    //------------------------//

    /**
     * Return the float value.
     * @return the float value
     */
    public float floatValue() { return floatValue; }

    /**
     * Return the double value.
     * @return the double value
     */
    public double doubleValue() { return doubleValue; }

    /**
     * Return the biased value of the exponent.
     * @return the unbiased exponent value
     */
    public int biasedExponent() { return biased; }

    /**
     * Return the unbiased value of the exponent.
     * @return the unbiased exponent value
     */
    public int unbiasedExponent()
    {
        return isDenormalized ? -bias + 1
                              : biased - bias;
    }
```

```java
/**
 * Return the sign as a string of '0' and '1'.
 * @return the string
 */
public String signBit() { return signBit; }

/**
 * Return the exponent as a string of '0' and '1'.
 * @return the string
 */
public String exponentBits() { return exponentBits; }

/**
 * Return the fraction as a string of '0' and '1'.
 * @return the string
 */
public String fractionBits() { return fractionBits; }

/**
 * Return the significand as a string of '0', '1' and '.'.
 * @return the string
 */
public String significandBits()
{
    return impliedBit + "." + fractionBits;
}

/**
 * Return whether or not the value is zero.
 * @return true if zero, else false
 */
public boolean isZero() { return isZero; }

/**
 * Return whether or not the value is a double.
 * @return true if a double, else false
 */
public boolean isDouble() { return isDouble; }

/**
 * Return whether or not the value is denormalized.
 * @return true if denormalized, else false
 */
public boolean isDenormalized() { return isDenormalized; }

/**
 * Return whether or not the exponent value is reserved.
 * @return true if reserved, else false
```

```
 */
public boolean isExponentReserved() { return isReserved; }

//-----------------------//
// Decomposition methods //
//-----------------------//

/**
 * Convert a long value into a character array of '0' and '1'
 * that represents the value in base 2.
 * @param value the long value
 * @param size the array size
 * @return the character array
 */
private static char[] toCharBitArray(long value, int size)
{
    char bits[] = new char[size];

    // Convert each bit from right to left.
    for (int i = size-1; i >= 0; = -i) {
        bits[i] = (value & 1) == 0 ? '0' : '1';
        value >>>= 1;
    }

    return bits;
}


/**
 * Decompose a floating-point value into its parts.
 * @param bits the character array of '0' and '1'
 *             that represents the value in base 2
 * @param bias the exponent bias value
 * @param reserved the reserved exponent value (other than 0)
 * @param signIndex the index of the sign bit
 * @param signSize the size  of the sign bit
 * @param exponentIndex the index of the exponent
 * @param exponentSize the size  of the exponent
 * @param fractionIndex the index of the fraction
 * @param fractionSize the size  of the fraction
 */
private void decompose(char bits[],
                       int bias,          int reserved,
                       int signIndex,     int signSize,
                       int exponentIndex, int exponentSize,
                       int fractionIndex, int fractionSize)
{
    this.bias = bias;

    // Extract the individual parts as strings of '0' and '1'.
```

```
    signBit       = new String(bits, signIndex,      signSize);
    exponentBits  = new String(bits, exponentIndex, exponentSize);
    fractionBits  = new String(bits, fractionIndex, fractionSize);

    try {
        biased   = Integer.parseInt(exponentBits, 2);
        fraction = Long.parseLong(fractionBits, 2);
    }
    catch(NumberFormatException ex) {}

    isZero        = (biased == 0) && (fraction == 0);
    isDenormalized = (biased == 0) && (fraction != 0);
    isReserved    = (biased == reserved);

    impliedBit = isDenormalized || isZero || isReserved ? "0" : "1";
}

/**
 * Print the decomposed parts of the value.
 */
public void print()
{
    System.out.println("-----------------------------");

    // Print the value.
    if (isDouble()) {
        System.out.println("double value = " + doubleValue());
    }
    else {
        System.out.println("float value = " + floatValue());
    }

    // Print the sign.
    System.out.print("sign = " + signBit());

    // Print the bit representation of the exponent and its
    // biased and unbiased values.  Indicate whether the value
    // is denormalized, or whether the exponent is reserved.
    System.out.print(", exponent = " + exponentBits() +
                     " (biased = " + biasedExponent());

    if (isZero()) {
        System.out.println(", zero)");
    }
    else if (isExponentReserved()) {
        System.out.println(", reserved)");
    }
    else if (isDenormalized()) {
        System.out.println(", denormalized, use " +
```

```
                                  unbiasedExponent() + ")");
    }
    else {
        System.out.println(", normalized, unbiased = " +
                               unbiasedExponent() + ")");
    }
    // Print the significand.
    System.out.println("significand = " + significandBits());
}

//----------------------------- //
// Compute and validate exponents //
//----------------------------- //

/**
 * Compute the value of the float biased exponent
 * given the unbiased value.
 * @param unbiased the unbiased exponent value
 * @return the biased exponent value
 */
public static int toFloatBiasedExponent(int unbiased)
{
    return unbiased + FLOAT_EXPONENT_BIAS;
}

/**
 * Compute the value of the float unbiased exponent
 * given the biased value.
 * @param biased the biased exponent value
 * @return the unbiased exponent value
 */
public static int toFloatUnbiasedExponent(int biased)
{
    return biased == 0 ? -FLOAT_EXPONENT_BIAS + 1
                       : biased - FLOAT_EXPONENT_BIAS;
}

/**
 * Compute the value of the double biased exponent
 * given the unbiased value.
 * @param unbiased the unbiased exponent value
 * @return the biased exponent value
 */
public static int toDoubleBiasedExponent(int unbiased)
{
    return unbiased + DOUBLE_EXPONENT_BIAS;
}

/**
```

```
 * Compute the value of the double unbiased exponent
 * given the biased value.
 * @param biased the biased exponent value
 * @return the unbiased exponent value
 */
public static int toDoubleUnbiasedExponent(int biased)
{
    return biased == 0 ? -DOUBLE_EXPONENT_BIAS + 1
                       : biased - DOUBLE_EXPONENT_BIAS;
}


/**
 * Validate the value of the float biased exponent value.
 * @param biased the biased exponent value
 * @throws numbercruncher.mathutils.IEEE754.Exception
 */
public static void validateFloatBiasedExponent(int biased)
    throws Exception
{
    if ((biased < 0) ||
        (biased > FLOAT_EXPONENT_RESERVED)) {
        throw new Exception("The biased exponent value should be " +
                            "0 through " + FLOAT_EXPONENT_RESERVED +
                            ".");
    }
}


/**
 * Validate the value of the float unbiased exponent value.
 * @param biased the unbiased exponent value
 * @throws numbercruncher.mathutils.IEEE754.Exception
 */
public static void validateFloatUnbiasedExponent(int unbiased)
    throws Exception
{
    if ((unbiased < -FLOAT_EXPONENT_BIAS + 1) ||
        (unbiased > FLOAT_EXPONENT_BIAS)) {
        throw new Exception("The unbiased exponent value should be " +
                            -(FLOAT_EXPONENT_BIAS - 1) + " through " +
                            FLOAT_EXPONENT_BIAS + ".");
    }
}


/**
 * Validate the value of the double biased exponent value.
 * @param biased the biased exponent value
 * @throws numbercruncher.mathutils.IEEE754.Exception
 */
public static void validateDoubleBiasedExponent(int biased)
```

```java
    throws Exception
{
    if ((biased < 0) ||
        (biased > DOUBLE_EXPONENT_RESERVED)) {
        throw new Exception("The biased exponent value should be " +
                            "0 through " +
                            DOUBLE_EXPONENT_RESERVED + ".");
    }
}


/**
 * Validate the value of the double unbiased exponent value.
 * @param biased the unbiased exponent value
 * @throws numbercruncher.mathutils.IEEE754.Exception
 */
public static void validateDoubleUnbiasedExponent(int unbiased)
    throws Exception
{
    if ((unbiased < -DOUBLE_EXPONENT_BIAS + 1) ||
        (unbiased > DOUBLE_EXPONENT_BIAS)) {
        throw new Exception("The unbiased exponent value should be " +
                            -(DOUBLE_EXPONENT_BIAS - 1) +
                            " through " +
                            DOUBLE_EXPONENT_BIAS + ".");
    }
}

//--------------------------- //
// Nested decomposition classes //
//--------------------------- //

/**
 * IEEE 754 exception.
 */
public static class Exception extends java.lang.Exception
{
    public Exception(String message) { super(message); }
}

/**
 * Abstract base class for the IEEE 754 part classes.
 */
private static abstract class Part
{
    /** the part buffer */  private StringBuffer part;

    /**
     * Constructor.
     * @param size the bit size of the part
```

```
    * @param bits the string of character bits '0' and '1'
    * @throws numbercruncher.mathutils.IEEE754.Exception
    */
private Part(int size, String bits) throws Exception
{
    if (size <= 0) {
        throw new Exception("Invalid part size: " + part);
    }

    int length = bits.length();
    part = new StringBuffer(size);

    // String length matches part size.
    if (length == size) {
        part.append(bits);
        validate();
    }

    // String length < part size:  Pad with '0'.
    else if (length < size) {
        part.append(bits);
        validate();
        for (int i = length; i < size; ++i) part.append('0');
    }

    // String length > part size:  Truncate at the right end.
    else {
        part.append(bits.substring(0, size));
        validate();
    }
}


/**
 * Convert the part to an integer value.
 * @return the integer value
 * @throws numbercruncher.mathutils.IEEE754.Exception if the
 *          binary number format is invalid
 */
protected int toInt() throws Exception
{
    try {
        return Integer.parseInt(part.toString(), 2);
    }
    catch(NumberFormatException ex) {
        throw new Exception("Invalid binary number format: " +
                            part.toString());
    }
}
```

```java
    /**
     * Convert the part to an long value.
     * @return the long value
     * @throws numbercruncher.mathutils.IEEE754.Exception if the
     *          binary number format is invalid
     */
    protected long toLong() throws Exception
    {
        try {
            return Long.parseLong(part.toString(), 2);
        }
        catch(NumberFormatException ex) {
            throw new Exception("Invalid binary number format: " +
                                part.toString());
        }
    }

    /**
     * Return the part as a string of characters '0' and '1'.
     */
    public String toString() { return part.toString(); }

    /**
     * Validate that the part consists only of '0' and '1'.
     * @throws numbercruncher.mathutils.IEEE754.Exception
     */
    private void validate() throws Exception
    {
        int length = part.length();

        for (int i = 0; i < length; ++i) {
            char bit = part.charAt(i);
            if ((bit != '0') && (bit != '1')) {
                throw new Exception("Invalid fraction bit string.");
            }
        }
    }
}

/**
 * The IEEE 754 fraction part for a float.
 */
public static class FloatFraction extends Part
{
    /**
     * Constructor.
     * @param bits the string of character bits '0' and '1'
```

```
        * @throws numbercruncher.mathutils.IEEE754.Exception
        */
      public FloatFraction(String bits) throws Exception
      {
          super(FLOAT_FRACTION_SIZE, bits);
      }
   }

   /**
    * The IEEE 754 fraction part for a double.
    */
   public static class DoubleFraction extends Part
   {
      /**
       * Constructor.
       * @param bits the string of character bits '0' and '1'
       * @throws numbercruncher.mathutils.IEEE754.Exception
       */
      public DoubleFraction(String bits) throws Exception
      {
          super(DOUBLE_FRACTION_SIZE, bits);
      }
   }
}
```

The class uses some of the conversion methods of the `Integer`, `Long`, `Float`, and `Double` wrapper classes. Methods `Integer.parseInt()` and `Long.parseLong()` parse a string representation of an `integer` value and a `long` value, respectively, in any base and return the value. Method `Float.floatToIntBits()` converts a `float` value to the `int` value that has the same bit representation. Similarly, method `Double.doubleToLongBits()` converts a `double` value to the `long` value that has the same bit representation. Methods `Float.intBitsToFloat()` and `Double.longBitsToDouble()` work the other way by converting an `int` value and a `long` value, respectively, to the `float` value and the `double` value that has the same bit representation.

The primary method of the class is `decompose()`. It takes a floating-point value that is represented as a character array of `'0'`s and `'1'`s and breaks the value into its various parts according to the standard.

The nested class `Part` and its subclasses `FloatFraction` and `DoubleFraction` support creating, validating, and manipulating the fraction parts of floating-point values.

Listing 3-1 shows Program 3–1, which uses class `IEEE754` to decompose, reconstitute, and print the parts of various `float` and `double` values.

Listing 3–1 Using class `IEEE754` to decompose, reconstitute, and print the parts of various `float` and `double` values.

```
package numbercruncher.program3_1;

import numbercruncher.mathutils.IEEE754;
import numbercruncher.mathutils.IEEE754Constants;

/**
 * PROGRAM 3-1: IEEE 754 Standard Floating-Point Formats
 *
 * Demonstrate the IEEE 754 standard floating-point formats
 * with various float and double values.
 */
public class FPFormats implements IEEE754Constants
{
    private void display() throws IEEE754.Exception
    {
        // Floats
        float floats[] = {
            -0.0f, 0.0f, -1.0f, 1.0f, 0.75f, -0.375f,
            Float.MIN_VALUE, Float.MAX_VALUE,
            Float.NEGATIVE_INFINITY, Float.POSITIVE_INFINITY,
            Float.NaN,
        };
        for (int i = 0; i < floats.length; ++i) {
            new IEEE754(floats[i]).print();
        }

        // Doubles
        double doubles[] = {
            -0.375,
            Double.MIN_VALUE, Double.MAX_VALUE,
            Double.POSITIVE_INFINITY,
            Double.NaN,
        };
        for (int i = 0; i < doubles.length; ++i) {
            new IEEE754(doubles[i]).print();
        }

        System.out.println("-----------------------------");

        IEEE754 numbers[] = {

            // Floats
            new IEEE754(
                0,
                IEEE754.toFloatBiasedExponent(-FLOAT_EXPONENT_BIAS),
```

```
                        new IEEE754.FloatFraction("00101")),
                new IEEE754(
                    0,
                    IEEE754.toFloatBiasedExponent(-126),
                    new IEEE754.FloatFraction("0")),
                new IEEE754(
                    0,
                    IEEE754.toFloatBiasedExponent(-FLOAT_EXPONENT_BIAS),
                    new IEEE754.FloatFraction("11111111111111111111111")),

                // Doubles
                new IEEE754(
                    0,
                    IEEE754.toDoubleBiasedExponent(-DOUBLE_EXPONENT_BIAS),
                    new IEEE754.DoubleFraction("00101")),

                new IEEE754(
                    0,
                    IEEE754.toDoubleBiasedExponent(-1022),
                    new IEEE754.DoubleFraction("0")),
                new IEEE754(
                    0,
                    IEEE754.toDoubleBiasedExponent(-DOUBLE_EXPONENT_BIAS),
                    new IEEE754.DoubleFraction("111111111111111111111111111" +
                                              "1111111111111111111111111")),
            };

            for (int i = 0; i < numbers.length; ++i) {
                numbers[i].print();
            }
        }


        /**
         * Main.
         * @param args the string array of program arguments
         */
        public static void main(String args[])
        {
            FPFormats formats = new FPFormats();

            try {
                formats.display();
            }

            catch(IEEE754.Exception ex) {
                System.out.println("***** Error: " + ex.getMessage());
            }
        }
    }
}
```

Output:

```
----------------------------
float value = -0.0
sign=1, exponent=00000000 (biased=0, zero)
significand=0.00000000000000000000000
----------------------------
float value = 0.0
sign=0, exponent=00000000 (biased=0, zero)
significand=0.00000000000000000000000
----------------------------
float value = -1.0
sign=1, exponent=01111111 (biased=127, normalized, unbiased=0)
significand=1.00000000000000000000000
----------------------------
float value = 1.0
sign=0, exponent=01111111 (biased=127, normalized, unbiased=0)
significand=1.00000000000000000000000
----------------------------
float value = 0.75
sign=0, exponent=01111110 (biased=126, normalized, unbiased=-1)
significand=1.10000000000000000000000
----------------------------
float value = -0.375
sign=1, exponent=01111101 (biased=125, normalized, unbiased=-2)
significand=1.10000000000000000000000
----------------------------
float value = 1.4E-45
sign=0, exponent=00000000 (biased=0, denormalized, use -126)
significand=0.00000000000000000000001
----------------------------
float value = 3.4028235E38
sign=0, exponent=11111110 (biased=254, normalized, unbiased=127)
significand=1.11111111111111111111111
----------------------------
float value = -Infinity
sign=1, exponent=11111111 (biased=255, reserved)
significand=0.00000000000000000000000
----------------------------
float value = Infinity
sign=0, exponent=11111111 (biased=255, reserved)
significand=0.00000000000000000000000
----------------------------
float value = NaN
sign=0, exponent=11111111 (biased=255, reserved)
significand=0.10000000000000000000000
----------------------------
```

```
double value = -0.375
sign=1, exponent=01111111101 (biased=1021, normalized, unbiased=-2)
significand=1.1000000000000000000000000000000000000000000000000000
----------------------------
double value = 4.9E-324
sign=0, exponent=00000000000 (biased=0, denormalized, use -1022)
significand=0.0000000000000000000000000000000000000000000000000001
----------------------------
double value = 1.7976931348623157E308
sign=0, exponent=11111111110 (biased=2046, normalized, unbiased=1023)
significand=1.1111111111111111111111111111111111111111111111111111
----------------------------
double value = Infinity
sign=0, exponent=11111111111 (biased=2047, reserved)
significand=0.0000000000000000000000000000000000000000000000000000
----------------------------
double value = NaN
sign=0, exponent=11111111111 (biased=2047, reserved)
significand=0.1000000000000000000000000000000000000000000000000000
----------------------------
----------------------------
float value = 1.83671E-39
sign=0, exponent=00000000 (biased=0, denormalized, use -126)
significand=0.00101000000000000000000000
----------------------------
float value = 1.17549435E-38
sign=0, exponent=00000001 (biased=1, normalized, unbiased=-126)
significand=1.00000000000000000000000000
----------------------------
float value = 1.1754942E-38
sign=0, exponent=00000000 (biased=0, denormalized, use -126)
significand=0.11111111111111111111111111
----------------------------
double value = 3.4766779039175E-309
sign=0, exponent=00000000000 (biased=0, denormalized, use -1022)
significand=0.0010100000000000000000000000000000000000000000000000
----------------------------
double value = 2.2250738585072014E-308
sign=0, exponent=00000000001 (biased=1, normalized, unbiased=-1022)
significand=1.0000000000000000000000000000000000000000000000000000
----------------------------
double value = 2.225073858507201E-308
sign=0, exponent=00000000000 (biased=0, denormalized, use -1022)
significand=0.1111111111111111111111111111111111111111111111111111
```

Screen 3–1 A screen shot of an interactive version of Program 3–1 in action. By using class `IEEE754`, the program allows you to interactively enter a `float` or `double` value and then decompose it, or you can enter the parts of a value and reconstitute it.

Screen 3–1 is a screen shot of one of the interactive GUI-based versions of Program 3–1 in action.[2] There are two interactive versions—a Java applet and a standalone program—and they both also use class `IEEE754`. Because the interactive programs consist mostly of GUI code, we won't be looking at their source code. However, the Java source code for all the programs, interactive and noninteractive, can be downloaded. See the instructions in the preface.

3.4 The Floating-Point Operations

Java supports the same additive, multiplicative, postfix, and unary arithmetic operations that it supports for the integer types, which we saw in Chapter 2.

Java allows additive and multiplicative operations between an integer value and a floating-point value. If at least one operand is floating-point, then Java converts the integer operand to floating-point, and then it performs a floating-point operation.

---

[2]   GUI = graphical user interface. For Java programs, that generally means an applet that runs inside of a Web browser window or a standalone application. Such programs usually use the Abstract Window Toolkit (AWT) classes or the more sophisticated Java Foundation Classes (JFC), also known as "Swing." To avoid running into the limitations of older Web browsers, the GUI programs in this book use only the AWT classes.

Each of the interactive programs comes in two versions, an applet version and a standalone version. You can download the Java source code for all the programs in this book. See the downloading instructions in the preface.

Table 3–2 The type of the result depends on the types of the operands when performing the floating-point addition, subtraction, multiplication, division, and remainder arithmetic operations.

Operand 1	Operand 2	Result
float	float	float
float	double	double
double	float	double
double	double	double

The result type of a postfix or a unary operation is the same as the type of its single operand. Table 3–2 shows how the result type of an additive or a multiplicative operation depends on the types of its two operands. The result type is `float` only if both operands are type `float`. Adding 1 to `Float.MAX_VALUE` results in `Float.POSITIVE_INFINITY`, not a `double` value.

The Java floating-point remainder operation is worth special mention. The floating-point operation is analogous to the integer operation. For any real values x and y, the remainder r is defined by

$$r = x - qy$$

where q is an integer value whose sign is the same as the sign of $\frac{x}{y}$, and it is the integer value with the largest magnitude such that $|q| \leq \left|\frac{x}{y}\right|$. Program 3–2 demonstrates the operation with some examples. See Listing 3–2.

Listing 3–2 The `float` remainder operation.

```
package numbercruncher.program3_2;

/**
 * PROGRAM 3-2: Float Remainder
 *
 * Demonstrate the float remainder operation.
 */
public class FloatRemainder
{
    public static void main(String args[])
    {
        float values[] = {
            5f,    3f,
            5.5f, 1.1f,
           -5.5f, 2.1f,
            5.5f, -3.1f,
           -5.5f, -4.1f,
        };
```

```
        for (int i = 0; i < values.length/2; ++i) {
            float x = values[2*i];
            float y = values[2*i+1];

            System.out.println(x + " % " + y + " = " + x%y);
        }
    }
}
```

Output:

```
5.0 % 3.0 = 2.0
5.5 % 1.1 = 1.0999999
-5.5 % 2.1 = -1.3000002
5.5 % -3.1 = 2.4
-5.5 % -4.1 = -1.4000001
```

The output of Program 3–2 shows that 5.0 % 3.0 is 2.0, as in the integer version. -5.5 % 2.1 should be -1.3 exactly, because $q = -2$, and $5.5 - 2(-2.1) = -1.3$. However, whereas -5.5 is exactly representable as a floating-point number, the float representation of 2.1 is slightly less than 2.1, and so we have a roundoff error. Similarly, -5.5 % (-4.1) has a roundoff error. The roundoff error is most evident in 5.5 % 1.1, which should be exactly 0. The floating-point representation of 1.1 is slightly *greater* than 1.1, and so $q = 4$ instead of 5. (We can confirm these number representations and subsequent roundoff errors using Program 3–1.)

Java's definition of the floating-point remainder operation differs from the IEEE 754 standard. Instead of using q as defined in the previous paragraph, the standard uses the integer value *closest* to $\frac{x}{y}$. Java has the library routine Math.IEEEremainder() for computing the standard's remainder operation.

3.5 ±0, ±∞, and NaN

Program 3–3 tabulates the results of the floating-point additive and multiplicative operations involving positive or negative 0, positive or negative infinity, Not-a-Number, and a "regular" floating-point values such as -1.0 and 1.0. See Listing 3–3a.

Listing 3–3a Zero, infinity, and Not-a-Number.

```
package numbercruncher.program3_3;

import numbercruncher.mathutils.AlignRight;

/**
 * PROGRAM 3-3: Zero, Infinity, and Not-a-Number
 *
 * Investigate the results of floating-point arithmetic
 * involving zero, infinity, and NaN.
```

```
 */
public class ZeroInfinityNaN
{
    public static void main(String args[])
    {
        AlignRight ar = new AlignRight();

        float operands[] = {
            -0f, +0f, -1f, 1f,
            Float.NEGATIVE_INFINITY, Float.POSITIVE_INFINITY, Float.NaN,
        };

        ar.print("x", 10); ar.print("y", 10); ar.print("|", 2);
        ar.print("x+y", 10); ar.print("x-y", 10);
        ar.print("x*y", 10); ar.print("x/y", 10); ar.print("x%y", 10);
        ar.underline();

        for (int i = 0; i < operands.length; ++i) {
            for (int j = 0; j < operands.length; ++j) {
                float x = operands[i];
                float y = operands[j];

                ar.print(x, 10); ar.print(y, 10); ar.print("|", 2);
                ar.print(x+y, 10); ar.print(x-y, 10);
                ar.print(x*y, 10); ar.print(x/y, 10); ar.print(x%y, 11);
                ar.println();
            }
        }
    }
}
```

Output:

x	y			x+y	x-y	x*y	x/y	x%y
-0.0	-0.0	|	-0.0	0.0	0.0	NaN	NaN
-0.0	0.0	|	0.0	-0.0	-0.0	NaN	NaN
-0.0	-1.0	|	-1.0	1.0	0.0	0.0	-0.0
-0.0	1.0	|	1.0	-1.0	-0.0	-0.0	-0.0
-0.0	-Infinity	|	-Infinity	Infinity	NaN	0.0	-0.0
-0.0	Infinity	|	Infinity	-Infinity	NaN	-0.0	-0.0
-0.0	NaN	|	NaN	NaN	NaN	NaN	NaN
0.0	-0.0	|	0.0	0.0	-0.0	NaN	NaN
0.0	0.0	|	0.0	0.0	0.0	NaN	NaN
0.0	-1.0	|	-1.0	1.0	-0.0	-0.0	0.0
0.0	1.0	|	1.0	-1.0	0.0	0.0	0.0
0.0	-Infinity	|	-Infinity	Infinity	NaN	-0.0	0.0
0.0	Infinity	|	Infinity	-Infinity	NaN	0.0	0.0
0.0	NaN	|	NaN	NaN	NaN	NaN	NaN

```
   -1.0        -0.0 |        -1.0        -1.0         0.0   Infinity          NaN
   -1.0         0.0 |        -1.0        -1.0        -0.0  -Infinity          NaN
   -1.0        -1.0 |        -2.0         0.0         1.0        1.0         -0.0
   -1.0         1.0 |         0.0        -2.0        -1.0       -1.0         -0.0
   -1.0   -Infinity |   -Infinity    Infinity    Infinity        0.0         -1.0
   -1.0    Infinity |    Infinity   -Infinity   -Infinity       -0.0         -1.0
   -1.0         NaN |         NaN         NaN         NaN        NaN          NaN
    1.0        -0.0 |         1.0         1.0        -0.0  -Infinity          NaN
    1.0         0.0 |         1.0         1.0         0.0   Infinity          NaN
    1.0        -1.0 |         0.0         2.0        -1.0       -1.0          0.0
    1.0         1.0 |         2.0         0.0         1.0        1.0          0.0
    1.0   -Infinity |   -Infinity    Infinity   -Infinity       -0.0          1.0
    1.0    Infinity |    Infinity   -Infinity    Infinity        0.0          1.0
    1.0         NaN |         NaN         NaN         NaN        NaN          NaN
-Infinity      -0.0 |   -Infinity   -Infinity         NaN   Infinity          NaN
-Infinity       0.0 |   -Infinity   -Infinity         NaN  -Infinity          NaN
-Infinity      -1.0 |   -Infinity   -Infinity    Infinity   Infinity          NaN
-Infinity       1.0 |   -Infinity   -Infinity   -Infinity  -Infinity          NaN
-Infinity -Infinity |   -Infinity         NaN    Infinity        NaN          NaN
-Infinity  Infinity |         NaN   -Infinity   -Infinity        NaN          NaN
-Infinity       NaN |         NaN         NaN         NaN        NaN          NaN
 Infinity      -0.0 |    Infinity    Infinity         NaN  -Infinity          NaN
 Infinity       0.0 |    Infinity    Infinity         NaN   Infinity          NaN
 Infinity      -1.0 |    Infinity    Infinity   -Infinity  -Infinity          NaN
 Infinity       1.0 |    Infinity    Infinity    Infinity   Infinity          NaN
 Infinity -Infinity |         NaN    Infinity   -Infinity        NaN          NaN
 Infinity  Infinity |    Infinity         NaN    Infinity        NaN          NaN
 Infinity       NaN |         NaN         NaN         NaN        NaN          NaN
      NaN      -0.0 |         NaN         NaN         NaN        NaN          NaN
      NaN       0.0 |         NaN         NaN         NaN        NaN          NaN
      NaN      -1.0 |         NaN         NaN         NaN        NaN          NaN
      NaN       1.0 |         NaN         NaN         NaN        NaN          NaN
      NaN -Infinity |         NaN         NaN         NaN        NaN          NaN
      NaN  Infinity |         NaN         NaN         NaN        NaN          NaN
      NaN       NaN |         NaN         NaN         NaN        NaN          NaN
```

Program 3–3 uses a useful class `AlignRight` in package `numbercruncher.`
`mathutils` for printing text and numbers right-aligned in columns. The class is shown in Listing 3–3b.

Listing 3-3b Utility class `AlignRight` for printing text and numbers right-aligned in columns.

```
package numbercruncher.mathutils;

/**
 * Print text and numbers right-aligned in columns.
 */
```

```java
public class AlignRight
{
    /** line size */   private int lineSize;

    /**
     * Constructor.
     */
    public AlignRight() {}

    /**
     * Print text right-aligned in the column.
     * @param text the text to print
     * @param width the column width
     */
    public void print(String text, int width)
    {
        int padding = width - text.length();
        while (- padding >= 0) System.out.print(" ");
        System.out.print(text);

        lineSize += width;
    }

    /**
     * Print an integer value right-aligned in the column.
     * @param value the value to print
     * @param width the column width
     */
    public void print(int value, int width)
    {
        print(Integer.toString(value), width);
    }

    /**
     * Print a float value right-aligned in the column.
     * @param value the value to print
     */
    public void print(float value, int width)
    {
        print(Float.toString(value), width);
    }

    /**
     * Print a double value right-aligned in the column.
     * @param value the value to print
     * @param width the column width
     */
    public void print(double value, int width)
    {
        print(Double.toString(value), width);
```

```
    }
    /**
     * Print a line.
     */
    public void println()
    {
        System.out.println();
        lineSize = 0;
    }

    /**
     * Print an underline.
     */
    public void underline()
    {
        System.out.println();
        for (int i = 0; i < lineSize; ++i) System.out.print("-");
        System.out.println();
        lineSize = 0;
    }
}
```

Some floating-point comparisons are a bit tricky. -0.0 is always equal to $+0.0$, and so the value of the relational expression $-0.0 < +0.0$ is false. $-$Infinity is *not* equal to $+$Infinity. Finally, NaN is never equal to another number, not even to another NaN.

3.6 No Exceptions!

What happens when "bad" things occur during floating-point operations? The IEEE 754 standard specifies standard responses to five kinds of exceptions, as shown in Table 3–3.

Java provides the standard responses. The result of an overflow is either $-$Infinity or $+$Infinity, and the result of an underflow is either a denormalized number, -0.0, or $+0.0$.

The IEEE 754 standard also specifies that, when an exception occurs, the computer must signal it by setting an associated status flag, and this flag must stay set until the program clears it. The standard also specifies that a program be able to trap the exception or ignore it by masking it.

Table 3–3   Standard responses to floating-point exceptions, as specified by the IEEE 754 standard.

Exception	Standard Response
Invalid operation	Set the result to Not-a-Number.
Division by zero	Set the result to $\pm\infty$.
Overflow	Set the result to the largest possible normalized number or to $\pm\infty$.
Underflow	Set the result to ± 0, the smallest possible normalized number, or a denormalized number.
Inexact value	Set the result to the correctly rounded value.

Java deviates from this standard. *Java's floating-point operations never throw exceptions.* They are nonstop. Programs must check for the exceptions indirectly, such as by testing for NaN using the `Float.isNaN()` and `Double.isNaN()` methods, and we must be especially wary when results become −Infinity or +Infinity.

3.7 Another Look at Roundoff Errors

In Chapter 1, we saw that the float value of $\frac{1}{3}$ printed as 0.33333334. What happens if we assign the float value to a double variable and then print the double variable's value? Will we get 0.3333333400000000 ? Actually, what we get is 0.3333333432674408. Where did the last eight digits come from? Are they random garbage? Program 3–4 attempts to find some answers. See Listing 3–4.

Listing 3–4 Roundoff errors of the number $\frac{1}{3}$.

```java
package numbercruncher.program3_4;

import numbercruncher.mathutils.IEEE754;

/**
 * PROGRAM 3-4: One Third
 *
 * Investigate the floating-point representation of 1/3.
 */
public class OneThird
{
    public static void main (String args[])
    {
        float  fThird     = 1/3f;
        double dConverted = fThird;
        double dThird     = 1/3d;

        System.out.println("          Float 1/3 = " + fThird);
        System.out.println("Converted to double = " + dConverted);
        System.out.println("         Double 1/3 = " + dThird);

        IEEE754 ieeeFThird     = new IEEE754(fThird);
        IEEE754 ieeeDConverted = new IEEE754(dConverted);
        IEEE754 ieeeDThird     = new IEEE754(dThird);

        ieeeFThird.print();
        ieeeDConverted.print();
        ieeeDThird.print();

        // Prepend the leading 0 bits of the converted 1/3.
        int    unbiased = ieeeDConverted.unbiasedExponent();
        String bits     = "1" + ieeeDConverted.fractionBits();
        while (++unbiased < 0) bits = "0" + bits;
```

```
    // Sum the indicated negative powers of 2.
    double sum   = 0;
    double power = 0.5;
    for (int i = 0; i < bits.length(); ++i) {
        if (bits.charAt(i) == '1') sum += power;
        power /= 2;
    }

    System.out.println();
    System.out.println("Converted 1/3 by summation = " + sum);
    }
}
```

Output:

```
        Float 1/3 = 0.33333334
Converted to double = 0.3333333432674408
       Double 1/3 = 0.3333333333333333
------------------------------
float value = 0.33333334
sign=0, exponent=01111101 (biased=125, normalized, unbiased=-2)
significand=1.01010101010101010101011
------------------------------
double value = 0.3333333432674408
sign=0, exponent=01111111101 (biased=1021, normalized, unbiased=-2)
significand=1.0101010101010101010101011000000000000000000000000000
------------------------------
double value = 0.3333333333333333
sign=0, exponent=01111111101 (biased=1021, normalized, unbiased=-2)
significand=1.0101010101010101010101010101010101010101010101010101

Converted 1/3 by summation = 0.3333333432674408
```

Let's examine $\frac{1}{3}$. Its unbiased exponent value is -2, so we need to shift the implied point of its significand two places to the left, giving us the value 0.01010101010101010101011 in base 2. We can verify it by doing base 2 division:

$$
\begin{array}{r}
0.010101\ldots \\
11\overline{)1.000000} \\
\underline{11} \\
100 \\
\underline{11} \\
100 \\
\underline{11} \\
1\ldots
\end{array}
$$

The IEEE 754 representation of $\frac{1}{3}$ rounded up the last bit from 0 to 1, thus introducing a very small positive error. We see this error as the final digit 4 (instead of 3) when we print out the `float` value.

Program 3–4's output also shows what really happens when we convert the `float` value to a `double`. This widening operation is exact: It appends 29 ($= 53 - 24$) zero bits at the right. But when we converted that `double` value to a decimal number for printing, we didn't get eight decimal zeros at the end; instead, we got what appear to be the garbage digits. For comparison, Program 3–4 also computes and displays the `double` value of $\frac{1}{3}$.

In fact, though, that "garbage" is quite valid, as the latter part of the program demonstrates. Using the binary representation of $\frac{1}{3}$, we add the indicated negative powers of 2. The printed sum matches what was printed for the converted value.

As we saw in Chapter 1, a roundoff error occurs when an exact value, such as $\frac{1}{3}$, lies between two representable floating-point values. How does Java decide which of the two floating-point values to choose? In the case of the `float` representation of $\frac{1}{3}$, how did Java decide the last bit should be 1 instead of 0?

When an exact values lies between two representable floating-point values, Java picks the floating-point value that is closest to the exact value. If the exact value lies exactly halfway between two floating-point values, Java picks the floating-point value whose least significant (rightmost) bit is 0. This corresponds to the default rounding mode called *round to nearest* in the IEEE 754 standard.

The IEEE 754 standard defines several other rounding modes for floating-point: *round down, round up,* and *round toward zero.* Once again, Java deviates from the standard. *Java does not implement the nondefault rounding modes defined by the standard.* If you want your Java program to use these other rounding modes, you can write methods that emulate the floating-point operations with the desired modes, or your program can invoke floating-point routines written in other languages.

3.8 Strict or Nonstrict Floating-Point Arithmetic

Whenever Java performs a floating-point operation, we know that the final result will be in the IEEE 754 single-precision or double-precision format, after being properly rounded to the nearest representable value. But if an expression contains multiple operations, what happens to the intermediate values?

Java provides two modes for evaluating floating-point expressions, *FP-strict* and *non-FP-strict.* In FP-strict mode, all the intermediate values of a computation must also be properly rounded and be in the appropriate IEEE 754 format. One important consequence of FP-strict is that your program is guaranteed to produce exactly the same results across all Java virtual machine implementations.

On the other hand, non-FP-strict mode allows the Java virtual machine, during the calculation of the intermediate values, to take better advantage of the underlying floating-point hardware, such as any "extended formats" that differ from the IEEE 754 standard. This may result in fewer overflows, perhaps less precision, or faster floating-point arithmetic. The final result value must still be properly rounded and be in the appropriate IEEE 754 format. However, there is no longer a guarantee that the final values will be exactly the same across all virtual machine implementations.

Compile-time constant floating-point expressions are always evaluated in FP-strict mode. Otherwise, by using the `strictfp` keyword, you can indicate which mode you want to be in effect when an expression is evaluated at run time. You can apply the keyword as a modifier of a class, an interface, or a method. Some examples are

```
public strictfp class MatrixMath { ... }

strictfp interface Integrand { ... }

public class ComplexMath
{
    public strictfp float norm() { ... }
    ...
}
```

If a method is modified by `strictfp`, then all the floating-point expressions in the method will be evaluated in FP-strict mode. If a class or an interface is modified by `strictfp`, then all the expressions in the class will be evaluated in FP-strict mode. A class that is FP-strict does not necessarily mean that its subclasses are—each subclass needs to be modified (or not) individually.

A particular Java virtual machine implementation may choose to always use the FP-strict mode, even in the absence of the `strictfp` modifier. Non-FP-strict mode is an option, not a requirement, for a virtual machine.

3.9 The Machine Epsilon ϵ

We conclude this chapter by computing approximations to the *machine epsilon* ϵ for types `float` and `double`. ϵ is the largest positive value that, when added to 1, produces a sum that is equal to 1. In other words, we want, because of roundoff, $1 + \epsilon = 1$ to be true. Any larger value for ϵ would have $1 + \epsilon > 1$.

Listing 3–5a shows `Epsilon` in package `numbercruncher.mathutils`. It computes the value of its two static class variables, `floatEpsilon` and `doubleEpsilon`, and it has methods to return each value.

Listing 3–5a Class `Epsilon`, which computes and returns machine ϵ for the `float` and `double` types.

```
package numbercruncher.mathutils;

/**
 * Compute the machine epsilon for the float and double types,
```

```
 * the largest positive floating-point value that, when added to 1,
 * results in a value equal to 1 due to roundoff.
 */
public final class Epsilon
{
    private static final float  floatEpsilon;
    private static final double doubleEpsilon;

    static {

        // Loop to compute the float epsilon value.
        float fTemp = 0.5f;
        while (1 + fTemp > 1) fTemp /= 2;
        floatEpsilon = fTemp;

        // Loop to compute the double epsilon value.
        double dTemp = 0.5;
        while (1 + dTemp > 1) dTemp /= 2;
        doubleEpsilon = dTemp;
    };

    /**
     * Return the float epsilon value.
     * @returns the value
     */
    public static float floatValue() { return floatEpsilon; }

    /**
     * Return the double epsilon value.
     * @returns the value
     */
    public static double doubleValue() { return doubleEpsilon; }
}
```

Program 3–5, shown in Listing 3–5b, imports both classes IEEE754 and Epsilon in order to decompose and print the machine ε values.

Listing 3–5b Printing the decomposed machine ε values.

```
package numbercruncher.program3_5;

import numbercruncher.mathutils.IEEE754;
import numbercruncher.mathutils.Epsilon;

/**
 * PROGRAM 3-5: Print Machine Epsilon
```

```
 *
 * Decompose and print the machine epsilon
 * for the float and double types.
 */
public class PrintEpsilon
{
    public static void main(String args[])
    {
        (new IEEE754(Epsilon.floatValue())).print();
        (new IEEE754(Epsilon.doubleValue())).print();
    }
}
```

Output:

```
------------------------------
float value = 5.9604645E-8
sign=0, exponent=01100111 (biased=103, normalized, unbiased=-24)
significand=1.00000000000000000000000
------------------------------
double value = 1.1102230246251565E-16
sign=0, exponent=01111001010 (biased=970, normalized, unbiased=-53)
significand=1.0000000000000000000000000000000000000000000000000000
```

In the float case, we have $1 + \epsilon$ is

$$
\begin{array}{r}
1.00000000000000000000000 \\
+\,0.00000000000000000000001 \\
\hline
1.00000000000000000000000
\end{array}
$$

Since the significand has 24 bits, the round to nearest mode rounds the sum down to 1. Any value larger than ϵ would result in a sum greater than 1. The double case is similar, except with a 53-bit significand. Table 3–4 summarizes the epsilon values.

One key point is that whenever we add two float numbers whose binary exponents differ by more than the bitsize of the significand, the smaller addend is lost in the roundoff. We'll discuss this further in Chapter 4. In subsequent chapters, we can use ϵ (or multiples of ϵ) during computations as the upper bound on relative roundoff errors.

Table 3–4 float and double epsilon values, which are the smallest floating-point values that, when added to 1, produce a sum that is greater than 1.

Type	Approximate ϵ	Unbiased Binary Exponent
float	6.0×10^{-8}	-24
double	1.1×10^{-16}	-53

3.10 Error Analysis

Floating-point error analysis analytically examines the sources of roundoff errors in arithmetic expressions and proves theorems about error propagation and error bounds. That topic is beyond the scope of this book. The references at the end of each chapter will list books that explain the error analyses of that chapter's topics.

References

Arnold, Ken, James Gosling, and David Holmes, *The Java Programming Language,* 3rd edition, New York: Addison-Wesley, 2000.

This text discusses floating-point arithmetic in Section 6.6.2, as well as the strict and nonstrict modes in Section 6.6.3.

Gosling, James, Bill Joy, Guy Steele, and Gilad Bracha, *The Java Language Specification,* 2nd edition, New York: Addison-Wesley, 2000.

This book specifies how Java does floating-point arithmetic in Sections 4.2.3 and 4.2.4. Section 15.4 contains the specification of FP-strict expressions. Sections 15.17 and 15.18.2 specifies the multiplicative and additive operators, respectively.

Kahan, W., and Joseph D. Darcy, "How Java's Floating-Point Hurts Everyone Everywhere," Department of Electrical Engineering and Computer Science, University of California, Berkeley. Originally presented March 1, 1998, at the ACM 1998 Workshop on Java for High-Performance Network Computing.

William Kahan, a computer science professor at the University of California at Berkeley, was one of the leaders of the development of the IEEE 754 standard. In this text, he and his coauthor criticize Java's deviations from the standard.

Knuth, Donald E., *The Art of Computer Programming, Volume 2: Seminumerical Algorithms,* 3rd edition, Reading, MA: Addison-Wesley, 1998.

This text contains a good introduction to floating-point arithmetic and error analysis, especially of the associative and commutative laws of addition, in Section 4.2.

Overton, Michael L., *Numerical Computing with IEEE Floating Point Arithmetic,* Philadelphia: Society for Industrial and Applied Mathematics, 2001.

This book is an excellent overview of floating-point, in general, in Chapters 1 through 3 and of the IEEE 754 standard, in particular, in Chapters 4 through 7. Another good description of the standard is Goldberg, David, "What Every Computer Scientist Should Know about Floating-Point Arithmetic," in *ACM Computing Surveys,* Volume 12, Number 1, March 1991. Of course, the standard itself is short but worthwhile reading.

PART II

ITERATIVE COMPUTATIONS

Computers are certainly good at looping, and many computations are iterative. But loops are where errors can build up and overwhelm the chance for any meaningful results.

Chapter 4 shows that even seemingly innocuous operations, such as summing a list of numbers, can get us into trouble. Examples show how running floating-point sums can gradually lose precision and offer some ways to prevent this from happening.

Chapter 5 is about finding the roots of an algebraic equation, which is another way of saying, "Solve for *x*." It introduces several iterative algorithms that converge upon solutions: bisection, *regula falsi,* improved *regula falsi,* secant, Newton's, and fixed-point. This chapter also discusses how to decide which algorithm is appropriate.

Chapter 6 poses the question, Given a set of points in a plane, can we construct a smooth curve that passes through all the points, or how about a straight line that passes the closest to all the points? This chapter presents algorithms for polynomial interpolation and linear regression.

Chapter 7 tackles some integration problems from freshman calculus, but it solves them numerically. It introduces two basic algorithms, the trapezoidal algorithm and Simpson's algorithm.

Finally, Chapter 8 is about solving differential equations numerically. It covers several popular algorithms, Euler's, predictor-corrector, and Runge-Kutta.

CHAPTER 4

SUMMING LISTS OF NUMBERS

A typical assignment in Computer Programming 101 is to write a program that sums a list of numbers. If you add many numbers, say hundreds or thousands of them, and there are no overflows, then you might reasonably expect that the roundoff errors will cancel each other out, and the sum will be fairly accurate. What could possibly go wrong?

This chapter shows that even such a simple operation *can* go wrong if we're careless about floating-point arithmetic. Several summation problems will illustrate some of the typical pitfalls. We'll take an *experimental* approach by writing programs that try different summation techniques to find ones that either compensate for the roundoff errors or reduce the opportunities for the errors to occur. (After all, isn't this computer *science?*)

4.1 A Summing Mystery—the Magnitude Problem

Let's start with a simple summing problem. The formula for the sum s_n of the first n counting numbers, 1 through n, is

$$s_n = \sum_{i=1}^{n} i = \frac{n(n + 1)}{2}$$

For example, the sum of the first 10 counting numbers is 55.

Program 4-1 adds a slight twist to the summation. See Listing 4–1. It adds fractions instead, where, for each summation, the numerators are the first n counting numbers and the denominator is the sum s_n. Therefore, the sum should be 1. For example, the fraction sum for s_{10} is

$$\frac{1}{55} + \frac{2}{55} + \frac{3}{55} + \frac{4}{55} + \frac{5}{55} + \frac{6}{55} + \frac{7}{55} + \frac{8}{55} + \frac{9}{55} + \frac{10}{55} = \frac{55}{55} = 1$$

The program computes the fraction sums with denominators s_{10}, s_{100}, s_{1000}, and so on through $s_{100,000,000}$.

We can see from the output that things go fairly smoothly, with the computed sums close to 1, until denominator $s_{100,000,000}$—and disaster strikes. In the last line of output, how did the sum manage to be 0.5? That's not even close!

Listing 4–1 Fraction sums.

```
package numbercruncher.program4_1;

import numbercruncher.mathutils.AlignRight;

/**
 * PROGRAM 4-1: Fraction Sums
 *
 * For each n, compute the sum 1/d + 2/d + 3/d + ... + n/d = d/d
 * where:
 *      n = 10, 100, 1000, ..., 100,000,000
 *      d = 1 + 2 + 3 + ... + n = (n/2)(n + 1)
 *
 * See how close each sum is to 1.
 */
public class FractionSums
{
    public static void main(String args[])
    {
        AlignRight ar = new AlignRight();

        ar.print("n", 9); ar.print("Denom", 14);
        ar.print("1/Denom", 14); ar.print("n/Denom", 13);
        ar.print("Sum", 11); ar.print("% Error", 13);
        ar.underline();

        for (int n = 10; n <= 100000000; n *= 10) {
            float sum   = 0;
            float denom = (0.5f*n)*(n + 1);

            // Sum fractions.
            for (int i = 1; i <= n; ++i) sum += i/denom;

            ar.print(n, 9); ar.print(denom, 14); ar.print(1/denom, 14);
```

```
        ar.print(n/denom, 13); ar.print(sum, 11);
        ar.print(100*Math.abs(sum - 1), 13);
        ar.println();
    }
  }
}
```

Output:

n	Denom	1/Denom	n/Denom	Sum	% Error
10	55.0	0.018181818	0.18181819	0.99999994	5.9604645E-6
100	5050.0	1.980198E-4	0.01980198	1.0	0.0
1000	500500.0	1.998002E-6	0.001998002	0.99999994	5.9604645E-6
10000	5.0005E7	1.9998E-8	1.9998E-4	0.9999999	1.1920929E-5
100000	5.0000502E9	1.9999799E-10	1.99998E-5	0.99999875	1.2516975E-4
1000000	5.00000489E11	1.999998E-12	1.999998E-6	0.9998997	0.010031462
10000000	5.0000004E13	1.9999998E-14	1.9999999E-7	1.002663	0.26630163
100000000	5.0000001E15	1.9999999E-16	2.0E-8	0.5	50.0

Why should the fraction sum for denominator $s_{100,000,000}$ fail so miserably when the previous sums all did so well? It isn't underflow or overflow. For each sum, the program prints out the values of the first fraction and last fraction, and their exponent values are well within the range (-45 through $+38$) for the float type. Each sum is computed from many addends, and so we might expect most of the high and low roundoff errors to cancel each other out.

For one possible source of the problem, recall our computation of the machine epsilon ϵ at the end of Chapter 3. Since the sum is supposed to be 1, and the float ϵ value is around 6.0×10^{-8}, we can see that, with denominator $s_{100,000,000}$, a significant percentage of the addends may have no effect on the sum as it approaches 1.

Program 4–2 provides some insight. See Listing 4–2. It computes the fraction sum for denominator $s_{100,000,000}$ by dividing the series of fractions into 20 equal-sized groups, and at the end of each group it prints the current fraction and the current value of the running sum. Before adding each fraction to the running sum, it calculates the difference between the fraction's binary exponent and the running sum's binary exponent. At the end of each group, it also prints the minimum exponent difference of that group and the percentage of exponent differences within the group that exceeded 24. (Recall that, at the end of Chapter 3, we saw that, for type float, the unbiased binary exponent of the machine epsilon is -24.)

Listing 4–2 Fraction sums for $n = 100,000,000$.

```
package numbercruncher.program4_2;

import numbercruncher.mathutils.AlignRight;

/**
```

```
 * PROGRAM 4-2: Fraction Sum 100M
 *
 * Compute the sum 1/d + 2/d + 3/d + ... + n/d = d/d
 * where:
 *      n = 100,000,000
 *      d = 1 + 2 + 3 + ... + n = (n/2)(n + 1)
 *
 * See why the sum ends up being 0.5
 */
public class FractionSum100M
{
    private static final int GROUPS = 20;
    private static final int MAX     = 100000000;     // 100M

    public static void main(String args[])
    {
        AlignRight ar = new AlignRight();

        ar.print("i", 9);
        ar.print("Fraction", 15);
        ar.print("Running sum", 15);
        ar.print("Min exp diff", 15);
        ar.print("% ExpDiff>24", 15);
        ar.underline();

        float sum   = 0;
        float denom = (0.5f*MAX)*(MAX + 1);

        int gSize   = MAX/GROUPS;               // group size
        int gEnd    = gSize;                    // index of group end
        int minDiff = Integer.MAX_VALUE;        // min exponent difference
        int exceeds = 0;                        // # of exponent diff > 24

        // Loop to sum the fractions.
        for (int i = 1; i <= MAX; ++i) {
            float fraction = i/denom;

            // Compute the exponent difference.
            int expSum      = Float.floatToIntBits(sum)      >> 23;
            int expFraction = Float.floatToIntBits(fraction) >> 23;
            int diff        = Math.abs(expSum - expFraction);

            if (i > 1) {
                minDiff = Math.min(minDiff, diff);
                if (diff > 24) ++exceeds;
            }

            sum += fraction;
```

```
            // Printout at the end of each group.
            if (i == gEnd) {
                ar.print(i, 9);
                ar.print(fraction, 15);
                ar.print(sum, 15);
                ar.print(minDiff, 15);
                ar.print((100*exceeds)/gSize, 15);
                ar.println();

                minDiff = Integer.MAX_VALUE;
                exceeds = 0;
                gEnd += gSize;
            }
        }
    }
}
```

Output:

i	Fraction	Running sum	Min exp diff	% ExpDiff>24
5000000	1.0E-9	0.002493547	0	0
10000000	2.0E-9	0.009991142	21	0
15000000	3.0E-9	0.022081949	22	0
20000000	4.0E-9	0.0407084	23	0
25000000	5.0E-9	0.05933485	23	0
30000000	6.0E-9	0.09342261	23	0
35000000	6.9999997E-9	0.125	24	15
40000000	8.0E-9	0.16593489	24	45
45000000	9.0E-9	0.2404407	24	0
50000000	1.0E-8	0.25	24	87
55000000	1.1E-8	0.25	25	100
60000000	1.2E-8	0.25	25	100
65000000	1.2999999E-8	0.25	25	100
70000000	1.3999999E-8	0.25	25	100
75000000	1.5E-8	0.26472795	24	90
80000000	1.6E-8	0.41373956	24	0
85000000	1.7E-8	0.5	24	42
90000000	1.8E-8	0.5	25	100
95000000	1.9E-8	0.5	25	100
100000000	2.0E-8	0.5	25	100

Now we begin to see what happened. *If the difference in magnitude between two addends is too great, the smaller addend loses much of its contribution to the sum.* Indeed, as we saw at the end of Chapter 3, smaller addends will have no effect at all on the sum if the difference between their binary exponents is greater than 24 when doing float addition.

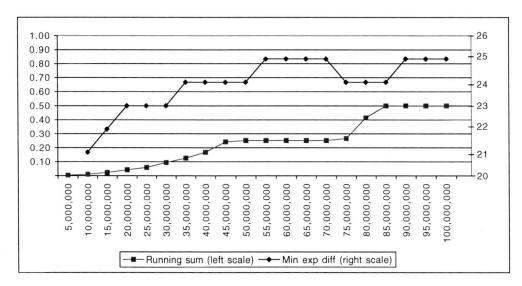

Figure 4–1 A graph of the output of Program 4–2. The running sum "stalls" at 0.25 and at 0.5 when the minimum exponent differences exceed 24.

Program 4–2 shows that, whenever the value of the running sum reaches the next power of 2, the sum's binary exponent increases by 1. If that widens the exponent difference between the sum and the upcoming fractions to more than 24, then those fractions have no effect on the sum until they become large enough to lower the exponent difference. Thus, the running sum "stalls" at 0.25 and again at 0.5 when the minimum exponent differences are 25. Figure 4–1 shows this clearly by graphing the values of the running sum versus the minimum exponent differences in each group.

Would it make a difference if we summed the fractions in the reverse order, from the largest down to the smallest? Program 4–3 shows that the running sum still stalls at 0.5, and we have even greater percentages of exponent differences exceeding 24. See Listing 4–3. So we've made the problem worse—the values of the running sum increase while the fractions decrease, making the exponent differences even larger.

In general, when adding a sorted list of numbers all of the same sign, it is better to add them in the order from the smallest magnitude up to the largest.

Listing 4–3 Fraction sums for $n = 100,000,000$ in reversed order.

```
package numbercruncher.program4_3;

import numbercruncher.mathutils.AlignRight;

/**
 * PROGRAM 4-3: Fraction Sum 100M in the Reversed Order
```

```
 *
 * Compute the sum n/d + (n-1)/d + (n-2)/d + ... + 2/d + 1/d = d/d
 * where:
 *     n = 100,000,000
 *     d = 1 + 2 + 3 + ... + n = (n/2)(n + 1)
 *
 * See if the sum is closer to 1.
 */
public class FractionSum100MReversed
{
    private static final int GROUPS = 20;
    private static final int MAX    = 100000000;     // 100M

    public static void main(String args[])
    {
        AlignRight ar = new AlignRight();

        ar.print("i", 9);
        ar.print("Fraction", 15);
        ar.print("Running sum", 15);
        ar.print("Min exp diff", 15);
        ar.print("% ExpDiff>24", 15);
        ar.underline();

        float sum   = 0;
        float denom = (0.5f*MAX)*(MAX + 1);

        int gSize   = MAX/GROUPS;            // group size
        int gStart  = (MAX + 1) - gSize;     // index of group start
        int minDiff = Integer.MAX_VALUE;     // min exponent difference
        int exceeds = 0;                     // # of exponent diff > 24

        // Loop to sum the fractions.
        for (int i = MAX; i >= 1; - i) {
            float fraction = i/denom;

            int expSum      = Float.floatToIntBits(sum)      >> 23;
            int expFraction = Float.floatToIntBits(fraction) >> 23;
            int diff        = Math.abs(expSum - expFraction);

            if (i < MAX) {
                minDiff = Math.min(minDiff, diff);
                if (diff > 24) ++exceeds;
            }

            sum += fraction;

            // Printout at the start of each group.
```

```
            if (i == gStart) {
                ar.print(i, 9);
                ar.print(fraction, 15);
                ar.print(sum, 15);
                ar.print(minDiff, 15);
                ar.print((100*exceeds)/gSize, 15);
                ar.println();

                minDiff = Integer.MAX_VALUE;
                exceeds = 0;
                gStart -= gSize;
            }
        }
    }
}
```

Output:

i	Fraction	Running sum	Min exp diff	% ExpDiff>24
95000001	1.9E-8	0.10206167	0	0
90000001	1.8E-8	0.18421358	22	0
85000001	1.7E-8	0.26743877	23	0
80000001	1.6E-8	0.41645038	24	0
75000001	1.5E-8	0.5	24	43
70000001	1.3999999E-8	0.5	25	100
65000001	1.2999999E-8	0.5	26	100
60000001	1.2E-8	0.5	26	100
55000001	1.1E-8	0.5	26	100
50000001	1.0E-8	0.5	26	100
45000001	9.0E-9	0.5	26	100
40000001	8.0E-9	0.5	26	100
35000001	6.9999997E-9	0.5	26	100
30000001	6.0E-9	0.5	27	100
25000001	5.0E-9	0.5	27	100
20000001	4.0E-9	0.5	27	100
15000001	3.0E-9	0.5	27	100
10000001	2.0000002E-9	0.5	28	100
5000001	1.0000002E-9	0.5	28	100
1	1.9999999E-16	0.5	29	100

We have a clear challenge. In order for a summation to be accurate, we need to keep the running sum and each addend sufficiently close together in magnitude, so that the difference between their binary exponents is not greater than 24.

Program 4–4 shows one way to do this. See Listing 4–4. The program partitions the fractions into 20 equal-sized groups. It computes a separate subtotal for each group; then it adds the subtotal to the running sum. Each group's fractions are closer in magnitude to the group subtotal, so the minimum difference between the binary exponents of a fraction and its group subtotal is under 24. Each group subtotal has enough "heft" to make its contribution to the overall sum. The trick is to get the right size for the groups. The final sum is very close to 1.

Listing 4–4 Fraction sums for $n = 100,000,000$ using group subtotals.

```
package numbercruncher.program4_4;

import numbercruncher.mathutils.AlignRight;
/**
 * PROGRAM 4-4: Fraction Sum 100M Using Group Subtotals
 *
 * Compute the sum 1/d + 2/d + 3/d + ... + n/d = d/d
 * where:
 *     n = 100,000,000
 *     d = 1 + 2 + 3 + ... + n = (n/2)(n + 1)
 *
 * Compute the sum by adding the group subtotals.
 * See if the final sum is closer to 1.
 */
public class FractionSum100MGrouped
{
    private static final int GROUPS = 20;
    private static final int MAX    = 100000000;     // 100M

    public static void main(String args[])
    {
        AlignRight ar = new AlignRight();

        ar.print("i", 9);
        ar.print("Group sum", 15);
        ar.print("Running sum", 15);
        ar.print("% ExpDiff>24", 15);
        ar.underline();

        float sum      = 0;             // running sum
        float subtotal = 0;             // group subtotal
        int   gSize    = MAX/GROUPS;    // group size
        int   gEnd     = gSize;         // index of group end
        int   exceeds  = 0;             // # of exponent diff > 24

        float denom = (0.5f*MAX)*(MAX + 1);

        // Sum the fractions by groups.
        for (int i = 1; i <= MAX; ++i) {
            float fraction = i/denom;

            int expSubtotal = Float.floatToIntBits(subtotal) >> 23;
```

```
        int expFraction = Float.floatToIntBits(fraction) >> 23;
        int diff        = Math.abs(expSubtotal - expFraction);

        if ((subtotal > 0) && (diff > 24)) ++exceeds;
        subtotal += fraction;

        // Subtotal and printout at the end of each group.
        if (i == gEnd) {
            sum += subtotal;

            ar.print(i, 9);
            ar.print(subtotal, 15);
            ar.print(sum, 15);
            ar.print((100*exceeds)/gSize, 15);
            ar.println();

            subtotal = 0;
            exceeds  = 0;
            gEnd += gSize;
        }
    }
    System.out.println("\n% error = " + 100*Math.abs(sum - 1));
    }
}
```

Output:

i	Group sum	Running sum	% ExpDiff>24
5000000	0.002493547	0.002493547	0
10000000	0.007556428	0.0100499755	0
15000000	0.012413543	0.02246352	0
20000000	0.017349107	0.039812624	0
25000000	0.023679595	0.06349222	0
30000000	0.02718998	0.0906822	0
35000000	0.034128636	0.12481084	0
40000000	0.036770158	0.161581	0
45000000	0.04185812	0.20343912	0
50000000	0.049500026	0.25293913	0
55000000	0.05435951	0.30729866	0
60000000	0.055825584	0.36312425	0
65000000	0.05929653	0.42242077	0
70000000	0.07003953	0.4924603	0
75000000	0.07346739	0.5659277	0
80000000	0.07455075	0.64047843	0
85000000	0.07784402	0.71832246	0
90000000	0.08436947	0.80269194	0
95000000	0.098553196	0.9012451	0

```
100000000      0.09986824      1.0011134              0

% error = 0.11134148
```

4.2 The Kahan Summation Algorithm

What if we don't have much prior knowledge of the numbers we're about to sum, such as how many there are and whether or not they're sorted? Perhaps the numbers are generated dynamically, and we need to know the current running sum at all times. Is there a way to add these numbers and avoid the magnitude problem?

Figure 4–2 illustrates one solution to the magnitude problem, the Kahan Summation Algorithm, which is named after its developer.[1] This method is also called *compensated summation.*

The algorithm uses feedback from the previous addition. During each addition, the new addend is "corrected" by adding to it an amount computed from the previous addition. The correction is the magnitude error, the rightmost bits of the previous addend that were lost when it was added to the running sum. By continuously recovering the lost bits from the previous addition, this summation algorithm manages to keep the running sum true despite the magnitude problems.

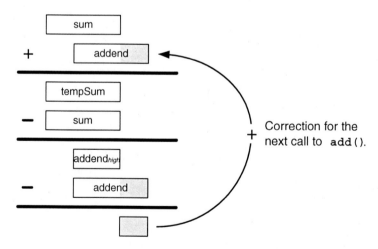

Figure 4-2   How the Kahan Summation Algorithm works.

---

[1]   William Kahan, a professor of computer science at the Berkeley campus of the University of California, does important work in the field of numerical computing. In the early 1980s, he led the group of computer scientists on the committee that wrote the IEEE 754 standard. He continues to consult with the computer industry to improve numerical computation.

Class `Summation` in package `numbercruncher.mathutils` implements this algo-rithm. See Listing 4–5a. Each call to method `add()` adds an addend and the correction to the run-ning sum, and then it computes the correction for the next call.

Listing 4–5a Kahan's Summation Algorithm for the `float` type.

```
package numbercruncher.mathutils;

/**
 * Implement Kahan's Summation Algorithm for the float type.
 */
public class KahanSummation
{
    /** the current running sum */      private float sum;
    /** the current correction */       private float correction;
    /** the current corrected addend */ private float correctedAddend;

    /**
     * Constructor.
     */
    public KahanSummation() {}

    /**
     * Return the current corrected value of the running sum.
     * @return the running sum's value
     */
    public float value() { return sum + correction; }

    /**
     * Return the corrected value of the current addend.
     * @return the corrected addend value
     */
    public float correctedAddend() { return correctedAddend; }

    /**
     * Add the value of an addend to the running sum.
     * @param the addend value
     */
    public void add(float addend)
    {
        // Correct the addend value and add it to the running sum.
        correctedAddend = addend + correction;
        float tempSum    = sum + correctedAddend;

        // Compute the next correction and set the running sum.
        // The parentheses are necessary to compute the high-order
        // bits of the addend.
        correction = correctedAddend - (tempSum - sum);
```

```
        sum         = tempSum;
    }

    /**
     * Clear the running sum and the correction.
     */
    public void clear()
    {
        sum         = 0;
        correction = 0;
    }
}
```

Program 4–5, shown in Listing 4–5b, uses class `Summation` to compute our fraction sum for denominator $s_{100,000,000}$. As we can see from the output, there is a significant improvement in the accuracy of the final sum, despite the high percentages of exponent differences within each group that exceed 24.

Listing 4–5b Fraction sums for $n = 100,000,000$ by the Kahan Summation Algorithm.

```
package numbercruncher.program4_5;

import numbercruncher.mathutils.KahanSummation;
import numbercruncher.mathutils.AlignRight;

/**
 * PROGRAM 4-5: Fraction Sum 100M by the Kahan Summation Algorithm
 *
 * Use the Kahan Summation Algorithm to compute
 * the sum 1/d + 2/d + 3/d + ... + n/d = d/d
 * where:
 *      n = 100,000,000
 *      d = 1 + 2 + 3 + ... + n = (n/2)(n + 1)
 *
 * See if the sum is closer to 1.
 */
public class FractionSum100MKahan
{
    private static final int GROUPS = 20;
    private static final int MAX     = 100000000;     // 100M

    public static void main(String args[])
    {
        AlignRight ar = new AlignRight();

        ar.print("i", 9); ar.print("Running sum", 16);
```

```
        ar.print("% ExpDiff>24", 16);
        ar.underline();

        float           denom = (0.5f*MAX)*(MAX + 1);
        KahanSummation kSum  = new KahanSummation();

        int gSize    = MAX/GROUPS;   // group size
        int gEnd     = gSize;        // index of group end
        int exceeds  = 0;            // # of exponent diff > 24

        // Sum the corrected fractions.
        for (int i = 1; i <= MAX; ++i) {
            float fraction = i/denom;

            int expSum = Float.floatToIntBits(kSum.value()) >> 23;
            kSum.add(fraction);

            int expFraction = Float.floatToIntBits(
                                kSum.correctedAddend()) >> 23;
            int diff        = Math.abs(expSum - expFraction);

            if ((i > 1) && (diff > 24)) ++exceeds;

            // Printout at the start of each group.
            if (i == gEnd) {
                ar.print(i, 9); ar.print(kSum.value(), 16);
                ar.print((100*exceeds)/gSize, 16);
                ar.println();

                exceeds = 0;
                gEnd += gSize;
            }
        }
        System.out.println("\n% error = " +
                        100*Math.abs(kSum.value() - 1));
    }
}
```

Output:

```
        i       Running sum    % ExpDiff>24
----------------------------------------
  5000000    0.0025000004              0
 10000000    0.010000001               0
 15000000         0.0225               0
 20000000           0.04               0
 25000000         0.0625               0
 30000000           0.09              26
 35000000         0.1225              12
 40000000           0.16              46
```

45000000	0.2025	42
50000000	0.25	36
55000000	0.3025	64
60000000	0.35999998	61
65000000	0.42249998	58
70000000	0.48999998	54
75000000	0.5625	72
80000000	0.64	73
85000000	0.72249997	72
90000000	0.81	70
95000000	0.9025	68
100000000	1.0	67

```
% error = 0.0
```

Figure 4–3 shows this improvement dramatically—the running sum of Program 4–5 smoothly increases to 1.

4.3 Summing Numbers in a Random Order

Before we leave our fraction summation problem, we should ask ourselves another question. What if the addends were not sorted but, instead, were in random order? How would the summation algorithms fare?

Program 4–6 performs the summation for denominator $s_{10,000,000}$. See Listing 4–6. It puts the counting numbers into an array, which it then scrambles. It does a simple straight summation

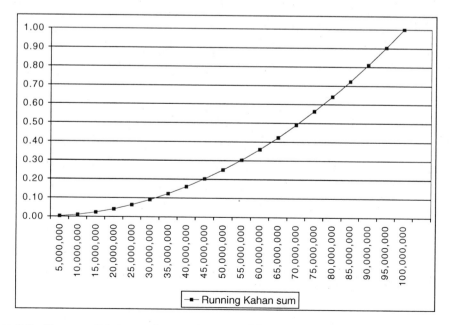

Figure 4-3   The smoothly increasing running sum of Program 4–5, thanks to the Kahan Summation Algorithm.

of the fractions in the random order; then, as in our previous programs, at the end of each equal-sized group, it prints the current value of the running sum and the percentage of exponent differences greater than 24 within the group. Finally, the program sums the fractions again using Kahan's Summation Algorithm on the same randomized ordering.

Listing 4–6 Fraction sums for $n = 10,000,000$ in a random order, with simple straight summation and the Kahan Summation Algorithm.

```
package numbercruncher.program4_6;

import java.util.Random;

import numbercruncher.mathutils.KahanSummation;
import numbercruncher.mathutils.AlignRight;

/**
 * PROGRAM 4-6: Fraction Sum 10M with Randomized Order
 *
 * Compute the sum 1/d + 2/d + 3/d + ... + n/d = d/d
 * where:
 *      n = 10,000,000
 *      d = 1 + 2 + 3 + ... + n = (n/2)(n + 1)
 *
 * Randomize the order of the fractions, and then compute their
 * sum by simple straight summation and by Kahan's Summation Algorithm.
 */
public class FractionSum10MRandom
{
    private static final int GROUPS = 20;
    private static final int MAX    = 10000000;      // 10M

    public static void main(String args[])
    {
        int     counting[] = new int[MAX + 1];  // array of counting #s
        Random random      = new Random(0);     // random # generator

        AlignRight ar = new AlignRight();

        // Initialize the array of counting numbers.
        for (int i = 1; i <= MAX; ++i) counting[i] = i;

        // Randomize the array.
        for (int i = 0; i < (MAX/2); ++i) {
            int j = random.nextInt(MAX) + 1;
            int k = random.nextInt(MAX) + 1;

            // Exchange random elements.
            int temp    = counting[j];
```

```
        counting[j] = counting[k];
        counting[k] = temp;
    }

    System.out.println("STRAIGHT SUMMATION:\n");
    ar.print("i", 9); ar.print("Running sum", 16);
    ar.print("% ExpDiff>24", 16);
    ar.underline();

    float sum   = 0;
    float denom = (0.5f*MAX)*(MAX + 1);

    int gSize     = MAX/GROUPS;    // group size
    int gEnd      = gSize;         // index of group end
    int exceeds   = 0;            // # of exponent diff > 24

    // Sum the fractions using simple straight summation.
    for (int i = 1; i <= MAX; ++i) {
        float fraction = counting[i]/denom;
        sum += fraction;

        int expSum      = Float.floatToIntBits(sum)      >> 23;
        int expFraction = Float.floatToIntBits(fraction) >> 23;
        int diff        = Math.abs(expSum - expFraction);

        if ((sum > 0) && (diff > 24)) ++exceeds;

        // Subtotal and printout at the end of each group.
        if (i == gEnd) {
            ar.print(i, 9); ar.print(sum, 16);
            ar.print((100*exceeds)/gSize, 16);
            ar.println();

            exceeds = 0;
            gEnd += gSize;
        }
    }
    System.out.println("\nStraight summation % error = " +
                    100*Math.abs(sum - 1));
    System.out.println("\nKAHAN SUMMATION ALGORITHM:\n");
    ar.print("i", 9); ar.print("Running sum", 16);
    ar.print("% ExpDiff>24", 16);
    ar.underline();

    KahanSummation kSum = new KahanSummation();

    exceeds = 0;
    gEnd    = gSize;
```

```
        // Sum the corrected fractions using
        // the Kahan Summation Algorithm.
        for (int i = 1; i <= MAX; ++i) {
            float fraction = counting[i]/denom;

            int expSum = Float.floatToIntBits(kSum.value()) >> 23;
            kSum.add(fraction);

            int expFraction = Float.floatToIntBits(
                              kSum.correctedAddend()) >> 23;
            int diff       = Math.abs(expSum - expFraction);

            if ((i > 1) && (diff > 24))
                ++exceeds;

            // Printout at the start of each group.
            if (i == gEnd) {
                ar.print(i, 9); ar.print(kSum.value(), 16);
                ar.print((100*exceeds)/gSize, 16);
                ar.println();

                exceeds = 0;
                gEnd += gSize;
            }
        }
        System.out.println("\nKahan summation % error = " +
                           100*Math.abs(kSum.value() - 1));
    }
}
```

Output:

```
STRAIGHT SUMMATION:
         i       Running sum     % ExpDiff>24
----------------------------------------
    500000       0.03253527           0
   1000000       0.06698631           0
   1500000       0.10321888           1
   2000000       0.14138556           1
   2500000       0.18116862           2
   3000000       0.22312914           2
   3500000       0.26563966           3
   4000000       0.31117648           4
   4500000       0.35919634           4
   5000000       0.40717205           4
   5500000       0.45824587           4
   6000000       0.5116293            5
   6500000       0.5648118            9
   7000000       0.6180561            9
```

```
  7500000          0.67235166                    9
  8000000          0.73646766                    9
  8500000           0.8006135                    9
  9000000           0.8647307                    9
  9500000           0.9288819                    9
 10000000           0.9929972                    9


Straight summation % error = 0.7002771

KAHAN SUMMATION ALGORITHM:

        i        Running sum    % ExpDiff>24
---------------------------------------------
   500000         0.032521274                   0
  1000000          0.06689266                   0
  1500000          0.10307682                   1
  2000000          0.14115047                   1
  2500000          0.18101728                   2
  3000000          0.22275041                   2
  3500000          0.26629776                   3
  4000000          0.31170923                   4
  4500000          0.35897893                   4
  5000000          0.40804166                   4
  5500000          0.45892397                   4
  6000000          0.51166385                   5
  6500000           0.566273                    9
  7000000           0.6227702                   9
  7500000          0.68106335                   9
  8000000          0.74115884                   9
  8500000           0.8031232                   9
  9000000          0.86690027                   9
  9500000           0.9325508                   9
 10000000               1.0                     9

Kahan summation % error = 0.0
```

If we compare the straight summation results with the output of Program 4–1 with denominator $s_{10,000,000}$, we see that the random order had worse results—an error of 0.70% vs. 0.27%. It's not hard to figure out why. When the fractions were sorted in ascending order, both the fractions and the running sum steadily increased in value (albeit not at the same rate). Therefore, at least in the beginning, the exponents of the fractions and of the running sum didn't differ by more than 24. But when the fractions were added in a random order, as the running sum grew, there was an increasing chance that the exponent difference between a fraction and the running sum was greater than 24. We can see that in the group percentages.

On the other hand, the Kahan Summation Algorithm worked well in this case even when the addends were unsorted.

4.4 Summing Addends with Different Signs

The previous example involved addends that were all of the same sign. What happens when we sum both positive and negative numbers?

Our next two programs experiment with the following series:

$$0 = \sum_{k=0}^{\infty} (-1)^k \frac{(2k+1)^2 + (2k+1)^3}{k!} = \frac{1^2+1^3}{0!} - \frac{3^2+3^3}{1!} + \frac{5^2+5^3}{2!} - \frac{7^2+7^3}{3!} + \dots$$

which has alternating signs.[2]

Program 4–7 performs a simple straight summation of the series. See Listing 4–7. The summation stops as soon as the fractions are too small to change the value of the running sum.

Listing 4–7 Summing numbers with mixed signs.

```
package numbercruncher.program4_7;

import numbercruncher.mathutils.AlignRight;

/**
 * Program 4-7: Sum Numbers with Mixed Signs
 *
 * Sum a sequence numbers with alternating signs.  The sum should be 0.
 */
public class SumMixedSigns
{
    private static AlignRight ar = new AlignRight();

    public static void main(String args[])
    {
        int     k          = 0;
        int     odd        = 1;      // odd number
        float   kFactorial = 1;      // k!
        boolean subtract   = false;  // true if subtract, false if add

        float   sum        = 0;      // running sum
        float   prevSum    = -1;     // previous value of running sum
        ar.print("k", 2);
        ar.print("Numerator", 11);
        ar.print("Factorial", 16);
        ar.print("Fraction", 16);
        ar.print("Running sum", 16);
        ar.underline();

        // Loop until the running sum stops changing.
        do {
```

---

[2] This equation is due to the Indian mathematician Ramanujan. We'll see more of his formulas in Chapter 13.

```
        float numerator = odd*odd;
        numerator += odd*numerator;

        float fraction = numerator/kFactorial;
        prevSum = sum;

        // Add or subtract the next fraction.
        if (subtract) fraction = -fraction;
        sum += fraction;

        ar.print(k, 2);
        ar.print(numerator, 11);
        ar.print(kFactorial, 16);
        ar.print(fraction, 16);
        ar.print(sum, 16);
        ar.println();

        ++k;
        kFactorial *= k;
        odd += 2;
        subtract = !subtract;
    } while (sum != prevSum);
  }
}
```

Output:

k	Numerator	Factorial	Fraction	Running sum
0	2.0	1.0	2.0	2.0
1	36.0	1.0	-36.0	-34.0
2	150.0	2.0	75.0	41.0
3	392.0	6.0	-65.333336	-24.333336
4	810.0	24.0	33.75	9.416664
5	1452.0	120.0	-12.1	-2.6833363
6	2366.0	720.0	3.286111	0.60277486
7	3600.0	5040.0	-0.71428573	-0.11151087
8	5202.0	40320.0	0.12901786	0.017506987
9	7220.0	362880.0	-0.019896384	-0.0023893975
10	9702.0	3628800.0	0.002673611	2.8421357E-4
11	12696.0	3.99168E7	-3.1806156E-4	-3.3847988E-5
12	16250.0	4.790016E8	3.392473E-5	7.674316E-8
13	20412.0	6.2270208E9	-3.277972E-6	-3.2012288E-6
14	25230.0	8.7178289E10	2.8940693E-7	-2.9118219E-6
15	30752.0	1.30767428E12	-2.351656E-8	-2.9353384E-6
16	37026.0	2.09227885E13	1.7696494E-9	-2.9335688E-6
17	44100.0	3.55687415E14	-1.2398527E-10	-2.9336927E-6
18	52022.0	6.4023735E15	8.125424E-12	-2.9336845E-6
19	60840.0	1.21645096E17	-5.001435E-13	-2.933685E-6
20	70602.0	2.43290202E18	2.9019664E-14	-2.933685E-6

The values of the running sum are supposed to oscillate about 0, alternating between positive and negative in step with the signs of the fractions. After the first couple of values, the running sum values should steadily decrease in magnitude. However, the pattern breaks when $k = 12$. The running sum's value seems smaller than expected, the next value has a greater magnitude, and all subsequent values are negative.

The pattern breaks when the exponents of the fraction and of the running sum are the same. Because the fraction and the running sum have opposite signs, cancellation error is the culprit. When $k = 12$, we subtract

$$3.3924730 \times 10^{-5} \text{ (running sum)}$$
$$-3.3847988 \times 10^{-5} \text{ (fraction)}$$

Losing the leading significant digits throws off the remaining values of the running sum. It is also at this point that the factorial values (and hence the fraction values) begin to lose accuracy due to insufficient digits of precision.

Program 4–8 uses `double` arithmetic to show one solution to the cancellation problem. See Listing 4–8. It computes separate subtotals for the positive fractions and for the negative fractions, thus removing the cancellation problem. Then, it computes the correct final sum by adding together the two subtotals. So we see that, *when summing numbers with mixed signs, it is better to sum the positive numbers and the negative numbers separately.*

Listing 4–8 Summing numbers with mixed signs using separate positive and negative subtotals.

```
package numbercruncher.program4_8;

import numbercruncher.mathutils.AlignRight;

/**
 * Program 4-8: Sum Numbers with Mixed Signs,
 *              Positive and Negative Subtotals
 *
 * Sum a sequence of double numbers with alternating signs.
 * Compute separate positive and negative subtotals.  The final sum
 * should be 0.
 */
public class SumMixedSignsPosNeg
{
    public static void main(String args[])
    {
        AlignRight ar = new AlignRight();
        int    k       = 0;
        int    odd      = 1;    // odd number
```

```
        double kFactorial = 1;    // k!
        double posSum       = 0;    // running subtotal of pos fractions
        double negSum       = 0;    // running subtotal of neg fractions
        double prevPosSum = -1;    // previous value of positive sum
        double prevNegSum = 1;     // previous value of negative sum

        ar.print("k", 2);
        ar.print("Fraction", 25);
        ar.print("Positive subtotal", 20);
        ar.print("Negative subtotal", 21);
        ar.underline();

        // Loop until the positive and negative subtotals
        // no longer change.
        do {
            // Positive fraction and subtotal.
            double posNumerator = odd*odd;
            posNumerator += odd*posNumerator;
            double posFraction = posNumerator/kFactorial;
            prevPosSum = posSum;
            posSum += posFraction;

            ar.print(k, 2);
            ar.print(posFraction, 25);
            ar.print(posSum, 20);
            ar.println();

            ++k;
            kFactorial *= k;
            odd += 2;

            // Negative fraction and subtotal.
            double negNumerator = odd*odd;
            negNumerator += odd*negNumerator;
            double negFraction = -negNumerator/kFactorial;
            prevNegSum = negSum;
            negSum += negFraction;

            ar.print(k, 2);
            ar.print(negFraction, 25);
            ar.print(" ", 20);
            ar.print(negSum, 21);
            ar.println();

            ++k;
            kFactorial *= k;
            odd += 2;
        } while ((posSum != prevPosSum) || (negSum != prevNegSum));
```

```
        System.out.println("\nFinal sum = " + (posSum + negSum));
    }
}
```

Output:

k	Fraction	Positive subtotal	Negative subtotal
0	2.0	2.0	
1	-36.0		-36.0
2	75.0	77.0	
3	-65.33333333333333		-101.33333333333333
4	33.75	110.75	
5	-12.1		-113.43333333333332
6	3.286111111111111	114.03611111111111	
7	-0.7142857142857143		-114.14761904761903
8	0.12901785714285716	114.16512896825397	
9	-0.019896384479717814		-114.16751543209875
10	0.002673611111111111	114.16780257936507	
11	-3.1806156806156807E-4		-114.16783349366682
12	3.392473010528566E-5	114.16783650409518	
13	-3.277972027972028E-6		-114.16783677163885
14	2.89406911430721E-7	114.16783679350209	
15	-2.35165579080923E-8		-114.16783679515541
16	1.7696492770897533E-9	114.16783679527174	
17	-1.2398526491663746E-10		-114.1678367952794
18	8.125423849197927E-12	114.16783679527987	
19	-5.001434484046243E-13		-114.1678367952799
20	2.901966448410855E-14	114.1678367952799	
21	-1.5923761931532594E-15		-114.1678367952799
22	8.287361182067708E-17	114.1678367952799	
23	-4.101498195323127E-18		-114.1678367952799

Final sum = 0.0

4.5 Insightful Computing

At this point, you may be asking yourself, Why don't we just do everything with double-precision arithmetic and not worry about roundoff, magnitude, and cancellation errors? Double-precision numbers have larger exponent range (good for preventing underflow and overflow errors) and greater precision (good for minimizing roundoff errors). But they take up twice as much memory (bad for arrays), and their arithmetic is slower (bad for repeated computations). Double-precision arithmetic will not hide the sins of bad design. *Using double-precision arithmetic with carelessly designed computations will only delay the onset of floating-point errors.*

We need to study the nature of the problem to gain some insight, and then we may have to try several methods before we find one that works. To illustrate, the next few programs will compute the value of e^x using its Taylor series at $x = -19.5$:

$$e^x = \sum_{k=0}^{\infty} \frac{x^k}{k!} = \frac{x^0}{0!} + \frac{x^1}{1!} + \frac{x^2}{2!} + \frac{x^3}{3!} + \cdots$$

Program 4–9 shows a first attempt and some of its output. See Listing 4–9.

Listing 4-9 Computation of $e^{-19.5}$ using the Taylor series.

```
package numbercruncher.program4_9;

import numbercruncher.mathutils.AlignRight;

/**
 * PROGRAM 4-9: e to x
 *
 * Compute e^x using the Taylor series with x = -19.5
 * The final value should be approximately 3.4e-9
 */
public class EtoX
{
    private static final double x = -19.5;

    public static void main(String args[])
    {
        AlignRight ar = new AlignRight();

        int    k           = 0;
        double numerator   = 1;
        double denominator = 1;
        double sum         = 1;    // running sum
        double prevSum     = 0;    // previous value of running sum

        ar.print("k", 2);
        ar.print("Numerator", 24);
        ar.println();
        ar.print("Denominator", 26);
        ar.print("Fraction", 24);
        ar.print("Running sum", 23);
        ar.underline();

        // Loop to compute and sum the terms of the Taylor series.
        do {
            numerator   *= x;      // x^k
```

```
            denominator *= ++k;   // k!

            double fraction = numerator/denominator;
            prevSum = sum;
            sum += fraction;

            ar.print(k, 2);
            ar.print(numerator, 24);
            ar.println();
            ar.print(denominator, 26);
            ar.print(fraction, 24);
            ar.print(sum, 23);
            ar.println();
        } while (prevSum != sum);
        double correct = Math.exp(x);

        System.out.println("\ne^" + x + " = " + sum);
        System.out.println("% error = " +
                        100*Math.abs(sum - correct)/correct);
    }
}
```

Output:

k	Numerator Denominator	Fraction	Running sum
1	-19.5		
	1.0	-19.5	-18.5
2	380.25		
	2.0	190.125	171.625
3	-7414.875		
	6.0	-1235.8125	-1064.1875
4	144590.0625		
	24.0	6024.5859375	4960.3984375
...			
17	-8.522919630788428E21		
	3.55687428096E14	-2.3961824224183973E7	-1.2635486167179534E7
18	1.6619693280037435E23		
	6.402373705728E15	2.595864290953264E7	1.3323156742353106E7
19	-3.2408401896073E24		
	1.21645100408832E17	-2.6641765091362443E7	-1.3318608349009337E7
20	6.319638369734235E25		
	2.43290200817664E18	2.5975720964078385E7	1.2657112615069048E7
...			
49	-1.6281557854172669E63		
	6.082818640342675E62	-2.676646932425302	-0.754026189305919
50	3.1749037815636704E64		

```
        3.0414093201713376E64        1.0438923036458678         0.2898661143399488
51      -6.191062374049157E65
        1.5511187532873822E66       -0.39913529257047886       -0.10926917823053006
52      1.2072571629395856E67
        8.065817517094388E67         0.14967573471392956        0.0404065564833995
...
90      1.2679876471392079E116
        1.4857159644817607E138       8.534522596864606E-23      9.498996099055442E-9
91     -2.4725759119214553E117
        1.3520015276784023E140      -1.828826270756701E-23      9.498996099055424E-9
92      4.821523028246838E118
        1.24384140546413E142         3.876316552147356E-24      9.498996099055428E-9
93     -9.401969905081333E119
        1.1567725070816409E144      -8.127760512567037E-25      9.498996099055428E-9

e^-19.5 = 9.498996099055428E-9
% error = 179.52464619068274
```

We immediately notice several things. The series converges very slowly, requiring 93 iterations before the fraction no longer affects the running sum. Because $e^{-19.5} \approx 3.398267819495071 \times 10^{-9}$, the final computed value, although of the correct magnitude, is very wrong. The values of the running sum oscillate wildly before converging to its final (incorrect) value. Their magnitudes initially grow dramatically ($k = 0$ through 18), decrease almost as dramatically ($k = 19$ through 50), and then finally start their slow convergence. This is caused by the magnitude of the fractions, which in turn is affected by their numerators and denominators. The magnitudes of the numerators initially exceed those of the denominators, and then the tide turns (at $k = 51$). Only when the absolute values of the fractions are decreasing can the values of the running sums converge.

The graph in Figure 4–4 plots the first 40 values of the running sum.

Thus, the value to which the running sum finally converges was determined by the "coarse tuning" that occurred earlier when its values first began to converge. The "fine tuning" at the end could not compensate for the earlier inaccuracies. The inaccuracies were due to roundoff errors (especially with the very large numerator and denominator values), magnitude errors (many values of the running sum were several orders of magnitude greater than the final value of the sum), and cancellation errors (because of the alternating signs of the fractions). In fact, the roundoff errors in the large running sum values greatly exceed the final sum value. Also, if the series converges too slowly, the denominator will eventually overflow. Although it did not happen here with $x = -19.5$, larger absolute values of x will cause the numerator to overflow.

Fixing the cancellation problem is easy. Since

$$e^x = \frac{1}{e^{-x}}$$

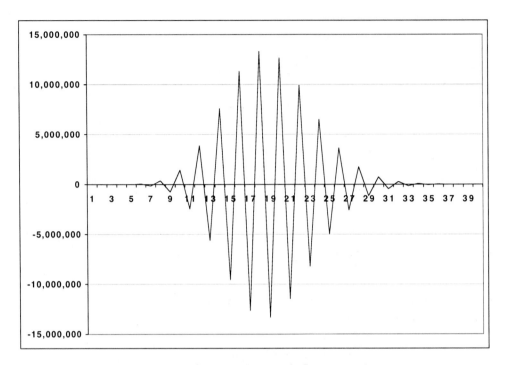

Figure 4–4   The oscillating values of the running sum in Program 4–9.

we can use the Taylor series with |x| and then take the inverse of the final sum if *x* is negative. Program 4–10 performs this computation. See Listing 4–10.

Listing 4–10 Computation of $e^{-19.5}$ by inverting the result of the Taylor series at $x = +19.5$.

```
package numbercruncher.program4_10;

import numbercruncher.mathutils.AlignRight;

/**
 * PROGRAM 4-10: e to x Inverse
 *
 * Compute e^x at x = -19.5 by using the Taylor series
 * with x = 19.5 and then taking the inverse of the result.
 * The final value should be approximately 3.4e-9
 */
public class EtoXInverse
{
```

```java
    private static final double x = -19.5;

    public static void main(String args[])
    {
        AlignRight ar = new AlignRight();

        int    k           = 0;
        double numerator   = 1;
        double denominator = 1;
        double sum         = 1;      // running sum
        double prevSum     = 0;      // previous value of running sum
        double xInverse    = -x;

        ar.print("k", 2);
        ar.print("Numerator", 24);
        ar.println();
        ar.print("Denominator", 26);
        ar.print("Fraction", 24);
        ar.print("Running sum", 23);
        ar.underline();

        // Loop to compute and sum the terms of the Taylor series.
        do {
            numerator   *= xInverse;     // xInverse^k
            denominator *= ++k;          // k!

            double fraction = numerator/denominator;
            prevSum = sum;
            sum += fraction;

            ar.print(k, 2);
            ar.print(numerator, 24);
            ar.println();
            ar.print(denominator, 26);
            ar.print(fraction, 24);
            ar.print(sum, 23);
            ar.println();
        } while (prevSum != sum);

        double result  = 1/sum;
        double correct = Math.exp(x);
        System.out.println("\ne^" + x + " = " + result);
        System.out.println("% error = " +
                        100*Math.abs(result - correct)/correct);
    }
}
```

Output:

k	Numerator Denominator	Fraction	Running sum
1	19.5		
	1.0	19.5	20.5
2	380.25		
	2.0	190.125	210.625
3	7414.875		
	6.0	1235.8125	1446.4375
4	144590.0625		
	24.0	6024.5859375	7471.0234375
...			
63	1.871459856776355E81		
	1.98260831540444E87	9.4393826669419E-7	2.9426756604150844E8
64	3.649346720713892E82		
	1.2688693218588417E89	2.87606190633386E-7	2.9426756604150873E8
65	7.116226105392089E83		
	8.247650592082472E90	8.628185719001579E-8	2.942675660415088E8
66	1.3876640905514574E85		
	5.443449390774431E92	2.5492366897050122E-8	2.942675660415088E8

```
e^-19.5 = 3.3982678194950715E-9
% error = 1.217062127663519E-14
```

The final value is much improved. But the convergence is still quite slow, and we still run the risk of overflows in the numerator and in the denominator with larger absolute values of x.

We need to increase the convergence rate, and we can accomplish that by reducing the sizes of the numerators. If the fractions are smaller, we'll reach the point sooner when the fractions are too small to affect the value of the running sum.

Now for a bit of insight. We can split an exponent x into its whole w and fraction f components, where $0 \leq f < 1$:

$$e^x = e^{w + f}$$

If w is nonzero, we can reduce the size of the exponent by factoring out the whole part w:

$$e^x = e^{w+f} = e^{\left(1 + \frac{f}{w}\right)w} = \left[e^{\left(1 + \frac{f}{w}\right)}\right]^w$$

Since $1 \leq \left(1 + \frac{f}{w}\right) < 2$, the Taylor series for $e^{\left(1 + \frac{f}{w}\right)}$ converges fairly rapidly, and then we raise the result to the integer power of w. Of course, if w is 0, we just compute e^f with the Taylor series.

Program 4–11 computes $e^{-19.5}$ using this split exponent technique. See Listing 4–11. It uses the numbercruncher.mathutils.IntPower class from Chapter 2.

Listing 4–11 Computation of $e^{-19.5}$ by splitting the exponent before using the Taylor series.

```java
package numbercruncher.program4_11;

import numbercruncher.mathutils.IntPower;
import numbercruncher.mathutils.AlignRight;

/**
 * PROGRAM 4-11: e to x with Split Exponent
 *
 * Compute e^x by splitting the exponent x into its whole and
 * fraction components before using the Taylor series.
 */
public class EtoXSplit
{
    private static final double x = -19.5;

    private static AlignRight ar = new AlignRight();

    public static void main(String args[])
    {

        double result;

        // Split off the whole part of |x|.
        double xAbs    = Math.abs(x);
        int    xWhole = (int) xAbs;

        // x is only a fraction.
        if (xWhole == 0) {
            result = taylor(xAbs);
        }

        // x has a whole part.
        else {
            // Split off the fraction part of x,
            // compute e^(1 + fraction/whole) ...
            double xFraction = xAbs - xWhole;
            double temp = taylor(1 + xFraction/xWhole);

            // ... and raise it to the whole power.
            result = IntPower.raise(temp, xWhole);
        }

        // Invert the result if x < 0.
        if (x < 0) result = 1/result;

        double correct = Math.exp(x);
```

```
    System.out.println("\ne     " + x + " = " + result);
    System.out.println("% error = " +
                       100*Math.abs(result - correct)/correct);
}


/**
 * Compute e^x, x > 0 using the Taylor series.
 * @param x the exponent
 * @return the value to which the series converged
 */
private static double taylor(double x)
{
    ar.print("k", 2);
    ar.print("Numerator", 20);
    ar.println();
    ar.print("Denominator", 22);
    ar.print("Fraction", 24);
    ar.print("Running sum", 20);
    ar.underline();

    int    k            = 0;
    double numerator    = 1;
    double denominator  = 1;
    double sum          = 1;
    double prevSum      = 0;

    // Loop until the terms have no effect on the sum.
    do {
        numerator    *= x;      // x^k
        denominator  *= ++k;    // k!

        double fraction = numerator/denominator;
        prevSum = sum;
        sum += fraction;

        ar.print(k, 2);
        ar.print(numerator, 20);
        ar.println();
        ar.print(denominator, 22);
        ar.print(fraction, 24);
        ar.print(sum, 20);
        ar.println();
    } while (prevSum != sum);

    return sum;
}
}
```

Output:

```
k            Numerator
             Denominator            Fraction            Running sum
----------------------------------------------------------------------
1   1.0263157894736843
                 1.0      1.0263157894736843   2.026315789473684
2   1.0533240997229918
                 2.0      0.5266620498614959    2.55297783933518
3   1.0810431549788602
                 6.0      0.18017385916314335   2.733151698498323
4   1.1094916590572512
                24.0      0.04622881912738547   2.7793805176257087
5   1.1386888079798105
               120.0      0.009489073399831755  2.7888695910255406
6   1.1686543029266478
               720.0      0.0016231309762870108 2.7904927220018276
7   1.1994083635299808
              5040.0      2.3797784990674224E-4 2.7907306998517343
8   1.230971741517612
             40320.0      3.053005311303601E-5  2.7907612299048474
9   1.263365734715444
            362880.0      3.4814972848198965E-6 2.790764711402132
10  1.2966122014184822
           3628800.0      3.5731156344204206E-7 2.7907650687136956
11  1.3307335751400213
             3.99168E7    3.333768175655416E-8  2.7907651020513775
12  1.3657528797489693
            4.790016E8    2.8512490976000275E-9 2.7907651049026265
13  1.4016937450055214
            6.2270208E9   2.2509861296842326E-10 2.790765105127725
14  1.4385804225056669
           8.71782912E10  1.6501590048437045E-11 2.7907651051442266
15  1.4764378020452897
          1.307674368E12  1.1290561612088505E-12 2.7907651051453555
16  1.5152914284149028
         2.0922789888E13  7.24230103406993E-14  2.790765105145428
17  1.5551675186363478
        3.55687428096E14  4.372287001992683E-15 2.7907651051454323
18  1.596092979653094
       6.402373705728E15  2.4929706590309163E-16 2.7907651051454327
19  1.6380954264860703
     1.21645100408832E17  1.3466185000305503E-17 2.7907651051454327

e^-19.5 = 3.398267819495072E-9
% error = 2.434124255327038E-14
```

So our bit of insight has improved the convergence rate and produced a very accurate result. The error percentage is a bit higher here than in Program 4–10. But in general, splitting the exponent is the better technique. With a smaller numerator and faster convergence, the effects of accumulated roundoff errors and the chances for overflow are both reduced.

4.6 Summation Summary

We can sum up, so to speak, the lessons of this chapter:

- When summing lists of numbers with the same sign, add them in the sorted order of the smallest magnitude to the largest.
- Avoid magnitude errors that occur whenever the differences between the binary exponents of the addends exceed 24 for `float` and 53 for `double`. The Kahan Summation Algorithm works well despite magnitude errors.
- When summing lists of numbers with mixed signs, avoid cancellation errors by subtotaling the positive and negative numbers separately.
- Double-precision arithmetic is not a cure-all.
- Sometimes we may have to try several summation algorithms before we find one that works.
- The best strategy of all is to gain some insight into the nature of the problem.

References

Forsythe, George, Michael A. Malcolm, and Cleve B. Moler, *Computer Methods for Mathematical Computations,* Englewood Cliffs, NJ: Prentice-Hall, 1977.

This book describes the computation of e^x using the Taylor series in Section 2.3.

Goldberg, David, "What Every Computer Scientist Should Know about Floating-Point Arithmetic," in *ACM Computing Surveys,* Volume 23, Number 1, March 1991.

Higham, Nicolas J., *Accuracy and Stability of Numerical Algorithms,* Philadelphia: Society for Industrial and Applied Mathematics, 1996.

Kahan, W., *Implementation of Algorithms, Part I,* Technical Report 20, lecture notes by W.S. Haugeland and D. Hough, Department of Computer Science, University of California, Berkeley, 1973.

Goldberg, Higham, and Kahan describe the Kahan Summation Algorithm. Goldberg contains a detailed analysis and proof of the method. Higham also analyzes the method and describes the even more ingenious *doubly compensated summation;* his Chapter 4 is entirely on summation.

Monahan, John F., *Numerical Methods of Statistics,* Cambridge, UK: Cambridge University Press, 2001.

This text discusses cancellation errors while computing a sample variance in Section 2.5.

CHAPTER 5

FINDING ROOTS

"**S**olve for *x*" is typically what we're asked to do when given an equation involving *x* as the unknown. One way to do it is to rewrite the equation into the form $f(x) = 0$, and then find the *roots,* or the *zeros,* of the function. In other words, we want to find the values of *x* such that $f(x) = 0$. Depending on the function, there may be more than one root, and they can be either real or complex, or there may be no roots at all. If we draw a graph of $f(x)$ in the *xy* plane, then the real roots are those values of *x* wherever the plot crosses the *x* axis. This chapter explores various algorithms for finding real roots that are suitable for a computer.

Traditionally, these algorithms are called *methods,* as in bisection method and Newton's method. However, to avoid confusion with the methods of Java classes, we'll use the word *algorithm* instead.

5.1 Analytical versus Computer Solutions

If the function is linear, then there is at most one root, and we can easily find it analytically with simple algebra. For example, if

$$f(x) = 3x - 6$$

then we just have to "do the math":

$$3x - 6 = 0$$
$$3x = 6$$
$$x = 2$$

So 2 is the root of the function $3x - 6$, and finding it is the solution to the problem "Solve the equation $3x = 6$ for *x*."

There are even formulas for roots. For the quadratic function $f(x) = ax^2 + bx + c$, where a, b, and c are real, and $a \neq 0$, we can use the quadratic formula we saw in Chapter 1

$$x = \frac{-b \pm \sqrt{b^2 - 4ac}}{2a}$$

to obtain the roots. If the discriminant $b^2 - 4ac$ is positive, the two roots are real and unequal. If it's 0, the two roots are real and equal, and if it's negative, the two roots are complex.

If the function f is a general polynomial, we may be able to solve it by factoring. For example, if

$$f(x) = 3x^3 - 18x^2 + 33x - 18$$

then we can factor it to

$$f(x) = (x - 1)(x - 3)(3x - 6)$$

and so $x = 1$, $x = 3$, and $x = 2$ are all roots.

But how do we program the computer to find roots? An analytical solution, such as by factoring and other algebraic manipulations, is fine to do by hand but difficult to program. The quadratic formula is easy to code, but it's only for quadratic functions.

The algorithms in this chapter take advantage of a computer's computational speed—they use brute force to find real roots iteratively by using trial and error. If we apply such algorithms intelligently, we'll maximize the chances that the trial x values (the *successive approximations*) converge to a root, and converge quickly. We hope that each trial decreases the error.

For each algorithm, we'll first write a simple program that illustrates the technique by printing out the successive approximations to a function's root. Next, we'll use an interactive program that animates the algorithm for a set of functions. You select the function, and then by clicking and dragging the mouse, you can set the value of the first trial value for x and watch the program converge (or fail to converge) to a root of the function.

5.2 The Functions

Before we start looking at the algorithms, we need to create some functions whose roots we're going to find and enter them all into a global function table. Listing 5–0a shows the abstract base class `Function` in package `numbercruncher.mathutils`.

Listing 5–0a The abstract base `Function` class.

```
package numbercruncher.mathutils;

/**
 * The base class for functions that can have derivatives.
```

```
 */
public abstract class Function implements Evaluatable
{
    /**
     * Return the value of the function at x.
     * (Implementation of Evaluatable.)
     * @param x the value of x
     * @return the function value
     */
    public abstract float at(float x);

    /**
     * Return the value of the function's derivative at x.
     * @param x the value of x
     * @return the derivative value
     */
    public float derivativeAt(float x) { return 0; }
}
```

This base class delegates to its subclasses the implementation of method at(), which will return the value of the function at *x*. By default, method derivativeAt() returns 0. This method may be overridden by a subclass, where it can return the value of the function's first derivative at *x*.

Listing 5–0b Interface Evaluatable.

```
package numbercruncher.mathutils;

/**
 * Interface implement by function classes.
 */
public interface Evaluatable
{
    /**
     * Return the value of the function at x.
     * @param x the value of x
     * @return the value of the function at x
     */
    float at(float x);
}
```

The base class implements interface Evaluatable in package numbercruncher. mathutils. See Listing 5–0b. This interface specifies the at() method. The interface will be useful when we develop classes that work with different function classes, such as the regression and interpolation function classes in Chapter 6.

Now we're ready to create some Function objects. Listing 5–0c shows parts of class RootFunctions in package numbercruncher.rootutils. It statically creates the function objects and enters them into the global hash table named TABLE.

Listing 5–0c Parts of class RootFunctions , which creates Function objects and enters them into a global hash table.

```
package numbercruncher.rootutils;

import java.util.Hashtable;
import numbercruncher.mathutils.Function;

/**
 * Load into a global table the functions whose roots we want to find.
 */
public class RootFunctions
{
    /** global function table */
    private static Hashtable TABLE = new Hashtable(32);

    // Enter the functions into the global function table.
    static {
        enterFunctions();
    }

    /**
     * Return the function with the given hash key
     * @param key the hash key
     * @return the function
     */
    public static Function function(String key)
    {
        return (Function) TABLE.get(key);
    }

    /**
     * Enter all the functions into the global function table.
     */
    private static void enterFunctions()
    {
        // Function f(x)  = x^2 - 4
        //          f'(x) = 2x
        TABLE.put(
            "x^2 - 4",
            new Function()
            {
                public float at(float x)
                {
                    return x*x - 4;
                }
            }
```

```
            public float derivativeAt(float x)
            {
                return 2*x;
            }
        });


...


    // Function g(x) = (x + 4/x)/2
    TABLE.put(
        "(x + 4/x)/2",
        new Function()
        {
            public float at(float x)
            {
                return (x + 4/x)/2;
            }
        });


...


}
```

The class enters each `Function` object into `TABLE`, using a string representation of the function's expression as the hash key. Some of the functions also have a defined first derivative $f'(x)$. Given a key, the `function()` method returns the corresponding `Function` object from `TABLE`, or null if the key is invalid.

Table 5–1 shows all the functions created by class `RootFunctions`. The reason some of the functions are named g will be explained later in this chapter.

5.3 The Bisection Algorithm

We begin with the simplest algorithm. Suppose we have a continuous function (its values have no breaks) over the interval between x_{neg} and x_{pos}. If $f(x_{neg}) < 0$ and $f(x_{pos}) > 0$, then we know that $f(x)$ must cross the x axis an odd number of times (and hence it must have at least one root) in the interval.[1] Note that x_{neg} itself is not necessarily negative, nor is x_{pos} itself necessarily positive, and that either $x_{neg} < x_{pos}$ or $x_{neg} > x_{pos}$. We can use the bisection algorithm, which reminds us of a binary search for an element of a sorted array of numbers.

The algorithm starts with the entire interval, and for each iteration, it performs the following actions:

- **Test the number of iterations** to check if the maximum was exceeded. If so, the algorithm has failed to find a root.

---

[1] We recall from freshman calculus the Intermediate Value Theorem, which states that, if function f is continuous over the interval $[a, c]$, and $f(a) = A$ and $f(c) = C$, and B is any number between A and C, then there must be least one number b between a and c such that $f(b) = B$. For the bisection algorithm, let $A < 0$ and $C > 0$ and $B = 0$. Then we're looking for a value b such that $f(b) = 0$.

Table 5–1   Functions used by the programs in this chapter.

$f(x) = x^2 - 4$	$g(x) = \dfrac{2}{x} + 1$
$f(x) = -x^2 + 4x + 5$	$g(x) = x^2 - 2$
$f(x) = x^3 + 3x^2 - 9x - 10$	$g(x) = e^{-x}$
$f(x) = x^2 - 2x + 3$	$g(x) = -\ln x$
$f(x) = 2x^3 - 10x^2 + 11x - 5$	$g(x) = e^{\left[\frac{1}{x}\right]}$
$f(x) = e^{-x}$	$g(x) = \dfrac{1}{\ln x}$
$f(x) = e^{\left[\frac{1}{x}\right]}$	$g(x) = \dfrac{x + e^{\left[\frac{1}{x}\right]}}{2}$
$g(x) = \dfrac{\left[x + \frac{4}{x}\right]}{2}$	$g(x) = \dfrac{\sin x}{2} + 1$
$g(x) = \dfrac{4}{x}$	$g(x) = 1 + \dfrac{1}{x} + \dfrac{1}{x^2}$
$g(x) = \sqrt{x + 2}$	$g(x) = \dfrac{20}{x^2 + 2x + 10}$

- **Compute the next position.** For the bisection algorithm, this means computing by bisecting the current interval and setting x_{mid} to the midpoint between the two ends of the interval.
- **Test for convergence.** If the algorithm has converged to a root, then it has successfully found that root.
- **Check the new position.** If the new position is the same as the previous one, and the algorithm still hasn't converged, then it has failed to find a root. For the bisection algorithm, if $f(x_{mid})$ is zero, or "sufficiently close" to zero, then the algorithm stops, and the final value of x_{mid} is the root it managed to trap.
- **Perform the iteration procedure to adjust the interval.** For the bisection algorithm, if $f(x_{mid}) < 0$, then the root must be in the x_{pos} half of the interval, so the algorithm sets x_{neg} to x_{mid} for the next iteration. On the other hand, if $f(x_{mid}) > 0$, then the root must be in the x_{neg} half of the interval, and so the algorithm sets x_{pos} to x_{mid} for the next iteration.

Even though we described these actions in the specific terms of the bisection algorithm, they apply in general to all the root-finding algorithms covered in this chapter. Therefore, can build a framework for these algorithms by creating an abstract RootFinder base class in package numbercruncher.mathutils. From this class, we can derive subclasses that implement the algorithms. Listing 5–0d shows this base class.

Listing 5–0d The abstract base class for the subclasses that implement root-finding algorithms.

```
package numbercruncher.mathutils;

/**
 * Abstract base class for the root finder classes.
 */
public abstract class RootFinder
{
    /** the function whose roots to find */ protected Function function;
    /** iteration counter */                 private   int       n;
    /** maximum number of iterations */      private   int       maxIters;

    /**
     * Constructor.
     * @param function the function whose roots to find
     * @param maxIters the maximum number of iterations
     */
    public RootFinder(Function function, int maxIters)
    {
        this.function = function;
        this.maxIters = maxIters;
    }

    /**
     * Check the interval.
     * @param xMin x-coordinate of the left of the interval
     * @param xMax x-coordinate of the right end of the interval
     * @throws InvalidIntervalException
     */
    public void checkInterval(float x1, float x2)
        throws InvalidIntervalException
    {
        float y1 = function.at(x1);
        float y2 = function.at(x2);

        // The interval is invalid if y1 and y2 have the same signs.
        if (y1*y2 > 0) throw new InvalidIntervalException();
    }

    /**
     * Return the iteration count.
     * @return the count
     */
    public int getIterationCount() { return n; }

    /**
     * Perform one iteration step.
```

```
     * @return true if the algorithm converged, else false
     * @throws IterationCountExceededException
     * @throws PositionUnchangedException
     */
    public boolean step() throws IterationCountExceededException,
                                 PositionUnchangedException
    {
        checkIterationCount();
        doIterationProcedure(n);

        computeNextPosition();
        checkPosition();

        return hasConverged();
    }

    /**
     * Check the iteration count to see if it has exeeded
     * the maximum number of iterations.
     * @throws IterationCountExceededException
     */
    protected void checkIterationCount()
        throws IterationCountExceededException
    {
        if (++n > maxIters) {
            throw new IterationCountExceededException()';
        }
    }

    /**
     * Reset.
     */
    protected void reset() { n = 0; }

    //------------------//
    // Subclass methods //
    //------------------//

    /**
     * Do the iteration procedure.
     * @param n the iteration count
     */
    protected abstract void doIterationProcedure(int n);

    /**
     * Compute the next position of x.
     */
    protected abstract void computeNextPosition();
```

```
    /**
     * Check the position of x.
     * @throws PositionUnchangedException
     */
    protected abstract void checkPosition()
        throws PositionUnchangedException;

    /**
     * Indicate whether or not the algorithm has converged.
     * @return true if converged, else false
     */
    protected abstract boolean hasConverged();

    //-----------------------//
    // Root finder exceptions //
    //-----------------------//

    /**
     * Invalid interval exception.
     */
    public class InvalidIntervalException
        extends java.lang.Exception {}

    /**
     * Iteration count exceeded exception.
     */
    public class IterationCountExceededException
        extends java.lang.Exception {}

    /**
     * Position unchanged exception.
     */
    public class PositionUnchangedException
        extends java.lang.Exception {}
}
```

The key method of the base class is step(), which performs one iteration step of the root-finding algorithm. It invokes methods to do the actions described on page 112, and returns true if the algorithm has converged, or false otherwise. Except for checkIterationCount(), all of these methods will be implemented by the subclasses.

The base class also defines several exceptions, RootFinder.InvalidInterval Exception, RootFinder.IterationCountExceededException, and RootFinder. PositionUnchangedException. Certain methods throw these exceptions. Method check IterationCount() can throw RootFinder.IterationCountExceededException. The subclass implementation of checkPosition() can throw RootFinder.Position

UnchangedException if necessary. Therefore, method step(), which invokes both methods, can also throw either of these two exceptions.

Some of the algorithms, including the bisection algorithm, require that the function value have different signs at the two ends of the interval. The base class provides the handy method check Interval() to test an interval, and it can throw RootFinder.InvalidIntervalException.

From the RootFinder base class, we can derive our first root-finding algorithm class, BisectionRootFinder. Like all the root-finding classes, it will be in the number-cruncher.mathutils package. See Listing 5–1a.

Listing 5–1a The class that implements the bisection algorithm.

```
package numbercruncher.mathutils;

/**
 * The root finder class that implements the bisection algorithm.
 */
public class BisectionRootFinder extends RootFinder
{
    private static final int   MAX_ITERS = 50;
    private static final float TOLERANCE = 100*Epsilon.floatValue();

    /** x-negative value */          private float    xNeg;
    /** x-middle value */            private float    xMid = Float.NaN;
    /** x-positive value */          private float    xPos;
    /** previous x-middle value */   private float    prevXMid;
    /** f(xNeg) */                   private float    fNeg;
    /** f(xMid) */                   private float    fMid;
    /** f(xPos) */                   private float    fPos;

    /**
     * Constructor.
     * @param function the functions whose roots to find
     * @param xMin the initial x-value where the function is negative
     * @param xMax the initial x-value where the function is positive
     * @throws RootFinder.InvalidIntervalException
     */
    public BisectionRootFinder(Function function,
                               float xMin, float xMax)
        throws RootFinder.InvalidIntervalException
    {
        super(function, MAX_ITERS);
        checkInterval(xMin, xMax);

        float yMin = function.at(xMin);
        float yMax = function.at(xMax);

        // Initialize xNeg, fNeg, xPos, and fPos.
        if (yMin < 0) {
```

```
            xNeg = xMin; xPos = xMax;
            fNeg = yMin; fPos = yMax;
        }
        else {
            xNeg = xMax; xPos = xMin;
            fNeg = yMax; fPos = yMin;
        }
    }


    //---------//
    // Getters //
    //---------//


    /**
     * Return the current value of x-negative.
     * @return the value
     */
    public float getXNeg() { return xNeg; }


    /**
     * Return the current value of x-middle.
     * @return the value
     */
    public float getXMid() { return xMid; }


    /**
     * Return the current value of x-positive.
     * @return the value
     */
    public float getXPos() { return xPos; }


    /**
     * Return the current value of f(x-negative).
     * @return the value
     */
    public float getFNeg() { return fNeg; }


    /**
     * Return the current value of f(x-middle).
     * @return the value
     */
    public float getFMid() { return fMid; }


    /**
     * Return the current value of f(x-positive).
     * @return the value
     */
    public float getFPos() { return fPos; }
```

```
//----------------------------//
// RootFinder method overrides //
//----------------------------//

/**
 * Do the bisection iteration procedure.
 * @param n the iteration count
 */
protected void doIterationProcedure(int n)
{
    if (n == 1) return;      // already initialized

    if (fMid < 0) {
        xNeg = xMid;         // the root is in the xPos half
        fNeg = fMid;
    }
    else {
        xPos = xMid;         // the root is in the xNeg half
        fPos = fMid;
    }
}

/**
 * Compute the next position of xMid.
 */
protected void computeNextPosition()
{
    prevXMid = xMid;
    xMid     = (xNeg + xPos)/2;
    fMid     = function.at(xMid);
}

/**
 * Check the position of xMid.
 * @throws PositionUnchangedException
 */
protected void checkPosition()
    throws RootFinder.PositionUnchangedException
{
    if (xMid == prevXMid) {
        throw new RootFinder.PositionUnchangedException();
    }
}

/**
 * Indicate whether or not the algorithm has converged.
 * @return true if converged, else false
 */
```

```
protected boolean hasConverged()
{
    return Math.abs(fMid) < TOLERANCE;
}
}
```

As we can see, other than the constructor that initializes the instance variables and the getter methods for these variables, the class mostly implements the abstract methods of the RootFinder base class.

Method doIterationProcedure() adjusts one or the other end of the interval, depending on whether the value of the function at x_{mid} is positive or negative. The method makes no changes during the first iteration, since values passed into the constructor determine the initial interval.

Method computeNextPosition() computes the next value of x_{mid} by finding the current interval's midpoint. Method checkPosition() makes sure that this midpoint is still changing. Finally, method hasConverged() checks to see if the value of the function at x_{mid} is "sufficiently close" to zero.

For this algorithm and the others in this chapter, we chose 50 as the maximum number of iterations, and 100ε as the tolerance for being close to zero, where ε is the machine epsilon value we computed at the end of Chapter 3. These two values are somewhat arbitrary—we chose them after some experimentation. If we set the tolerance too low, we run the risk of an algorithm never reaching it. The maximum number of iterations prevents a failing algorithm from running away.

Program 5–1 instantiates a BisectionRootFinder object to demonstrate the bisection algorithm on a Function object. But before we see its source listing and the output, let's look at an interactive GUI-based version of the program.[2] The interactive version allows you to select any of the functions listed in Table 5–1 that are named *f*. Screen 5–1 shows screen shots of the first three iterations of the bisection algorithm applied to $f(x) = x^2 - 4$, starting with the interval $[-0.25, 3.25]$. For each iteration, notice how either x_{neg} or x_{pos} changes, depending on whether the value of $f(x_{mid})$ was positive or negative in the previous iteration. (The interactive program can automatically run through its iteration steps with a short pause at the end of each one, or you can manually single-step one iteration at a time. The screen shots in Screen 5–1 were made from the single-step mode.)

Because of the ever-shrinking interval, the bisection algorithm is a *bracketing algorithm*.

The noninteractive version of Program 5–1 prints out, for each iteration, the current values of x_{neg}, $f(x_{neg})$, x_{mid}, $f(x_{mid})$, x_{pos}, and $f(x_{pos})$. The values of x_{mid} converge to the root trapped by x_{neg} and x_{pos}. The main() method simply loops until the algorithm either succeeds or fails. See Listing 5–1b.

---

[2] Each interactive program in this book has two versions, an applet and a standalone application. You can download all the Java source code. See the downloading instructions in the preface of this book.

Screen 5-1 The first three iterations of the bisection algorithm applied to the function $f(x) = x^2 - 4$ in the initial interval $[-0.25, 3.25]$. The tall vertical lines mark the current ends of the interval, and the short vertical line marks the current value of x_{mid}. These screen shots are from the interactive version of Program 5-1.

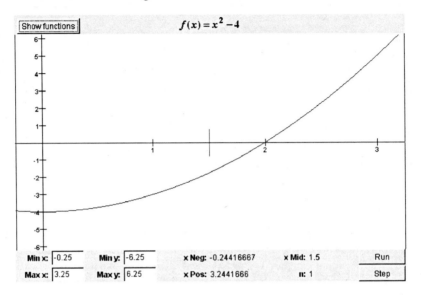

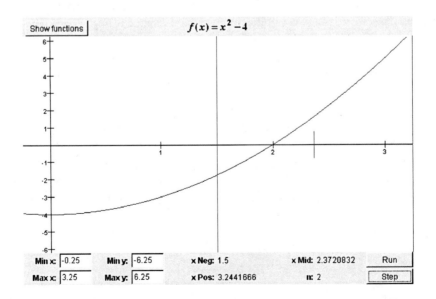

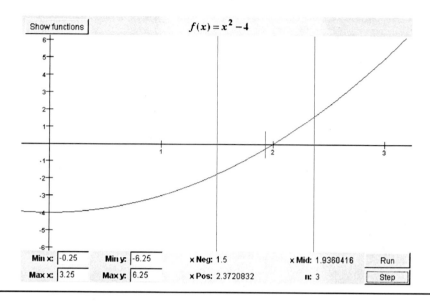

$$f(x) = x^2 - 4$$

Min x: -0.25	Min y: -6.25	x Neg: 1.5	x Mid: 1.9360416	Run
Max x: 3.25	Max y: 6.25	x Pos: 2.3720832	n: 3	Step

Listing 5–1b The noninteractive version of Program 5–1 applies the bisection algorithm to the function $f(x) = x^2 - 4$ in the initial interval $[-0.25, 3.25]$.

```
package numbercruncher.program5_1;

import numbercruncher.mathutils.Function;
import numbercruncher.mathutils.BisectionRootFinder;
import numbercruncher.mathutils.AlignRight;
import numbercruncher.rootutils.RootFunctions;

/**
 * PROGRAM 5-1: Bisection Algorithm
 *
 * Demonstrate the Bisection Algorithm on a function.
 */
public class BisectionAlgorithm
{
    /**
     * Main program.
     * @param args the array of runtime arguments
     */
    public static void main(String args[])
    {
        try {
            BisectionRootFinder finder =
                new BisectionRootFinder(
                        RootFunctions.function("x^2 - 4"),
                                -0.25f, 3.25f);
```

```
            AlignRight ar = new AlignRight();

            ar.print("n", 2);
            ar.print("xNeg", 10); ar.print("f(xNeg)", 14);
            ar.print("xMid", 10); ar.print("f(xMid)", 14);
            ar.print("xPos", 10); ar.print("f(xPos)", 13);
            ar.underline();

            // Loop until convergence or failure.
            boolean converged;
            do {
                converged = finder.step();

                ar.print(finder.getIterationCount(), 2);
                ar.print(finder.getXNeg(), 10);
                ar.print(finder.getFNeg(), 14);
                ar.print(finder.getXMid(), 10);
                ar.print(finder.getFMid(), 14);
                ar.print(finder.getXPos(), 10);
                ar.print(finder.getFPos(), 13);
                ar.println();
            } while (!converged);
            System.out.println("\nSuccess! Root = " +
                                finder.getXMid());
        }
        catch(Exception ex) {
            System.out.println("***** Error: " + ex);
        }
    }
}
```

Output:

```
 n     xNeg       f(xNeg)      xMid      f(xMid)      xPos      f(xPos)
----------------------------------------------------------------------
 1    -0.25       -3.9375       1.5       -1.75        3.25       6.5625
 2     1.5         -1.75       2.375     1.640625      3.25       6.5625
 3     1.5         -1.75      1.9375   -0.24609375     2.375     1.640625
 4    1.9375    -0.24609375   2.15625   0.64941406     2.375     1.640625
 5    1.9375    -0.24609375   2.046875  0.18969727    2.15625   0.64941406
 6    1.9375    -0.24609375  1.9921875 -0.031188965   2.046875  0.18969727
 7  1.9921875  -0.031188965  2.0195312  0.07850647    2.046875  0.18969727
 8  1.9921875  -0.031188965  2.0058594  0.023471832  2.0195312  0.07850647
 9  1.9921875  -0.031188965  1.9990234 -0.0039052963 2.0058594  0.023471832
10  1.9990234  -0.0039052963 2.0024414  0.009771347  2.0058594  0.023471832
11  1.9990234  -0.0039052963 2.0007324  0.0029301643 2.0024414  0.009771347
12  1.9990234  -0.0039052963 1.9998779 -4.8828125E-4 2.0007324  0.0029301643
13  1.9998779  -4.8828125E-4  2.0003052  0.0012207031 2.0007324  0.0029301643
14  1.9998779  -4.8828125E-4  2.0000916  3.6621094E-4 2.0003052  0.0012207031
```

```
15 1.9998779 -4.8828125E-4 1.9999847 -6.1035156E-5 2.0000916 3.6621094E-4
16 1.9999847 -6.1035156E-5 2.0000381  1.5258789E-4 2.0000916 3.6621094E-4
17 1.9999847 -6.1035156E-5 2.0000114  4.5776367E-5 2.0000381 1.5258789E-4
18 1.9999847 -6.1035156E-5 1.9999981 -7.6293945E-6 2.0000114 4.5776367E-5
19 1.9999981 -7.6293945E-6 2.0000048  1.9073486E-5 2.0000114 4.5776367E-5
20 1.9999981 -7.6293945E-6 2.0000014  5.722046E-6  2.0000048 1.9073486E-5

Success! Root = 2.0000014
```

The bisection algorithm is very easy to program, but how well does it work? Much more like the tortoise than the hare, if there is at least one real root in an interval, the algorithm will eventually find one of them. Of course, how fast the algorithm converges depends on the function and on the initial interval. Also, if there is more than one real root, which one the algorithm will converge to depends on the initial interval.

The bisection algorithm uses a very simple formula to determine the next approximation of the root: the midpoint of the current interval. Thus, its convergence rate is linear—the absolute error between the latest value of x_{mid} and the root is decreased at best by one half of the size of the current interval per iteration.

5.4 The *Regula Falsi* Algorithm

Obviously, a root-finding algorithm would converge faster if somehow the approximations were to get closer to the root faster. The algorithm of *regula falsi* (Latin for *false position*) attempts to do just that with a smarter algorithm for generating the approximations (false positions). We'll implement this algorithm in class `RegulaFalsiRootFinder`.

The basic idea is not hard to explain. Like the bisection algorithm, it is a bracketing algorithm that begins with an initial interval containing the root, and each iteration shrinks the interval to trap the root. For each iteration, we have x_{neg} and x_{pos}, the endpoints of interval, and we draw the secant (a line connecting two points on a curve) from the point $(x_{neg}, f(x_{neg}))$ to the point $(x_{pos}, f(x_{pos}))$. Then the new position x_{false} is where the secant crosses the x axis. See Figure 5–1.

We can compute the value of x_{false} using similar triangles. Because

$$\frac{x_{false} - x_{neg}}{f(x_{neg})} = \frac{x_{false} - x_{pos}}{f(x_{pos})}$$

we can cross-multiply and solve for x_{false}:

$$\left(x_{false} - x_{neg}\right)f(x_{pos}) = \left(x_{false} - x_{pos}\right)f(x_{neg})$$

$$x_{false}\left[f(x_{neg}) - f(x_{pos})\right] = x_{pos}f(x_{neg}) - x_{neg}f(x_{pos})$$

$$x_{false} = \frac{x_{pos}f(x_{neg}) - x_{neg}f(x_{pos})}{f(x_{neg}) - f(x_{pos})}$$

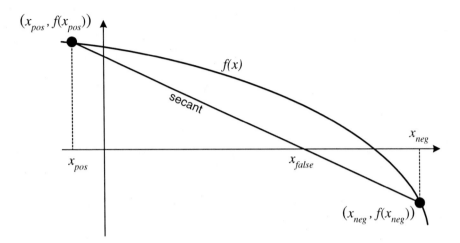

Figure 5–1   A secant line for the function $f(x)$ in the interval $[x_{pos}, x_{neg}]$, where $f(x_{pos}) > 0$ and $f(x_{neg}) < 0$.

To simplify the right-hand side, we break apart the fraction, add and subtract x_{pos}, and manipulate the terms inside the square brackets:

$$x_{false} = x_{pos} + \left[\frac{x_{pos}f(x_{neg})}{f(x_{neg}) - f(x_{pos})} - x_{pos} \right] - \frac{x_{neg}f(x_{pos})}{f(x_{neg}) - f(x_{pos})}$$

$$= x_{pos} + \left[\frac{x_{pos}f(x_{neg})}{f(x_{neg}) - f(x_{pos})} - \frac{x_{pos}f(x_{neg}) - x_{pos}f(x_{pos})}{f(x_{neg}) - f(x_{pos})} \right] - \frac{x_{neg}f(x_{pos})}{f(x_{neg}) - f(x_{pos})}$$

$$= x_{pos} + \left[\frac{x_{pos}f(x_{pos})}{f(x_{neg}) - f(x_{pos})} \right] - \frac{x_{neg}f(x_{pos})}{f(x_{neg}) - f(x_{pos})}$$

$$= x_{pos} - \frac{f(x_{pos})(x_{neg} - x_{pos})}{f(x_{neg}) - f(x_{pos})}$$

The iteration procedure for the *regula falsi* algorithm is similar to that for the bisection algorithm. If $f(x_{false}) < 0$, then the root must be in the x_{pos} half of the interval, so the algorithm sets x_{neg} to x_{false} for the next iteration. On the other hand, if $f(x_{false}) > 0$, then the root must be in the x_{neg} half of the interval, so the algorithm sets x_{pos} to x_{false} for the next iteration. If $f(x_{false})$ is 0, or sufficiently close to 0, then the algorithm stops, and the final value of x_{false} is the root it managed to trap.

Screen 5–2 is a screen shot of the interactive version of Program 5–2, which instantiates a `RegulaFalsiRootFinder` object. Screen 5–2 shows the first three iterations of the *regula falsi* algorithm applied to the function $f(x) = x^2 - 4$ in the initial interval $[-0.25, 3.25]$. Notice that the algorithm tends to converge toward the root from one side only.

Screen 5–2 The first three iterations of the *regula falsi* algorithm applied to the function $f(x)$ = $x^2 - 4$ in the initial interval $[-0.25, 3.25]$. The three secant lines (and the short vertical lines marking the positions of x_{false}) are superimposed on each other. This screen shot is from the interactive version of Program 5–2.

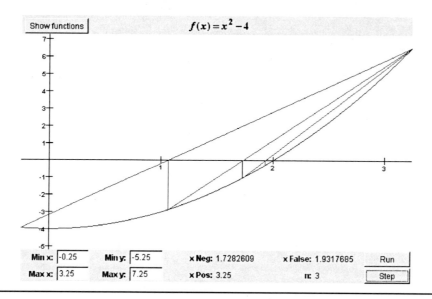

Listing 5–2a shows the class `RegulaFalsiRootFinder` , which implements this algorithm. It is very similar to class `BisectionRootFinder`.

Listing 5–2a The class that implements the *regula falsi* algorithm.

```
package numbercruncher.mathutils;

/**
 * The root finder class that implements the regula falsi algorithm.
 */
public class RegulaFalsiRootFinder extends RootFinder
{
    private static final int   MAX_ITERS = 50;
    private static final float TOLERANCE = 100*Epsilon.floatValue();

    /** x-negative value */        protected float xNeg;
    /** x-false value */           protected float xFalse = Float.NaN;
    /** x-positive value */        protected float xPos;
    /** previous x-false value */  protected float prevXFalse;
    /** f(xNeg)  */                protected float fNeg;
```

```
/** f(xFalse) */              protected float fFalse = Float.NaN;
/** f(xPos) */                protected float fPos;

/**
 * Constructor.
 * @param function the functions whose roots to find
 * @param xMin the initial x-value where the function is negative
 * @param xMax the initial x-value where the function is positive
 * @throws RootFinder.InvalidIntervalException
 */
public RegulaFalsiRootFinder(Function function,
                             float xMin, float xMax)
    throws RootFinder.InvalidIntervalException
{
    super(function, MAX_ITERS);
    checkInterval(xMin, xMax);

    float yMin = function.at(xMin);
    float yMax = function.at(xMax);

    // Initialize xNeg, fNeg, xPos, and fPos.
    if (yMin < 0) {
        xNeg = xMin; xPos = xMax;
        fNeg = yMin; fPos = yMax;
    }
    else {
        xNeg = xMax; xPos = xMin;
        fNeg = yMax; fPos = yMin;
    }
}

//---------//
// Getters //
//---------//

/**
 * Return the current value of x-negative.
 * @return the value
 */
public float getXNeg() { return xNeg; }

/**
 * Return the current value of x-false.
 * @return the value
 */
public float getXFalse() { return xFalse; }

/**
 * Return the current value of x-positive.
 * @return the value
```

```
     */
    public float getXPos() { return xPos; }

    /**
     * Return the current value of f(x-negative).
     * @return the value
     */
    public float getFNeg() { return fNeg; }

    /**
     * Return the current value of f(x-false).
     * @return the value
     */
    public float getFFalse() { return fFalse; }

    /**
     * Return the current value of f(x-positive).
     * @return the value
     */
    public float getFPos() { return fPos; }

    //---------------------------//
    // RootFinder method overrides //
    //---------------------------//

    /**
     * Do the regula falsi iteration procedure.
     * @param n the iteration count
     */
    protected void doIterationProcedure(int n)
    {
        if (n == 1) return;     // already initialized

        if (fFalse < 0) {
            xNeg = xFalse;      // the root is in the xPos side
            fNeg = fFalse;
        }
        else {
            xPos = xFalse;      // the root is in the xNeg side
            fPos = fFalse;
        }
    }

    /**
     * Compute the next position of x-false.
     */
    protected void computeNextPosition()
    {
        prevXFalse = xFalse;
```

```
        xFalse      = xPos - fPos*(xNeg - xPos)/(fNeg - fPos);
        fFalse      = function.at(xFalse);
    }

    /**
     * Check the position of x-false.
     * @throws PositionUnchangedException
     */
    protected void checkPosition()
        throws RootFinder.PositionUnchangedException
    {
        if (xFalse == prevXFalse) {
            throw new RootFinder.PositionUnchangedException();
        }
    }

    /**
     * Indicate whether or not the algorithm has converged.
     * @return true if converged, else false
     */
    protected boolean hasConverged()
    {
        return Math.abs(fFalse) < TOLERANCE;
    }
}
```

The noninteractive version of Program 5–2 instantiates a RegulaFalsiRootFinder object, and it shows that, for the same function $f(x) = x^2 - 4$ and the same initial interval $[-0.25, 3.25]$, the *regula falsi* algorithm converges faster than the bisection algorithm. See Listing 5–2b.

Listing 5–2b The noninteractive version of Program 5–2 applies the *regula falsi* algorithm applied to the function $f(x) = x^2 - 4$ in the initial interval $[-0.25, 3.25]$.

```
package numbercruncher.program5_2;

import numbercruncher.mathutils.Function;
import numbercruncher.mathutils.RegulaFalsiRootFinder;
import numbercruncher.mathutils.AlignRight;
import numbercruncher.rootutils.RootFunctions;

/**
 * PROGRAM 5-2: Regula Falsi Algorithm
 *
 * Demonstrate the Regula Falsi Algorithm on a function.
```

```
 */
public class RegulaFalsiAlgorithm
{
    /**
     * Main program.
     * @param args the array of runtime arguments
     */
    public static void main(String args[])
    {
        try {
            RegulaFalsiRootFinder finder =
                new RegulaFalsiRootFinder(
                        RootFunctions.function("x^2 - 4"),
                                          -0.25f, 3.25f);

            AlignRight ar = new AlignRight();

            ar.print("n", 2);
            ar.print("xNeg", 11); ar.print("f(xNeg)", 15);
            ar.print("xFalse", 11); ar.print("f(xFalse)", 15);
            ar.print("xPos", 6); ar.print("f(xPos)", 9);
            ar.underline();

            // Loop until convergence or failure.
            boolean converged;
            do {
                converged = finder.step();

                ar.print(finder.getIterationCount(), 2);
                ar.print(finder.getXNeg(), 11);
                ar.print(finder.getFNeg(), 15);
                ar.print(finder.getXFalse(), 11);
                ar.print(finder.getFFalse(), 15);
                ar.print(finder.getXPos(), 6);
                ar.print(finder.getFPos(), 9);
                ar.println();
            } while (!converged);

            System.out.println("\nSuccess! Root = " +
                               finder.getXFalse());
        }
        catch(Exception ex) {
            System.out.println("***** Error: " + ex);
        }
    }
}
```

Output:

n	xNeg	f(xNeg)	xFalse	f(xFalse)	xPos	f(xPos)
1	-0.25	-3.9375	1.0625	-2.8710938	3.25	6.5625
2	1.0625	-2.8710938	1.7282609	-1.0131145	3.25	6.5625
3	1.7282609	-1.0131145	1.9317685	-0.26827025	3.25	6.5625
4	1.9317685	-0.26827025	1.9835405	-0.06556702	3.25	6.5625
5	1.9835405	-0.06556702	1.9960688	-0.015709162	3.25	6.5625
6	1.9960688	-0.015709162	1.9990634	-0.0037455559	3.25	6.5625
7	1.9990634	-0.0037455559	1.999777	-8.921623E-4	3.25	6.5625
8	1.999777	-8.921623E-4	1.9999468	-2.1266937E-4	3.25	6.5625
9	1.9999468	-2.1266937E-4	1.9999874	-5.054474E-5	3.25	6.5625
10	1.9999874	-5.054474E-5	1.999997	-1.1920929E-5	3.25	6.5625
11	1.999997	-1.1920929E-5	1.9999992	-3.33786E-6	3.25	6.5625

Success! Root = 1.9999992

The output shows that the value of x_{pos} never changed—the algorithm converged to the root from one side only.

5.5 The Improved *Regula Falsi* Algorithm

We can greatly improve the *regula falsi* algorithm with a simple trick. At the end of each iteration, if the sign of $f(x_{false})$ did not change from the previous iteration (or if this is the first iteration), we decrease the slope of the secant. We do this by halving the height of the secant's endpoint at the end of the interval that is not going to move. This trick also encourages the algorithm to approach a root from both sides. Class `ImprovedRegulaFalsiRootFinder` will implement the improved *regula falsi* algorithm.

Program 5–3 instantiates an object of this class. Screen 5–3 is a screen shot of the interactive version of the program. It shows the first three iterations for the function $f(x) = x^2 - 4$ in the initial interval $[-0.25, 3.25]$. For clarity, the program doesn't draw the vertical line that marks each position of x_{false}. Notice that, in the second iteration, x_{false} is to the right of the root.

Listing 5–3a shows class `ImprovedRegulaFalsiRootFinder`. Since the algorithm is an improvement of the original *regula falsi* algorithm, the class simply extends class `RegulaFalsiRootFinder`. It overrides methods `doIterationProcedure()` and `computeNextPosition()` in order to decrease the secant slope when appropriate.

Listing 5–3a The class that implements the improved *regula falsi* algorithm.

```
package numbercruncher.mathutils;

/**
 * The root finder class that implements the
 * improved regula falsi algorithm.
```

Screen 5–3 The first three iterations of the improved *regula falsi* algorithm applied to the function $f(x) = x^2 - 4$ in the initial interval $[-0.25, 3.25]$. This screen shot is from the interactive version of Program 5–3.

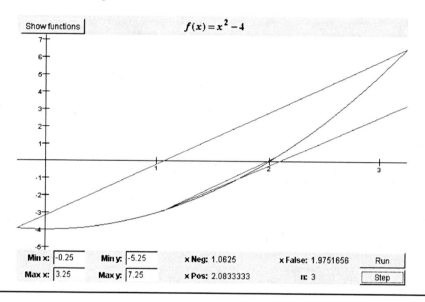

```
    */
public class ImprovedRegulaFalsiRootFinder
    extends RegulaFalsiRootFinder
{
    /** previous f(xFalse) value */  private float prevFFalse;

    private boolean decreasePos = false;
    private boolean decreaseNeg = false;

    /**
     * Constructor.
     * @param function the functions whose roots to find
     * @param xMin the initial x-value where the function is negative
     * @param xMax the initial x-value where the function is positive
     * @throws RootFinder.InvalidIntervalException
     */
    public ImprovedRegulaFalsiRootFinder(Function function,
                                        float xMin, float xMax)
        throws RootFinder.InvalidIntervalException
    {
        super(function, xMin, xMax);
    }
```

```
//----------------------------------------//
// Override RegulaFalsiRootFinder methods //
//----------------------------------------//

/**
 * Do the improved regula falsi iteration procedure.
 * @param n the iteration count
 */
protected void doIterationProcedure(int n)
{
    super.doIterationProcedure(n);

    // Decrease the slope of the secant?
    if (decreasePos) fPos /= 2;
    if (decreaseNeg) fNeg /= 2;
}

/**
 * Compute the next position of xFalse.
 */
protected void computeNextPosition()
{
    prevXFalse = xFalse;
    prevFFalse = fFalse;
    xFalse     = xPos - fPos*(xNeg - xPos)/(fNeg - fPos);
    fFalse     = function.at(xFalse);

    decreasePos = decreaseNeg = false;

    // If there was no sign change in f(xFalse),
    // or if this is the first iteration step,
    // then decrease the slope of the secant.
    if (Float.isNaN(prevFFalse) || (prevFFalse*fFalse > 0)) {
        if (fFalse < 0) decreasePos = true;
        else            decreaseNeg = true;
    }
}
}
```

The noninteractive version of Program 5–3 shows that, for the same function $f(x) = x^2 - 4$ and the same initial interval $[-0.25, 3.25]$, the improved *regula falsi* algorithm has the best convergence rate so far. See Listing 5–3b.

Listing 5–3b The noninteractive version of Program 5–3 applies the improved *regula falsi* algorithm applied to the function $f(x) = x^2 - 4$ in the initial interval $[-0.25, 3.25]$.

```
package numbercruncher.program5_3;

import numbercruncher.mathutils.Function;
```

```java
import numbercruncher.mathutils.ImprovedRegulaFalsiRootFinder;
import numbercruncher.mathutils.AlignRight;
import numbercruncher.rootutils.RootFunctions;

            /**
 * PROGRAM 5-3: Improved Regula Falsi Algorithm
 *
 * Demonstrate the Improved Regula Falsi Algorithm on a function.
 */
public class ImprovedRegulaFalsiAlgorithm
{
    /**
     * Main program.
     * @param args the array of runtime arguments
     */
    public static void main(String args[])
    {
        try {
            ImprovedRegulaFalsiRootFinder finder =
                new ImprovedRegulaFalsiRootFinder(
                        RootFunctions.function("x^2 - 4"),
                                            -0.25f, 3.25f);

            AlignRight ar = new AlignRight();

            ar.print("n", 2);
            ar.print("xNeg", 10); ar.print("f(xNeg)", 13);
            ar.print("xFalse", 10); ar.print("f(xFalse)", 13);
            ar.print("xPos", 10); ar.print("f(xPos)", 13);
            ar.underline();

            // Loop until convergence or failure.
            boolean converged;
            do {
                converged = finder.step();

                ar.print(finder.getIterationCount(), 2);
                ar.print(finder.getXNeg(), 10);
                ar.print(finder.getFNeg(), 13);
                ar.print(finder.getXFalse(), 10);
                ar.print(finder.getFFalse(), 13);
                ar.print(finder.getXPos(), 10);
                ar.print(finder.getFPos(), 13);
                ar.println();
            } while (!converged);

            System.out.println("\nSuccess! Root = " +
                            finder.getXFalse());
```

```
        }
        catch(Exception ex) {
            System.out.println("***** Error: " + ex);
        }
    }
}
```

Output:

n	xNeg	f(xNeg)	xFalse	f(xFalse)	xPos	f(xPos)
1	-0.25	-3.9375	1.0625	-2.8710938	3.25	6.5625
2	1.0625	-2.8710938	2.0833335	0.34027863	3.25	3.28125
3	1.0625	-2.8710938	1.9751655	-0.098721266	2.0833335	0.34027863
4	1.9751655	-0.098721266	1.99949	-0.002039671	2.0833335	0.34027863
5	1.99949	-0.002039671	2.0004833	0.0019330978	2.0833335	0.17013931
6	1.99949	-0.002039671	2.0	0.0	2.0004833	0.0019330978

```
Success! Root = 2.0
```

5.6 The Secant Algorithm

Unlike the bracketing bisection and *regula falsi* algorithms, the secant algorithm is our first example of an *open algorithm,* which does not work with ever shrinking intervals. It begins with two arbitrarily chosen values x_0 and x_1, and for the first iteration, it draws the secant through $(x_0, f(x_0))$ and $(x_1, f(x_1))$. The next false position is x_2, where the secant crosses the x axis. For the next iteration, it draws the secant through $(x_1, f(x_1))$ and $(x_2, f(x_2))$ to obtain the next false position x_3. Each subsequent iteration n proceeds similarly, using the x_{n-1} and x_n to obtain x_{n+1}. Because this is an open algorithm, $f(x_{n-1})$ and $f(x_n)$ do not need to have opposite signs. The iterations continue until $f(x_{n+1})$ is sufficiently close to 0, and then x_{n+1} is the root.

As we did for the *regula falsi* algorithm, we use similar triangles to compute x_{n+1}:

$$x_{n+1} = x_n - \frac{f(x_n)(x_{n-1} - x_n)}{f(x_{n-1}) - f(x_n)}$$

Class SecantRootFinder, shown in Listing 5–4a, implements the secant algorithm.

Listing 5–4a The class that implements the secant algorithm.

```
package numbercruncher.mathutils;

/**
 * The root finder class that implements the secant algorithm.
 */
public class SecantRootFinder extends RootFinder
{
    private static final int   MAX_ITERS = 50;
    private static final float TOLERANCE = 100*Epsilon.floatValue();
```

```
/** x[n-1] value */              private float xnm1;
/** x[n] value */                private float xn;
/** x[n+1] value */              private float xnp1 = Float.NaN;
/** previous value of x[n+1] */  private float prevXnp1;
/** f(x[n-1]) */                 private float fnm1;
/** f([n]) */                    private float fn;
/** f(x[n+1]) */                 private float fnp1;

/**
 * Constructor.
 * @param function the functions whose roots to find
 * @param x0 the first initial x-value
 * @param x1 the second initial x-value
 */
public SecantRootFinder(Function function, float x0, float x1)
{
    super(function, MAX_ITERS);

    // Initialize x[n-1], x[n], f(x[n-1]), and f(x[n]).
    xnm1 = x0;   fnm1 = function.at(xnm1);
    xn   = x1;   fn   = function.at(xn);
}

//---------//
// Getters //
//---------//

/**
 * Return the current value of x[n-1].
 * @return the value
 */
public float getXnm1() { return xnm1; }

/**
 * Return the current value of x[n].
 * @return the value
 */
public float getXn() { return xn; }

/**
 * Return the current value of x[n+1].
 * @return the value
 */
public float getXnp1() { return xnp1; }

/**
 * Return the current value of f(x[n-1]).
 * @return the value
 */
public float getFnm1() { return fnm1; }
```

```
/**
 * Return the current value of f(x[n]).
 * @return the value
 */
public float getFn() { return fn; }

/**
 * Return the current value of f(x[n+1]).
 * @return the value
 */
public float getFnp1() { return fnp1; }

//----------------------------//
// RootFinder method overrides //
//----------------------------//

/**
 * Do the secant iteration procedure.
 * @param n the iteration count
 */
protected void doIterationProcedure(int n)
{
    if (n == 1) return;      // already initialized

    // Use the latest two points.
    xnm1 = xn;       // x[n-1]    = x[n]
    xn   = xnp1;     // x[n]      = x[n+1]
    fnm1 = fn;       // f(x[n-1]) = f(x[n])
    fn   = fnp1;     // f(x[n])   = f(x[n+1])
}

/**
 * Compute the next position of x[n+1].
 */
protected void computeNextPosition()
{
    prevXnp1 = xnp1;
    xnp1     = xn - fn*(xnm1 - xn)/(fnm1 - fn);
    fnp1     = function.at(xnp1);
}

/**
 * Check the position of x[n+1].
 * @throws PositionUnchangedException
 */
protected void checkPosition()
    throws RootFinder.PositionUnchangedException
{
```

```
        if (xnp1 == prevXnp1) {
            throw new RootFinder.PositionUnchangedException();
        }
    }

    /**
     * Indicate whether or not the algorithm has converged.
     * @return true if converged, else false
     */
    protected boolean hasConverged()
    {
        return Math.abs(fnp1) < TOLERANCE;
    }
}
```

Program 5–4 instantiates a `SecantRootFinder` object. Screen 5–4 shows the first two iterations of the interactive version of the program. This version requires you to set the values of x_0 and x_1 by clicking the mouse on their positions.

The noninteractive version of Program 5–4 shows that, if we pick good starting values x_0 and x_1, the secant algorithm can converge quickly. See Listing 5–4b.

Listing 5–4b The noninteractive version of Program 5–4 applies the secant algorithm applied to the function $f(x) = x^2 - 4$ with the initial values $x_0 = 0.3625$ and $x_1 = 1.3625001$.

```
package numbercruncher.program5_4;

import numbercruncher.mathutils.Function;
import numbercruncher.mathutils.SecantRootFinder;
import numbercruncher.mathutils.AlignRight;
import numbercruncher.rootutils.RootFunctions;

/**
 * PROGRAM 5-4: Secant Algorithm
 *
 * Demonstrate the Secant Algorithm on a function.
 */
public class SecantAlgorithm
{
    /**
     * Main program.
     * @param args the array of runtime arguments
     */
    public static void main(String args[])
    {
        try {
            SecantRootFinder finder =
```

```
                    new SecantRootFinder(
                            RootFunctions.function("x^2 - 4"),
                                            0.3625f, 1.3625001f);

            AlignRight ar = new AlignRight();

            ar.print("n", 2);
            ar.print("x[n-1]", 10); ar.print("f(x[n-1])", 12);
            ar.print("x[n]", 10); ar.print("f(x[n])", 13);
            ar.print("x[n+1]", 10); ar.print("f(x[n+1])", 14);
            ar.underline();

            // Loop until convergence or failure.
            boolean converged;
            do {
                converged = finder.step();

                ar.print(finder.getIterationCount(), 2);
                ar.print(finder.getXnm1(), 10);
                ar.print(finder.getFnm1(), 12);
                ar.print(finder.getXn(), 10);
                ar.print(finder.getFn(), 13);
                ar.print(finder.getXnp1(), 10);
                ar.print(finder.getFnp1(), 14);
                ar.println();
            } while (!converged);

            System.out.println("\nSuccess! Root = " +
                                finder.getXnp1());
        }
        catch(Exception ex) {
            System.out.println("***** Error: " + ex);
        }
    }
}
```

Output:

```
n    x[n-1]    f(x[n-1])      x[n]      f(x[n])     x[n+1]      f(x[n+1])
----------------------------------------------------------------------
1    0.3625   -3.8685937  1.3625001   -2.1435935  2.6051629     2.7868733
2  1.3625001  -2.1435935  2.6051629    2.7868733  1.9027661    -0.37948108
3  2.6051629   2.7868733  1.9027661   -0.37948108 1.986947     -0.05204177
4  1.9027661  -0.37948108 1.986947    -0.05204177 2.0003262     0.0013046265
5   1.986947  -0.05204177 2.0003262   0.0013046265 1.9999989   -4.2915344E-6

Success! Root = 1.9999989
```

Screen 5–4 The first two iterations of the secant algorithm applied to the function $f(x) = x^2 - 4$. The user sets the initial values of x_0 and x_1 with the mouse. At each iteration n, the two vertical lines mark the positions of x_{n-1} and x_n. These screen shots are from the interactive version of Program 5–4.

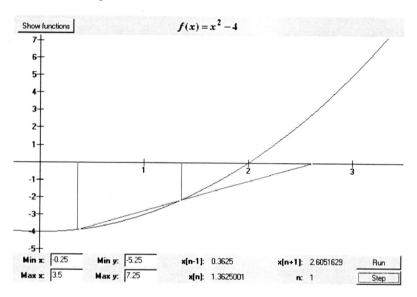

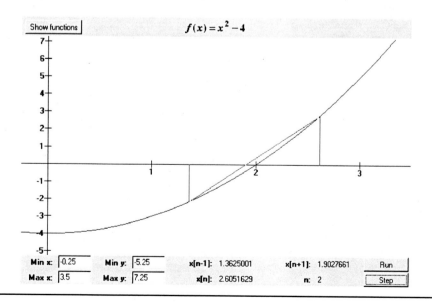

5.7 Newton's Algorithm

Let's take another look at the iteration formula for the secant algorithm:

$$x_{n+1} = x_n - \frac{f(x_n)(x_{n-1} - x_n)}{f(x_{n-1}) - f(x_n)}$$

Suppose the function f is differentiable (and hence continuous) over the interval $[x_{n-1}, x_n]$:

$$f'(x_n) = \lim_{x_{n-1} \to x_n} \frac{f(x_{n-1}) - f(x_n)}{x_{n-1} - x_n}$$

By making x_{n-1} be the same point as x_n, we can replace the slope of the secant by the slope of the tangent at x_n, and then we have the formula for Newton's algorithm:[3]

$$x_{n+1} = x_n - \frac{f(x_n)}{f'(x_n)}$$

Figure 5–2 makes this clear. We draw the tangent line through the point $(x_n, f(x_n))$. The tangent line intercepts the x axis at x_{n+1}, which is closer to the root than x_n.

Listing 5–5a shows class `NewtonsRootFinder`, which implements Newton's algorithm. Notice that it invokes the `derivativeAt()` method of a `Function` object in order to evaluate a function's derivative.

Listing 5–5a The class that implements Newton's algorithm.

```
package numbercruncher.mathutils;

/**
 * The root finder class that implements Newton's algorithm.
 */
public class NewtonsRootFinder extends RootFinder
{
    private static final int   MAX_ITERS = 50;
    private static final float TOLERANCE = 100*Epsilon.floatValue();

    /** x[n] value */            private float xn;
    /** x[n+1] value */          private float xnp1;
    /** previous x[n+1] value */ private float prevXnp1;
    /** f(x[n]) */               private float fn;
    /** f(x[n+1]) */             private float fnp1;
```

---

[3] Sir Isaac Newton (1643–1727) was an English scientist, astronomer, and mathematician who is famous for his work on optics, his laws of motion and of gravitation, his development of the calculus, and his book *Principia*, published in 1687. We shall encounter Newton again in Chapters 6 and 7.

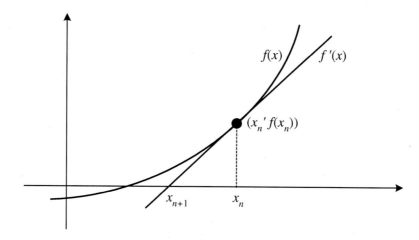

Figure 5–2 One iteration step of Newton's algorithm. The tangent line is at $(x_n, f(x_n))$.

```
/** f'(x[n]) */                    private float fpn;

/**
 * Constructor.
 * @param function the functions whose roots to find
 */
public NewtonsRootFinder(Function function)
{
    super(function, MAX_ITERS);
}

/**
 * Reset.
 * @param x0 the initial x-value
 */
public void reset(float x0)
{
    super.reset();

    xnp1 = x0;
    fnp1 = function.at(xnp1);
}

//---------//
// Getters //
//---------//

/**
 * Return the current value of x[n].
 * @return the value
 */
```

```
public float getXn() { return xn; }

/**
 * Return the current value of x[n+1].
 * @return the value
 */
public float getXnp1() { return xnp1; }

/**
 * Return the current value of f(x[n]).
 * @return the value
 */
public float getFn() { return fn; }

/**
 * Return the current value of f(x[n+1]).
 * @return the value
 */
public float getFnp1() { return fnp1; }

/**
 * Return the current value of f'(x[n]).
 * @return the value
 */
public float getFpn() { return fpn; }

//---------------------------//
// RootFinder method overrides //
//---------------------------//

/**
 * Do Newton's iteration procedure.
 * @param n the iteration count
 */
protected void doIterationProcedure(int n)
{
    xn = xnp1;
}

/**
 * Compute the next position of x[n+1].
 */
protected void computeNextPosition()
{
    fn  = fnp1;
    fpn = function.derivativeAt(xn);

    // Compute the value of x[n+1].
    prevXnp1 = xnp1;
```

```
    xnp1       = xn - fn/fpn;

    fnp1 = function.at(xnp1);
}


/**
 * Check the position of x[n+1].
 * @throws PositionUnchangedException
 */
protected void checkPosition()
    throws RootFinder.PositionUnchangedException
{
    if (xnp1 == prevXnp1) {
        throw new RootFinder.PositionUnchangedException();
    }
}


/**
 * Indicate whether or not the algorithm has converged.
 * @return true if converged, else false
 */
protected boolean hasConverged()
{
    return Math.abs(fnp1) < TOLERANCE;
}
}
```

Program 5–5 instantiates a NewtonsRootFinder object. Screen 5–5a is a screen shot of the interactive version of the program, which allows you to dynamically set the value of the starting point x_0 by dragging the mouse along the x axis. It animates the algorithm by tracing the algorithm's path toward the root. At x_0 and each subsequent value of x, the program draws the vertical line from the x axis to $f(x)$ and the tangent line at $f(x)$. Where the tangent crosses the x axis is the next value of x. The iterations stop when $f(x)$ is sufficiently close to zero.

The noninteractive version of Program 5–5 shows that, if we pick a good starting value x_0, Newton's algorithm can have a very good convergence rate. See Listing 5–5b. Actually, the algorithm has the best convergence rate of all the algorithms we've looked at so far. Once it starts to converge to a root, the number of correct significant digits in the approximation doubles with each iteration. But one drawback is that it requires the computation of the function's derivative. This may be expensive, or not even possible, for some functions.

Listing 5–5b The noninteractive version of Program 5–5 applies Newton's algorithm applied to the function $f(x) = x^2 - 4$ with the initial value $x_0 = 5.130833$.

```
package numbercruncher.program5_5;

import numbercruncher.mathutils.Function;
```

Screen 5–5a Newton's algorithm applied to the function $f(x) = x^2 - 4$ with the initial value $x_0 = 5.130833$. The vertical lines mark the values of x, and the slanted lines are the tangents at $f(x)$. This screen shot is from the interactive version of Program 5–5.

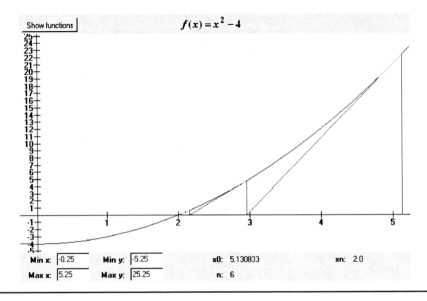

```
import numbercruncher.mathutils.NewtonsRootFinder;
import numbercruncher.mathutils.AlignRight;
import numbercruncher.rootutils.RootFunctions;

/**
 * PROGRAM 5-5: Newton's Algorithm
 *
 * Demonstrate Newton's Algorithm on a function.
 */
public class NewtonsAlgorithm
{
    /**
     * Main program.
     * @param args the array of runtime arguments
     */
    public static void main(String args[])
    {
        try {
            NewtonsRootFinder finder =
                new NewtonsRootFinder(
                    RootFunctions.function("x^2 - 4"));
            finder.reset(5.130833f);
```

```
        AlignRight ar = new AlignRight();

        ar.print("n", 2);
        ar.print("x[n]", 11); ar.print("f(x[n])", 14);
        ar.print("f'(x[n])", 11); ar.print("x[n+1]", 11);
        ar.print("f(x[n+1])", 14);
        ar.underline();

        // Loop until convergence or failure.
        boolean converged;
        do {
            converged = finder.step();

            ar.print(finder.getIterationCount(), 2);
            ar.print(finder.getXn(), 11);
            ar.print(finder.getFn(), 14);
            ar.print(finder.getFpn(), 11);
            ar.print(finder.getXnp1(), 11);
            ar.print(finder.getFnp1(), 14);
            ar.println();
        } while (!converged);

        System.out.println("\nSuccess! Root = " + finder.getXnp1());
    }
    catch(Exception ex) {
        System.out.println("***** Error: " + ex);
    }
  }
}
```

Output:

```
n       x[n]          f(x[n])      f'(x[n])      x[n+1]        f(x[n+1])
---------------------------------------------------------------------------
1     5.130833       22.325449    10.261666    2.955217        4.733307
2     2.955217        4.733307     5.910434    2.1543777       0.6413431
3     2.1543777       0.6413431    4.3087554   2.0055313       0.022155762
4     2.0055313       0.022155762  4.0110626   2.0000076       3.0517578E-5
5     2.0000076       3.0517578E-5 4.0000153   2.0            0.0

Success! Root = 2.0
```

Because of the derivative f', we need to be extra careful when applying Newton's algorithm. The screen shots in Screen 5–5b show what can happen if the derivative $f'(x) = 0$. The approximations to the root can shoot off to infinity, or they may oscillate and fail to converge.

Screen 5–5b Pathological behavior of Newton's algorithm when the function derivative $f'(x) = 0$.

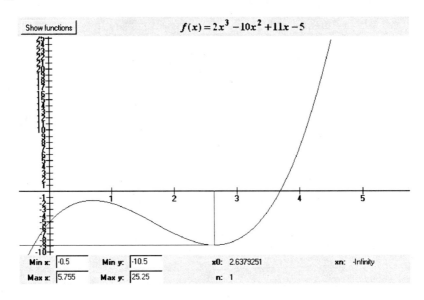

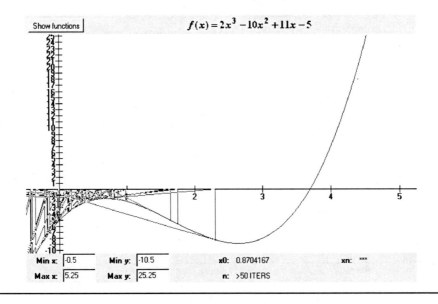

5.8 Fixed-Point Iteration

Enter any value greater than 0 into a calculator, and then repeatedly press the $\sqrt{}$ key. The value in the display steadily converges to 1. For the square root function $g(x) = \sqrt{x}$, the value 1 is its *fixed point* for any starting x value in the interval $0 < x < \infty$. Similarly, 0 is the fixed point for the function $g(x) = x^2$, but only for a starting x value in the interval $-1 < x < 1$. If a function has a fixed point for a starting x value, then the process of repeatedly applying the function is called *fixed-point iteration.* For reasons that will soon become clear, we'll use g as the name of a function with which we'll do fixed-point iteration.

If we plot fixed-point iteration the same way we plotted Newton's algorithm, we can generate some particularly beautiful graphs, as shown in Figure 5–3. The first graph shows the function $g(x) = \sqrt{x}$, and the second graph shows the function $g(x) = e^{[\frac{1}{x}]}$. To convey that each value of $g(x)$ is "fed back" to become the next value of x—that is, $x_{n+1} = g(x_n)$—we draw the line $x = y$ and reflect each value of $g(x)$ onto the next value for x. The fixed-point iteration trace for the first function is a staircase that leads to the fixed-point value of 1, and the trace for the second function spirals down to the fixed-point value of approximately 1.76.

The concept of fixed-point iteration will play a major role when we examine fractals in Chapter 16. But for now, we'll consider fixed-point iteration as another open algorithm for finding roots.

So what root have we found by computing the fixed point of $g(x) = \sqrt{x}$? Starting with the iteration formula $x = g(x)$, we have

$$x = \sqrt{x}$$
$$x^2 = x$$
$$x^2 - x = 0$$

and so if we set $f(x) = x^2 - x$, we can find one of its roots, namely the value 1, by deriving the function $g(x) = \sqrt{x}$ and doing fixed-point iteration with the latter. The fixed-point value of $g(x)$ is then one of the roots of $f(x)$.

Similarly, for the function $g(x) = e^{[\frac{1}{x}]}$, we have

$$x = e^{[\frac{1}{x}]},$$
$$x - e^{[\frac{1}{x}]} = 0$$

and so $f(x) = x - e^{[\frac{1}{x}]}$, and its root is approximately 1.76.

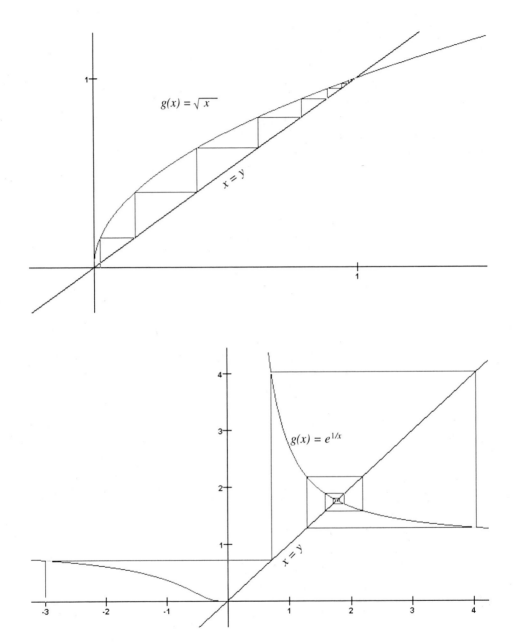

Figure 5–3 Fixed-point iteration traces for the functions $g(x) = \sqrt{x}$ and $g(x) = e^{\left[\frac{1}{x}\right]}$.

Class `FixedPointRootFinder`, shown in Listing 5–6a, implements the fixed-point iteration algorithm. Given a function $f(x)$, we must manually derive a function $g(x)$ that is suitable for fixed-point iteration. For our original example function $f(x) = x^2 - 4$, we can derive $g(x)$ by solving for x:

$$x^2 - 4 = 0$$
$$x^2 = 4$$
$$2x^2 = x^2 + 4$$
$$2x = x + \frac{4}{x}$$
$$x = \frac{\left[x + \dfrac{4}{x}\right]}{2}$$

and so $g(x) = \dfrac{\left[x + \frac{4}{x}\right]}{2}$

The algorithm iteratively computes $x_{n+1} = g(x_n)$ until two successive values of x are sufficiently close to each other:

$$\left|\frac{x_{n+1} - x_n}{x_n}\right| < 100\varepsilon$$

where ε is the machine epsilon value. We cannot use a smaller tolerance because the values generated by fixed-point iteration can oscillate near the fixed point, with x and $g(x)$ exchanging values for each iteration.

Listing 5–6a The class that implements the fixed-point iteration algorithm.

```
package numbercruncher.mathutils;

/**
 * The root finder class that implements
 * the fixed-point iteration algorithm.
 */
public class FixedPointRootFinder extends RootFinder
{
    private static final int   MAX_ITERS = 50;
    private static final float TOLERANCE = 100*Epsilon.floatValue();

    /** x[n] value */          private float xn = Float.NaN;
```

```java
/** previous x[n] value */   private float prevXn;
/** g(x[n]) */               private float gn;

/**
 * Constructor.
 * @param function the functions whose roots to find
 */
public FixedPointRootFinder(Function function)
{
    super(function, MAX_ITERS);
}

/**
 * Reset.
 * @param x0 the initial x-value
 */
public void reset(float x0)
{
    super.reset();
    gn = x0;
}

//---------//
// Getters //
//---------//

/**
 * Return the current value of x[n].
 * @return the value
 */
public float getXn() { return xn; }

/**
 * Return the current value of g(x[n]).
 * @return the value
 */
public float getGn() { return gn; }

//----------------------------//
// RootFinder method overrides //
//----------------------------//

/**
 * Do the fixed point iteration procedure. (Nothing to do!)
 * @param n the iteration count
 */
protected void doIterationProcedure(int n) {}
```

```
/**
 * Compute the next position of xn.
 */
protected void computeNextPosition()
{
    prevXn = xn;
    xn     = gn;
    gn     = function.at(xn);
}


/**
 * Check the position of xn.
 * @throws PositionUnchangedException
 */
protected void checkPosition()
    throws RootFinder.PositionUnchangedException
{
    if (xn == prevXn) {
        throw new RootFinder.PositionUnchangedException();
    }
}


/**
 * Indicate whether or not the algorithm has converged.
 * @return true if converged, else false
 */
protected boolean hasConverged()
{
    return Math.abs((gn - xn)/xn) < TOLERANCE;
}
}
```

As we can see, the class does the least work of all the root-finding classes, but then, of course, we had to work hard ourselves to derive the function $g(x)$.

Program 5–6 instantiates a `FixedPointRootFinder` object. Screen 5–6a is a screen shot of the interactive version of the program performing fixed-point iteration on the function $g(x) = \dfrac{\left[x + \frac{4}{x}\right]}{2}$. Like the interactive version of Program 5–5 for Newton's method, it allows you to dynamically set the starting value for x by dragging the mouse along the x axis.

In Screen 5–6a, we see that, if the initial value for x is negative, fixed-point iteration will find the other fixed-point value of -2, which is the other root of $f(x) = x^2 - 4$.

The noninteractive version of Program 5–6, which performs fixed-point iteration also on the function $g(x) = e^{\left[\frac{1}{x}\right]}$, shows that the convergence of the fixed-point algorithm is not as good as that of Newton's algorithm, especially in the spiral case. See Listing 5–6b.

Screen 5–6a Fixed-point iteration applied to the function $g(x) = \dfrac{\left[x + \frac{4}{x}\right]}{2}$ with the initial value $x_0 = 10.325$. This screen shot is from the interactive version of Program 5–6.

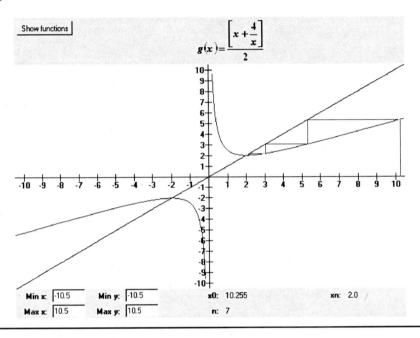

Listing 5–6b The noninteractive version of Program 5–1 applies fixed-point iteration applied to the function $g(x) = \dfrac{\left[x + \frac{4}{x}\right]}{2}$ with the initial value $x_0 = 10.325$ and to the function $g(x) = e^{\left[\frac{1}{x}\right]}$ with the initial value $x_0 = -3$.

```
package numbercruncher.program5_6;

import numbercruncher.mathutils.Function;
import numbercruncher.mathutils.FixedPointRootFinder;
import numbercruncher.mathutils.AlignRight;
import numbercruncher.rootutils.RootFunctions;

/**
 * PROGRAM 5-6: Fixed-Point Iteration
 *
 * Demonstrate Fixed-Point Iteration on a function.
 */
public class FixedPointIteration
{
```

```
/**
 * Main program.
 * @param args the array of runtime arguments
 */
public static void main(String args[])
{
    doFunction("(x + 4/x)/2", 10.325f);
    doFunction("exp(1/x)", -3f);
}


/**
 * Apply fixed-point iteration to a function.
 * @param key the function key
 * @param x0 the starting value
 */
private static void doFunction(String key, float x0)
{
    try {
        FixedPointRootFinder finder;
        AlignRight ar = new AlignRight();

        System.out.println("\ng(x) = " + key + "\n");
        finder = new FixedPointRootFinder(
                        RootFunctions.function(key));
        finder.reset(x0);

        ar.print("n", 2); ar.print("x[n]", 15);
        ar.print("g(x[n])", 15);
        ar.underline();

        // Loop until convergence or failure.
        boolean converged;
        do {
            converged = finder.step();

            ar.print(finder.getIterationCount(), 2);
            ar.print(finder.getXn(), 15);
            ar.print(finder.getGn(), 15);
            ar.println();
        } while (!converged);

        System.out.println("\nSuccess! Fixed point = " +
                        finder.getXn());
    }
    catch(Exception ex) {
        System.out.println("***** Error: " + ex);
    }
}
}
```

Output:

```
g(x) = (x + 4/x)/2
  n          x[n]          g(x[n])
-------------------------------
  1         10.325        5.3562045
  2       5.3562045       3.051501
  3       3.051501        2.1811657
  4       2.1811657       2.0075238
  5       2.0075238       2.000014
  6       2.000014           2.0
  7          2.0             2.0
Success! Fixed point = 2.0


g(x) = exp(1/x)

  n          x[n]          g(x[n])
-------------------------------
  1         -3.0          0.7165313
  2       0.7165313       4.0374465
  3       4.0374465       1.2810516
  4       1.2810516       2.1828005
  5       2.1828005       1.5811099
  6       1.5811099       1.8822485
  7       1.8822485       1.7011074
  8       1.7011074       1.8001182
  9       1.8001182       1.7428454
 10       1.7428454       1.7749537
 11       1.7749537       1.7566261
 12       1.7566261       1.7669822
 13       1.7669822       1.7610966
 14       1.7610966       1.7644305
 15       1.7644305       1.7625386
 16       1.7625386       1.7636112
 17       1.7636112       1.7630026
 18       1.7630026       1.7633477
 19       1.7633477       1.763152
 20       1.763152        1.763263
 21       1.763263        1.7632
 22       1.7632          1.7632357
 23       1.7632357       1.7632155
 24       1.7632155       1.763227
 25       1.763227        1.7632204

Success! Fixed point = 1.763227
```

Table 5–2 Example functions $f(x)$ and derived convergent and nonconvergent iteration functions $g(x)$.

$f(x)$	Roots	Convergent $g(x)$	Divergent $g(x)$
$f(x) = x^2 - 4$	-2.00 2.00	$g(x) = \dfrac{\left[x + \frac{4}{x}\right]}{2}$	$g(x) = \dfrac{4}{x}$
$f(x) = x^2 - x - 2$	-1.00 2.00	$g(x) = \sqrt{x + 2}$ $g(x) = \dfrac{2}{x} + 1$	$g(x) = x^2 - 2$
$f(x) = x - e^{-x}$	0.567	$g(x) = e^{-x}$	$g(x) = -\ln x$
$f(x) = x - e^{\left[\frac{1}{x}\right]}$	1.76	$g(x) = e^{\left[\frac{1}{x}\right]}$ $g(x) = \dfrac{x + e^{\left[\frac{1}{x}\right]}}{2}$	$g(x) = \dfrac{1}{\ln x}$
$f(x) = 2x - \sin x - 2$	1.50	$g(x) = \dfrac{\sin x}{2} + 1$	
$f(x) = x^3 - x^2 - x - 1$	1.84	$g(x) = 1 + \dfrac{1}{x} + \dfrac{1}{x^2}$	
$f(x) = x^3 + 2x^2 + 10x - 20$	1.37	$g(x) = \dfrac{20}{x^2 + 2x + 10}$	

There are several ways to define the iteration function $g(x)$ for a given function $f(x)$. For the function $f(x) = x^2 - 4$ we could have chosen the simpler function $g(x) = \frac{4}{x}$, and for the function $f(x) = x - e^{\left[\frac{1}{x}\right]}$ we could have chosen $g(x) = \frac{1}{\ln x}$. Does it matter which definition of $g(x)$ to use?

If we do not derive the appropriate iteration function $g(x)$, the algorithm can diverge, as shown in Screen 5–6b. We must derive $g(x)$ such that, for all values of x within an interval that contains the fixed point value, $|g'(x)| < 1$ for the derivative $g'(x)$. Then the algorithm will converge within that interval to the fixed point.

Table 5–2 shows examples of functions $f(x)$ and corresponding convergent and nonconvergent fixed-point iteration functions $g(x)$ that can be derived. You can try all of the iteration functions using the interactive version of Program 5–6.

Screen 5–6b Fixed-point iteration applied to nonconvergent functions $g(x) = \frac{4}{x}$ and $g(x) = \frac{1}{\ln x}$.

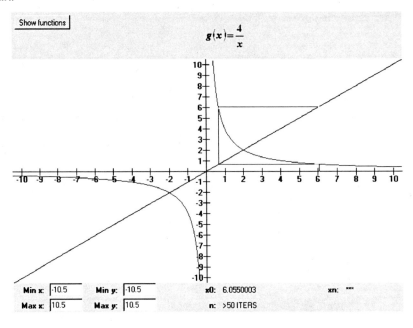

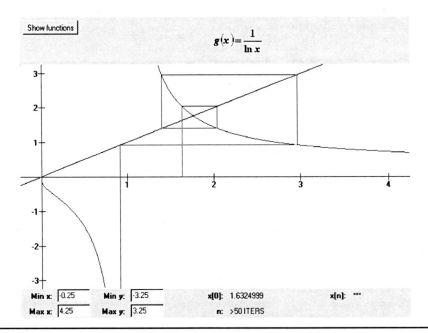

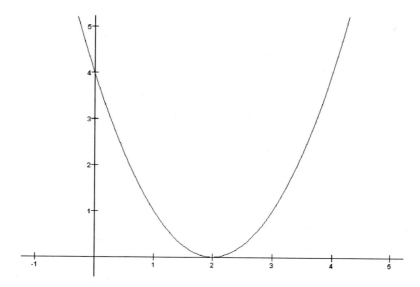

Figure 5–4   The graph of $f(x) = x^2 - 4x + 4$ with a double root at $x = 2$.

5.9 Double Trouble with Multiple Roots

If the graph of function $f(x)$ touches or crosses the x axis tangentially, then there are multiple roots at that point. In other words, if $f(x_r) = 0$ and $f'(x_r) = 0$, then x_r is a multiple root. For example, 2 is a double root of the function

$$f(x) = (x - 2)(x - 2)$$
$$= x^2 - 4x + 4$$

Multiple roots are problematic for Newton's algorithm and the secant algorithm because the derivative value is 0. The function plot does not cross the x axis at an even degree (double, quadruple, etc.) multiple root. Figure 5–4 shows that the function $f(x) = x^2 - 4x + 4$ is always positive, so the bracketing algorithms, which require a sign change, won't work, either.

5.10 Comparing the Root-Finder Algorithms

We've considered six algorithms of finding roots in this chapter: bisection, *regula falsi*, improved *regula falsi*, secant, Newton's, and fixed-point iteration. How do we decide which algorithm is the best one to use on any given function?

It should be obvious by now that, before choosing an algorithm, *you must know what the graph of the function looks like* in the interval in which you want to find a root. You need at least a rough idea of where the roots are and how the function behaves near the roots.

Each algorithm requires the function to be continuous near a root. Before looking for a root, be sure there is at least one root to find. Sign changes in the value of the function indicate the presence of a root. Some roots may actually be multiple roots.

We can use several criteria to judge a root-finding algorithm:

- **Reliability.** Will it find the root?
- **Rate of convergence.** How quickly does the algorithm converge to a root?
- **Complexity.** How hard is it to program?
- **Performance.** How much work is necessary during each iteration?
- **Safety.** What can go wrong? How likely will it diverge, cycle, or shoot off into infinity?

Before we compare convergence rates, let's start with some definitions.

> DEFINITION: Suppose we have a root-finding algorithm that generates a sequence of successive approximations $x_0, x_1, x_2, \ldots, x_n, \ldots$ to a root. Let Δ_n be the difference between x_n and the root. If
>
> $$\lim_{n \to \infty} \frac{|\Delta_{n+1}|}{|\Delta_n|^p} = C$$
>
> where C is a nonzero constant, then p is the algorithm's **order of convergence.**
>
> DEFINITION: If $p = 1$, then the algorithm has a **linear convergence rate.**
>
> DEFINITION: If $1 < p < 2$, then the algorithm has a **superlinear convergence rate.**
>
> DEFINITION: If $p = 2$, then the algorithm has a **quadratic convergence rate.**

We won't do the proofs here, but of the algorithms we've examined in this chapter, the bisection algorithm and fixed-point iteration have linear convergence rates, the *regula falsi* and secant algorithms have superlinear convergence rates, and Newton's algorithm has a quadratic convergence rate.

The easiest and safest algorithm to program is the bisection algorithm. Once the initial conditions are met (continuous function, different signs at the interval ends), the algorithm is guaranteed to find a root. Unfortunately, its convergence rate is the slowest.

The *regula falsi* algorithm usually converges faster than the bisection algorithm, and it is very safe. Because it tends to approach a root from only one side, certain pathological functions may cause its convergence to get slower as it gets closer to the root. The *regula falsi* algorithm requires more computation for each iteration than the bisection algorithm. The improved *regula falsi* algorithm converges faster, but at the cost of even more computation per iteration.

The secant algorithm requires you to pick two initial points. With good starting points, it can converge even faster than the improved *regula falsi* algorithm. Bad starting points, however, can send the algorithm wandering before it converges, or it may diverge altogether, so safety can be an issue. As for programming and execution complexity, it is very similar to the *regula falsi* algorithm.

Fixed-point iteration requires you to derive an iteration function $g(x)$ based on the original function $f(x)$. The algorithm converges only if you define $g(x)$ carefully to meet certain criteria, as explained earlier.

With its quadratic convergence rate, Newton's algorithm is generally the fastest of all the algorithms, especially if the initial value is already close to the root. However, it does require the computation of both the function and its derivative during each iteration, and that can be expensive. Also, as we saw earlier, the algorithm's behavior can be dangerously erratic with certain pathological functions.

Perhaps the best way to find roots is a combination of two algorithms. Start with the bisection or the *regula falsi* algorithm to quickly find a narrow interval around the root. Then use Newton's algorithm to refine the search if the function's derivative is not too expensive to compute; otherwise, finish off with the improved *regula falsi* or the secant algorithm.

References

Atkinson, L.V., and P.J. Harley, *An Introduction to Numerical Methods with Pascal,* London: Addison-Wesley, 1983.

Chapra, Seven C., and Raymond P. Canale, *Numerical Methods for Engineers,* 3rd edition, New York: WCB/McGraw-Hill, 1998.

Conte, Samuel D., and Carl de Boor, *Elementary Numerical Analysis: An Algorithmic Approach,* New York: McGraw-Hill, 1980.

Scheid, Francis, *Numerical Analysis,* New York: McGraw-Hill, 1988.

Woodford, C., and C. Phillips, *Numerical Methods with Worked Examples,* London: Chapman and Hall, 1997.

The topic of finding roots is covered well in these books. See Chapters 5 and 6 in the Chapra book, Chapter 3 in the Conte book, and Chapter 2 in the Woodford book. The Chapra and Conte books discuss error analyses of the various root-finding algorithms. Conte also includes proofs of their convergence rates. Some of this chapter's example functions, especially the ones for fixed-point iteration, are from these books (some modified). See Section 3.1.4 in Atkinson and Chapter 25 in Scheid.

CHAPTER 6

INTERPOLATION AND APPROXIMATION

If you're given a set of data values, the following are questions you might ask. Is there a good way to represent these data in a meaningful way, so that I can see what's the overall shape or trend of the values? How can I estimate new data values that lie between the given values, so that the new ones "fit in" with this shape or trend? Can I generate new values that approximate the original values?

If you can cast the data as a set of points in the xy plane, a very useful way to answer these questions is to draw a graph of the data. There are two types of graphs you can draw. If the set of data values is small, say 10 values or fewer, you can try to plot a curve that goes *through* all of the points. Or if there are many data values, you can plot a curve that goes as "near" as possible *among* the points, but not necessarily going through any of them.

Both types of graphs will allow you to generate new data values. Our job, then, is to define the function for the graph. By plugging new x values into the function, it will generate new values that fit in with the existing values.

In this chapter, given a set of data points, we will create a polynomial function that goes through each point. Because the function passes through the points, it is an *interpolation* function. With this function, we can *estimate* a new data point between two original adjacent data points by plugging in a new x coordinate that lies between the x coordinates of the two original points.

We'll also create a line function that passes closely among a given set of data points (and, of course, we'll have to define what "close" means). This *regression function* defines a *regression line*. By plugging in new x coordinates into the function, we can generate new data points that *approximate* the original data. We'll defer polynomial regression functions of a higher degree until Chapter 10, since they require solving sets of simultaneous equations.

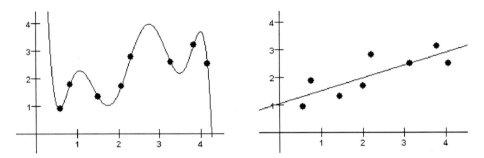

Figure 6–1   Graphs of a polynomial interpolation function of degree 7 (left) and a regression line (right) for the same set of data points.

Figure 6–1 graphs examples of a polynomial interpolation function and a regression line.

6.1 The Power Form versus the Newton Form

We are familiar with the *power form* of a polynomial of degree *n:*

$$f_n(x) = a_0 + a_1x + a_2x^2 + \ldots + a_nx^n$$

We'll use the subscript *n* after the name of the function to indicate the function's degree, its highest exponent of *x.*

Another polynomial form is the *Newton form:*

$$f_n(x) = b_0 + b_1 (x - x_0)$$
$$+b_2 (x - x_0)(x - x_1)$$
$$+b_3 (x - x_0)(x - x_1)(x - x_2)$$
$$+ \ldots$$
$$+b_n (x - x_0)(x - x_1)(x - x_2) \ldots (x - x_{n-1})$$

which is computationally convenient because of the way the $(x - x_i)$ products accumulate from one term to the next—we simply multiply the previous product by the next $(x - x_i)$. The x_i constants are called *centers.* We'll use the Newton form to represent polynomial interpolation functions.[1]

6.2 Polynomial Interpolation Functions

If we are given two data points in the *xy* plane, there is one, and only one, polynomial interpolation function $f_1(x)$ of degree 1 that will pass through both points—a line function.

---

[1]   The Newton form is actually equivalent to the power form, which you can discover by multiplying out the terms and reorganizing them. And, yes, this is the same Isaac Newton of the algorithm for finding roots described in Chapter 5.

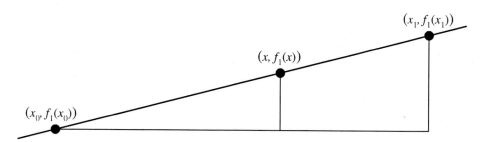

Figure 6–2 A line in the *xy* plane.

As shown in Figure 6–2, let the two points be $(x_0, f_1(x_0))$ and $(x_1, f_1(x_1))$. Then, using similar triangles, we have

$$\frac{f_1(x) - f_1(x_0)}{x - x_0} = \frac{f_1(x_1) - f_1(x_0)}{x_1 - x_0}$$

and so

$$f_1(x) = f_1(x_0) + \left[\frac{f_1(x_1) - f_1(x_0)}{x_1 - x_0}\right](x - x_0)$$

Notice that we have derived the Newton form of the polynomial

$$f_1(x) = b_0 + b_1 (x - x_0)$$

where the coefficients $b_0 = f_1(x_0)$ and $b_1 = $ the quantity in the square brackets. The quantity in the square brackets is called a *divided difference,* and it happens to be the slope of the line. As we'll soon see, divided differences play a major computational role in determining polynomial interpolation functions.

If there are three points in the *xy* plane, then there is a polynomial interpolation function $f_2(x)$ of degree 2 that will pass through all three points. This is a quadratic function, which describes a parabola. Although we won't prove it here, this parabola is unique for any three given points.

The Newton form of the parabola is

$$f_2(x) = b_0 + b_1(x - x_0) + b_2(x - x_0)(x - x_1)$$

where the centers x_0 and x_1 are the x coordinates of two of our three given points. The coefficients b_i are constant—their values are the same for any value of x. So to compute b_0, first set x to the value x_0 to get rid of the terms containing b_1 and b_2, and we see that

$$b_0 = f_2(x_0)$$

Now set x to the value x_1 to get rid of the term containing b_2 and substitute in the value we just computed for b_0:

$$f_2(x_1) = f_2(x_0) + b_1(x_1 - x_0)$$

and so

$$b_1 = \frac{f_2(x_1) - f_2(x_0)}{(x_1 - x_0)}$$

Finally, set x to the center value x_2 (the x coordinate of the third point) and substitute in the values for b_0 and b_1:

$$f_2(x_2) = f_2(x_0) + \left[\frac{f_2(x_1) - f_2(x_0)}{(x_1 - x_0)}\right](x_2 - x_0) + b_2(x_2 - x_0)(x_2 - x_1)$$

Subtract $f_2(x_1)$ from both sides:

$$f_2(x_2) - f_2(x_1) = \left[f_2(x_0) - f_2(x_1)\right] + \left[\frac{f_2(x_1) - f_2(x_0)}{(x_1 - x_0)}\right](x_2 - x_0) + b_2(x_2 - x_0)(x_2 - x_1)$$

But since

$$[f_2(x_0) - f_2(x_1)] + \left[\frac{f_2(x_1) - f_2(x_0)}{(x_1 - x_0)}\right](x_2 - x_0)$$

$$= \left[\frac{f_2(x_1) - f_2(x_0)}{(x_1 - x_0)}\right](-1)(x_1 - x_0) + \left[\frac{f_2(x_1) - f_2(x_0)}{(x_1 - x_0)}\right](x_2 - x_0)$$

$$= \left[\frac{f_2(x_1) - f_2(x_0)}{(x_1 - x_0)}\right][(-x_1 + x_0) + (x_2 - x_0)]$$

$$= \left[\frac{f_2(x_1) - f_2(x_0)}{(x_1 - x_0)}\right](x_2 - x_1)$$

we have

$$f_2(x_2) - f_2(x_1) = \left[\frac{f_2(x_1) - f_2(x_0)}{(x_1 - x_0)}\right](x_2 - x_1) + b_2(x_2 - x_0)(x_2 - x_1)$$

Divide both sides by $(x_2 - x_1)$, and we get

$$\frac{f_2(x_2) - f_2(x_1)}{(x_2 - x_1)} = \left[\frac{f_2(x_1) - f_2(x_0)}{(x_1 - x_0)}\right] + b_2(x_2 - x_0)$$

and finally

$$b_2 = \frac{\left[\dfrac{f_2(x_2) - f_2(x_1)}{(x_2 - x_1)}\right] - \left[\dfrac{f_2(x_1) - f_2(x_0)}{(x_1 - x_0)}\right]}{(x_2 - x_0)}$$

Notice that the values of b_0 and b_1 are similar to the corresponding values we had computed for the first degree polynomial. The definition of b_2 is recursive—it's a divided difference that is composed of two divided differences.

In general, if we are given $n+1$ points, then there exists a unique polynomial function $f_n(x)$ of degree n that passes through all the points.

6.3 Divided Differences

We can use the notation $f[x_i, x_j]$ to represent the first divided difference:

$$f[x_i, x_j] = \frac{f(x_i) - f(x_j)}{x_i - x_j}$$

For the second divided difference:

$$f[x_i, x_j, x_k] = \frac{\dfrac{f(x_i) - f(x_j)}{x_i - x_j} - \dfrac{f(x_j) - f(x_k)}{x_j - x_k}}{x_i - x_k}$$

$$= \frac{f[x_i, x_j] - f[x_j, x_k]}{x_i - x_k}$$

In general, we can define the nth divided difference recursively:

$$f[x_n, x_{n-1}, \ldots, x_1, x_0] = \frac{f[x_n, x_{n-1}, \ldots, x_1] - f[x_{n-1}, x_{n-2}, \ldots, x_0]}{x_n - x_0}$$

although they can be computed more efficiently by starting with the first divided differences, then computing the second, then the third, and so on.

Now, here's our payoff. For a polynomial interpolation functions in Newton form, we have

$$b_0 = f_n(x_0)$$
$$b_1 = f_n[x_1, x_0]$$
$$b_2 = f_n[x_2, x_1, x_0]$$

$$\cdots$$

$$b_n = f_n[x_n, x_{n-1}, \ldots, x_1, x_0]$$

Thus, an interpolating line is

$$f_1(x) = f_1(x_0) + f_1[x_1, x_0](x - x_0)$$

and an interpolating parabola is

$$f_2(x) = f_2(x_0) + f_2[x_1, x_0](x - x_0) + f_2[x_2, x_1, x_0](x - x_0)(x - x_1)$$

Adding another data point means we simply compute and add another term to the interpolation function. The data points do not have to be in any particular order, nor do they need to be spaced evenly along the x axis.

We can visualize the computation of divided differences using a divided difference table, as shown in Table 6–1.

Table 6–1   A divided difference table showing the first through the fourth divided differences for a function $f(x)$ and five data points x_0, x_1, x_2, x_3, and x_4. The gray shading shows an example of how to "fan back" diagonally from a divided difference to see how it is recursively defined and to determine its denominator:

$$f[x_3, x_2, x_1, x_0] = \frac{f[x_3, x_2, x_1] - f[x_2, x_1, x_0]}{x_3 - x_0}$$

i	x	$f(x)$	First	Second	Third	Fourth
0	x_0	$f(x_0)$				
			$f[x_1, x_0]$			
1	x_1	$f(x_1)$		$f[x_2, x_1, x_0]$		
			$f[x_2, x_1]$		$f[x_3, x_2, x_1, x_0]$	
2	x_2	$f(x_2)$		$f[x_3, x_2, x_1]$		$f[x_4, x_3, x_2, x_1, x_0]$
			$f[x_3, x_2]$		$f[x_4, x_3, x_2, x_1]$	
3	x_3	$f(x_3)$		$f[x_4, x_3, x_2]$		
			$f[x_4, x_3]$			
4	x_4	$f(x_4)$				

6.4 Constructing the Interpolation Function

From the equations for the b_i coefficients in the previous section, we see that they are values at the top of each column of the divided difference table, starting with the column labeled $f(x)$ in Table 6–1.

We start with the small DataPoint class in package numbercruncher.mathutils that represents a data point constructed from an x value and a y value. See Listing 6–0.

Listing 6–0 A data point.

```
package numbercruncher.mathutils;

/**
 * A data point for interpolation and regression.
 */
public class DataPoint
{
    /** the x value */  public float x;
    /** the y value */  public float y;

    /**
     * Constructor.
     * @param x the x value
     * @param y the y value
     */
    public DataPoint(float x, float y)
    {
        this.x = x;
        this.y = y;
    }
}
```

The InterpolationPolynomial class in package numbercruncher.mathutils represents a polynomial interpolation function in Newton form. It uses divided differences to compute the coefficients. See Listing 6–1a.

The class builds the divided difference table incrementally—each new data point allows a new entry to be appended at the bottom of each column. Method addDataPoint() augments the table with each new data point.

The class implements the Evaluatable interface described at the beginning of Chapter 5. Method at() returns the value of the interpolation function at a given value of x by computing the terms of the Newton form.

Listing 6–1a A class that implements a polynomial interpolation function.

```
package numbercruncher.mathutils;

/**
 * A polynomial interpolation function.
 */
public class InterpolationPolynomial implements Evaluatable
{
```

```java
/** number of data points */       private int       n;
/** array of data points */        private DataPoint data[];
/** divided difference table */     private float     dd[][];

/**
 * Constructor.
 * @param data the array of data points
 */
public InterpolationPolynomial(DataPoint data[])
{
    this.data = data;
    this.dd   = new float[data.length] [data.length];

    for (int i = 0; i < data.length; ++i) {
        addDataPoint(data[i]);
    }
}

/**
 * Constructor.
 * @param maxPoints the maximum number of data points
 */
public InterpolationPolynomial(int maxPoints)
{
    this.data = new DataPoint[maxPoints];
    this.dd   = new float[data.length][data.length];
}

/**
 * Return the data points.
 * @return the array of data points
 */
public DataPoint[] getDataPoints() { return data; }

/**
 * Return the divided difference table.
 * @return the table
 */
public float[][] getDividedDifferenceTable() { return dd; }

/**
 * Return the current number of data points.
 * @return the count
 */
public int getDataPointCount() { return n; }

/**
 * Add new data point: Augment the divided difference table
 * by appending a new entry at the bottom of each column.
```

```
      * @param dataPoint the new data point
      */
    public void addDataPoint(DataPoint dataPoint)
    {
        if (n >= data.length) return;

        data[n]   = dataPoint;
        dd[n][0]  = dataPoint.y;

        ++n;

        for (int order = 1; order < n; ++order) {
            int   bottom       = n - order - 1;
            float numerator    = dd[bottom+1][order-1]
                                   - dd[bottom][order-1];
            float denominator = data[bottom + order].x
                                   - data[bottom].x;

            dd[bottom][order] = numerator/denominator;
        }
    }

    /**
     * Return the value of the polynomial
     * interpolation function at x.
     * (Implementation of Evaluatable.)
     * @param x the value of x
     * @return the value of the function at x
     */
    public float at(float x)
    {
        if (n < 2) return Float.NaN;

        float y = dd[0][0];
        float xFactor = 1;

        // Compute the value of the function.
        for (int order = 1; order < n; ++order) {
            xFactor = xFactor*(x - data[order-1].x);
            y = y + xFactor*dd[0][order];
        }

        return y;
    }

    /**
     * Reset.
     */
    public void reset() { n = 0; }
}
```

Program 6–1 instantiates an `InterpolationPolynomial` object. As shown in Listing 6–1b, the noninteractive version of the program constructs the interpolation function from a set of five data points from e^x in the interval $1 < x < 2$ as computed by `Math.exp()`. With each new data point, the interpolation function can estimate the value $e^{1.4}$ with greater accuracy. Note that the data points are not sorted, and they are not evenly spaced.

Listing 6–1b The noninteractive version of Program 6–1 estimates $e^{1.4}$ with increasing accuracy as new data points are added to the polynomial interpolation function.

```
package numbercruncher.program6_1;

import numbercruncher.mathutils.DataPoint;
import numbercruncher.mathutils.InterpolationPolynomial;
import numbercruncher.mathutils.AlignRight;

/**
 * PROGRAM 6-1: Polynomial Interpolation
 *
 * Demonstrate polynomial interpolation by using a divided difference
 * table to construct an interpolation function for a set of data points.
 * Use the function to estimate new values.
 */
public class Interpolation
{
    private static final int MAX_POINTS = 10;

    private static AlignRight ar = new AlignRight();

    /**
     * Main program.
     * @param args the array of runtime arguments
     */
    public static void main(String args[])
    {
        InterpolationPolynomial p =
                        new InterpolationPolynomial(MAX_POINTS);
        float x = 1.4f;

        p.addDataPoint(new DataPoint(1.12f, (float) Math.exp(1.12f)));
        p.addDataPoint(new DataPoint(1.55f, (float) Math.exp(1.55f)));
        printEstimate(p, x);

        p.addDataPoint(new DataPoint(1.25f, (float) Math.exp(1.25f)));
        printEstimate(p, x);

        p.addDataPoint(new DataPoint(1.92f, (float) Math.exp(1.92f)));
        printEstimate(p, x);
```

```
        p.addDataPoint(new DataPoint(1.33f, (float) Math.exp(1.33f)));
        printEstimate(p, x);

        p.addDataPoint(new DataPoint(1.75f, (float) Math.exp(1.75f)));
        printEstimate(p, x);
    }

    /**
     * Print the value of p(x).
     * @param p the polynomial interpolation function
     * @param x the value of x
     */
    private static void printEstimate(InterpolationPolynomial p,
                                      float x)
    {
        printTable(p);

        float est      = p.at(x);
        float exp      = (float) Math.exp(x);
        float errorPct = (float) Math.abs(100*(est - exp)/exp);

        System.out.println("\nEstimate e^" + x + "  = " + est);
        System.out.println("  Math.exp(" + x + ") = " + exp);
        System.out.println("          % error = " + errorPct + "\n");
    }

    /**
     * Print the divided difference table.
     */
    private static void printTable(InterpolationPolynomial p)
    {
        int       n    = p.getDataPointCount();
        DataPoint data[] = p.getDataPoints();

        float     dd[][] = p.getDividedDifferenceTable();
        ar.print("i", 1); ar.print("x", 5); ar.print("f(x)", 10);
        if (n > 1) ar.print("First", 10);
        if (n > 2) ar.print("Second", 10);
        if (n > 3) ar.print("Third", 12);
        if (n > 4) ar.print("Fourth", 12);
        if (n > 5) ar.print("Fifth", 12);
        ar.underline();

        for (int i = 0; i < n; ++i) {
            ar.print(i, 1);
            ar.print(data[i].x, 5);
            ar.print(dd[i][0], 10);

            for (int order = 1; order < n-i; ++order) {
                ar.print(dd[i][order], (order < 3) ? 10 : 12);
            }
```

```
            ar.println();
        }
    }
}
```

Output:

```
i    x      f(x)      First
------------------------
0 1.12 3.0648541    3.82934
1 1.55    4.71147

Estimate e^1.4  = 4.137069
  Math.exp(1.4) = 4.0552
        % error = 2.0188677


i    x      f(x)      First     Second
----------------------------------
0 1.12 3.0648541    3.82934 1.8545004
1 1.55    4.71147  4.070425
2 1.25 3.4903429

Estimate e^1.4  = 4.0591803
  Math.exp(1.4) = 4.0552
        % error = 0.09814953


i    x      f(x)      First     Second      Third
------------------------------------------------
0 1.12 3.0648541    3.82934 1.8545004    0.724587
1 1.55    4.71147  4.070425    2.43417
2 1.25 3.4903429  4.971068
3 1.92   6.820958

Estimate e^1.4  = 4.0546155
  Math.exp(1.4) = 4.0552
        % error = 0.014416116


i    x      f(x)      First     Second      Third      Fourth
------------------------------------------------------------
0 1.12 3.0648541    3.82934 1.8545004    0.724587 0.17594407
1 1.55    4.71147  4.070425    2.43417 0.7615353
2 1.25 3.4903429  4.971068 2.2666323
3 1.92   6.820958 5.1523986
4 1.33 3.7810435

Estimate e^1.4  = 4.055192
  Math.exp(1.4) = 4.0552
        % error = 1.998972E-4
```

```
i    x       f(x)      First     Second      Third       Fourth        Fifth
-----------------------------------------------------------------------------
0 1.12 3.0648541    3.82934 1.8545004    0.724587  0.17594407 0.037198737
1 1.55   4.71147   4.070425    2.43417   0.7615353  0.19937928
2 1.25 3.4903429  4.971068 2.2666323   0.80141115
3 1.92  6.820958 5.1523986   2.667338
4 1.33 3.7810435 4.6989512
5 1.75   5.754603


Estimate e^1.4  = 4.0552006
  Math.exp(1.4) = 4.0552
        % error = 1.1758659E-5
```

It is often the case, however, that the given set of data points will not come from any known function. Or the function is so expensive to compute that using an interpolation function is preferable.

The interactive version[2] of Program 6–1 allows you to set up to 10 arbitrary data points by clicking the mouse on the graph, and the program will then create and plot the polynomial interpolation function through the data points. Screen 6–1a shows a screen shot with 5 data points.

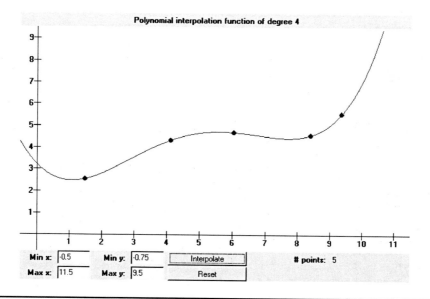

Screen 6–1a A graph of a polynomial interpolation function created by the interactive version of Program 6–1.

---

[2]   Each interactive program in this book has two versions, an applet and a standalone application. You can download all the Java source code. See the downloading instructions in the preface of this book.

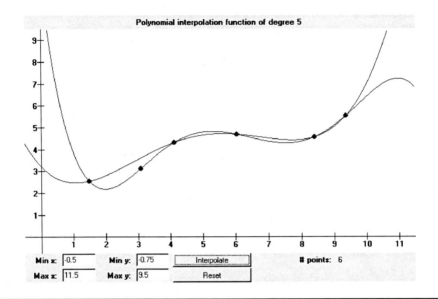

Screen 6–1b The result of adding another data point (the second one from the left).

Screen 6–1b shows the plot of the modified interpolation function after adding a new data point.

With an interpolation function, it is important that we use it to *interpolate,* not *extrapolate.* Attempting to use the function to estimate values outside of the domain of the original data values can be very precarious. Screens 6–1a and 6–1b show how the function can shoot off in the positive or negative *y* directions with *x* values less than or greater than the original data points. This is especially true with higher degree functions.

6.5 Least-Squares Linear Regression

If we're given a set of data points, we might not want an interpolation function that passes through all the points. But, instead, we're interested in a trend line that passes closely among the points, especially if there are a large number of data points. We can use the function that describes the trend line to generate approximations of the original data points. These approximations "smooth out" the original data, which is desirable if the original data contained some experimental error.

The trend line that we will compute is the regression line. Since we're looking for the line that passes the most closely among the data points, it is unique for a given set of points. What remains is to define what we mean by "close."

Figure 6–3 shows a regression line passing among three data points, (x_1, y_1), (x_2, y_2), and (x_3, y_3). The line function is in the power form, $f(x) = a_0 + a_1 x$. This is also known as the *slope-intercept* form of the line function, where a_0 is where the line intercepts the *y* axis, and a_1 is the slope of the line.

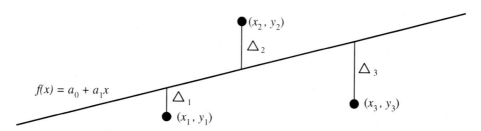

Figure 6–3 A linear regression line passing "closely" among three points. Each Δ represents the error, or vertical difference, between the point and the line.

The figure also shows Δ_1, Δ_2, and Δ_3, which are the differences between the y values of the data points and the y values computed by the line function. For example,

$$\Delta_3 = y_3 - f(x_3)$$
$$= y_3 - a_0 - a_1 x_3$$

Therefore, each Δ represents the *vertical* difference between the point and the line, *not* the perpendicular distance. We can also consider each Δ to be the error between the actual value (the data point) and the predicted value (computed on the regression line).

Thus, to get the regression line function $f(x) = a_0 + a_1 x$, we need to compute the values of its coefficients a_0 and a_1 such that the line is the one that is closest to the data points: The line that we'll consider to be the closest is the *least-squares regression line,* because it's the one that minimizes the sum of the squares of all the Δs. In other words, we want values for a_0 and a_1 that minimize the value of the error function $E(a_0, a_1)$ defined as

$$E(a_0, a_1) = \sum \Delta_i^2 = \sum (y_i - f(x_i))^2 = \sum (y_i - a_0 - a_1 x_i)^2$$

By squaring the Δ values, the least-squares algorithm places a heavy penalty on large errors. Therefore, the algorithm tries to avoid many large Δ's.

6.6 Constructing the Regression Line

Our problem of finding the regression line for a given set of data points has become one of finding the values for a_0 and a_1 that minimize the value of the error function $E(a_0, a_1)$.

$E(a_0, a_1)$ is a function of the two variables a_0 and a_1, and its value is always nonnegative. Its graph will be the surface of a smooth, three-dimensional shape sitting above (or possibly touching) the $a_0 a_1$ plane. The region near its minimum would be like the bottom of a round bowl. At the minimum point, tangent lines drawn parallel to the a_0 axis and parallel to the a_1 axis will both have zero slopes.[3]

---

[3]   In other words, in order for the error function $E(a_0, a_1)$ to have a local minimum at some point in the $a_0 a_1$ plane, it is necessary that the partial derivatives $\partial E/\partial a_0 = 0$ and $\partial E/\partial a_1 = 0$ at that point.

So we differentiate $E(a_0, a_1)$ twice, first with respect to a_0 and then with respect to a_1. To start, multiply out the squared expression:

$$E(a_0, a_1) = \sum(y_i - a_0 - a_1 x_i)^2$$
$$= \sum(y_i^2 - 2a_0 y_i - 2a_1 x_i y_i + a_0^2 + 2a_0 a_1 x_i + a_1^2 x_i^2)$$

Differentiate with respect to a_0:

$$\sum(-2y_i + 2a_0 + 2a_1 x_i) = -2\sum(y_i - a_0 - a_1 x_i)$$

and then differentiate with respect to a_1:

$$\sum(-2x_i y_i + 2a_0 x_i + 2a_1 x_i^2) = -2\sum(x_i y_i - a_0 x_i - a_1 x_i^2)$$

Since the slopes are 0, set both derivatives equal to 0 and divide all sides by -2. For the first equation,

$$0 = \sum(y_i - a_0 - a_1 x_i)$$
$$= \sum y_i - \sum a_0 - a_1 \sum x_i$$

and then for the second equation,

$$0 = \sum(x_i y_i - a_0 x_i - a_1 x_i^2)$$
$$= \sum x_i y_i - a_0 \sum x_i - a_1 \sum x_i^2$$

If n is the total number of data points, then in the first equation, $\sum a_0$ is simply $n a_0$. If we rearrange the terms of the two equations, we have the *normal equations,* a system of two linear equations with the two unknowns a_0 and a_1:

$$n a_0 + \left(\sum x_i\right) a_1 = \sum y_i$$
$$\left(\sum x_i\right) a_0 + \left(\sum x_i^2\right) a_1 = \sum x_i y_i$$

Solve the first equation for a_0:

$$a_0 = \frac{\sum y_i - \left(\sum x_i\right) a_1}{n}$$

and substitute it into the second equation:

$$\left(\sum x_i\right)\left[\frac{\sum y_i - \left(\sum x_i\right) a_1}{n}\right] + \left(\sum x_i^2\right) a_1 = \sum x_i y_i$$

Multiply through by n and rearrange the terms:

$$\left(\sum x_i\right)\left[\sum y_i - \left(\sum x_i\right)a_1\right] + n\left(\sum x_i^2\right)a_1 = n\sum x_i y_i$$

$$\sum x_i \sum y_i - \left(\sum x_i\right)^2 a_1 + n\left(\sum x_i^2\right)a_1 = n\sum x_i y_i$$

$$a_1\left[n\sum x_i^2 - \left(\sum x_i\right)^2\right] = n\sum x_i y_i - \sum x_i \sum y_i$$

and so

$$a_1 = \frac{n\sum x_i y_i - \sum x_i \sum y_i}{n\sum x_i^2 - \left(\sum x_i\right)^2}$$

If we let $\bar{x}$ represent $\dfrac{\sum x_i}{n}$, the average of the x_i values, and $\bar{y}$ represent $\dfrac{\sum y_i}{n}$, the average of the y_i values, we can simplify the expression for a_0:

$$a_0 = \bar{y} - a_1\bar{y}$$

So to calculate the least-squares regression line for a given set of data points, we need to compute the following quantities: $\sum x_i$, $\sum y_i$, $\sum x_i^2$, $\sum x_i y_i$, $\bar{x}$, and $\bar{y}$.

Listing 6–2a shows the RegressionLine class in package numbercruncher. mathutils. It computes these quantities for a set of data points—method addData() updates the sums for each new data point. Before methods getA0() and getA1() return the values of the coefficients a_0 and a_1, respectively, each invokes method validateCoefficients(), which uses the formulas to compute the current values of the coefficients. The class implements the Evaluatable interface.

Listing 6–2a A class that implements a least-squares regression line.

```
package numbercruncher.mathutils;

/**
 * A least-squares regression line function.
 */
public class RegressionLine implements Evaluatable
{
    /** sum of x */       private double sumX;
    /** sum of y */       private double sumY;
    /** sum of x*x */     private double sumXX;
    /** sum of x*y */     private double sumXY;
```

```java
/** line coefficient a0 */  private float a0;
/** line coefficient a1 */  private float a1;

/** number of data points */        private int     n;
/** true if coefficients valid */   private boolean coefsValid;

/**
 * Constructor.
 */
public RegressionLine() {}

/**
 * Constructor.
 * @param data the array of data points
 */
public RegressionLine(DataPoint data[])
{
    for (int i = 0; i < data.length; ++i) {
        addDataPoint(data[i]);
    }
}

/**
 * Return the current number of data points.
 * @return the count
 */
public int getDataPointCount() { return n; }

/**
 * Return the coefficient a0.
 * @return the value of a0
 */
public float getA0()
{
    validateCoefficients();
    return a0;
}

/**
 * Return the coefficient a1.
 * @return the value of a1
 */
public float getA1()
{
    validateCoefficients();
    return a1;
}

/**
 * Return the sum of the x values.
 * @return the sum
```

```
 */
public double getSumX() { return sumX; }

/**
 * Return the sum of the y values.
 * @return the sum
 */
public double getSumY() { return sumY; }

/**
 * Return the sum of the x*x values.
 * @return the sum
 */
public double getSumXX() { return sumXX; }

/**
 * Return the sum of the x*y values.
 * @return the sum
 */
public double getSumXY() { return sumXY; }

/**
 * Add a new data point: Update the sums.
 * @param dataPoint the new data point
 */
public void addDataPoint(DataPoint dataPoint)
{
    sumX  += dataPoint.x;
    sumY  += dataPoint.y;
    sumXX += dataPoint.x*dataPoint.x;
    sumXY += dataPoint.x*dataPoint.y;

    ++n;
    coefsValid = false;
}

/**
 * Return the value of the regression line function at x.
 * (Implementation of Evaluatable.)
 * @param x the value of x
 * @return the value of the function at x
 */
public float at(float x)
{
    if (n < 2) return Float.NaN;

    validateCoefficients();
    return a0 + a1*x;
}
```

```
    /**
     * Reset.
     */
    public void reset()
    {
        n = 0;
        sumX = sumY = sumXX = sumXY = 0;
        coefsValid = false;
    }

    /**
     * Validate the coefficients.
     */
    private void validateCoefficients()
    {
        if (coefsValid) return;

        if (n >= 2) {
            float xBar = (float) sumX/n;
            float yBar = (float) sumY/n;

            a1 = (float) ((n*sumXY - sumX*sumY)
                            /(n*sumXX - sumX*sumX));
            a0 = (float) (yBar - a1*xBar);
        }
        else {
            a0 = a1 = Float.NaN;
        }

        coefsValid = true;
    }
}
```

There could be some computational problems with the sums. If the data points have both positive and negative x and y values, then sumX and sumY may have cancellation errors. If the data points are spread far apart from one another, there may be magnitude errors with all the sums, especially sumXX and sumXY . Of course, there is also the danger of overflow. Therefore, we may need to rewrite method addData() to employ some of the summation algorithms described in Chapter 4.

Program 6–2 instantiates a RegressionLine object and uses a set of seven data points to construct and print the equation for a least-squares regression line. Listing 6–2b shows the noninteractive version of the program.

Listing 6–2b The noninteractive version of Program 6–2 constructs a regression line for a set of data points.

```
package numbercruncher.program6_2;

import numbercruncher.mathutils.DataPoint;
import numbercruncher.mathutils.RegressionLine;
```

```java
/**
 * PROGRAM 6-2: Linear Regression
 *
 * Demonstrate linear regression by constructing
 * the regression line for a set of data points.
 */
public class LinearRegression
{
    private static final int MAX_POINTS = 10;

    /**
     * Main program.
     * @param args the array of runtime arguments
     */
    public static void main(String args[])
    {
        RegressionLine line = new RegressionLine();

        line.addDataPoint(new DataPoint(6.2f, 6.0f));
        line.addDataPoint(new DataPoint(1.3f, 0.75f));
        line.addDataPoint(new DataPoint(5.5f, 3.05f));
        line.addDataPoint(new DataPoint(2.8f, 2.96f));
        line.addDataPoint(new DataPoint(4.7f, 4.72f));
        line.addDataPoint(new DataPoint(7.9f, 5.81f));
        line.addDataPoint(new DataPoint(3.0f, 2.49f));

        printSums(line);
        printLine(line);
    }

    /**
     * Print the computed sums.
     * @param line the regression line
     */
    private static void printSums(RegressionLine line)
    {
        System.out.println("n      = " + line.getDataPointCount());
        System.out.println("Sum x  = " + line.getSumX());
        System.out.println("Sum y  = " + line.getSumY());
        System.out.println("Sum xx = " + line.getSumXX());
        System.out.println("Sum xy = " + line.getSumXY());
    }

    /**
     * Print the regression line function.
     * @param line the regression line
     */
    private static void printLine(RegressionLine line)
    {
```

```
        System.out.println("\nRegression line:  y = " +
                           line.getA1() +
                           "x + " + line.getA0());
    }
}
```

Output:

```
n     = 7
Sum x  = 31.399999618530273
Sum y  = 25.77999973297119
Sum xx = 171.71999621391296
Sum xy = 138.7909932732582

Regression line:  y = 0.74993044x + 0.31888318
```

The interactive version of Program 6–2 allows you to set up to 100 arbitrary data points by clicking the mouse on the graph, and the program will then create and plot the regression line through the data points. Screen 6–2a shows a screen shot.

You can add new data points to see their effect on the regression line. Screen 6–2b is a screen shot after new data points have been added, and it shows the new regression line.

The fact that the least-squares algorithm minimizes the vertical distances between the data points and the regression line, instead of their perpendicular distances from the line, causes pathological behavior when most of the data points are stacked vertically. Screen 6–2c shows an example. Fortunately, most data points, such as from experiments, are spread more horizontally than vertically.

Screen 6–2a A least-squares regression line created by the interactive version of Program 6–2.

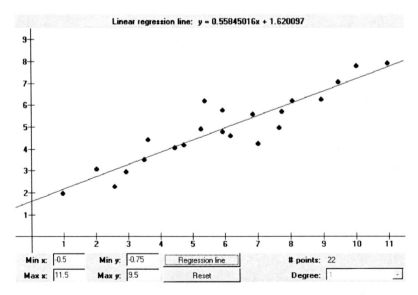

A regression line that is nearly vertical (as the data points in Screen 6–2c suggest that it should be) would cause very large Δ values.

Screen 6–2b The result of adding new data points.

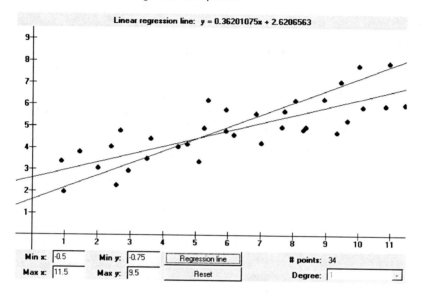

Screen 6–2c A pathological regression line when most of the data points are stacked vertically.

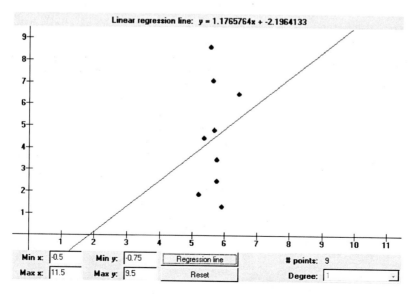

References

Atkinson, L.V., and P.J. Harley, *An Introduction to Numerical Methods with Pascal,* London: Addison-Wesley, 1983.

Chapra, Seven C., and Raymond P. Canale, *Numerical Methods for Engineers,* 3rd edition, New York: WCB/McGraw-Hill, 1998.

Cheny, Ward, and David Kincaid, *Numerical Mathematics and Computing,* 4th edition, Pacific Grove, CA: Brooks/Cole, 1999.

Woodford, C., and C. Phillips, *Numerical Methods with Worked Examples,* London: Chapman and Hall, 1997.

Polynomial interpolation and linear regression are topics covered by most books on numerical methods, such as these. See Sections 17.1 and 18.1 in Chapra, Sections 4.1 and 10.1 in Cheney, Chapter 3 in Woodford, and Chapter 6 in Atkinson.

Monahan, John F., *Numerical Methods of Statistics,* Cambridge, UK: Cambridge University Press, 2001.

Spiegel, Murray R., and Larry J. Stephens, *Statistics,* 3rd edition, New York: McGraw-Hill, 1999.

Books on statistics also include polynomial interpolation and linear regression, such as Chapter 13 in Spiegel. Monahan presents matrix-oriented computational algorithms for least-squares regression in Sections 5.1 through 5.3.

CHAPTER **7**

NUMERICAL INTEGRATION

Freshman calculus classes would have us believe that integration is mostly algebraic manipulation—if the integrand (the function we want to integrate) fits a certain pattern, perform a prescribed set of transformations and then plug in the values to get the answer. For example, if the integrand is $f(x) = x^n$ and $n \neq -1$, then, we were taught,

$$\int_a^b f(x)dx = \int_a^b x^n dx$$

$$= \frac{1}{n+1}x^{n+1}\Big|_a^b$$

$$= \frac{1}{n+1}(b^{n+1} - a^{n+1})$$

Unfortunately, in the real world, these patterns aren't always apparent, and so we use the computer to do *numerical integration.*

7.1 Back to Basics

Numerical integration returns us to the basic definition of integration: finding the area under a curve in a piecewise manner. Figure 7–1 shows how we can use rectangles to estimate the area under a curve defined by some integrand $f(x)$. We can make the computation easier by making all the rectangles have the same width.

7.2 The Trapezoidal Algorithm

As we can see in Figure 7–1, there is error at the top of each rectangle, since the rectangles don't fit exactly under the curve. These errors are smaller for narrower rectangles, but with a greater number of rectangles, we'll have a greater number of roundoff errors. Figure 7–2 shows how we can decrease the errors by using trapezoids instead of rectangles.

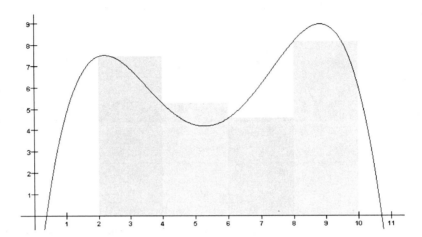

Figure 7–1   Using rectangles to estimate the area under a curve defined by a function $f(x)$.

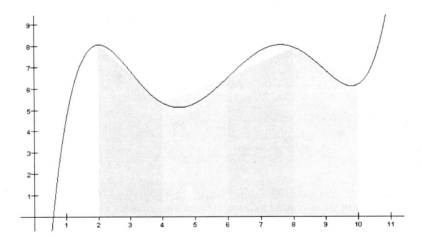

Figure 7–2   Using trapezoids to estimate the area under a curve defined by a function $f(x)$.

Trapezoids are handy because there is a simple formula for computing their areas. If the heights of the two sides of a trapezoid are y_1 and y_2, and its width is h, then the formula for the area A is

$$A = \frac{1}{2}(y_1 + y_2)h$$

Or, in other words, it is the width times the average of the two heights.[1]

---

[1]   In calculus, the letter h is traditionally used to represent the width of an interval.

That's the basic idea behind the trapezoidal integration algorithm. It simply fits a number of equal-width trapezoids under the curve of the integrand $f(x)$. The heights of a trapezoid's sides are given by the integrand—if the sides are at x_1 and x_2, then the heights are $f(x_1)$ and $f(x_2)$. If we want to use n trapezoids to estimate the total area under the curve in the interval $[a, b]$, then their common width is $h = \frac{b-a}{n}$.

In theory, increasing n will increase the accuracy of the area estimate. However, in reality, a very large n (and hence a very small h) will cause so many roundoff errors to accumulate that the accuracy will actually decrease. We will see this occurring in Program 7–1. Listing 7–1a shows the class `TrapezoidalIntegrator` in package `numbercruncher.mathutils` that implements the trapezoidal integration algorithm.

Listing 7–1a The class that implements the trapezoidal integration algorithm.

```
package numbercruncher.mathutils;

/**
 * Function integrator that implements the trapezoidal algorithm.
 */
public class TrapezoidalIntegrator implements Integrator
{
    /** the function to integrate */  private Evaluatable integrand;

    /**
     * Constructor.
     * @param integrand the function to integrate
     */
    public TrapezoidalIntegrator(Evaluatable integrand)
    {
        this.integrand = integrand;
    }

    /**
     * Integrate the function from a to b using the trapezoidal
     * algorithm, and return an approximation to the area.
     * (Integrator implementation.)
     * @param a the lower limit
     * @param b the upper limit
     * @param intervals the number of equal-width intervals
     * @return an approximation to the area
     */
    public float integrate(float a, float b, int intervals)
    {
        if (b <= a) return 0;

        float h         = (b - a)/intervals;    // interval width
        float totalArea = 0;
```

```
        // Compute the area using the current number of intervals.
        for (int i = 0; i < intervals; ++i) {
            float x1 = a + i*h;
            totalArea += areaOf(x1, h);
        }
        return totalArea;
    }

    /**
     * Compute the area of the ith trapezoidal region.
     * @param x1 the left bound of the region
     * @param h the interval width
     * @return the area of the region
     */
    private float areaOf(float x1, float h)
    {
        float x2    = x1 + h;                // right bound of the region
        float y1    = integrand.at(x1);      // value at left bound
        float y2    = integrand.at(x2);      // value at right bound
        float area = h*(y1 + y2)/2;          // area of the region

        return area;
    }
}
```

The constructor takes an `Evaluator` argument, and so the argument can be a `Function`, `InterpolationPolynomial`, or `RegressionLine` object. Its second argument is the number of intervals. Method `integrate()` performs the integration by invoking method `areaOf()` for each region, summing the areas, and returning an approximation to the total area. Method `areaOf()` implements the formula for the area of a trapezoid.

Class `TrapezoidalIntegrator` implements interface `Integrator`, which is also defined in package `numbercruncher.mathutils`. See Listing 7–1b.

Listing 7–1b Interface integrator.

```
package numbercruncher.mathutils;

/**
 * Interface implemented by integrator classes.
 */
public interface Integrator
{
    /**
     * Integrate the function from a to b,
     * and return an approximation to the area.
     * @param a the lower limit
```

```
     * @param b the upper limit
     * @param intervals the number of equal-width intervals
     * @return an approximation to the area
     */
    float integrate(float a, float b, int intervals);
}
```

If we give Program 7–1 the command-line argument "trapezoidal," it instantiates a `Trape-zoidalIntegrator` object. (We'll use the same program later when we examine Simpson's integration algorithm.) The noninteractive version of the program uses the object to compute an approximation to π (≈ 3.1415926) in the following way. The area of the unit circle (its radius is 1) is π, and its equation is $x^2 + y^2 = 1$. Therefore,

$$\frac{\pi}{4} = \int_0^1 \sqrt{1 - x^2}\,dx$$

since it integrates over the upper right quadrant of the circle. See Listing 7–1c.

Listing 7–1c The noninteractive version of Program 7–1 computes an approximation to the value of π with the trapezoidal integration algorithm when given the command-line argument "trapezoidal."

```
package numbercruncher.program7_1;

import numbercruncher.mathutils.Function;
import numbercruncher.mathutils.Integrator;
import numbercruncher.mathutils.TrapezoidalIntegrator;
import numbercruncher.mathutils.SimpsonsIntegrator;
import numbercruncher.mathutils.Epsilon;
import numbercruncher.mathutils.AlignRight;

/**
 * PROGRAM 7-1: Integration
 *
 * Demonstrate numerical integration algorithms.
 */
public class Integration
{
    private static final int    MAX_INTERVALS = Integer.MAX_VALUE/2;
    private static final float  TOLERANCE     = 100*Epsilon.floatValue();

    private static final float  FROM_LIMIT    = 0;
    private static final float  TO_LIMIT      = 1;

    private static final int    TRAPEZOIDAL   = 0;
    private static final int    SIMPSONS      = 1;
```

```java
    private static final String ALGORITHMS[] = {"Trapezoidal",
                                                "Simpson's"};
/**
 * Main program.
 * @param args the array of runtime arguments
 */
public static void main(String args[])
{
    String arg       = args[0].toLowerCase();
    int    algorithm = arg.startsWith("tra") ? TRAPEZOIDAL
                                              : SIMPSONS;

    System.out.println("ALGORITHM: " + ALGORITHMS[algorithm]);
    System.out.println();

    // The function to integrate.
    Function integrand = new Function() {
        public float at(float x)
        {
            return (float) Math.sqrt(1 - x*x);
        }
    };

    integrate(algorithm, integrand);
}
/**
 * Do the integration with either the trapezoidal algorithm
 * or Simpson's algorithm.
 * @param algorithm 0 for trapezoidal, 1 for Simpson's
 * @param integrand the function to integrate
 * @return an approximation to the area
 */
private static void integrate(int algorithm, Function integrand)
{
    int   intervals = 1;                 // number of intervals
    float area      = 0;                 // total area
    float errorPct  = Float.MAX_VALUE;   // % error

    float prevArea;
    float prevErrorPct;

    Integrator integrator =
        (algorithm == TRAPEZOIDAL)
            ? (Integrator) new TrapezoidalIntegrator(integrand)
            : (Integrator) new SimpsonsIntegrator(integrand);

    AlignRight ar = new AlignRight();
```

```
        ar.print("n", 5); ar.print("pi", 15); ar.print("% Error", 15);
        ar.underline();

        do {
            prevArea = area;
            area       = integrator.integrate(FROM_LIMIT, TO_LIMIT,
                                               intervals);
            float pi = 4*area;

            prevErrorPct = errorPct;
            errorPct = (float) Math.abs(100*(pi - Math.PI)/Math.PI);

            ar.print(intervals, 5);
            ar.print(pi, 15);
            ar.print(errorPct, 15);
            ar.println();

            intervals *= 2;
        } while ((errorPct > TOLERANCE)
                && (errorPct  < prevErrorPct)
                && (intervals < MAX_INTERVALS));
    }
}
```

Output:

```
ALGORITHM: Trapezoidal


    n           pi        % Error
---------------------------------
    1          2.0       36.338024
    2     2.732051       13.036119
    4     2.995709        4.643623
    8     3.089819        1.648008
   16    3.1232529       0.5837735
   32    3.1351023      0.20659526
   64    3.1392965     0.073087834
  128    3.1407807     0.025845688
  256    3.1413052     0.009149671
  512    3.1414926     0.003184639
 1024    3.1415575    0.0011204039
 2048    3.1415784      4.525632E-4
 4096    3.1415865     1.9453382E-4
 8192    3.1415906      6.551914E-5
16384    3.1415942     4.8317346E-5
32768    3.1415963     1.1661924E-4
```

The program begins with one interval ($n = 1$) and doubles the number for each iteration. Notice that it has three stopping criteria: (1) the number of intervals has exceeded the maximum, (2) the error percentage is below the tolerance, or (3) the error percentage has begun to rise. The error percentage starts to rise when the accumulated roundoff errors overwhelm the computation.

Screen 7–1a shows screen shots of the first three iterations of the interactive version[2] of Program 7–1 using the trapezoidal algorithm, with one, two, and four intervals. This program also uses polynomial interpolation (see Chapter 6) to allow you to define an arbitrary integrand.

7.3 Simpson's Algorithm

Just as trapezoids fit better under a curve than rectangles do, parabolas fit even better than trapezoids. This is the basis for Simpson's algorithm,[3] which can extend beyond parabolas (second-degree polynomials) to higher degree polynomials. Figure 7–3 shows how to use parabolic regions (their tops are parabolas) to estimate the area under a curve.

Screen 7–1a The first three iterations of the interactive version of Program 7–1 using the trapezoidal algorithm.

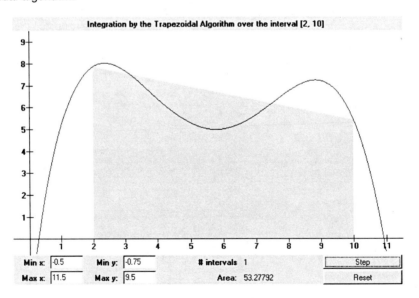

---

[2]   Each interactive program in this book has two versions, an applet and a standalone application. You can download all the Java source code. See the downloading instructions in the preface of this book.

[3]   Also known as Simpson's rule. Thomas Simpson (1710–1761) was a self-taught mathematician who developed this algorithm in 1743.

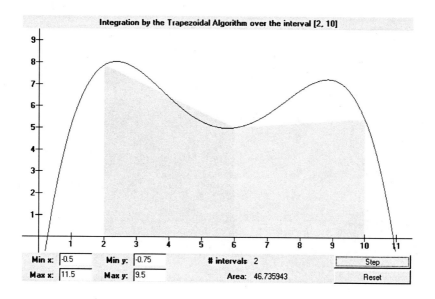

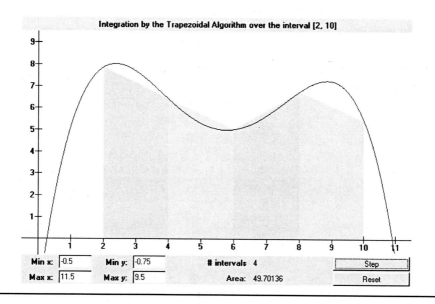

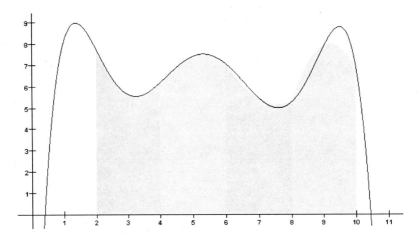

Figure 7–3   Using parabolic regions to estimate the area under a curve defined by a function $f(x)$.

We need to derive the formula for the area of a single parabolic region. From Chapter 6, we know that we can define a unique parabola with three points. Let h be the common width of each region, and we'll define the parabola over two adjacent regions. Since it doesn't matter where along the x axis the parabolic region lies, it is computationally convenient to set the x values of the three points to $-h$, 0, and h.

The power form of a parabolic function is $f(x) = a_0 + a_1x + a_2x^2$. That gives us

$$f(-h) = a_0 - a_1h + a_2h^2$$
$$f(0) = a_0$$
$$f(h) = a_0 + a_1h + a_2h^2$$

Subtract the first equation from the third:

$$f(h) - f(-h) = 2a_1h$$
$$a_1 = \frac{f(h) - f(-h)}{2h}$$

Add the first and third equations and substitute the value of a_0:

$$f(h) + f(-h) = 2f(0) + 2a_2h^2$$

$$a_2 = \frac{f(h) + f(-h) - 2f(0)}{2h^2}$$

The integral of a second-degree polynomial is something we can compute analytically:

$$\int_{-h}^{h} (a_0 + a_1x + a_2x^2)dx = \left[a_0x + \frac{a_1}{2}x^2 + \frac{a_2}{3}x^3 \right]_{-h}^{h}$$

$$= \left(a_0h + \frac{a_1}{2}h^2 + \frac{a_2}{3}h^3 \right) - \left(-a_0h + \frac{a_1}{2}h^2 - \frac{a_2}{3}h^3 \right)$$

$$= 2a_0h + \frac{2}{3}a_2h^3$$

Now substitute the values for a_0 and a_2:

$$2a_0h + \frac{2}{3}a_2h^3 = 2hf(0) + \frac{2}{3}\left[\frac{f(h) + f(-h) - 2f(0)}{2h^2} \right]h^3$$

$$= 2hf(0) + \frac{h}{3}\left[f(h) + f(-h) - 2f(0) \right]$$

$$= \frac{h}{3}\left[6f(0) + f(h) + f(-h) - 2f(0) \right]$$

$$= \frac{h}{3}\left[f(-h) + 4f(0) + f(h) \right]$$

Let the x values of three points of the parabola be x_1, x_2, and x_3, where $x_1 = -h$, $x_2 = 0$, and $x_3 = h$. Then the area of the parabolic region is

$$\frac{h}{3}\left[f(x_1) + 4f(x_2) + f(x_3) \right]$$

Class `SimpsonsIntegrator` in package `numbercruncher.mathutils` implements Simpson's integration algorithm with parabolas. See Listing 7–1d.

Listing 7–1d The class that implements Simpson's integration algorithm with parabolas.

```
package numbercruncher.mathutils;

/**
 * Function integrator that implements
 * Simpson's algorithm with parabolas.
 */
public class SimpsonsIntegrator implements Integrator
{
    /** the function to integrate */  private Evaluatable integrand;

    /**
```

```
  * Constructor.
  * @param integrand the function to integrate
  */
 public SimpsonsIntegrator(Evaluatable integrand)
 {
      this.integrand = integrand;
 }


 /**
  * Integrate the function from a to b using Simpson's algorithm,
  * and return an approximation to the area.
  * (Integrator implementation.)
  * @param a the lower limit
  * @param b the upper limit
  * @param intervals the number of equal-width intervals
  * @return an approximation to the area
  */
 public float integrate(float a, float b, int intervals)
 {
      if (b <= a) return 0;

      float h         = (b - a)/intervals/2;  // interval width
                                              //   (split in two)
      float totalArea = 0;

      // Compute the area using the current number of intervals.
      for (int i = 0; i < intervals; ++i) {
          float x1 = a + 2*i*h;
          totalArea += areaOf(x1, h);
      }

      return totalArea;
 }


 /**
  * Compute the area of the ith parabolic region.
  * @param x1 the left bound of the region
  * @param h the interval width
  * @return the area of the region
  */
 private float areaOf(float x1, float h)
 {
      float x2   = x1 + h;                // middle
      float x3   = x2 + h;                // right bound of the region
      float y1   = integrand.at(x1);      // value at left bound
      float y2   = integrand.at(x2);      // value at the middle
```

```
            float y3   = integrand.at(x3);      // value at right bound
            float area = h*(y1 + 4*y2+ y3)/3;   // area of the region

            return area;
        }
    }
}
```

Like the constructor for class `TrapezoidalIntegrator` we saw earlier, the constructor for class `SimpsonsIntegrator` takes an `Evaluatable` argument and the number of intervals. Method `integrate()` performs the integration and returns an approximation to the area.

Instead of working with pairs of adjacent regions, method `integrate()` splits each region in half, so that method `areaOf()` has three points to work with. This latter method implements the formula for the area of a parabolic region.

If we give the noninteractive version of Program 7–1 the command-line argument "simpsons," it instantiates a `SimpsonsIntegrator` object to compute the approximate value of π. See the output in Listing 7–1e.

Simpson's integration algorithm converges faster than the trapezoidal integration algorithm. But the computation of each region's area is a bit more complicated, and so there is more opportunity for roundoff errors. In this example, the errors prevent the estimate for π to be more accurate than that from the trapezoidal integration algorithm.

Listing 7–1e The output of the noninteractive version of Program 7–1, which computes an approximation to the value of π with Simpson's integration algorithm when given the command-line argument "simpsons."

Output:

```
ALGORITHM: Simpson's


     n           pi        % Error
 - - - - - - - - - - - - - - - - -
     1      2.9760678      5.2688203
     2      3.0835953      1.8461139
     4       3.121189      0.6494647
     8      3.1343977      0.22902104
    16      3.1390526      0.08085148
    32       3.140695      0.028570175
    64      3.1412754      0.010098308
   128      3.1414802      0.003579272
   256      3.1415539      0.0012342404
   512      3.1415799      4.070286E-4
  1024      3.1415892      1.11053734E-4
  2048      3.1415887      1.2623193E-4
```

Screen 7–1b shows screen shots of the first three iterations of the interactive version of Program 7–1 using Simpson's algorithm.

Screen 7–1b The first three iterations of the interactive version of Program 7–1 using Simpson's algorithm.

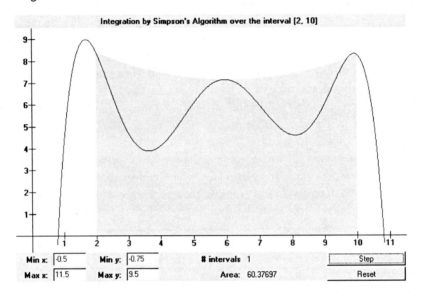

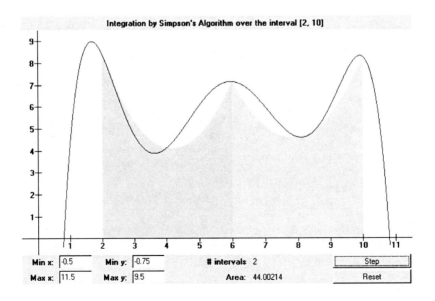

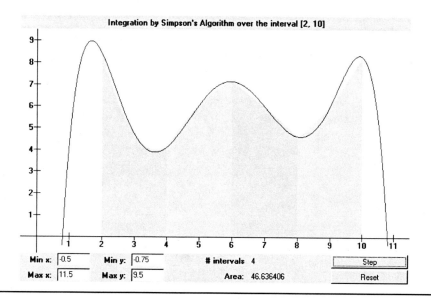

References

Chapra, Seven C., and Raymond P. Canale, *Numerical Methods for Engineers,* 3rd edition, New York: WCB/McGraw-Hill, 1998.

Cheny, Ward, and David Kincaid, *Numerical Mathematics and Computing,* 4th edition, Pacific Grove, CA: Brooks/Cole, 1999.

Woodford, C., and C. Phillips, *Numerical Methods with Worked Examples,* London: Chapman and Hall, 1997.

Sections 21.1 and 21.2 of Chapra and Chapter 4 of Woodford provide excellent introductions to the trapezoidal and Simpson's integration algorithms. Chapra also has good coverage of other integration algorithms in the rest of Chapter 21 and in Chapter 22. Cheney, in Section 5.4, presents an adaptive Simpson's algorithm, which dynamically determines whether or not to subdivide intervals based on the nature of the integrand.

Hamming, Richard W., *Methods of Mathematics Applied to Calculus, Probability, and Statistics,* Englewood Cliffs, NJ: Prentice-Hall, 1985.

This book contains a very clear derivation of Simpson's formula for parabolas in Section 11.11.

CHAPTER 8

SOLVING DIFFERENTIAL EQUATIONS NUMERICALLY

We can think of solving differential equations as the inverse of finding the derivative of a function. Given a differential equation (the derivative), a solution is any function that has that derivative. In this chapter, we will deal with only first-order ordinary differential equations (that is, first derivatives only).

For example, a solution of the differential equation[1]

$$y' = 6x^2 - 20x + 11$$

is

$$y = 2x^3 - 10x^2 + 11x + C$$

where C is an arbitrary constant. The latter is a solution because its derivative is the differential equation.

Because of the arbitrary constant C, there are an infinite number of solutions. In order to have a particular solution, we need to add an *initial condition*. Therefore, if we modify the problem in the previous paragraph to finding a solution to the differential equation with the initial condition $y(0) = -5$, then we have an *initial value problem,* and its solution is

$$y = 2x^3 - 10x^2 + 11x - 5$$

---

[1]   Differential equation problems traditionally use y and y' to name a function and its derivative.

Like integration problems in freshman calculus, solving initial value problems is straightforward only if the differential equations fit certain well-known patterns. Very often, they don't, and so we resort to using computers to generate numerical solutions.

As you may have guessed, a numerical solution of an initial value problem is only an approximation to the true, analytical solution. Also, we won't get a solution written out symbolically, like the one shown earlier. A numerical solution generally is a set of points that lie on the approximation. Our goal is to devise algorithms that generate the most accurate solutions in the least amount of time. In this chapter, we'll investigate three algorithms that solve initial value problems numerically.

8.1 Back to Basics

What does the derivative of a function tell us? If our function is $y(x)$, then its derivative $y'(x)$ gives us the value of the slope of $y(x)$ for each value of x (assuming, of course, that $y(x)$ is continuous and has a derivative there). In other words, the derivative of a function tells us, at each point, the *direction* of the function at that point.

So, if we're given the differential equation $y'(x)$ with the initial condition $y(x_0) = y_0$, we can use the values of $y'(x)$ to get approximations to the values of $y(x)$ over an interval from x_0 to x_n.

The basic idea behind solving differential equations is really that simple. If we're given the initial condition $y(x_0) = y_0$, we start with the point (x_0, y_0), since the solution must go through that point. The value of $y'(x_0)$ tells us which direction to go, and so we go in that direction until we reach x_1, giving us point (x_1, y_1). See Figure 8–1. At (x_1, y_1), we change direction according to the value of $y'(x_1)$ and go in that new direction until we reach x_2, giving us the point (x_2, y_2). There, we change direction according to the value of $y'(x_2)$ and go until we reach x_3. This continues until we reach x_n. Then our entire path, the points (x_0, y_0), (x_1, y_1), and so on through (x_n, y_n), is our approximation to the solution function $y(x)$ over the interval $[x_0, x_n]$.

How accurate can this solution be? Let's assume that we always go the same horizontal distance h before we change direction:

$$h = \left| x_1 - x_0 \right| = \left| x_2 - x_1 \right| = \ldots = \left| x_n - x_{n-1} \right|$$

Then, of course, smaller values of h will result in more accurate solutions, since we'll have more frequent "course corrections" as we trace out the approximation to the solution function. However, smaller h values mean more steps from x_0 to x_n, and the increased amount of computation not only requires more time but also can generate more roundoff errors.

Besides roundoff errors, there are other sources of error. If the true solution $y(x)$ is a curve (instead of a straight line), then when we head off from the initial point (x_0, y_0), we're going to go off course from the $y(x)$—how big this *local error* is depends on the size of h. We see this error in Figure 8–1 as the vertical distance between (x_1, y_1) and $(x_1, y(x_1))$. But at (x_1, y_1), we don't get to make up for that local error. We simply head off in the new direction from the already off-course (x_1, y_1) according to the value of $y'(x_1)$, and so we make a new local error on top of the previous one. Thus, at the end, we have a *cumulative error.*

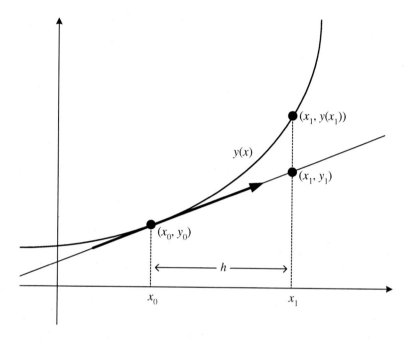

Figure 8–1 Using the slope value $y'(x_0)$ to provide the direction (bold arrow) to get from the point (x_0, y_0) to the point (x_1, y_1).

Figure 8–2 shows the effects of these errors (albeit with a relatively large value of h) solving the differential equation

$$y' = 2x$$

with the initial condition $y(2) = 0$. The actual solution is

$$y = x^2 - 4$$

Figure 8–2 shows the numerical approximation of the solution function on both sides of the initial point.

8.2 A Differential Equation Class

In general, a first-order differential equation is a function that involves not only the variable x but also the variable y. In other words, $y' = f(x, y)$ for some function f. For example, the differential equation

$$y' = f(x, y) = 8x - 2y + 8$$

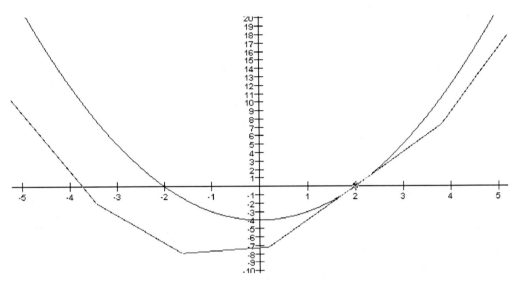

Figure 8–2   The effects of cumulative error in the numerical solution of an initial value problem. The dot represents initial condition $y(2) = 0$. The analytical solution $y = x^2 - 4$ is the smooth curve. Compare that to the numerical solution consisting of the line segments. The width of each interval $h = 1.825$, resulting in the large error. The error would be less with a smaller value of h.

with the initial condition $y(0) = -1$ has the solution

$$y = 4x - 3e^{-2x} + 2$$

which we can confirm by taking the derivative of the solution and then performing some algebraic manipulations:

$$
\begin{aligned}
y &= 4x - 3e^{-2x} + 2 \\
y' &= 4 + 6e^{-2x} \\
&= 8x - 8x + 6e^{-2x} - 4 + 8 \\
&= 8x - 2(4x - 3e^{-2x} + 2) + 8 \\
&= 8x - 2y + 8
\end{aligned}
$$

Listing 8–0a shows class `DifferentialEquation` in package `numbercruncher.mathutils`, which is analogous to the class `numbercruncher.mathutils.Function` introduced in Chapter 5. We'll use this class for solving initial value problems in this chapter, and so the class includes an `initialCondition` instance variable. It also has the instance variable `solutionLabel`, which is a string label for the true, analytical solution function.

Listing 8–0a Class `DifferentialEquation`.

```
package numbercruncher.mathutils;

import java.util.Hashtable;

/**
 * The base class for functions that can have derivatives.
 * Initialize the static function table with some sample functions.
 */
public abstract class DifferentialEquation implements Evaluatable
{
    /** initial condition */         private DataPoint initialCondition;
    /** solution function label */   private String    solutionLabel;

    /**
     * Constructor.
     * @param initialCondition the initial condition data point
     * @param solutionLabel the solution function label
     */
    public DifferentialEquation(DataPoint initialCondition,
                                String solutionLabel)
    {
        this.initialCondition = initialCondition;
        this.solutionLabel    = solutionLabel;
    }

    /**
     * Return the initial condition data point.
     * @return the initial condition
     */
    public DataPoint getInitialCondition() { return initialCondition; }

    /**
     * Return the solution label.
     * @return the label
     */
    public String getSolutionLabel() { return solutionLabel; }

    /**
     * Return the value of the differential equation at x.
     * (Implementation of Evaluatable.)
     * @param x the value of x
     * @return the solution value
     */
    public abstract float at(float x);
```

```
    /**
     * Return the value of the differential equation at (x, y).
     * @return the solution value
     */
    public float at(float x, float y) { return at(x); }

    /**
     * Return the value of the solution at x.
     * @return the solution value
     */
    public abstract float solutionAt(float x);
}
```

The class implements interface `numbercruncher.mathutils.Evaluatable` (see Chapter 5), and so it has a method `at()` that takes a single x parameter. The class also has a method `at()` that takes both x and y parameters, which we'll use to evaluate the differential equation, and a method `solutionAt()` to evaluate the true solution.

Listing 8–0b shows parts of the class `DiffEqsToSolve`, which is analogous to class `numbercruncher.rootutils.RootFunctions`. This class enters into its static table the differential equations, initial conditions, and analytical solutions that we'll use in this chapter. Table 8–1 shows these contents.

Table 8–1 The differential equations and initial conditions used in this chapter as entered by the class `DiffEqsToSolve`.

$y' = f(x, y)$	Initial Condition	Solution
$y' = 2x$	$y(2) = 0$	$y = x^2 - 4$
$y' = 3x^2 + 6x - 9$	$y(-4.5050397) = 0$	$y = x^3 + 3x^2 - 9x - 10$
$y' = 6x^2 - 20x + 11$	$y(0) = -5$	$y = 2x^3 - 10x^2 + 11x - 5$
$y' = 2xe^{2x} + y$	$y(0) = 1$	$y = 3e^x - 2e^{2x} + 2xe^{2x}$
$y' = 8x - 2y + 8$	$y(0) = -1$	$y = 4x - 3e^{-2x} + 2$
$y' = xe^{-2x} - 2y$	$y(0) = -0.5$	$y = \dfrac{x^2e^{-2x} - e^{-2x}}{2}$

Listing 8–0b A partial listing of class `DiffEqsToSolve` .

```
package numbercruncher.program8_1;

import java.util.Hashtable;
import numbercruncher.mathutils.DataPoint;
import numbercruncher.mathutils.DifferentialEquation;

/**
 * Load into a global table the differential equations
```

```
 * we want to solve.
 */
public class DiffEqsToSolve
{
    /** global function table */
    private static Hashtable TABLE = new Hashtable(32);

    // Enter the differential equations into the global table.
    static {
        enterDifferentialEquations();
    }

    /**
     * Return the differential equation with the given hash key
     * @param key the hash key
     * @return the differential equation
     */
    public static DifferentialEquation equation(String key)
    {
        return (DifferentialEquation) TABLE.get(key);
    }

    /**
     * Enter the differential equations into the global table.
     */
    private static void enterDifferentialEquations()
    {

...

        // Differential equation f(x, y) = 6x^2 - 20x + 11
        //         Initial condition y(0) = -5
        //                   Solution y  = 2x^3 - 10x^2 + 11x - 5
        TABLE.put(
            "6x^2 - 20x + 11",
            new DifferentialEquation(new DataPoint(0, -5),
                                "2x^3 - 10x^2 + 11x - 5")
            {
                public float at(float x)
                {
                    return 6*x*x - 20*x + 11;
                }

                public float solutionAt(float x)
                {
                    return 2*x*x*x - 10*x*x + 11*x - 5;
                }
            });
```

```
// Differential equation f(x, y) = 2xe^2x + y
//          Initial condition y(0) = 1
//                  Solution y = 3e^x - 2e^2x + 2xe^2x
TABLE.put(
    "2xe^2x + y",
    new DifferentialEquation(new DataPoint(0, 1),
                        "3e^x - 2e^2x + 2xe^2x")
    {
        public float at(float x)
        {
            return (float) (2*x*Math.exp(2*x) + solutionAt(x));
        }

        public float at(float x, float y)
        {
            return (float) (2*x*Math.exp(2*x) + y);
        }

        public float solutionAt(float x)
        {
            return (float) (3*Math.exp(x) +
                            2*Math.exp(2*x)*(x - 1));
        }
    });

...


    }
}
```

8.3 Euler's Algorithm

The algorithm described at the beginning of this chapter is Euler's algorithm.[2] As we've seen, the algorithm divides the region of interest into equal-sized intervals of horizontal size h, starting with the point representing the initial condition. Then off it goes, using the slope—the value of $y' = f(x_i, y_i)$—at the beginning of each interval to get to the point (x_{i+1}, y_{i+1}) at the other side of that interval. The set of all these points lies on the approximation to the solution function $y(x)$. Until roundoff errors from the increased amount of computation overwhelms the solution, smaller values of h will result in better approximate solutions.

----

[2] This is more traditionally called Euler's *method,* but we'll use the word *algorithm* here to avoid confusion with Java methods. Leonard Euler (1707–1783) was a brilliant and prolific mathematician whose career spanned more than 60 years. He contributed to number theory, geometry, and calculus, as well as several areas of science.

We can compute the next point (x_{i+1}, y_{i+1}) from the previous point (x_i, y_i) and the value of the slope $y_i' = f(x_i, y_i)$ at the previous point. Review Figure 8–1.

$$f(x_i, y_i) = \frac{y_{i+1} - y_i}{h}$$

$$y_{i+1} = y_i + f(x_i, y_i)h$$

and, of course, $x_{i+1} = x_i + h$.

Listing 8–0c shows the class `DiffEqSolver` in package `numbercruncher. mathutils` that will be the base class of the differential equation solver classes.

Listing 8–0c The base class `DiffEqSolver` for the differential equation solver classes.

```java
package numbercruncher.mathutils;

/**
 * The base class for differential equation solvers.
 */
public abstract class DiffEqSolver
{
    /** the differential equation to solve */
    protected DifferentialEquation equation;

    /** the initial condition data point */
    protected DataPoint initialCondition;

    /** current x value */      protected float x;
    /** current y value */      protected float y;

    /**
     * Constructor.
     * @param equation the differential equation to solve
     */
    public DiffEqSolver(DifferentialEquation equation)
    {
        this.equation        = equation;
        this.initialCondition = equation.getInitialCondition();

        reset();
    }

    /**
     * Reset x and y to the initial condition data point.
     */
    public void reset()
    {
```

```
        this.x = initialCondition.x;
        this.y = initialCondition.y;
    }

    /**
     * Return the next data point in the
     * approximation of the solution.
     * @param h the width of the interval
     */
    public abstract DataPoint nextPoint(float h);
}
```

Instances of this abstract class store the differential equation and the initial condition, and they keep track of the current values of x and y. The abstract method nextPoint() will be implemented by the subclasses, where the method will compute and return the next data point based on the current values of x and y and value of the horizontal interval width h .

Listing 8–1a Class EulersDiffEqSolver, the differential equation solver that implements Euler's algorithm.

```
package numbercruncher.mathutils;

/**
 * Differential equation solver that implements Euler's algorithm.
 */
public class EulersDiffEqSolver extends DiffEqSolver
{
    /**
     * Constructor.
     * @param equation the differential equation to solve
     */
    public EulersDiffEqSolver(DifferentialEquation equation)
    {
        super(equation);
    }

    /**
     * Return the next data point in the
     * approximation of the solution.
     * @param h the width of the interval
     */
    public DataPoint nextPoint(float h)
    {
        y += h*equation.at(x, y);
        x += h;

        return new DataPoint(x, y);
    }
}
```

Listing 8–1a shows our first subclass of DiffEqSolver, class EulersDiffEqSolver in package numbercruncher.mathutils. As we can see, its nextPoint() method implements Euler's algorithm. The value of equation.at(x, y) is the slope at a point at one side of an interval, and the method returns the point at the other side of the interval.

The noninteractive version of Program 8–1 works with different subclasses of DiffEq-Solver, and which subclass it instantiates depends on the command-line argument processed by main(). In Listing 8–1b, we see its output with the command-line argument "eulers," which causes the program to instantiate a EulersDiffEqSolver object.

Listing 8–1b The noninteractive version of Program 8–1 with the command-line argument "eulers" for Euler's algorithm.

```
package numbercruncher.program8_1;

import numbercruncher.mathutils.DifferentialEquation;
import numbercruncher.mathutils.DataPoint;
import numbercruncher.mathutils.DiffEqSolver;
import numbercruncher.mathutils.EulersDiffEqSolver;
import numbercruncher.mathutils.PredictorCorrectorDiffEqSolver;
import numbercruncher.mathutils.RungeKuttaDiffEqSolver;
import numbercruncher.mathutils.AlignRight;

/**
 * PROGRAM 8-1: Solve Differential Equations
 *
 * Demonstrate algorithms for solving differential equations.
 */
public class SolveDiffEq
{
    private static final int MAX_INTERVALS = Integer.MAX_VALUE/2;

    private static final int EULER               = 0;
    private static final int PREDICTOR_CORRECTOR = 1;
    private static final int RUNGE_KUTTA         = 2;

    private static final String ALGORITHMS[] = {
        "Euler's", "Predictor-Corrector", "Runge-Kutta"
    };

    /**
     * Main program.
     * @param args the array of runtime arguments
     */
    public static void main(String args[])
    {
        String arg = args[0].toLowerCase();
        int algorithm =   arg.startsWith("eul") ? EULER
```

```
                        : arg.startsWith("pre") ? PREDICTOR_CORRECTOR
                        :                          RUNGE_KUTTA;

    System.out.println("ALGORITHM:"+ ALGORITHMS[algorithm]);

    solve(algorithm, "6x^2 - 20x + 11", 6);
    solve(algorithm, "2xe^2x + y", 1);
    solve(algorithm, "xe^-2x - 2y", 1);
}

private static void solve(int algorithm, String key, float x)
{
    DifferentialEquation equation = DiffEqsToSolve.equation(key);
    DataPoint initialCondition = equation.getInitialCondition();
    String    solutionLabel    = equation.getSolutionLabel();

    float    initX    = initialCondition.x;
    float    initY    = initialCondition.y;
    float    trueValue = equation.solutionAt(x);

    System.out.println();
    System.out.println("Differential equation: f(x,y) ="+ key);
    System.out.println("    Initial condition: y(" +
                    initX + ") ="+ initY);
    System.out.println("  Analytical solution: y ="+
                    solutionLabel);
    System.out.println("           True value: y(" +
                    x + ") ="+ trueValue);
    System.out.println();

    DiffEqSolver solver;

    switch (algorithm) {

        case EULER: {
            solver = new EulersDiffEqSolver(equation);
            break;
        }

        case PREDICTOR_CORRECTOR: {
            solver = new PredictorCorrectorDiffEqSolver(equation);
            break;
        }

        default: {
            solver = new RungeKuttaDiffEqSolver(equation);
            break;
        }
    }
```

```
        AlignRight ar = new AlignRight();

        ar.print("n", 8);                    ar.print("h", 15);
        ar.print("y(" + x + ")", 15); ar.print("Error", 15);
        ar.underline();
        int intervals = 2;
        float h = Math.abs(x - initX)/intervals;

        float error = Float.MAX_VALUE;
        float prevError;

        do {
            DataPoint nextPoint = null;

            for (int i = 0; i < intervals; ++i) {
                nextPoint = solver.nextPoint(h);
            }

            prevError = error;
            error     = nextPoint.y - trueValue;

            ar.print(intervals, 8);     ar.print(h, 15);
            ar.print(nextPoint.y, 15); ar.print(error, 15);
            ar.println();

            intervals *= 2;
            h /= 2;
            solver.reset();
        } while ((intervals < MAX_INTERVALS) &&
                (Math.abs(prevError) > Math.abs(error)));
    }
}
```

Output:

```
ALGORITHM: Euler's

Differential equation: f(x,y) = 6x^2 - 20x + 11
    Initial condition: y(0.0) = -5.0
  Analytical solution: y = 2x^3 - 10x^2 + 11x - 5
           True value: y(6.0) = 133.0
```

n	h	y(6.0)	Error
2	3.0	43.0	-90.0
4	1.5	74.5	-58.5
8	0.75	100.375	-32.625

16	0.375	115.84375	-17.15625
32	0.1875	124.21094	-8.7890625
64	0.09375	128.55273	-4.4472656
128	0.046875	130.76318	-2.2368164
256	0.0234375	131.87823	-1.1217651
512	0.01171875	132.43834	-0.56166077
1024	0.005859375	132.719	-0.28100586
2048	0.0029296875	132.85947	-0.14053345
4096	0.0014648438	132.92973	-0.07026672
8192	7.324219E-4	132.96489	-0.035110474
16384	3.6621094E-4	132.98236	-0.01763916
32768	1.8310547E-4	132.99138	-0.008621216
65536	9.1552734E-5	132.99562	-0.0043792725
131072	4.5776367E-5	132.99786	-0.0021362305
262144	2.2888184E-5	132.99792	-0.0020751953
524288	1.1444092E-5	133.0011	0.0010986328
1048576	5.722046E-6	133.00006	6.1035156E-5
2097152	2.861023E-6	133.03824	0.038238525

```
Differential equation: f(x,y) = 2xe^2x + y
   Initial condition: y(0.0) = 1.0
 Analytical solution: y = 3e^x - 2e^2x + 2xe^2x
          True value: y(1.0) = 8.154845
```

n	h	y(1.0)	Error
2	0.5	3.6091409	-4.5457044
4	0.25	5.293519	-2.8613262
8	0.125	6.5289307	-1.6259146
16	0.0625	7.284655	-0.87019014
32	0.03125	7.7041717	-0.45067358
64	0.015625	7.9254375	-0.22940779
128	0.0078125	8.039102	-0.11574364
256	0.00390625	8.09671	-0.058135033
512	0.001953125	8.1257105	-0.02913475
1024	9.765625E-4	8.140253	-0.014592171
2048	4.8828125E-4	8.147548	-0.007297516
4096	2.4414062E-4	8.151206	-0.0036392212
8192	1.2207031E-4	8.153012	-0.001832962
16384	6.1035156E-5	8.15396	-8.8500977E-4
32768	3.0517578E-5	8.154387	-4.5776367E-4
65536	1.5258789E-5	8.154611	-2.3460388E-4
131072	7.6293945E-6	8.154683	-1.6212463E-4
262144	3.8146973E-6	8.154706	-1.3923645E-4
524288	1.9073486E-6	8.154436	-4.0912628E-4

```
Differential equation: f(x,y) = xe^-2x - 2y
   Initial condition: y(0.0) = -0.5
 Analytical solution: y = (x^2e^-2x - e^-2x)/2
          True value: y(1.0) = 0.0
```

n	h	y(1.0)	Error
2	0.5	0.09196986	0.09196986
4	0.25	0.043056414	0.043056414
8	0.125	0.02059899	0.02059899
16	0.0625	0.010078897	0.010078897
32	0.03125	0.00498614	0.00498614
64	0.015625	0.0024799863	0.0024799863
128	0.0078125	0.0012367641	0.0012367641
256	0.00390625	6.176049E-4	6.176049E-4
512	0.001953125	3.0862397E-4	3.0862397E-4
1024	9.765625E-4	1.5423674E-4	1.5423674E-4
2048	4.8828125E-4	7.712061E-5	7.712061E-5
4096	2.4414062E-4	3.8514103E-5	3.8514103E-5
8192	1.2207031E-4	1.9193667E-5	1.9193667E-5
16384	6.1035156E-5	9.6256945E-6	9.6256945E-6
32768	3.0517578E-5	4.7721633E-6	4.7721633E-6
65536	1.5258789E-5	2.3496477E-6	2.3496477E-6
131072	7.6293945E-6	9.0182266E-7	9.0182266E-7
262144	3.8146973E-6	-3.8416E-7	-3.8416E-7
524288	1.9073486E-6	4.7914605E-6	4.7914605E-6

Method solve() solves each initial value problem several times, each iteration with twice the number of intervals and half the horizontal interval width h . For each value of h, it repeatedly calls the nextPoint() method of the differential equation solver object. After each iteration, it tests the accuracy of the solution by evaluating the numerical solution function at a value of x some distance away from the initial x_0 and then comparing the numerical solution with the true, analytical solution.

The method has a unique stopping criterion. The error between the numerical solution and the true solution diminishes as the value of h decreases, until roundoff errors begin to dominate. The method stops the iteration when the error stops decreasing and begins to increase.

The output of Listing 8–1b shows that Euler's algorithm converges slowly, and its accuracy can be low.

Screen 8–1a shows screen shots of the interactive version[3] of Program 8–1, which can also work with different subclasses of DiffEqSolver. Here, we see the first three iterations of Euler's algorithm numerically solving the differential equation

$$y' = xe^{-2x} - 2y$$

with the initial condition $y(0) = -0.5$.

---

[3]   Each interactive program in this book has two versions, an applet and a standalone application. You can download all the Java source code. See the downloading instructions in the preface of this book.

Screen 8–1a The first three iterations of Program 8–1 using Euler's algorithm to solve the initial value problem $y' = xe^{-2x} - 2y$ and $y(0) = -0.5$. The analytical solution is the smooth curve, and the numerical solution consists of the line segments. The dot represents the initial condition.

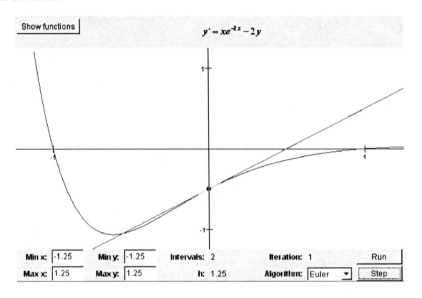

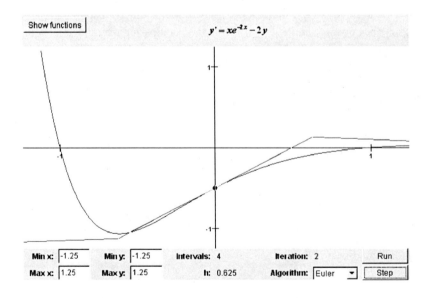

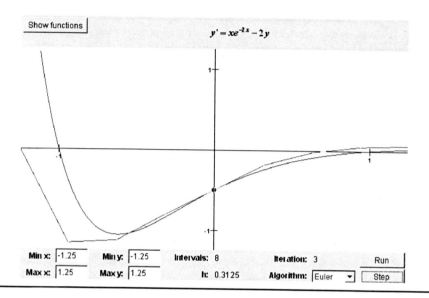

8.4 A Predictor-Corrector Algorithm

How can we improve upon Euler's algorithm? Evidently, using the slope at a point on one side of an interval to compute a point at the other side introduces too great a local error, and so the algorithm converges too slowly before it is overwhelmed by roundoff errors.

A simple *predictor-corrector* type of algorithm starts out as Euler's algorithm does:

$$y^0_{i+1} = y_i + f(x_i, y_i)h$$

where $y' = f(x, y)$. However, the algorithm considers this to be only a *predictor* for the next value of y, so we mark it with the 0 superscript. We use this predicted y value (which is at the other side of the interval) to compute the slope there: $f(x_{i+i}, y^0_{i+i})$, where $x_{i+1} = x_i + h$. (Euler's algorithm would do this computation at the start of the next interval.)

Now we take the average of the two slopes from both sides of the interval, go back to the beginning of the interval, and use the average slope to compute the *corrected* next value of y at the other side of the interval:

$$y_{i+1} = y_i + \left[\frac{f(x_i, y_i) + f(x_{i+1}, y^0_{i+1})}{2} \right]h$$

and $x_{i+1} = x_i + h$.

Listing 8–1c shows class `PredictorCorrectorDiffEqSolver` in package `number-cruncher.mathutils`, our second subclass of `DiffEqSolver`. Its `nextPoint()` method implements the predictor-corrector algorithm.

Listing 8–1c Class `PredictorCorrectorDiffEqSolver`, the differential equation solver that implements a predictor-corrector algorithm.

```
package numbercruncher.mathutils;

/**
 * Differential equation solver that implements
 * a predictor-corrector algorithm.
 */
public class PredictorCorrectorDiffEqSolver extends DiffEqSolver
{

    /**
     * Constructor.
     * @param equation the differential equation to solve
     */
    public PredictorCorrectorDiffEqSolver(DifferentialEquation equation)
    {
        super(equation);
    }

    /**
     * Return the next data point in the
     * approximation of the solution.
     * @param h the width of the interval
     */
    public DataPoint nextPoint(float h)
    {
        float predictor = y + Math.abs(h)*equation.at(x);
        float avgSlope  = (equation.at(x, y)
                              + equation.at(x+h, predictor))/2;

        y += h*avgSlope;      // corrector
        x += h;

        return new DataPoint(x, y);
    }
}
```

If we change the command-line argument to the noninteractive version of Program 8–1 (review Listing 8–1b) to "predictor," we get output from instantiating a `PredictorCorrector DiffEqSolver` object. See Listing 8–1d.

Listing 8–1d Output from Program 8–1 with the command-line argument "predictor" for the predictor-corrector algorithm.

```
ALGORITHM: Predictor-Corrector

Differential equation: f(x,y) = 6x^2 - 20x + 11
```

Initial condition: y(0.0) = -5.0
Analytical solution: y = 2x^3 - 10x^2 + 11x - 5
True value: y(6.0) = 133.0

n	h	y(6.0)	Error
2	3.0	187.0	54.0
4	1.5	146.5	13.5
8	0.75	136.375	3.375
16	0.375	133.84375	0.84375
32	0.1875	133.21094	0.2109375
64	0.09375	133.05273	0.052734375
128	0.046875	133.01312	0.013122559
256	0.0234375	133.00331	0.0033111572
512	0.01171875	133.00082	8.239746E-4
1024	0.005859375	133.00023	2.2888184E-4
2048	0.0029296875	133.00005	4.5776367E-5
4096	0.0014648438	133.00005	4.5776367E-5

Differential equation: f(x,y) = 2xe^2x + y
Initial condition: y(0.0) = 1.0
Analytical solution: y = 3e^x - 2e^2x + 2xe^2x
True value: y(1.0) = 8.154845

n	h	y(1.0)	Error
2	0.5	8.449224	0.29437923
4	0.25	8.197649	0.042803764
8	0.125	8.160373	0.0055274963
16	0.0625	8.15547	6.246567E-4
32	0.03125	8.154899	5.340576E-5
64	0.015625	8.154848	2.861023E-6
128	0.0078125	8.154843	-1.9073486E-6
256	0.00390625	8.154846	9.536743E-7
512	0.001953125	8.154843	-1.9073486E-6

Differential equation: f(x,y) = xe^-2x - 2y
Initial condition: y(0.0) = -0.5
Analytical solution: y = (x^2e^-2x - e^-2x)/2
True value: y(1.0) = 0.0

n	h	y(1.0)	Error
2	0.5	-0.035143584	-0.035143584
4	0.25	-0.0086004995	-0.0086004995
8	0.125	-0.0020729005	-0.0020729005
16	0.0625	-5.0861575E-4	-5.0861575E-4
32	0.03125	-1.2598E-4	-1.2598E-4
64	0.015625	-3.135181E-5	-3.135181E-5

128	0.0078125	-7.822178E-6	-7.822178E-6
256	0.00390625	-1.9620056E-6	-1.9620056E-6
512	0.001953125	-4.900794E-7	-4.900794E-7
1024	9.765625E-4	-1.1298107E-7	-1.1298107E-7
2048	4.8828125E-4	-3.3578544E-8	-3.3578544E-8
4096	2.4414062E-4	-7.399285E-8	-7.399285E-8

We see that this predictor-corrector algorithm converges faster and produces more accurate solutions than Euler's algorithm. The penalty is a bit more computation at each interval.

Screen 8–1b shows the first three iterations of the interactive version of Program 8–1 using this algorithm to solve the same initial value problem as in Screen 8–1a.

8.5 The Fourth-Order Runge-Kutta Algorithm

The last algorithm we'll examine in this chapter is from a set of algorithms called Runge-Kutta.[4] The most popular one is the fourth-order Runge-Kutta algorithm. Like the predictor-corrector algorithm, it uses an average of slopes, but Runge-Kutta also uses slopes taken *within* the interval, not just at the sides.

Screen 8–1b The first three iterations of Program 8–1 using a predictor-corrector algorithm to solve the initial value problem $y' = xe^{-2x} - 2y$ and $y(0) = -0.5$. The analytical solution is the smooth curve, and the numerical solution consists of the line segments. The dot represents the initial condition.

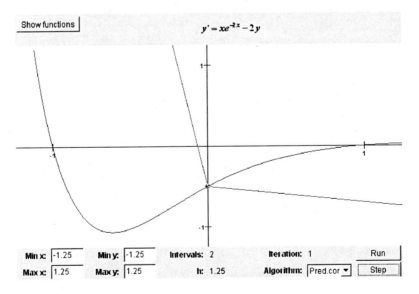

---

[4]   These algorithms are named after Carl Runge (1856–1927) and Martin Wilhelm Kutta (1867–1944), two German mathematicians who developed them.

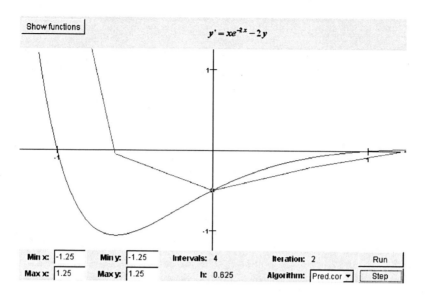

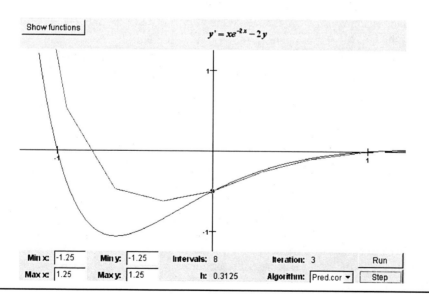

At each interval, Runge-Kutta starts out by computing in sequence four values, where $y' = f(x, y)$:

$$k_1 = f(x_i, y_i)$$

$$k_2 = f\left(x_i + \frac{h}{2}, y_i + \frac{h}{2}k_1\right)$$

$$k_3 = f\left(x_i + \frac{h}{2}, y_i + \frac{h}{2}k_2\right)$$

$$k_4 = f(x_i + h, y_i + hk_3)$$

The algorithm makes several "probes" into the interval and at the other side of the interval to get slope values:

- First, k_1 is the slope at the point (x_i, y_i) at the beginning of the interval.
- Using k_1, we find a point halfway into the interval and compute k_2, the slope at that point.
- Then we go back to the beginning point and use k_2 to find another point halfway into the interval and compute k_3, the slope at that point.
- Once again, we return to the beginning point and use k_3 to find a point at the other side of the interval and compute k_4, the slope at that point.
- Finally, from the beginning point (x_i, y_i), we use a weighted average of the four slopes to compute the next point at the other side of the interval:

$$y_{i+1} = y_i + \left(\frac{k_1 + 2k_2 + 2k_3 + k_4}{6}\right)h$$

and $x_{i+1} = x_i + h$.

Listing 8–1e shows class `RungeKuttaDiffEqSolver` in package `number-cruncher.mathutils`, a subclass of `DiffEqSolver`. Its `nextPoint()` method implements the fourth-order Runge-Kutta algorithm.

Listing 8–1e Class `RungeKuttaDiffEqSolver`, the differential equation solver that implements the fourth-order Runge-Kutta algorithm.

```
package numbercruncher.mathutils;

/**
 * Differential equation solver that implements
 * a fourth-order Runge-Kutta algorithm.
 */
public class RungeKuttaDiffEqSolver extends DiffEqSolver
{
```

```
/**
 * Constructor.
 * @param equation the differential equation to solve
 */
public RungeKuttaDiffEqSolver(DifferentialEquation equation)
{
    super(equation);
}

/**
 * Return the next data point in the
 * approximation of the solution.
 * @param h the width of the interval
 */
public DataPoint nextPoint(float h)
{
    float k1 = equation.at(x, y);
    float k2 = equation.at(x + h/2, y + k1*h/2);
    float k3 = equation.at(x + h/2, y + k2*h/2);
    float k4 = equation.at(x + h, y + k3*h);

    y += (k1 + 2*(k2 + k3) + k4)*h/6;
    x += h;

    return new DataPoint(x, y);
}
}
```

By changing the command-line argument to the noninteractive version of Program 8–1 (re-view Listing 8–1b) to "runge," we get output from instantiating a RungeKuttaDiffEqSolver object. See Listing 8–1f.

Listing 8–1f Output from Program 8–1 with the command-line argument "runge" for the fourth-order Runge-Kutta algorithm.

```
ALGORITHM: Runge-Kutta

Differential equation: f(x,y) = 6x^2 - 20x + 11
    Initial condition: y(0.0) = -5.0
  Analytical solution: y = 2x^3 - 10x^2 + 11x - 5
           True value: y(6.0) = 133.0
```

n	h	y(6.0)	Error
2	3.0	133.0	0.0
4	1.5	133.0	0.0

```
Differential equation: f(x,y) = 2xe^2x + y
   Initial condition: y(0.0) = 1.0
 Analytical solution: y = 3e^x - 2e^2x + 2xe^2x
          True value: y(1.0) = 8.154845


        n              h            y(1.0)              Error
   ---------------------------------------------------------
        2            0.5          8.148893     -0.0059518814
        4            0.25         8.154289       -5.559921E-4
        8            0.125        8.154804      -4.1007996E-5
       16            0.0625       8.154843      -1.9073486E-6
       32            0.03125      8.154845               0.0
       64            0.015625     8.154845               0.0


Differential equation: f(x,y) = xe^-2x - 2y
   Initial condition: y(0.0) = -0.5
 Analytical solution: y = (x^2e^-2x - e^-2x)/2
          True value: y(1.0) = 0.0


        n              h            y(1.0)              Error
   ---------------------------------------------------------
        2            0.5       -0.0027439892     -0.0027439892
        4            0.25      -1.2015179E-4      -1.2015179E-4
        8            0.125     -6.262213E-6       -6.262213E-6
       16            0.0625    -3.6507845E-7      -3.6507845E-7
       32            0.03125   -3.4924597E-8      -3.4924597E-8
       64            0.015625   1.7695129E-8       1.7695129E-8
      128            0.0078125  1.2805685E-9       1.2805685E-9
      256            0.00390625 6.9849193E-9       6.9849193E-9
```

Of the three algorithms we've examined, the fourth-order Runge-Kutta algorithm has the fastest convergence and generates the most accurate solutions. But, of course, it requires the most computation per interval.

Screen 8–1c shows the first three iterations of the interactive version of Program 8–1 using this algorithm to solve the same initial value problem as in Screens 8–1a and 8–1b.

Screen 8–1c The first three iterations of Program 8–1 using the fourth-order Runge-Kutta algorithm to solve the initial value problem $y' = xe^{-2x} - 2y$ and $y(0) = -0.5$. The analytical solution is the smooth curve, and the numerical solution consists of the line segments. The dot represents the initial condition.

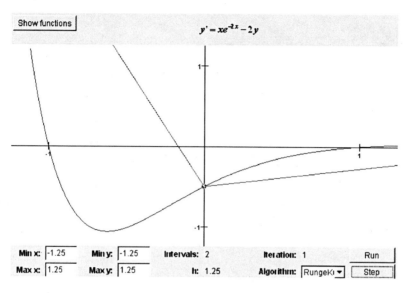

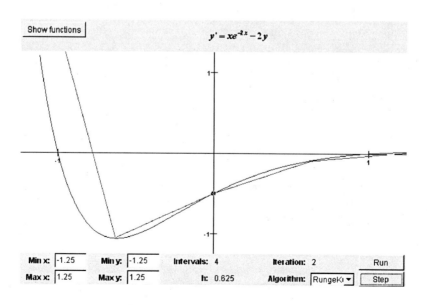

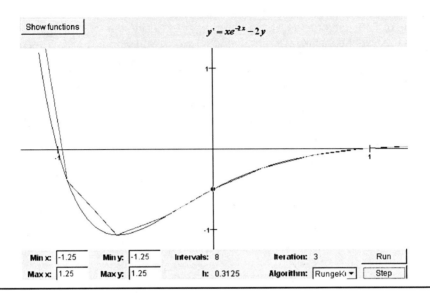

References

Boyce, William E., and Richard C. DiPrima, *Elementary Differential Equations,* 2nd edition, New York: John Wiley and Sons, 1969.

Some of the initial value problems used in this chapter are from this book.

Chapra, Seven C., and Raymond P. Canale, *Numerical Methods for Engineers,* 3rd edition, New York: WCB/McGraw-Hill, 1998.

Cheny, Ward, and David Kincaid, *Numerical Mathematics and Computing,* 4th edition, Pacific Grove, CA: Brooks/Cole, 1999.

Conte, Samuel D., and Carl de Boor, *Elementary Numerical Analysis: An Algorithmic Approach,* New York: McGraw-Hill, 1980.

Most textbooks on numerical methods discuss solving differential equations numerically, such as Chapra in Chapter 25, Cheney in Chapter 8, and Conte in Chapter 8. These books also cover other algorithms, including those for solving higher order differential equations. Chapra has an especially good discussion of the various Runge-Kutta algorithms.

PART III

A MATRIX PACKAGE

This part of the book incrementally develops a practical matrix package. We can then import the classes of this package into any Java application that uses matrices.

Chapter 9 develops the matrix class for the basic operations of addition, subtraction, and multiplication. It also covers subclasses for vectors and square matrices. The chapter's interactive demo uses graphic transformation matrices to animate a three-dimensional wire-frame cube.

Chapter 10 first reviews the manual procedure we learned in high school to solve systems of linear equations. It then introduces LU decomposition to solve linear systems using matrices. An interactive demo creates polynomial regression functions of any order from 1 through 9, which requires solving a system of "normal" equations.

Finally, Chapter 11 uses LU decomposition to compute the inverse of a matrix efficiently and reliably. A demo program tests how well we can invert the dreaded Hilbert matrices, which are notoriously difficult to invert accurately. The chapter also computes determinants and condition numbers of matrices, and it compares different algorithms for solving linear systems.

CHAPTER 9

BASIC MATRIX OPERATIONS

Even the most basic matrix operations of addition, subtraction, and, especially, multiplication can put a strain on a computer's computational capabilities. The matrix operands do not have to be very big before they generate large numbers of individual floating-point operations. This is prime breeding ground for accumulated roundoff errors.

In this chapter, we'll begin to develop the `numbercruncher.matrix` package. Its classes include `Matrix`, `SquareMatrix`, `IdentityMatrix`, `RowVector`, and `ColumnVector`. We'll add class `LinearSystem` for solving systems of simultaneous linear equations in Chapter 10 and class `InvertibleMatrix` in Chapter 11. Figure 9–1 shows the inheritance tree for these classes.[1]

Most of the math in this chapter is from high school algebra—we'll simply be implementing it as Java classes. The interactive program for this chapter will demonstrate the use of the `Matrix`, `SquareMatrix`, `IdentityMatrix`, and `RowVector` classes, along with matrix multiplication, to animate an object in three-dimensional space.

9.1 Matrix

We can represent a matrix in Java as an array of arrays. For example, the statement

```
float values[][] = new float[nRows][nCols]
```

---

[1] We won't make the claim that this class hierarchy is the most reasonable one—in fact, a commercial-quality matrix package would probably combine some of these classes. However, this hierarchy does break things up into more easily digestible chunks for the purposes of this book.

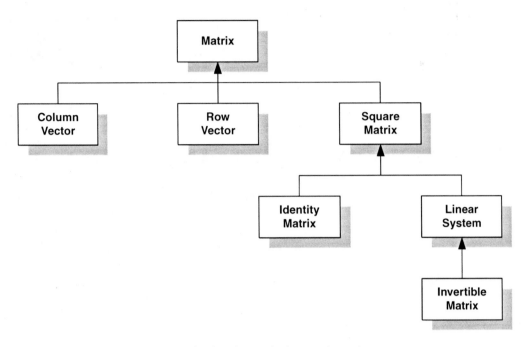

Figure 9–1   The inheritance tree for the classes in the matrix package.

will allocate such an array, assuming nRows is the number of rows and nCols is the number of columns. A matrix class would include nRows and nCols as instance variables, along with values.

Listing 9–0a shows the Matrix class in package numbercruncher.matrix. As we saw in Figure 9–1, it is the base class for all the matrix classes, but it also contains most of the methods that implement the matrix operations.

Listing 9–0a The Matrix class.

```
package numbercruncher.matrix;

import numbercruncher.mathutils.AlignRight;

/**
 * The matrix class.
 */
public class Matrix
{
    /** number of rows */        protected int    nRows;
    /** number of columns */     protected int    nCols;
    /** 2-d array of  values */  protected float values[][];

    //--------------//
    // Constructors //
    //--------------//
```

```
/**
 * Default constructor.
 */
protected Matrix() {}

/**
 * Constructor.
 * @param rowCount the number of rows
 * @param colCount the number of columns
 */
public Matrix(int rowCount, int colCount)
{
    nRows = (rowCount > 0) ? rowCount : 1;
    nCols = (colCount > 0) ? colCount : 1;
    values = new float[nRows][nCols];
}

/**
 * Constructor.
 * @param values the 2-d array of values
 */
public Matrix(float values[][]) { set(values); }

//---------//
// Getters //
//---------//

/**
 * Get the row count.
 * @return the row count
 */
public int rowCount() { return nRows; }

/**
 * Get the column count.
 * @return the column count
 */
public int columnCount() { return nCols; }
/**
 * Get the value of element [r,c] in the matrix.
 * @param r the row index
 * @param c the column index
 * @return the value
 * @throws numbercruncher.MatrixException for an invalid index
 */
public float at(int r, int c) throws MatrixException
{
    if ((r < 0) || (r >= nRows) || (c < 0) || (c >= nCols)) {
        throw new MatrixException(MatrixException.INVALID_INDEX);
```

```
        }
      return values[r][c];
    }

    /**
     * Get a row of this matrix.
     * @param r the row index
     * @return the row as a row vector
     * @throws numbercruncher.MatrixException for an invalid index
     */
    public RowVector getRow(int r) throws MatrixException
    {
        if ((r < 0) || (r >= nRows)) {
            throw new MatrixException(MatrixException.INVALID_INDEX);
        }

        RowVector rv = new RowVector(nCols);
        for (int c = 0; c < nCols; ++c) {
            rv.values[0][c] = this.values[r][c];
        }
        return rv;
    }
    /**
     * Get a column of this matrix.
     * @param c the column index
     * @return the column as a column vector
     * @throws numbercruncher.MatrixException for an invalid index
     */
    public ColumnVector getColumn(int c) throws MatrixException
    {
        if ((c < 0) || (c >= nCols)) {
            throw new MatrixException(MatrixException.INVALID_INDEX);
        }

        ColumnVector cv = new ColumnVector(nRows);
        for (int r = 0; r < nRows; ++r) {
            cv.values[r][0] = this.values[r][c];
        }
        return cv;
    }
    /**
     * Copy the values of this matrix.
     * @return the values
     */
    public float[][] values() { return values; }

    /**
     * Copy the values of this matrix.
     * @return the copied values
     */
```

```java
public float[][] copyValues2D()
{
    float v[][] = new float[nRows][nCols];

    for (int r = 0; r < nRows; ++r) {
        for (int c = 0; c < nCols; ++c) {
            v[r][c] = values[r][c];
        }
    }

    return v;
}

//---------//
// Setters //
//---------//

/**
 * Set the value of element [r,c].
 * @param r the row index
 * @param c the column index
 * @param value the value
 * @throws numbercruncher.MatrixException for an invalid index
 */
public void set(int r, int c, float value) throws MatrixException
{
    if ((r < 0) || (r >= nRows) || (c < 0) || (c >= nCols)) {
        throw new MatrixException(MatrixException.INVALID_INDEX);
    }

    values[r][c] = value;
}

/**
 * Set this matrix from a 2-d array of values.
 * If the rows do not have the same length, then the matrix
 * column count is the length of the shortest row.
 * @param values the 2-d array of values
 */
protected void set(float values[][])
{
    this.nRows  = values.length;
    this.nCols  = values[0].length;
    this.values = values;

    for (int r = 1; r < nRows; ++r) {
        nCols = Math.min(nCols, values[r].length);
    }
}
```

```java
/**
 * Set a row of this matrix from a row vector.
 * @param rv the row vector
 * @param r the row index
 * @throws numbercruncher.MatrixException for an invalid index or
 *                                          an invalid vector size
 */
public void setRow(RowVector rv, int r) throws MatrixException
{
    if ((r < 0) || (r >= nRows)) {
        throw new MatrixException(MatrixException.INVALID_INDEX);
    }
    if (nCols != rv.nCols) {
        throw new MatrixException(
                        MatrixException.INVALID_DIMENSIONS);
    }

    for (int c = 0; c < nCols; ++c) {
        this.values[r][c] = rv.values[0][c];
    }
}

/**
 * Set a column of this matrix from a column vector.
 * @param cv the column vector
 * @param c the column index
 * @throws numbercruncher.MatrixException for an invalid index or
 *                                          an invalid vector size
 */
public void setColumn(ColumnVector cv, int c)
    throws MatrixException
{
    if ((c < 0) || (c >= nCols)) {
        throw new MatrixException(MatrixException.INVALID_INDEX);
    }
    if (nRows != cv.nRows) {
        throw new MatrixException(
                        MatrixException.INVALID_DIMENSIONS);
    }

    for (int r = 0; r < nRows; ++r) {
        this.values[r][c] = cv.values[r][0];
    }
}

//-------------------//
// Matrix operations //
//-------------------//
```

```java
/**
 * Return the transpose of this matrix.
 * @return the transposed matrix
 */
public Matrix transpose()
{
    float tv[][] = new float[nCols][nRows];   // transposed values

    // Set the values of the transpose.
    for (int r = 0; r < nRows; ++r) {
        for (int c = 0; c < nCols; ++c) {
            tv[c][r] = values[r][c];
        }
    }

    return new Matrix(tv);
}

/**
 * Add another matrix to this matrix.
 * @param m the matrix addend
 * @return the sum matrix
 * @throws numbercruncher.MatrixException for invalid size
 */
public Matrix add(Matrix m) throws MatrixException
{
    // Validate m's size.
    if ((nRows != m.nRows) && (nCols != m.nCols)) {
        throw new MatrixException(
                        MatrixException.INVALID_DIMENSIONS);
    }

    float sv[][] = new float[nRows][nCols]; // sum values

    // Compute values of the sum.
    for (int r = 0; r < nRows; ++r) {
        for (int c = 0; c < nCols; ++c) {
            sv[r][c] = values[r][c] + m.values[r][c];
        }
    }

    return new Matrix(sv);
}

/**
 * Subtract another matrix from this matrix.
 * @param m the matrix subrrahend
 * @return the difference matrix
```

```
 * @throws numbercruncher.MatrixException for invalid size
 */
public Matrix subtract(Matrix m) throws MatrixException
{
    // Validate m's size.
    if ((nRows != m.nRows) && (nCols != m.nCols)) {
        throw new MatrixException(
                           MatrixException.INVALID_DIMENSIONS);
    }

    float dv[][] = new float[nRows][nCols]; // difference values

    // Compute values of the difference.
    for (int r = 0; r < nRows; ++r) {
        for (int c = 0; c < nCols; ++c) {
            dv[r][c] = values[r][c] - m.values[r][c];
        }
    }

    return new Matrix(dv);
}

/**
 * Multiply this matrix by a constant.
 * @param k the constant
 * @return the product matrix
 */
public Matrix multiply(float k)
{
    float pv[][] = new float[nRows][nCols]; // product values

    // Compute values of the product.
    for (int r = 0; r < nRows; ++r) {
        for (int c = 0; c < nCols; ++c) {
            pv[r][c] = k*values[r][c];
        }
    }

    return new Matrix(pv);
}

/**
 * Multiply this matrix by another matrix.
 * @param m the matrix multiplier
 * @return the product matrix
 * @throws numbercruncher.MatrixException for invalid size
 */
public Matrix multiply(Matrix m) throws MatrixException
{
```

```
        // Validate m's dimensions.
        if (nCols != m.nRows) {
            throw new MatrixException(
                            MatrixException.INVALID_DIMENSIONS);
        }

        float pv[][] = new float[nRows][m.nCols];  // product values

        // Compute values of the product.
        for (int r = 0; r < nRows; ++r) {
            for (int c = 0; c < m.nCols; ++c) {
                float dot = 0;
                for (int k = 0; k < nCols; ++k) {
                    dot += values[r][k] * m.values[k][c];
                }
                pv[r][c] = dot;
            }
        }

        return new Matrix(pv);
}
/**
 * Multiply this matrix by a column vector: this*cv
 * @param cv the column vector
 * @return the product column vector
 * @throws numbercruncher.MatrixException for invalid size
 */
public ColumnVector multiply(ColumnVector cv)
    throws MatrixException
{
    // Validate cv's size.
    if (nRows != cv.nRows) {
        throw new MatrixException(
                        MatrixException.INVALID_DIMENSIONS);
    }

    float pv[] = new float[nRows];    // product values

    // Compute the values of the product.
    for (int r = 0; r < nRows; ++r) {
        float dot = 0;
        for (int c = 0; c < nCols; ++c) {
            dot += values[r][c] * cv.values[c][0];
        }
        pv[r] = dot;
    }

    return new ColumnVector(pv);
}
```

```java
/**
 * Multiply a row vector by this matrix: rv*this
 * @param rv the row vector
 * @return the product row vector
 * @throws numbercruncher.MatrixException for invalid size
 */
public RowVector multiply(RowVector rv) throws MatrixException
{
    // Validate rv's size.
    if (nCols != rv.nCols) {
        throw new MatrixException(
                        MatrixException.INVALID_DIMENSIONS);
    }

    float pv[] = new float[nRows];  // product values

    // Compute the values of the product.
    for (int c = 0; c < nCols; ++c) {
        float dot = 0;
        for (int r = 0; r < nRows; ++r) {
            dot += rv.values[0][r] * values[r][c];
        }
        pv[c] = dot;
    }

    return new RowVector(pv);
}

/**
 * Print the matrix values.
 * @param width the column width
 */
public void print(int width)
{
    AlignRight ar = new AlignRight();

    for (int r = 0; r < nRows; ++r) {
        ar.print("Row ", 0); ar.print(r+1, 2); ar.print(":", 0);

        for (int c = 0; c < nCols; ++c) {
            ar.print(values[r][c], width);
        }

        ar.println();
    }
}
}
```

The `transpose()`, `add()`, and `subtract()` methods are straightforward. There are several `multiply()` methods to handle different types of multipliers and to return the correct product types.

If a nonrectangular, two-dimensional array of values passed to the `set(float values[][])` method, the method trims the ragged edges on the right by using the shortest row to determine the number of columns of the matrix.

The `multiply()` methods can involve large numbers of additions. Therefore, they may suffer from the summation problems described in Chapter 4. If these problems arise, then we may need to rewrite the methods to employ some of the techniques from that chapter. Then there will, of course, be a performance penalty.

The `RowVector multiply(RowVector rv)` method may be a bit confusing. You might think that it more properly belongs in the `RowVector` class, where its signature would be `RowVector multiply(Matrix m)`. But `RowVector` is a subclass of `Matrix`, and `Matrix` has a method with the signature `Matrix multiply(Matrix m)`. Java does not allow a subclass to override a method of its superclass with a method that differs only in its return type.

Many of the matrix methods throw `MatrixException`. As shown in Listing 9–0b, its error messages cover the various errors that can occur during matrix operations or in solving linear equations.

Listing 9–0b Matrix exceptions.

```
package numbercruncher.matrix;

public class MatrixException extends Exception
{
    public static final String INVALID_INDEX =
                                    "Invalid index.";
    public static final String INVALID_DIMENSIONS =
                                    "Invalid matrix dimensions.";
    public static final String ZERO_ROW =
                                    " Matrix has a zero row.";
    public static final String SINGULAR =
                                    "Matrix is singular.";
    public static final String NO_CONVERGENCE =
                                    "Solution did not converge.";

    /**
     * Constructor.
     * @param msg the error message
     */
    public MatrixException(String msg) { super(msg); }
}
```

9.2 Square Matrix

Listing 9–0c shows class `SquareMatrix`, a subclass of `Matrix`. This subclass overrides the `add()`, `subtract()`, and `multiply()` methods to each take a `SquareMatrix` argument and return a `SquareMatrix` value.

The overriding operations methods use the private `SquareMatrix(Matrix m)` constructor, which in turn invokes the private `void set(Matrix m)` method. These methods "convert" a general matrix into a square matrix by having the square matrix reference the general matrix's values. The `SquareMatrix` class does this safely because, in each case, the general matrix is only an intermediate value generated during a matrix operation.

Listing 9–0c The `SquareMatrix` class.

```
package numbercruncher.matrix;

/**
 * A square matrix.
 */
public class SquareMatrix extends Matrix
{
    //--------------//
    // Constructors //
    //--------------//

    /**
     * Constructor.
     * @param n the number of rows == the number of columns
     */
    public SquareMatrix(int n) { super(n, n); }

    /**
     * Constructor.
     * @param m the matrix (only the upper left square used)
     */
    private SquareMatrix(Matrix m) { set(m); }

    /**
     * Constructor.
     * @param values the array of values
     */
    public SquareMatrix(float values[][]) { set(values); }

    //---------//
    // Setters //
    //---------//

    /**
     * Set this square matrix from another matrix.  Note that this
```

```
    * matrix will reference the values of the argument matrix.  If
    * the values are not square, only the upper left square is used.
    * @param values the 2-d array of values
    */
   private void set(Matrix m)
   {
       this.nRows  = this.nCols = Math.min(m.nRows, m.nCols);
       this.values = m.values;
   }

   /**
    * Set this square matrix from a 2-d array of values.  If the
    * values are not square, only the upper left square is used.
    * @param values the 2-d array of values
    */
   protected void set(float values[][])
   {
       super.set(values);
       nRows = nCols = Math.min(nRows, nCols);
   }

   //-------------------//
   // Matrix operations //
   //-------------------//

   /**
    * Add another square matrix to this matrix.
    * @param sm the square matrix addend
    * @return the sum matrix
    * @throws numbercruncher.MatrixException for invalid size
    */
   public SquareMatrix add(SquareMatrix sm) throws MatrixException
   {
       return new SquareMatrix(super.add(sm));
   }

   /**
    * Subtract another square matrix from this matrix.
    * @param sm the square matrix subrrahend
    * @return the difference matrix
    * @throws numbercruncher.MatrixException for invalid size
    */
   public SquareMatrix subtract(SquareMatrix sm)
       throws MatrixException
   {
       return new SquareMatrix(super.subtract(sm));
   }

   /**
    * Multiply this square matrix by another square matrix.
```

```
     * @param sm the square matrix multiplier
     * @return the product matrix
     * @throws numbercruncher.MatrixException for invalid size
     */
    public SquareMatrix multiply(SquareMatrix sm)
        throws MatrixException
    {
        return new SquareMatrix(super.multiply(sm));
    }
}
```

9.3 Identity Matrix

Class `IdentityMatrix` is a subclass of `SquareMatrix`. It initializes the matrix by placing 1.0 values along the diagonal. See Listing 9–0d. It also has a static method `convert()` that resets the values of a general square matrix to make it an identity matrix.

Listing 9–0d The `IdentityMatrix` class.

```
package numbercruncher.matrix;

public class IdentityMatrix extends SquareMatrix
{
    /**
     * Constructor.
     * @param n the number of rows == the number of columns
     */
    public IdentityMatrix(int n)
    {
        super(n);
        for (int i = 0; i < n; ++i) values[i][i] = 1;
    }

    /**
     * Convert a square matrix into an identity matrix.
     * @param sm the square matrix to convert
     */
    public static void convert(SquareMatrix sm)
    {
        for (int r = 0; r < sm.nRows; ++r) {
            for (int c = 0; c < sm.nCols; ++c) {
                sm.values[r][c] = (r == c) ? 1 : 0;
            }
        }
    }
}
```

9.4 Row Vector

The `RowVector` class, shown in Listing 9–0e, is a subclass of `Matrix`. In many respects, `RowVector` is similar to `SquareMatrix`. It overrides the `add()` and `subtract()` methods to take `RowVector` arguments and return `RowVector` values. (Recall that multiplying a row vector by a matrix was taken care of in the `Matrix` class.)

The `norm()` method computes and returns the *Euclidean norm* of a row vector. The norm of a vector v is written $\|v\|$. This scalar value is the square root of the sum of the squares of the vector's values. We can think of a vector norm as the "absolute value" of a vector, or its "distance" from the origin in vector space.

Listing 9–0e The `RowVector` class.

```
package numbercruncher.matrix;

public class RowVector extends Matrix
{
    //--------------//
    // Constructors //
    //--------------//

    /**
     * Constructor.
     * @param n the number of elements
     */
    public RowVector(int n) { super(1, n); }

    /**
     * Constructor.
     * @param values the array of values
     */
    public RowVector(float values[]) { set(values); }

    /**
     * Constructor.
     * @param m the matrix (only the first row used)
     */
    private RowVector(Matrix m) { set(m); }

    //---------//
    // Getters //
    //---------//

    /**
     * Return the row vector's size.
     */
    public int size() { return nCols; }
```

```
/**
 * Copy the values of this matrix.
 * @return the copied values
 */
public float[] copyValues1D()
{
    float v[] = new float[nCols];

    for (int c = 0; c < nCols; ++c) {
        v[c] = values[0][c];
    }

    return v;
}

/**
 * Return the i'th value of the vector.
 * @param i the index
 * @return the value
 */
public float at(int i) { return values[0][i]; }

//---------//
// Setters //
//---------//

/**
 * Set this row vector from a matrix. Only the first row is used.
 * @param m the matrix
 */
private void set(Matrix m)
{
    this.nRows  = 1;
    this.nCols  = m.nCols;
    this.values = m.values;
}

/**
 * Set this row vector from an array of values.
 * @param values the array of values
 */
protected void set(float values[])
{
    this.nRows  = 1;
    this.nCols  = values.length;
    this.values = new float[1][];

    this.values[0] = values;
}
```

```java
/**
 * Set the i'th value of the vector.
 * @param i the index
 * @param value the value
 */
public void set(int i, float value) { values[0][i] = value; }

//-------------------//
// Vector operations //
//-------------------//

/**
 * Add another row vector to this row vector.
 * @param rv the other row vector
 * @return the sum row vector
 * @throws numbercruncher.MatrixException for invalid size
 */
public RowVector add(RowVector rv) throws MatrixException
{
    return new RowVector(super.add(rv));
}

/**
 * Subtract another row vector from this row vector.
 * @param rv the other row vector
 * @return the sum row vector
 * @throws numbercruncher.MatrixException for invalid size
 */
public RowVector subtract(RowVector rv) throws MatrixException
{
    return new RowVector(super.subtract(rv));
}

/**
 * Compute the Euclidean norm.
 * @return the norm
 */
public float norm()
{
    double t = 0;
    for (int c = 0; c < nCols; ++c) {
        float v = values[0][c];
        t += v*v;
    }

    return (float) Math.sqrt(t);
}

/**
 * Print the vector values.
```

```
    */
    public void print()
    {
        for (int c = 0; c < nCols; ++c) {
            System.out.print( "    " + values[0][c]);
        }
        System.out.println();
    }
}
```

9.5 Column Vector

The ColumnVector class is another subclass of Matrix, and it is nearly identical to the RowVector class. See Listing 9–0f. One difference is that, whereas in class RowVector the set(float values[]) method could have the matrix reference the values argument directly, the same method in class ColumnVector must copy the argument vector to the first (and only) element of the matrix rows.

Listing 9–0f The ColumnVector class.

```
package numbercruncher.matrix;

/**
 * A column vector.
 */
public class ColumnVector extends Matrix
{
    //--------------//
    // Constructors //
    //--------------//

    /**
     * Constructor.
     * @param n the number of elements
     */
    public ColumnVector(int n) { super(n, 1); }

    /**
     * Constructor.
     * @param values the array of values
     */
    public ColumnVector(float values[]) { set(values); }

    /**
     * Constructor.
     * @param m the matrix (only the first column used)
     */
    private ColumnVector(Matrix m) { set(m); }
```

```
//---------//
// Getters //
//---------//

/**
 * Return this column vector's size.
 */
public int size() { return nRows; }

/**
 * Return the i'th value of the vector.
 * @param i the index
 * @return the value
 */
public float at(int i) { return values[i][0]; }

/**
 * Copy the values of this matrix.
 * @return the copied values
 */
public float[] copyValues1D()
{
    float v[] = new float[nRows];

    for (int r = 0; r < nRows; ++r) {
        v[r] = values[r][0];
    }

    return v;
}

//---------//
// Setters //
//---------//

/**
 * Set this column vector from a matrix.
 * Only the first column is used.
 * @param m the matrix
 */
private void set(Matrix m)
{
    this.nRows  = m.nRows;
    this.nCols  = 1;
    this.values = m.values;
}

/**
 * Set this column vector from an array of values.
```

```
 * @param values the array of values
 */
protected void set(float values[])
{
    this.nRows  = values.length;
    this.nCols  = 1;
    this.values = new float[nRows][1];

    for (int r = 0; r < nRows; ++r) {
        this.values[r][0] = values[r];
    }
}

/**
 * Set the value of the i'th element.
 * @param i the index
 * @param value the value
 */
public void set(int i, float value) { values[i][0] = value; }

//-------------------//
// Vector operations //
//-------------------//

/**
 * Add another column vector to this column vector.
 * @param cv the other column vector
 * @return the sum column vector
 * @throws numbercruncher.MatrixException for invalid size
 */
public ColumnVector add(ColumnVector cv) throws MatrixException
{
    return new ColumnVector(super.add(cv));
}

/**
 * Subtract another column vector from this column vector.
 * @param cv the other column vector
 * @return the sum column vector
 * @throws numbercruncher.MatrixException for invalid size
 */
public ColumnVector subtract(ColumnVector cv)
    throws MatrixException
{
    return new ColumnVector(super.subtract(cv));
}
```

```
/**
 * Compute the Euclidean norm.
 * @ return the norm
 */
public float norm()
{
    double t = 0;

    for (int r = 0; r < nRows; ++r) {
        float v = values[r][0];
        t += v*v;
    }

    return (float) Math.sqrt(t);
}

/**
 * Print the vector values.
 */
public void print()
{
    for (int r = 0; r < nRows; ++r) {
        System.out.print("    " + values[r][0]);
    }
    System.out.println();
}
}
```

9.6 Graphic Transformation Matrices

With these matrix classes, we can write an interactive program that shows how matrices are used in computer graphics to control the motion of graphic images in three dimensions.

We can represent a three-dimensional graphic image as a set of *vertices* (corners) and *edges* (lines between the vertices). Vertices (and the edges between them) can define a flat *face*—three vertices define a triangle, four vertices define a square, and so on.

In three-dimensional space, each vertex has x, y, and z coordinates. We can assume that the z axis extends outward from and into the computer screen, with the positive direction toward the viewer.

We can transform, or alter, the coordinates of a vertex in several ways. The ways our program will use are

- **Translation.** Move the vertex to another location by adding values (positive or negative) to each coordinate value. If all the vertices of a graphic image are similarly translated, the entire image moves to a new location on the screen. We can represent translation mathematically as

$$x' = x + t_x$$
$$y' = y + t_y$$
$$z' = z + t_z$$

where t_x, t_y, and t_z are the translation values for each coordinate.

- **Scaling.** Move the vertex toward or away from the origin by multiplying each coordinate value by a scale factor greater than 1 (away from the origin) or between 0 and 1 (toward the origin). If a graphic image is centered about the origin, and all its vertices are scaled by the same amount in all three dimensions, the image shrinks or grows in size. Mathematically,

$$x' = x \times s_x$$
$$y' = y \times s_y$$
$$z' = z \times s_z$$

where s_x, s_y, and s_z are the scale factors for each coordinate.

- **Rotation.** Move the vertex to a new location on the screen by rotating it around its center of rotation. This rotation can be along the x, y, or z axis. If a graphic image is centered about the origin, and its center of rotation is the origin itself, then rotating all its vertices causes the image to spin along one of the axes. Mathematically, rotation of angle θ_x about the x axis is

$$x' = x$$
$$y' = y \times \cos(\theta_x) - z \times \sin(\theta_x)$$
$$z' = y \times \sin(\theta_x) + z \times \cos(\theta_x)$$

Rotation of angle θ_y about the y axis is

$$x' = x \times \cos(\theta_y) + z \times \sin(\theta_y)$$
$$y' = y$$
$$z' = -x \times \sin(\theta_y) + z \times \cos(\theta_y)$$

Rotation of angle θ_z about the z axis is

$$x' = x \times \cos(\theta_z) - y \times \sin(\theta_z)$$
$$y' = x \times \sin(\theta_z) + y \times \cos(\theta_z)$$
$$z' = z$$

If we represent a vertex as a row vector with an appended fourth element with value 1, then we can perform each of the preceding transformations by multiplying the vector by a 4×4 *transformation matrix*:

- Translation:

$$[x', y', z', 1] = [x, y, z, 1] \begin{bmatrix} 1 & 0 & 0 & 0 \\ 0 & 1 & 0 & 0 \\ 0 & 0 & 1 & 0 \\ t_x & t_y & t_z & 1 \end{bmatrix}$$

- Scaling:

$$[x', y', z', 1] = [x, y, z, 1] \begin{bmatrix} s_x & 0 & 0 & 0 \\ 0 & s_y & 0 & 0 \\ 0 & 0 & s_z & 0 \\ 0 & 0 & 0 & 1 \end{bmatrix}$$

- Rotation around the x axis:

$$[x', y', z', 1] = [x, y, z, 1] \begin{bmatrix} 1 & 0 & 0 & 0 \\ 0 & \cos\theta_x & -\sin\theta_x & 0 \\ 0 & \sin\theta_x & \cos\theta_x & 0 \\ 0 & 0 & 0 & 1 \end{bmatrix}$$

- Rotation around the y axis:

$$[x', y', z', 1] = [x, y, z, 1] \begin{bmatrix} \cos\theta_y & 0 & \sin\theta_y & 0 \\ 0 & 1 & 0 & 0 \\ -\sin\theta_y & 0 & \cos\theta_y & 0 \\ 0 & 0 & 0 & 1 \end{bmatrix}$$

- Rotation around the z axis:

$$[x', y', z', 1] = [x, y, z, 1] \begin{bmatrix} \cos\theta_z & -\sin\theta_z & 0 & 0 \\ \sin\theta_z & \cos\theta_z & 0 & 0 \\ 0 & 0 & 1 & 0 \\ 0 & 0 & 0 & 1 \end{bmatrix}$$

Since scaling is about the origin, we must first move the graphic image to the origin, apply the scaling, and then move the image back to its location. We can do the move to and from the origin with two translation operations. Similarly, to spin the image, it must be at the origin, since we want the center of rotation to be the origin. We can rotate it separately along each axis in turn.

Thus, we can end up multiplying each vertex several times by the various transformation matrices in order to get the sequence of motions we want for the entire image. But there's a wonderful feature of transformation matrices—we can multiply all the transformation matrices together *in the order that we want to apply them* and then multiply each vertex by this product matrix, called the *concatenated transformation matrix*. That causes the entire sequence of motions to be applied all at once to each vertex.

9.7 A Tumbling Cube in 3-D Space

Our interactive program will use the graphic image of a wire-frame cube. The program will animate this cube image by making it tumble in an enclosed three-dimensional space—it will move and rotate, bounce off the walls of the enclosed space, and grow larger and smaller to create the illusion that it is moving toward or away from the viewer. Screen 9–1 shows a couple of screen shots of this program in action. Besides the cube, the program also displays the current values of the concatenated transformation matrix.

We won't look at the entire program in this chapter, just the source files that use the matrix classes.

Listing 9–1a shows the Vertex class, which, as described previously, we'll make a subclass of RowVector . The constructor puts the *x, y,* and *z* coordinates into the first three elements and a 1 into the fourth element.

The class overrides the multiply() method to transform the vertex by multiplying it by a transformation matrix. This multiplication will give new values for the *x, y,* and *z* coordinates.

Listing 9–1a The Vertex class.

```
package numbercruncher.program9_1;

import numbercruncher.matrix.RowVector;
import numbercruncher.matrix.SquareMatrix;
import numbercruncher.matrix.MatrixException;

/**
 * Represent a vertex of the wire-frame cube in three dimensions.
 */
class Vertex extends RowVector
{
    /**
     * Constructor.
```

Screen 9–1 The tumbling cube and the concatenated transformation matrix of Program 9–1.

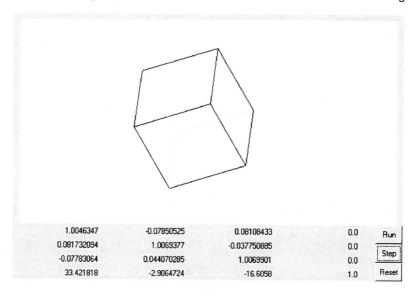

1.0046347	-0.07850525	0.08108433	0.0
0.081732094	1.0069377	-0.037750885	0.0
-0.07783064	0.044070285	1.0069901	0.0
33.421818	-2.9064724	-16.6058	1.0

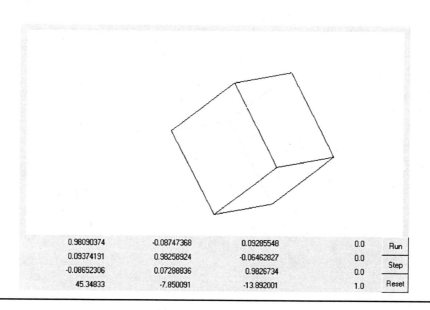

0.98090374	-0.08747368	0.09285548	0.0
0.09374191	0.98258924	-0.06462827	0.0
-0.08652306	0.07288836	0.9826734	0.0
45.34833	-7.850091	-13.892001	1.0

```
 * @param x the x value
 * @param y the y value
 * @param z the z value
 */
Vertex(float x, float y, float z)
{
    super(4);

    values[0][0] = x;
    values[0][1] = y;
    values[0][2] = z;
    values[0][3] = 1;
}

/**
 * Return this vertex's x value.
 * @return the x value
 */
float x() { return values[0][0]; }

/**
 * Return this vertex's y value.
 * @return the y value
 */
float y() { return values[0][1]; }

/**
 * Return this vertex's z value.
 * @return the z value
 */
float z() { return values[0][2]; }

/**
 * Transform this vector by multiplying it
 * by a transformation matrix.
 * @param t the transformation matrix
 */
void multiply(SquareMatrix t) throws MatrixException
{
    RowVector rv = t.multiply(this);
    this.values = rv.values();
}
}
```

Listing 9–1b shows class WireFrameCube, which represents our graphic cube. It consists of eight vertices and six faces. Each face is a square, which is represented by the indices of its four vertices. Initially, the cube is centered about the origin, and each edge has length 1.

Listing 9–1b The `WireFrameCube` class.

```
package numbercruncher.program9_1;

import java.awt.*;

/**
 * A wire-frame cube to transform and display.
 */
class WireFrameCube
{
    /**
     * Represent each face of the cube.
     */
    private class Face
    {
        /** indices of the face's vertices */   int indices[];

        /**
         * Constructor.
         * @param v1 the first vertex
         * @param v2 the second vertex
         * @param v3 the third vertex
         * @param v4 the fourth vertex
         */
        Face(int v1, int v2, int v3, int v4)
        {
            indices = new int[] {v1, v2, v3, v4};
        }
    }
    /** The cube's vertices. */
    private Vertex vertices[] = {
        new Vertex(-0.5f, -0.5f, -0.5f),
        new Vertex(+0.5f, -0.5f, -0.5f),
        new Vertex(-0.5f, +0.5f, -0.5f),
        new Vertex(+0.5f, +0.5f, -0.5f),
        new Vertex(-0.5f, -0.5f, +0.5f),
        new Vertex(+0.5f, -0.5f, +0.5f),
        new Vertex(-0.5f, +0.5f, +0.5f),
        new Vertex(+0.5f, +0.5f, +0.5f),
    };

    /** The cube's faces. */
    private Face faces[] = {
        new Face(0, 1, 3, 2),
        new Face(0, 1, 5, 4),
        new Face(2, 3, 7, 6),
        new Face(0, 4, 6, 2),
```

```
      new Face(1, 5, 7, 3),
      new Face(4, 5, 7, 6),
};

/**
 * Draw the transformed cube.
 * @param g the graphics context
 * @param transformation the transformation to apply
 */
void draw(Graphics g, Transformation transformation)
{
    // Transform the vertices.
    transformation.transform(vertices);

    // Loop for each face.
    for (int i = 0; i < faces.length; ++i) {
        int indices[] = faces[i].indices;

        // Draw the edges of the face.
        for (int j = 0; j < indices.length; ++j) {
            int k  = (j + 1)%indices.length;
            int c1 = Math.round(vertices[indices[j]].x());
            int r1 = Math.round(vertices[indices[j]].y());
            int c2 = Math.round(vertices[indices[k]].x());
            int r2 = Math.round(vertices[indices[k]].y());

            // Set the color based on the edge's position.
            Color color =
                transformation.behindCenter(vertices[indices[j]],
                                            vertices[indices[k]])
                    ? Color.lightGray : Color.black;

            // Draw the edge.
            g.setColor(color);
            g.drawLine(c1, r1, c2, r2);
        }
    }
}
}
```

The constructor receives a graphics context, so that the cube can draw itself, and a transformation object, which we'll examine next.

The cube's draw() method first asks the transformation object to transform all of its vertices. Then it proceeds to draw the edges between the transformed vertices. The transformation object has a behindCenter() method, which indicates whether or not an edge is behind the cube's center. To further create the illusion of a three-dimensional cube, the edges in front of the center are drawn in black, and those in back are drawn in light gray, as seen in Screen 9–1.

Listing 9–1c shows the Transformation class. This class contains all the transformation matrices needed to animate the cube image: a translation matrix (translate), a scaling matrix (scale) , and three rotation matrices, one for each axis (rotateX, rotateY, and rotateZ). It also has a matrix that concatenates the three rotations (rotate) and a matrix that concatenates all the transformations (transform). It uses a separate Vertex object (center) to keep track of the cube's center.

Listing 9–1c The Transformation class.

```
package numbercruncher.program9_1;

import numbercruncher.matrix.SquareMatrix;
import numbercruncher.matrix.IdentityMatrix;
import numbercruncher.matrix.MatrixException;

/**
 * Transformations of a graphic image.
 */
class Transformation
{
    /** translation matrix */
    private SquareMatrix translate = new IdentityMatrix(4);

    /** scaling matrix */
    private SquareMatrix scale = new IdentityMatrix(4);

    /** matrix to rotate about the x axis */
    private SquareMatrix rotateX = new IdentityMatrix(4);

    /** matrix to rotate about the y axis */
    private SquareMatrix rotateY = new IdentityMatrix(4);

    /** matrix to rotate about the z axis */
    private SquareMatrix rotateZ = new IdentityMatrix(4);

    /** concatenated rotation matrix */
    private SquareMatrix rotate = new IdentityMatrix(4);

    /** concatenated transformation matrix */
    private SquareMatrix transform = new IdentityMatrix(4);

    /** center of rotation */
    private Vertex center = new Vertex(0, 0, 0);
```

```java
/**
 * Initialize for a new set of transformations.
 */
void init()
{
    IdentityMatrix.convert(transform);
}

/**
 * Reset to the initial conditions.
 */
void reset()
{
    center = new Vertex(0, 0, 0);

    setTranslation(0, 0, 0);
    setScaling(1, 1, 1);
    setRotation(0, 0, 0);
}

/**
 * Set the translation matrix.
 * @param tx the change in the x direction
 * @param ty the change in the y direction
 * @param tz the change in the z direction
 */
void setTranslation(float tx, float ty, float tz)
{
    try {
        translate.set(3, 0, tx);
        translate.set(3, 1, ty);
        translate.set(3, 2, tz);
    }
    catch(MatrixException ex) {}
}
/**
 * Set the scaling matrix.
 * @param sx the scaling factor in the x direction
 * @param sy the scaling factor in the y direction
 * @param sz the scaling factor in the z direction
 */
void setScaling(float sx, float sy, float sz)
{
    try {
        scale.set(0, 0, sx);
        scale.set(1, 1, sy);
        scale.set(2, 2, sz);
    }
    catch(MatrixException ex) {}
```

```
    }
    /**
     * Set the rotation matrix.
     * @param thetaX amount (in radians) to rotate around the x axis
     * @param thetaY amount (in radians) to rotate around the y axis
     * @param thetaZ amount (in radians) to rotate around the z axis
     */
    void setRotation(float thetaX, float thetaY, float thetaZ)
    {
        try {
            float sin = (float) Math.sin(thetaX);
            float cos = (float) Math.cos(thetaX);

            // Rotate about the x axis.
            rotateX.set(1, 1,  cos);
            rotateX.set(1, 2, -sin);
            rotateX.set(2, 1,  sin);
            rotateX.set(2, 2,  cos);

            sin = (float) Math.sin(thetaY);
            cos = (float) Math.cos(thetaY);

            // Rotate about the y axis.
            rotateY.set(0, 0,  cos);
            rotateY.set(0, 2,  sin);
            rotateY.set(2, 0, -sin);
            rotateY.set(2, 2,  cos);

            sin = (float) Math.sin(thetaZ);
            cos = (float) Math.cos(thetaZ);

            // Rotate about the z axis.
            rotateZ.set(0, 0,  cos);
            rotateZ.set(0, 1, -sin);
            rotateZ.set(1, 0,  sin);
            rotateZ.set(1, 1,  cos);

            // Concatenate rotations.
            rotate = rotateX.multiply(rotateY.multiply(rotateZ));
        }
        catch(MatrixException ex) {}
    }

    /**
     * Transform a set of vertices based on previously-set
     * translation, scaling, and rotation.  Concatenate the
     * transformations in the order:  scale, rotate, translate.
     * @param vertices the vertices to transform
     */
```

```java
void transform(Vertex vertices[])
{
    // Scale and rotate about the origin.
    toOrigin();
    scale();
    rotate();
    reposition();

    translate();

    // Apply the concatenated transformations.
    try {

        // Do the vertices.
        for (int i = 0; i < vertices.length; ++i) {
            Vertex v = vertices[i];
            v.multiply(transform);
        }

        // Do the center of rotation.
        center.multiply(transform);
    }
    catch(MatrixException ex) {}
}

/**
 * Check for a bounce against any wall of the space.
 * Return true if bounced.
 * @param width the width of the space
 * @param height the height of the space
 * @param depth the depth of the space
 * @return true if bounced, else false
 */
boolean bounced(float width, float height, float depth)
{
    boolean b = false;

    try {

        // Bounced off the sides?
        if ((center.x() < 0) || (center.x() > width)) {
            translate.set(3, 0, -translate.at(3, 0));
            b = true;
        }

        // Bounced off the top or bottom?
        if ((center.y() < 0) || (center.y() > height)) {
            translate.set(3, 1, -translate.at(3, 1));
```

```
                b = true;
            }

            // Bounced off the front or back?
            if ((center.z() < 0) || (center.z() > depth)) {
                translate.set(3, 2, -translate.at(3, 2));

                // Invert the scale factor.
                float scaleFactor = 1/scale.at(0, 0);

                scale.set(0, 0, scaleFactor);
                scale.set(1, 1, scaleFactor);
                scale.set(2, 2, scaleFactor);

                b = true;
            }
        }
        catch(MatrixException ex) {}

        return b;
    }

    /**
     * Check if a line is behind the center of rotation.
     * @param v1 the vertex of one end of the line
     * @param v2 the vertex of the other end of the line
     * @return true if behind, else false
     */
    boolean behindCenter(Vertex v1, Vertex v2)
    {
        return (v1.z() < center.z()) && (v2.z() < center.z());
    }

    /**
     * Return a value from the concatenated transformation matrix.
     * @param r the value's row
     * @param c the value's column
     * @return the value
     */
    float at(int r, int c)
    {
        try {
            return transform.at(r, c);
        }
        catch(MatrixException ex) {
            return Float.NaN;
        }
    }
```

```java
/**
 * Concatenate a translation.
 * @param translate the translation matrix to use
 */
private void translate(SquareMatrix translate)
{
    try {
        transform = transform.multiply(translate);
    }
    catch(MatrixException ex) {}
}

/**
 * Concatenate the preset translation.
 */
private void translate()
{
    translate(translate);
}

/**
 * Concatenate the preset scaling.
 */
private void scale()
{
    try {
        transform = transform.multiply(scale);
    }
    catch(MatrixException ex) {}
}

/**
 * Concatenate the preset rotation.
 */
private void rotate()
{
    try {
        transform = transform.multiply(rotate);
    }
    catch(MatrixException ex) {}
}

/**
 * Translate back to the origin.
 */
private void toOrigin()
{
    try {
        SquareMatrix tempTranslate = new IdentityMatrix(4);
```

```
            tempTranslate.set(3, 0, -center.x());
            tempTranslate.set(3, 1, -center.y());
            tempTranslate.set(3, 2, -center.z());

            translate(tempTranslate);
        }
        catch(MatrixException ex) {}
    }

    /**
     * Translate back into position.
     */
    private void reposition()
    {
        try {
            SquareMatrix tempTranslate = new IdentityMatrix(4);

            tempTranslate.set(3, 0, center.x());
            tempTranslate.set(3, 1, center.y());
            tempTranslate.set(3, 2, center.z());

            translate(tempTranslate);
        }
        catch(MatrixException ex) {}
    }
}
```

Method `init()` initializes `transform` to the identity matrix to prepare it for a sequence of transformations. Method `reset()` puts the cube image back to its starting point at the origin and "clears" the translation, scaling, and rotation matrices.

Method `setTranslation()` sets the translation value into matrix `translate`. Similarly, method `setScaling()` sets the scale factors into matrix `scale`.

Method `setRotatation()` sets the rotation values into the three rotation matrices `rotateX`, `rotateY`, and `rotateZ`. Then it multiplies the matrices together to set the concatenated rotation matrix `rotate`.

Method `transform()`, which we saw in Listing 9–1b being called by the method `WireFrameCube.draw()`, transforms each vertex of the graphic image.

First, the method must concatenate all the transformations. It calls method `toOrigin()` to move the object back to the origin, and then it calls methods `scale()` and `rotate()` to scale and rotate the image about the origin. Next, it calls method `reposition()` to put the scaled and rotated image back to its location. Finally, a call to `translate()` moves the image to its new location. As we'll soon see, these calls concatenate all the transformations into matrix `transform`.

Now method `transform()` simply multiplies each vertex of the graphic image by the matrix `transform`. It also multiplies the `center` vertex by `transform` to move it along with the object.

Methods `toOrigin()` and `reposition()` use temporary translation matrices and the `center` vertex to move the graphic image to and from the origin. The methods `translate()`, `scale()`, and `rotate()` simply multiply the concatenated `transform` matrix by the individual transformation matrices `transform`, `scale`, and `rotate`, respectively.

Method `bounce()` checks whether or not the graphic image has bounced off any of the six walls of the enclosed three-dimensional space. Bouncing off a wall is achieved simply by negating the appropriate t_x, t_y, or t_z value in the `translate` matrix. If the object bounces off either the back or front wall, the method also replaces the scaling factors in the `scale` matrix by their reciprocals—we want the image to grow as it approaches the viewer and to shrink as it recedes from the viewer. The method returns `true` if a bounce occurred. Otherwise, it returns `false`.

Method `behindCenter()`, which we also saw in Listing 9–1b being called by method `WireFrameCube.draw()`, checks the two vertices of an edge. It deems the edge to be behind the graphic image's center if both vertices are behind the center, and then it returns `true`. Otherwise, it returns `false`.

Method `at()` simply returns the current values of the concatenated `transform` matrix. This allows our program to display the values.

Class `CubePanel` is a subclass of `java.awt.Panel`, and it represents the enclosed three-dimensional space for the tumbling wire-frame cube image. Its constructor receives a `Transformation` object, and it creates a `WireFrameCube` object. See Listing 9–1d.

Listing 9–1d Class `CubePanel`.

```
package numbercruncher.program9_1;

import java.awt.*;

/**
 * The panel that represents the enclosed 3-D space
 * for the tumbling wire-frame cube.
 */
public class CubePanel extends Panel
{
    private static final float MAX_TRANSLATE = 5;
    private static final float MAX_SCALING   = 3;
    /** width of space */    private int width;
    /** height of space */   private int height;
    /** depth of space */    private int depth;

    /** image buffer */              private Image     buffer;
    /** buffer graphics context */   private Graphics  bg;

    /** true for first draw */   private boolean first = true;

    /** wire frame cube */   private WireFrameCube   cube;
    /** transformation */    private Transformation  transformation;
    /** parent panel */      private TransformationPanel parent;
```

```java
    /**
     * Constructor.
     * @param transformation the graphics transformation
     * @param parent the parent panel
     */
    CubePanel(Transformation transformation,
              TransformationPanel parent)
    {
        this.transformation = transformation;
        this.parent         = parent;
        this.cube           = new WireFrameCube();

        setBackground(Color.white);
    }

    /**
     * Reset the cube to its starting position.
     */
    public void reset()
    {
        cube  = new WireFrameCube();
        first = true;
        bg    = null;

        repaint();
    }

    /**
     * Draw the contents of the panel.
     */
    public void draw()
    {
        if (bg == null) return;
        bg.clearRect(0, 0, width, height);

        transformation.init();

        if (first) {
            firstDraw();

        }
        else {
            subsequentDraw();
        }

        repaint();
        parent.updateMatrixDisplay();
    }
```

```java
/**
 * Paint without first clearing.
 * @param g the graphics context
 */
public void update(Graphics g) { paint(g); }

/**
 * Paint the contents of the image buffer.
 * @param g the graphics context
 */
public void paint(Graphics g)
{
    // Has the buffer been created?
    if (bg == null) {
        Rectangle r = getBounds();

        width  = r.width;
        height = r.height;
        depth  = width;

        // Create the image buffer and get its graphics context.
        buffer = createImage(width, height);
        bg     = buffer.getGraphics();

        draw();
    }

    // Paint the buffer contents.
    g.drawImage(buffer, 0, 0, null);
}

/**
 * First time drawing.
 */
private void firstDraw()
{
    // Scale and move to the center.
    transformation.setScaling(50, 50, 50);
    transformation.setTranslation(width/2, height/2, depth/2);

    cube.draw(bg, transformation);

    // Random subsequent translations.
    float xDelta = (float) (2*MAX_TRANSLATE*Math.random()
                            - MAX_TRANSLATE);
    float yDelta = (float) (2*MAX_TRANSLATE*Math.random()
                            - MAX_TRANSLATE);
    float zDelta = (float) (2*MAX_TRANSLATE*Math.random()
                            - MAX_TRANSLATE);
```

```
        transformation.setTranslation(xDelta, yDelta, zDelta);

        // Set the scale factor based on the space's depth and
        // whether the cube is moving towards or away from the viewer.
        // At maximum z, the cube should be twice its original size,
        // and at minimum z, it should be half its original size.
        float steps       = (depth/2)/Math.abs(zDelta);
        float scaleFactor = (float) Math.pow(MAX_SCALING, 1/steps);
        if (zDelta < 0) scaleFactor = 1/scaleFactor;
        transformation.setScaling(
                        scaleFactor, scaleFactor, scaleFactor);

        setRandomRotation();
        first = false;
    }

    /**
     * Subsequent drawing.
     */
    private void subsequentDraw()
    {
        // Draw the transformed cube.
        cube.draw(bg, transformation);

        // If there was a bounce, set new random rotation angles.
        if (transformation.bounced(width, height, depth)) {
            setRandomRotation();
        }
    }

    /**
     * Set random rotation angles about the axes.
     */
    private void setRandomRotation()
    {
        transformation.setRotation(
                    (float) (0.1*Math.random()),     // x axis
                    (float) (0.1*Math.random()),     // y axis
                    (float) (0.1*Math.random()));    // z axis
    }
}
```

The class uses an off-screen image buffer to draw the image. Method draw() first initializes the Transformation object. Then, if this is the very first time it will draw the cube, or the first time after the cube has been reset, it calls method firstDraw(). Otherwise, it calls method subsequentDraw(). In either case, it finishes by causing a repaint and an update of the displayed values of the concatenated transformation matrix.

Method `firstDraw()` scales the cube (which, when created, is centered at the origin and has edges of length 1) and moves it to the center of the panel. Then, the method sets random translation values. Next, it computes and sets the proper scaling factors, so that the cube will appear to be half its size at the back of the space and twice its size at the front of the space. Finally, the method calls method `setRandomRotation()` to set random rotation values.

Method `subsequentDraw()` invokes the cube's `draw()` method, passing it the graphics context of the off-screen image buffer and the `Transformation` object. The cube will then transform and draw itself, as we saw in Listing 9–1b. Method `subsequentDraw()` then checks for a bounce, and if one occurred, it makes things a bit more interesting by setting new random rotation values.

References

Bronson, Richard, *Matrix Operations,* New York: McGraw-Hill, 1989.

Golub, Gene H., and Charles F. Van Loan, *Matrix Computations,* Baltimore: The John Hopkins University Press, 1996.

   Basic matrix operations are covered in Golub and Van Loan in Section 1.1 and in Bronson in Chapter 1.

Newman, William M., and Robert F. Sproull, *Principles of Interactive Computer Graphics,* 2nd edition, New York: McGraw-Hill, 1979.

Xiang, Zhigang, and Roy Plastock, *Computer Graphics,* 2nd edition, New York: McGraw-Hill, 2000.

   Many books on computer graphics discuss graphic transformation matrices, such as Newman and Sproull in Section 22–1 and Xiang and Plastock in Chapter 6.

CHAPTER 10

SOLVING SYSTEMS OF LINEAR EQUATIONS

A mong the least fond memories of high school algebra are the lessons on solving systems of linear equations, with the drudgery of the repetitious hand calculations. This must be one of the algorithms we would most want to implement on a computer.

In this chapter, we'll first review the algorithm behind the hand calculations, and then we'll make some improvements to this algorithm. Finally, we'll implement this algorithm as a Java class that uses matrices.

10.1 The Gaussian Elimination Algorithm

Let's start with the following example of a system of four linear equations in four unknowns x_1, x_2, x_3, and x_4:

$$3x_1 + x_2 - 5x_3 + 4x_4 = -18$$
$$2x_1 - 3x_2 + 3x_3 - 2x_4 = 19$$
$$5x_1 - 3x_2 + 4x_3 + x_4 = 22$$
$$-2x_1 + 4x_2 - 3x_3 - 3x_4 = -14$$

The correct solution is $x_1 = 1$, $x_2 = -2$, $x_3 = 3$, and $x_4 = -1$.

The first set of operations is called *forward elimination*. The goal is to systematically remove one unknown at a time from the system. To keep things simpler, we'll do all the arithmetic with three significant digits.

- **Eliminate x_1 from the second, third, and fourth equations.** Designate the first equation as the *pivot equation* and its leading coefficient, 3, the *pivot element*. To eliminate x_1 from the second equation, multiply the pivot equation by the multiplier $\frac{2}{3}$ (the ratio of the coefficients of x_1) and subtract the result from the second equation. To eliminate x_1 from the third equation, multiply the pivot equation by the multiplier $\frac{5}{3}$ and subtract the result from the third equation. To eliminate x_1 from the fourth equation, multiply the pivot equation by the multiplier $\frac{-2}{3}$ and subtract the result from the fourth equation. After these operations, the system becomes

$$3.00x_1 + 1.00x_2 - 5.00x_3 + 4.00x_4 = -18.0$$
$$-3.67x_2 + 6.33x_3 - 4.67x_4 = 31.0$$
$$-4.67x_2 + 12.3x_3 - 5.67x_4 = 52.0$$
$$4.67x_2 - 6.33x_3 - 2.33x_4 = -26.0$$

Note that the pivot element was the common divisor for each pivot equation multiplier, and that the pivot equation (after the multiplication) is subtracted from each of the equations below it.

• **Eliminate x_2 from the third and fourth equations.** Now the second equation is the pivot equation, and -3.67 is the pivot element. To eliminate x_2 from the third equation, multiply the pivot equation by the multiplier $\frac{-4.67}{-3.67}$ and subtract the result from the third equation. To eliminate x_2 from the fourth equation, multiply the pivot equation by the multiplier $\frac{4.67}{-3.67}$ and subtract the result from the fourth equation. After these operations, the system becomes

$$3.00x_1 + 1.00x_2 - 5.00x_3 + 4.00x_4 = -18.0$$
$$-3.67x_2 + 6.33x_3 - 4.67x_4 = 31.0$$
$$4.25x_3 + 0.272x_4 = 12.6$$
$$1.72x_3 - 8.27x_4 = 13.4$$

• **Eliminate x_3 from the fourth equation.** The third equation is the pivot equation, and 4.25 becomes the pivot element. Multiply the pivot equation by the multiplier $\frac{1.72}{4.25}$ and subtract the result from the fourth equation. After this operation, the system becomes

$$3.00x_1 + 1.00x_2 - 5.00x_3 + 4.00x_4 = -18.0$$
$$-3.67x_2 + 6.33x_3 - 4.67x_4 = 31.0$$
$$4.25x_3 + 0.272x_4 = 12.6$$
$$-8.38x_4 = 8.30$$

The system is now in *upper triangular form.*

Once the system is in upper triangular form, it is easy to solve for each unknown, starting with x_4 at the bottom equation, and moving up one equation at a time for each of the other unknowns. This process is called *back substitution:*

$$x_4 = \frac{8.30}{-8.38} = -0.990$$

$$x_3 = \frac{12.6 - [0.272(-0.990)]}{4.25} = 3.03$$

$$x_2 = \frac{31.0 - [6.33(3.03) - 4.67(-0.990)]}{-3.67} = -1.96$$

$$x_1 = \frac{-18.0 - [1.00(-1.96) - 5.00(3.03) + 4.00(-0.990)]}{3.00} = 1.02$$

We see that there are some roundoff errors.

This algorithm, forward elimination followed by back substitution, is known as *Gaussian elimination.*

10.2 Problems with Gaussian Elimination

As we've seen, the Gaussian elimination algorithm, with its large number of arithmetic operations, is prone to roundoff errors. These errors become worse with larger systems of equations. Note that there are a number of subtractions and divisions, and as we saw back in Chapter 1, subtractions can lead to a loss of significant digits, and division by small values can magnify errors.

Some systems of equations are especially sensitive to roundoff errors. Slight changes in the coefficients of the intermediate systems during forward elimination can cause large changes in the final solution.

DEFINITION: A system of linear equations is **ill-conditioned** if small changes in the coefficients result in large changes in the solution.

DEFINITION: A system is **well-conditioned** if small changes in the coefficients result only in small changes in the solution.

In Chapter 11, we'll compute a scalar value that measures a system's condition.

Figure 10–1 shows a simple example of an ill-conditioned system. Two lines are very nearly coincident. Even a tiny wiggle in either or both lines, caused by small changes in the coefficients of the two line equations, will cause a large change in the point where the lines cross.

Another pitfall of Gaussian elimination is division by zero. If a pivot element is zero, then we're in trouble.

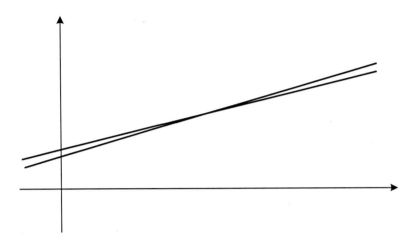

Figure 10–1   A simple example of an ill-conditioned system. A tiny wiggle in either or both lines will greatly change where the two lines cross.

Gaussian elimination will fail if a system has no solution or if it has an infinite number of solutions. For example, in the simple case of two lines, the lines may be exactly coincident (an infinite number of solutions), or they may be parallel to each other (no solution).

> DEFINITION: A system of linear equations is **singular** if it has no solution or an infinite number of solutions.

Thus, the straightforward form of the Gaussian elimination algorithm as shown in Section 10.1 is not enough. We need to make some improvements.

10.3 Partial Pivoting

We can improve the Gaussian elimination algorithm by adding an operation called *partial pivoting.*

Partial pivoting prevents dividing by zero during forward elimination, and it helps with the problem of dividing by a small pivot element. At each elimination step, partial pivoting exchanges the equations in order to choose the best pivot equation. (Full pivoting includes changing the order of the coefficients of the equations and is usually not done.)

As we saw in Section 10.1 during forward elimination, we designate one equation the pivot equation, and then we subtract multiples of that equation from the equations below it to eliminate one unknown. The multiplier is a fraction whose divisor is the pivot element, the leading coefficient of the pivot equation. Therefore, if we want to avoid dividing by a small number, we want the pivot element to be the largest possible. To make this happen, we pivot (exchange) equations if necessary.

The following is a simple system to illustrate the need for partial pivoting:

$$0.000100x_1 + 2.00x_2 = 2.00$$
$$1.00x_1 + 1.00x_2 = 2.00$$

The solution is approximately $x_1 = 1.00005$ and $x_2 = 0.99995$, or, with three significant digits, $x_1 = 1.00$ and $x_2 = 1.00$.

Forward elimination produces (with three significant digits)

$$0.000100x_1 + 2.00x_2 = 2.00$$
$$-2000x_2 = -2000$$

and back substitution yields

$$x_2 = \frac{-2000}{-2000} = 1.00$$

$$x_1 = \frac{2.00 - [2.00(1.00)]}{0.000100} = 0.00$$

which is completely wrong for x_1. The error occurred during forward elimination—dividing by the small pivot element 0.000100 generated large values, which were then subtracted from much smaller values, causing magnitude errors like the ones we examined in Chapter 4.

Before we try to eliminate x_1 in the first step, we should make the pivot element as large as possible in absolute value. Certainly, the coefficient of x_1 in the second equation, 1.00, is greater than 0.000100, so we do a partial pivot by exchanging the two rows:

$$1.00x_1 + 1.00x_2 = 2.00$$
$$0.000100x_1 + 2.00x_2 = 2.00$$

Now forward elimination yields (with three significant digits)

$$1.00x_1 + 1.00x_2 = 2.00$$
$$2.00x_2 = 2.00$$

and back substitution gives us the much more accurate solution

$$x_2 = \frac{2.00}{2.00} = 1.00$$

$$x_1 = \frac{2.00 - [1.00(1.00)]}{1.00} = 1.00$$

10.4 Scaling

Even partial pivoting is not always enough, however. The following is another simple system:

$$3.00x_1 + 10,000x_2 = 10,000$$
$$2.00x_1 + 1.00x_2 = 3.00$$

The approximate answer is $x_1 = 1.0002$ and $x_2 = 0.9997$, or, with three significant digits, $x_1 = 1.00$ and $x_2 = 1.00$.

Forward elimination gives us (with three significant digits)

$$3.00x_1 + 10,000x_2 = 10,000$$
$$-6,700x_2 = -6,700$$

and back substitution produces the inaccurate solution

$$x_2 = \frac{-6,700}{-6,700} = 1.00$$

$$x_1 = \frac{10,000 - [10,000(1.00)]}{3.00} = 0.00$$

So we failed, even though the pivot element was the largest possible. After forward elimination, we still have magnitude errors from the greatly different coefficient values.

Scaling helps with this problem. To scale an equation, divide through by the coefficient with the largest absolute value in that equation. Thus, we divide the first equation through by 10,000 and the second equation through by 2.00:

$$0.000300x_1 + 1.00x_2 = 1.00$$
$$1.00x_1 + 0.500x_2 = 1.50$$

Now we must partially pivot:

$$1.00x_1 + 0.500x_2 = 1.50$$
$$0.000300x_1 + 1.00x_2 = 1.00$$

Forward elimination gives us

$$1.00x_1 + 0.500x_2 = 1.50$$
$$1.00x_2 = 1.00$$

And, finally, back substitution produces

$$x_2 = \frac{1.00}{1.00} = 1.00$$

$$x_1 = \frac{1.50 - [0.500(1.00)]}{1.00} = 1.00$$

We can improve the Gaussian elimination algorithm with a combination of scaling and partial pivoting.

10.5 LU Decomposition

Now let's see how we can implement the Gaussian elimination algorithm using matrices. Our original system of linear equations will serve as an example.

If we collect the coefficients of the system into a square matrix A, put the values after the equal signs on the right-hand side into a column vector b, and represent the unknowns x_i as the column vector x, then we have the matrix equation $Ax = b$. For example, our system of linear equations becomes

$$\begin{bmatrix} 3 & 1 & -5 & 4 \\ 2 & -3 & 3 & -2 \\ 5 & -3 & 4 & 1 \\ -2 & 4 & -3 & -5 \end{bmatrix} \begin{bmatrix} x_1 \\ x_2 \\ x_3 \\ x_4 \end{bmatrix} = \begin{bmatrix} -18 \\ 19 \\ 22 \\ -14 \end{bmatrix}$$

If we do the matrix multiplication, we get

$$\begin{bmatrix} 3x_1 + x_2 - 5x_3 + 4x_4 \\ 2x_1 - 3x_2 + 3x_3 - 2x_4 \\ 5x_1 - 3x_2 + 4x_3 + x_4 \\ -2x_1 + 4x_2 - 3x_3 - 3x_4 \end{bmatrix} = \begin{bmatrix} -18 \\ 19 \\ 22 \\ -14 \end{bmatrix}$$

which is equivalent to the original system.

After we're done with forward elimination, we'll have an upper triangular matrix U. For our system of equations, U is

$$\begin{bmatrix} 3.00 & 1.00 & -5.00 & 4.00 \\ 0.00 & -3.67 & 6.33 & -4.67 \\ 0.00 & 0.00 & 4.25 & 0.272 \\ 0.00 & 0.00 & 0.00 & -8.38 \end{bmatrix}$$

The forward elimination process produces an upper triangular matrix by *subtracting* multiples of the pivot row from each row below the pivot row. So, to recover the original matrix A from U, we want to *add* those multiples of the pivot row. We can do that with a lower triangular matrix L that contains ones on the diagonal and the multiples below the diagonal. For our system of equations,

$$L = \begin{bmatrix} 1.00 & 0.00 & 0.00 & 0.00 \\ \frac{2.00}{3.00} & 1.00 & 0.00 & 0.00 \\ \frac{5.00}{3.00} & \frac{-4.67}{-3.67} & 1.00 & 0.00 \\ \frac{-2.00}{3.00} & \frac{4.67}{-3.67} & \frac{1.72}{4.25} & 1.00 \end{bmatrix} = \begin{bmatrix} 1.00 & 0.00 & 0.00 & 0.00 \\ 0.667 & 1.00 & 0.00 & 0.00 \\ 1.67 & 1.27 & 1.00 & 0.00 \\ -0.667 & -1.27 & 0.405 & 1.00 \end{bmatrix}$$

We can verify that, indeed (subject to roundoff errors), $LU = A$. The process of decomposing (factoring) matrix A into matrices L and U is called *LU decomposition.*

When we did the forward elimination by hand, the right-hand-side values participated in the process. From the matrix point of view, we started with the column vector

$$b = \begin{bmatrix} -18 \\ 19 \\ 22 \\ -14 \end{bmatrix}$$

and ended up with a new column vector, which we'll call *y:*

$$y = \begin{bmatrix} -18.0 \\ 31.0 \\ 12.6 \\ 8.30 \end{bmatrix}$$

We then performed back substitution with these values to compute the values of the solution vector *x.*

We began with the equation $Ax = b$, and by performing forward elimination, we transformed the equation to $Ux = y$:

$$\begin{bmatrix} 3.00 & 1.00 & -5.00 & 4.00 \\ 0.00 & -3.67 & 6.33 & -4.67 \\ 0.00 & 0.00 & 4.25 & 0.272 \\ 0.00 & 0.00 & 0.00 & -8.38 \end{bmatrix} \begin{bmatrix} x_1 \\ x_2 \\ x_3 \\ x_4 \end{bmatrix} = \begin{bmatrix} -18.0 \\ 31.0 \\ 12.6 \\ 8.30 \end{bmatrix}$$

which we can solve for x using back substitution.

If we think about it, having the right-hand-side values participate in the forward elimination process really isn't such a good idea. Here's why. Suppose then we're given a new set of right-hand-side values b', and we're asked to solve for x using these new values. We'd have to go through the forward elimination process again to compute the corresponding y'. We'd also end up with the same U, and so we would redo work we'd already done.

So, given a vector b, we want a quick way to compute the corresponding vector y without repeating work. But just as we have $LU = A$, we also have $Ly = b$:

$$\begin{bmatrix} 1.00 & 0.00 & 0.00 & 0.00 \\ 0.667 & 1.00 & 0.00 & 0.00 \\ 1.67 & 1.27 & 1.00 & 0.00 \\ -0.667 & -1.27 & 0.405 & 1.00 \end{bmatrix} \begin{bmatrix} y_1 \\ y_2 \\ y_3 \\ y_4 \end{bmatrix} = \begin{bmatrix} -18.0 \\ 19.0 \\ 22.0 \\ -14.0 \end{bmatrix}$$

Do the matrix multiplication and use a process similar to back substitution called *forward substitution*, which solves the y_i from the top down:

$$1.00y_1 = -18.0$$
$$y_1 = -18.0$$

$$0.667y_1 + 1.00y_2 = 0.667(-18.0) + 1.00y_2 = 19.0$$
$$y_2 = 31.0$$

$$1.67y_1 + 1.27y_2 + 1.00y_3 = 1.67(-18.0) + 1.27(31.0) + 1.00y_3 = 22.0$$
$$y_3 = 12.7$$

$$-0.667y_1 - 1.27y_2 + 0.405y_3 + 1.00y_4 = -0.667(-18.0) - 1.27(31.0) + 0.405(12.7) + 1.00y_4 = -14.0$$
$$y_4 = 8.22$$

Roundoff errors from using only three significant digits account for the discrepancies between these values and the ones we saw above in the equation $Ux = y$.

Then we go back to the equation $Ux = y$ and solve for x using back substitution.

Adding scaling and partial pivoting to these matrix operations is straightforward. Scaling is multiplying the elements of a row of matrix A by a nonzero value, and partial pivoting involves exchanging rows of the matrix.

10.6 Iterative Improvement

In Chapter 5, we examined root-finding algorithms, such as Newton's algorithm, that converge toward a correct solution. Each iteration step generated an approximate solution, which was then used in the next iteration to generate a better approximation. We stopped when we deemed an approximation to be "close enough." We can do something similar when we use matrices to solve systems of equations.

Let's say we use the matrix operations described in the previous section to solve a system of equations $Ax = b$, and we compute our first solution x_1. Most likely, this solution isn't exact because of roundoff errors, and so we can compute the *residual vector*

$$r_1 = b - Ax_1$$

We use r_1 to solve the system

$$Az_1 = r_1$$

for z_1.

The values of z_1 represent the discrepancies in the corresponding values of x_1 that caused the residual values in r_1. In other words, if we compute $x_2 = x_1 + z_1$, then x_2 is the correct solution to the original equation $Ax = b$. That's assuming z_1 was computed correctly, but, of course, it probably wasn't, either.

So we iterate again:

$$r_2 = b - Ax_2$$

We solve

$$Az_2 = r_2$$

for z_2, and then $x_3 = x_2 + z_2$.

We continue iterating, and if all goes well, the x_i will converge toward the correct solution. We stop when we decide we're "close enough."

10.7 A Class for Solving Systems of Linear Equations

We've covered a lot of ground so far in this chapter. We began by solving a system of linear equations with the Gaussian elimination algorithm, which involved forward elimination followed by back substitution. Then we recast the problem as the matrix equation $Ax = b$, and we used LU decomposition (forward elimination with scaled partial pivoting) to factor matrix A into matrices L and U. We used the equation $Ly = b$ and forward substitution to solve for y, and then we used the equation $Ux = y$ and back substitution to arrive at the solution x for the original system. With matrices L and U, we can quickly solve for x, given any new b. We can do iterative improvement on x.

Listing 10–0 shows class `LinearSystem` in package `numbercruncher.matrix`, which is a subclass of `SquareMatrix`. A `LinearSystem` object represents a coefficient matrix A. Its methods can perform LU decomposition and solve for x when given b, where x and b are represented by `ColumnVector` objects.

The class uses a couple of tricks. Instead of storing matrices L and U separately, it stores them together into a `SquareMatrix` object LU, which contains the elements of U in its upper triangle and the elements of **L** (without the ones on the diagonal) in its lower triangle. Thus, our matrices **L** and **U** from our example system would be stored in LU as

$$\begin{bmatrix} 3.00 & 1.00 & -5.00 & 4.00 \\ 0.667 & -3.67 & 6.33 & -4.67 \\ 1.67 & 1.27 & 4.25 & 0.272 \\ -0.667 & -1.27 & 0.405 & -8.38 \end{bmatrix}$$

The class does partial pivoting not by actually exchanging rows of the matrix but, instead, by keeping track of the exchanges in a *permutation vector,* implemented as the integer array permutation of row indices. Instead of exchanging rows, the class exchanges elements of permutation, and later, instead of indexing the rows directly, it goes through permutation. Thus, permutation also keeps a record of the row exchanges.

The class computes the scaling factors, but it does not actually scale the rows by multiplying them by the factors. It uses the scaling factors only to decide whether or not a row exchange is needed to choose the best possible pivot element.

Listing 10–0 The LinearSystem class.

```
package numbercruncher.matrix;

import java.util.Random;

import numbercruncher.mathutils.Epsilon;
import numbercruncher.mathutils.AlignRight;

/**
 * Solve a system of linear equations using LU decomposition.
 */
public class LinearSystem extends SquareMatrix
{
    private static final float TOLERANCE = Epsilon.floatValue();

    /** max iters for improvement = twice # of significant digits */
    private static final int MAX_ITER;
    static {
        int   i = 0;
        float t = TOLERANCE;
        while (t < 1) { ++i; t *= 10; }
        MAX_ITER = 2*i;
    }

    /** decomposed matrix A = LU */      protected SquareMatrix LU;
    /** row index permutation vector */  protected int permutation[];
    /** row exchange count */            protected int exchangeCount;
```

```
/**
 * Constructor.
 * @param n the number of rows = the number of columns
 */
public LinearSystem(int n)
{
    super(n);
    reset();
}

/**
 * Constructor.
 * @param values the array of values
 */
public LinearSystem(float values[][]) { super(values); }

/**
 * Set the values of the matrix.
 * @param values the 2-d array of values
 */
protected void set(float values[][])
{
    super.set(values);
    reset();
}

/**
 * Set the value of element [r,c] in the matrix.
 * @param r the row index, 0..nRows
 * @param c the column index, 0..nRows
 * @param value the value
 * @throws matrix.MatrixException for invalid index
 */
public void set(int r, int c, float value) throws MatrixException
{
    super.set(r, c, value);
    reset();
}

/**
 * Set a row of this matrix from a row vector.
 * @param rv the row vector
 * @param r the row index
 * @throws matrix.MatrixException for an invalid index or
 *                                an invalid vector size
 */
public void setRow(RowVector rv, int r) throws MatrixException
{
    super.setRow(rv, r);
```

```
        reset();
    }

    /**
     * Set a column of this matrix from a column vector.
     * @param cv the column vector
     * @param c the column index
     * @throws matrix.MatrixException for an invalid index or
     *                                an invalid vector size
     */
    public void setColumn(ColumnVector cv, int c)
        throws MatrixException
    {
        super.setColumn(cv, c);
        reset();
    }

    /**
     * Reset. Invalidate LU and the permutation vector.
     */
    protected void reset()
    {
        LU            = null;
        permutation   = null;
        exchangeCount = 0;
    }

    /**
     * Solve Ax = b for x using the Gaussian elimination algorithm.
     * @param b the right-hand-side column vector
     * @param improve true to improve the solution
     * @return the solution column vector
     * @throws matrix.MatrixException if an error occurred
     */
    public ColumnVector solve(ColumnVector b, boolean improve)
        throws MatrixException
    {
        // Validate b's size.
        if (b.nRows != nRows) {
            throw new MatrixException(
                            MatrixException.INVALID_DIMENSIONS);
        }

        decompose();

        // Solve Ly = b for y by forward substitution.
        // Solve Ux = y for x by back substitution.
        ColumnVector y = forwardSubstitution(b);
        ColumnVector x = backSubstitution(y);
```

```
        // Improve and return x.
        if (improve) improve(b, x);
        return x;
    }

    /**
     * Print the decomposed matrix LU.
     * @param width the column width
     * @throws matrix.MatrixException if an error occurred
     */
    public void printDecomposed(int width) throws MatrixException
    {
        decompose();

        AlignRight ar = new AlignRight();

        for (int r = 0; r < nRows; ++r) {
            int pr = permutation[r];    // permuted row index
            ar.print("Row ", 0); ar.print(r+1, 2); ar.print(":", 0);

            for (int c = 0; c < nCols; ++c) {
                ar.print(LU.values[pr][c], width);
            }
            ar.println();
        }
    }

    /**
     * Compute the upper triangular matrix U and lower triangular
     * matrix L such that A = L*U.  Store L and U together in
     * matrix LU.  Compute the permutation vector permutation of
     * the row indices.
     * @throws matrix.MatrixException for a zero row or
     *                                a singular matrix
     */
    protected void decompose() throws MatrixException
    {
        // Return if the decomposition is valid.
        if (LU != null) return;

        // Create a new LU matrix and permutation vector.
        // LU is initially just a copy of the values of this system.
        LU = new SquareMatrix(this.copyValues2D());
        permutation = new int[nRows];

        float scales[] = new float[nRows];
```

```
                // Loop to initialize the permutation vector and scales.
                for (int r = 0; r < nRows; ++r) {
                    permutation[r] = r;        // initially no row exchanges

                    // Find the largest row element.
                    float largestRowElmt = 0;
                    for (int c = 0; c < nRows; ++c) {
                        float elmt = Math.abs(LU.at(r, c));
                        if (largestRowElmt < elmt) largestRowElmt = elmt;
                    }

                    // Set the scaling factor for row equilibration.
                    if (largestRowElmt != 0) {
                        scales[r] = 1/largestRowElmt;
                    }
                    else {
                        throw new MatrixException(MatrixException.ZERO_ROW);
                    }
                }


            // Do forward elimination with scaled partial row pivoting.
            forwardElimination(scales);

            // Check bottom right element of the permuted matrix.
            if (LU.at(permutation[nRows - 1], nRows - 1) == 0) {
                throw new MatrixException(MatrixException.SINGULAR);
            }
    }


    /**
     * Do forward elimination with scaled partial row pivoting.
     * @parm scales the scaling vector
     * @throws matrix.MatrixException for a singular matrix
     */
    private void forwardElimination(float scales[])
        throws MatrixException
    {
        // Loop once per pivot row 0..nRows-1.
        for (int rPivot = 0; rPivot < nRows - 1; ++rPivot) {
            float largestScaledElmt = 0;
            int   rLargest          = 0;

            // Starting from the pivot row rPivot, look down
            // column rPivot to find the largest scaled element.
            for (int r = rPivot; r < nRows; ++r) {
```

```
    // Use the permuted row index.
    int   pr        = permutation[r];
    float absElmt    = Math.abs(LU.at(pr, rPivot));
    float scaledElmt = absElmt*scales[pr];

    if (largestScaledElmt < scaledElmt) {

        // The largest scaled element and
        // its row index.
        largestScaledElmt = scaledElmt;
        rLargest          = r;
    }
}

// Is the matrix singular?
if (largestScaledElmt == 0) {
    throw new MatrixException(MatrixException.SINGULAR);
}

// Exchange rows if necessary to choose the best
// pivot element by making its row the pivot row.
if (rLargest != rPivot) {
    int temp                = permutation[rPivot];
    permutation[rPivot]    = permutation[rLargest];
    permutation[rLargest] = temp;

    ++exchangeCount;
}

// Use the permuted pivot row index.
int   prPivot   = permutation[rPivot];
float pivotElmt = LU.at(prPivot, rPivot);

// Do the elimination below the pivot row.
for (int r = rPivot + 1; r < nRows; ++r) {

    // Use the permuted row index.
    int   pr        = permutation[r];
    float multiple = LU.at(pr, rPivot)/pivotElmt;

    // Set the multiple into matrix L.
    LU.set(pr, rPivot, multiple);

    // Eliminate an unknown from matrix U.
    if (multiple != 0) {
        for (int c = rPivot + 1; c < nCols; ++c) {
            float elmt = LU.at(pr, c);

            // Subtract the multiple of the pivot row.
            elmt -= multiple*LU.at(prPivot, c);
```

```
                            LU.set(pr, c, elmt);
                        }
                    }
                }
            }
        }


    /**
     * Solve Ly = b for y by forward substitution.
     * @param b the column vector b
     * @return the column vector y
     * @throws matrix.MatrixException if an error occurred
     */
    private ColumnVector forwardSubstitution(ColumnVector b)
        throws MatrixException
    {
        ColumnVector y = new ColumnVector(nRows);

        // Do forward substitution.
        for (int r = 0; r < nRows; ++r) {
            int   pr = permutation[r];       // permuted row index
            float dot = 0;
            for (int c = 0; c < r; ++c) {
                dot += LU.at(pr, c)*y.at(c);
            }
            y.set(r, b.at(pr) - dot);
        }

        return y;
    }

    /**
     * Solve Ux = y for x by back substitution.
     * @param y the column vector y
     * @return the solution column vector x
     * @throws matrix.MatrixException if an error occurred
     */
    private ColumnVector backSubstitution(ColumnVector y)
        throws MatrixException
    {
        ColumnVector x = new ColumnVector(nRows);

        // Do back substitution.
        for (int r = nRows - 1; r >= 0; --r) {
            int   pr = permutation[r];       // permuted row index
            float dot = 0;
            for (int c = r+1; c < nRows; ++c) {
                dot += LU.at(pr, c)*x.at(c);
            }
```

```
            x.set(r, (y.at(r) - dot)/LU.at(pr, r));
        }

        return x;
    }

    /**
     * Iteratively improve the solution x to machine accuracy.
     * @param b the right-hand side column vector
     * @param x the improved solution column vector
     * @throws matrix.MatrixException if failed to converge
     */
    private void improve(ColumnVector b, ColumnVector x)
        throws MatrixException
    {
        // Find the largest x element.
        float largestX = 0;
        for (int r = 0; r < nRows; ++r) {
            float absX = Math.abs(x.values[r][0]);
            if (largestX < absX) largestX = absX;
        }

        // Is x already as good as possible?
        if (largestX == 0) return;

        ColumnVector residuals = new ColumnVector(nRows);
        // Iterate to improve x.
        for (int iter = 0; iter < MAX_ITER; ++iter) {

            // Compute residuals = b - Ax.
            // Must use double precision!
            for (int r = 0; r < nRows; ++r) {
                double dot    = 0;
                float  row[] = values[r];
                for (int c = 0; c < nRows; ++c) {
                    double elmt = at(r, c);
                    dot += elmt*x.at(c);         // dbl.prec. *
                }
                double value = b.at(r) - dot;   // dbl.prec. -
                residuals.set(r, (float) value);
            }

            // Solve Az = residuals for z.
            ColumnVector z = solve(residuals, false);

            // Set x = x + z.
            // Find largest the largest difference.
            float largestDiff = 0;
            for (int r = 0; r < nRows; ++r) {
```

```
            float oldX = x.at(r);
            x.set(r, oldX + z.at(r));

            float diff = Math.abs(x.at(r) - oldX);
            if (largestDiff < diff) largestDiff = diff;
        }

        // Is any further improvement possible?
        if (largestDiff < largestX*TOLERANCE) return;
    }

    // Failed to converge because A is nearly singular.
    throw new MatrixException(MatrixException.NO_CONVERGENCE);
    }
}
```

Public method `solve()` returns a solution `ColumnVector` for a `ColumnVector` parameter b, assuming there were no exceptions, such as singularity. It calls method `decompose()`, `forwardSubstitution()`, and `backSubstitution()`. It calls method `improve()` to iteratively improve the solution vector x if the boolean parameter `improve` is true, and then it returns x.

Method `decompose()` computes the values of the decomposed matrix LU. This matrix is not recomputed unless any coefficient value of matrix *A* was changed by a call to method `set()`, `setRow()`, or `setColumn()`. Method `decompose()` calls method `forward-Elimination()`.

Method `improve()` uses double-precision arithmetic to compute the residual values, whose accuracy is crucial to ensure convergence. It iterates at most MAX_ITER times, which is statically computed to be twice the number of significant digits.

10.8 A Program to Test LU Decomposition

Listing 10–1 shows Program 10–1, which tests class `LinearSystem` by solving a randomly generated system of linear equations.

Listing 10–1 A program to test solving a system of linear equations by LU decomposition.

```
package numbercruncher.program10_1;

import java.util.Random;
import numbercruncher.matrix.LinearSystem;
import numbercruncher.matrix.ColumnVector;
import numbercruncher.matrix.MatrixException;

/**
 * PROGRAM 10-1: Test class LinearSystem by solving
```

```
 *                 a "random" system of linear equations.
 */
public class TestLinearSystem
{
    /**
     * Run the test.
     * @param correct the known correct solution vector
     * @throws matrix.MatrixException if an error occurred
     */
    private void run(ColumnVector correct) throws MatrixException
    {
        int    n      = correct.size();        // # of equations
        Random random = new Random(0);         // random # generator

        LinearSystem A = new LinearSystem(n);  // matrix A
        ColumnVector b = new ColumnVector(n);  // vector b

        // Randomly generate the values of matrix A
        // between -10 and 10.
        for (int r = 0; r < n; ++r) {
            for (int c = 0; c < n; ++c) {
                A.set(r, c, 20*random.nextFloat() - 10);
            }
        }

        // Compute the values of vector b using the correct solution.
        for (int r = 0; r < n; ++r) {
            float dot = 0;
            for (int c = 0; c < n; ++c) {
                dot += A.at(r, c)*correct.at(c);
            }
            b.set(r, dot);
        }

        System.out.println("Coefficient matrix A");
        A.print(13);

        System.out.print("\nb =");
        b.print();

        // Solve the system with iterative improvement.
        ColumnVector x = A.solve(b, true);

        System.out.println("\nDecomposed matrix LU");
        A.printDecomposed(13);

        System.out.print("\nx =");
        x.print();
```

```java
            // Compute the error vector and print its norm.
            System.out.println("Error vector norm = " +
                                x.subtract(correct).norm());
    }

    /**
     * Main.
     * @param args the array of arguments
     */
    public static void main(String args[])
    {
        // The known correct solution.
        ColumnVector correct =
                    new ColumnVector(new float[] {1, 2, 3, 4, 5});

        TestLinearSystem test = new TestLinearSystem();

        try {
            test.run(correct);
        }
        catch(MatrixException ex) {
            System.out.println("*** ERROR: " + ex.getMessage());
            ex.printStackTrace();
        }
    }
}
```

Output:

```
Coefficient matrix A
Row  1:     4.619355     6.6288204    -5.189272     2.1269035    2.7483473
Row  2:    -3.8189888    1.0087395    -7.6598682    1.9509048    5.6306925
Row  3:    -3.3356323   -4.944477     -2.2962165    2.2607145    9.696831
Row  4:     9.656389     7.5836506    -9.538363     8.824982    -6.480465
Row  5:    -4.500921    -3.741281     -7.422057    -2.6404858   -7.0679674

b =  24.558529  11.175966  37.413776  -0.8937969  -80.15143

Decomposed matrix LU
Row  1:     9.656389     7.5836506    -9.538363     8.824982    -6.480465
Row  2:    -0.3954883    4.007984    -11.432179     5.441082     3.0677445
Row  3:    -0.46610805  -0.051517297  -12.456921    1.7532192   -9.930522
Row  4:     0.47837293   0.7487573    -0.63687897  -5.0521903   -2.7731104
Row  5:    -0.34543267  -0.5800513     0.9811678   -1.3350756   15.278912

x =  1.0000005  1.9999993  2.9999995  3.9999998  5.0
Error vector norm = 1.0115243E-6
```

The program generates a random set of coefficients for matrix A. (It actually generates the same "random" values each time.) Then, using the known correct solution, it generates the values of vector b and then solves for vector x. We can see that, for these five equations, the norm of the error vector is very small.

10.9 Polynomial Regression

In Chapter 6, we started with the error function for the least-squares regression line:

$$E(a_0, a_1) = \sum (y_i - a_0 - a_1 x_i)^2$$

We differentiated this equation twice, first with respect to the unknown coefficient a_0 and then with respect to the unknown coefficient a_1. We set both derivatives to zero to arrive at the normal equations

$$na_0 + \left(\sum x_i\right)a_1 = \sum y_i$$
$$\left(\sum x_i\right)a_0 + \left(\sum x_i^2\right)a_1 = \sum x_i y_i$$

which we could solve by simple substitution.

Now that we've written a class that solves systems of equations, we can compute the coefficients of regression polynomials with higher degrees. For example, a second-degree regression parabola has the error function

$$E(a_0, a_1, a_2) = \sum (y_i - a_0 - a_1 x_i - a_2 x_i^2)^2$$

By differentiating with respect to a_0, a_1, and a_2 and setting the derivatives to zero, we get (after the usual algebraic manipulations) the system of three normal equations

$$na_0 + \left(\sum x_i\right)a_1 + \left(\sum x_i^2\right)a_2 = \sum y_i$$
$$\left(\sum x_i\right)a_0 + \left(\sum x_i^2\right)a_1 + \left(\sum x_i^3\right)a_2 = \sum x_i y_i$$
$$\left(\sum x_i^2\right)a_0 + \left(\sum x_i^3\right)a_1 + \left(\sum x_i^4\right)a_2 = \sum x_i^2 y_i$$

We can see a pattern emerging! Note that, in the multiplier for a_0 of each equation, the exponent of x_i is the row index 0, 1, or 2, and the same exponent for x_i appears in the right-hand-side value. (In the first equation, $\left(\sum x_i^0\right)a_0 = \left(\sum 1\right)a_0 = na_0$ and $\sum x_i^0 y_i = \sum 1 y_i = \sum y_i$). Subsequent x_i exponents within an equation are each one greater than the previous one. Also, note how the multipliers for the a_i repeat themselves along the diagonals running from lower left to upper right.

In general, if we want to fit an nth-degree polynomial to a set of at least $n+1$ data points, the error function is

$$E(a_0, a_1, a_2, \ldots, a_n) = \sum (y_i - a_0 - a_1 x_i - a_2 x_i^2 - \ldots - a_n x_i^n)^2$$

and in the resulting system of normal equations, the rth equation ($r = 0$ through n) has the form

$$\sum_{c=0}^{n}\left[\left(\sum x_i^{\,r+c}\right)a_c\right] = \sum x_i^{\,r}\, y_i$$

Note that, in this linear system, the unknowns are the a_i, and the x_i are data points used to compute the coefficients of the equations.

Class `RegressionPolynomial` in package `numbercruncher.mathutils` is analogous to the class `RegressionLine`, which we saw in Chapter 6. See Listing 10–2a.

Listing 10–2a Class `RegressionPolynomial`.

```
package numbercruncher.mathutils;

import numbercruncher.mathutils.IntPower;
import numbercruncher.matrix.LinearSystem;
import numbercruncher.matrix.ColumnVector;
import numbercruncher.matrix.MatrixException;

/**
 * A least-squares regression polynomial function.
 */
public class RegressionPolynomial implements Evaluatable
{
    /** number of data points */        private int     n;
    /** degree of the polynomial */     private int     degree;
    /** maximum no. of data points */   private int     maxPoints;
    /** true if coefficients valid */   private boolean coefsValid;
    /** warning message */              private String  warningMsg;

    /** data points */                  private DataPoint data[];

    /** coefficient matrix A */             private LinearSystem A;
    /** regression coefficients vector a */ private ColumnVector a;
    /** right-hand-side vector b */          private ColumnVector b;

    /**
     * Constructor.
     * @param degree the degree of the polynomial
     * @param maxPoints the maximum number of data points
     */
    public RegressionPolynomial(int degree, int maxPoints)
    {
        this.degree    = degree;
        this.maxPoints = maxPoints;
        this.data      = new DataPoint[maxPoints];
    }
```

```
/**
 * Constructor.
 * @param degree the degree of the polynomial
 * @param data the array of data points
 */
public RegressionPolynomial(int degree, DataPoint data[])
{
    this.degree    = degree;
    this.maxPoints = maxPoints;
    this.data      = data;
    this.n         = data.length;
}

/**
 * Return the degree of the polynomial.
 * @return the count
 */
public int getDegree() { return degree; }

/**
 * Return the current number of data points.
 * @return the count
 */
public int getDataPointCount() { return n; }

/**
 * Return the data points.
 * @return the count
 */
public DataPoint[] getDataPoints() { return data; }

/**
 * Return the coefficients matrix.
 * @return the A matrix
 * @throws matrix.MatrixException if a matrix error occurred
 * @throws Exception if an overflow occurred
 */
public LinearSystem getCoefficientsMatrix()
    throws Exception, MatrixException
{
    validateCoefficients();
    return A;
}

/**
 * Return the regression coefficients.
 * @return the a vector
 * @throws matrix.MatrixException if a matrix error occurred
 * @throws Exception if an overflow occurred
 */
```

```
public ColumnVector getRegressionCoefficients()
    throws Exception, MatrixException
{
    validateCoefficients();
    return a;
}

/**
 * Return the right hand side.
 * @return the b vector
 * @throws matrix.MatrixException if a matrix error occurred
 * @throws Exception if an overflow occurred
 */
public ColumnVector getRHS() throws Exception, MatrixException
{
    validateCoefficients();
    return b;
}

/**
 * Return the warning message (if any).
 * @return the message or null
 */
public String getWarningMessage() { return warningMsg; }

/**
 * Add a new data point: Update the sums.
 * @param dataPoint the new data point
 */
public void addDataPoint(DataPoint dataPoint)
{
    if (n == maxPoints) return;

    data[n++] = dataPoint;
    coefsValid = false;
}

/**
 * Return the value of the regression polynomial function at x.
 * (Implementation of Evaluatable.)
 * @param x the value of x
 * @return the value of the function at x
 */
public float at(float x)
{
    if (n < degree + 1) return Float.NaN;

    try {
        validateCoefficients();
```

```
            float xPower = 1;
            float y      = 0;

            // Compute y = a[0] + a[1]*x + a[2]*x^2 + ... + a[n]*x^n
            for (int i = 0; i <= degree; ++i) {
                y += a.at(i)*xPower;
                xPower *= x;
            }

            return y;
        }
        catch(MatrixException ex) {
            return Float.NaN;
        }
        catch(Exception ex) {
            return Float.NaN;
        }
    }

    /**
     * Reset.
     */
    public void reset()
    {
        n    = 0;
        data = new DataPoint[maxPoints];
        coefsValid = false;
    }

    /**
     * Compute the coefficients.
     * @throws matrix.MatrixException if a matrix error occurred
     * @throws Exception if an overflow occurred
     */
    public void computeCoefficients()
        throws Exception, MatrixException
    {
        validateCoefficients();
    }

    /**
     * Validate the coefficients.
     * @throws matrix.MatrixException if a matrix error occurred
     * @throws Exception if an overflow occurred
     */
    private void validateCoefficients()
        throws Exception, MatrixException
    {
        if (coefsValid) return;
```

```
    A = new LinearSystem(degree + 1);
    b = new ColumnVector(degree + 1);

    // Compute the multipliers of a[0] for each equation.
    for (int r = 0; r <= degree; ++r) {
        float sum = sumXPower(r);
        int    j   = 0;

        if (Float.isInfinite(sum)) {
            throw new Exception("Overflow occurred.");
        }

        // Set the multipliers along the diagonal.
        for (int i = r; i >= 0; --i) A.set(i, j++, sum);

        // Set the right-hand-side value.
        b.set(r, sumXPowerY(r));
    }

    // Compute the multipliers of a[c] for the last equation.
    for (int c = 1; c <= degree; ++c) {
        float sum = sumXPower(degree + c);
        int    i   = degree;

        if (Float.isInfinite(sum)) {
            throw new Exception("Overflow occurred.");
        }

        // Set the multipliers along the diagonal.
        for (int j = c; j <= degree; ++j) A.set(i--, j, sum);
    }

    warningMsg = null;

    // First try solving with iterative improvement.  If that
    // fails, then try solving without iterative improvement.
    try {
        a = A.solve(b, true);
    }
    catch(MatrixException ex) {
        warningMsg = ex.getMessage();
        a = A.solve(b, false);
    }

    coefsValid = true;
}

/**
 * Compute the sum of the x coordinates each raised
```

```
     * to an integer power.
     * @return the sum
     */
    private float sumXPower(int power)
    {
        float sum = 0;

        for (int i = 0; i < n; ++i) {
            sum += (float) IntPower.raise(data[i].x, power);
        }

        return sum;
    }

    /**
     * Compute the sum of the x coordinates each raised to an integer
     * power and multiplied by the corresponding y coordinate.
     * @return the sum
     */
    private float sumXPowerY(int power)
    {
        float sum = 0;

        for (int i = 0; i < n; ++i) {
            sum += (float) data[i].y*IntPower.raise(data[i].x, power);
        }

        return sum;
    }
}
```

This class keeps all the data points in array `data`. Method `addDataPoint()` appends a new data point to the array. `LinearSystem` A stores the values of the normal equations (the sums of the powers of the x coordinates), `ColumnVector` a stores the values of the unknown regression coefficients a_i, and `ColumnVector` b stores the right-hand-side values. In other words, we will be solving the system $Aa = b$ for a. Method `getRegressionCoefficients()` computes and returns `ColumnVector` a.

Method `validateCoefficients()` computes the values for A and b. It first tries solving for a with iterative improvement. The computations are especially prone to overflow with higher degrees, so there are special checks for that. If A is nearly singular (which can happen at higher degrees and a low number of data points), iterative improvement will fail to converge. In that case, the method tries solving for a again but without iterative improvement—the resulting regression polynomial will be less accurate. Method `at()` computes the value of the regression polynomial for a given value of x.

The noninteractive version of Program 10–2 creates 20 points along the sine wave from 0 to 2π. It creates a 3rd-degree regression polynomial for the data points, and then it uses the polynomial to estimate the value of sin π, which should be zero. See Listing 10–2b.

Listing 10–2b The noninteractive version of Program 10–2.

```
package numbercruncher.program10_2;

import numbercruncher.mathutils.DataPoint;
import numbercruncher.mathutils.RegressionPolynomial;
import numbercruncher.matrix.ColumnVector;
import numbercruncher.matrix.MatrixException;

/**
 * PROGRAM 10-2: Polynomial Regression
 *
 * Demonstrate polynomial regression by fitting a polynomial
 * to a set of data points.
 */
public class Regression
{
    private static final int   MAX_POINTS = 20;
    private static final float TWO_PI     = (float) (2*Math.PI);
    private static final float H          = TWO_PI/MAX_POINTS;

    /**
     * Main program.
     * @param args the array of runtime arguments
     */
    public static void main(String args[])
    {
        int   degree = 3;
        float testX  = (float) Math.PI;

        try {
            RegressionPolynomial poly =
                    new RegressionPolynomial(degree, MAX_POINTS);

            // Compute MAX_POINTS data points along the sine curve
            // between 0 and 2*pi.
            for (int i = 0; i < MAX_POINTS; ++i) {
                float x = i*H;
                float y = (float) Math.sin(x);
                poly.addDataPoint(new DataPoint(x, y));
            }
```

```
                // Compute and print the regression polynomial.
                System.out.print("y = ");
                ColumnVector a = poly.getRegressionCoefficients();
                System.out.print(a.at(0) + " + " + a.at(1) + "x");
                for (int i = 2; i <= degree; ++i) {
                    System.out.print(" + " + a.at(i) + "x^" + i);
                }
                System.out.println();

                // Compute an estimate.
                System.out.println("y(" + testX + ") = " +
                                   poly.at(testX));

                // Print the warning if there is one.
                String warning = poly.getWarningMessage();
                if (warning != null) {
                    System.out.println("WARNING: " + warning);
                }
            }
            catch(Exception ex) {
                System.out.println("\nERROR: " + ex.getMessage());
            }
        }
    }
}
```

Output

```
y = -0.14296114 + 1.8568094x + -0.87079257x^2 + 0.09318722x^3
y(3.1415927) = -0.014611721
```

The interactive version[1] of Program 10–2 allows you to plot up to 100 data points with mouse clicks and then create and plot a regression polynomial of degree 1 through 9 among the data points. Screen 10–2 shows screen shots of regression polynomials of various degrees within the same set of data points.

Just as we saw with the interpolation polynomial in Chapter 6, higher degree regression polynomials can have erratic behavior outside of the domain of the data points.

---

[1]   Each interactive program in this book has two versions, an applet and a standalone application. You can download all the Java source code. See the downloading instructions in the preface of this book.

Screen 10–2 Regression polynomials of degree 1, 4, and 9 within the same set of data points.

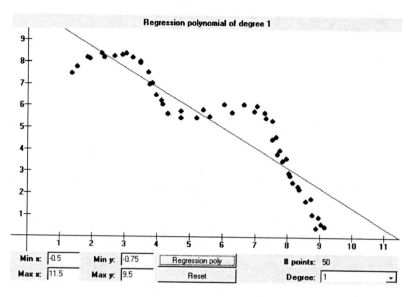

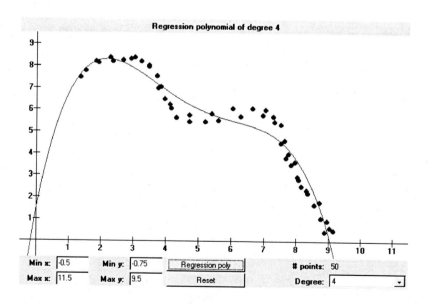

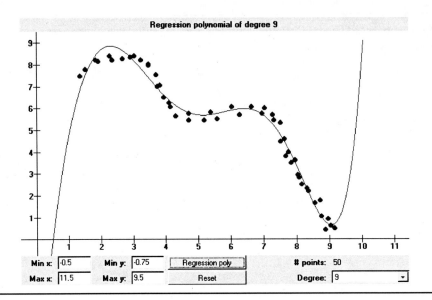

References

Atkinson, L.V., and P.J. Harley, *An Introduction to Numerical Methods with Pascal,* London: Addison-Wesley, 1983.

Chapra, Seven C., and Raymond P. Canale, *Numerical Methods for Engineers,* 3rd edition, New York: WCB/McGraw-Hill, 1998.

   Polynomial regression is discussed by Chapra and Canale in Section 17.2.

Cheny, Ward, and David Kincaid, *Numerical Mathematics and Computing,* 4th edition, Pacific Grove, CA: Brooks/Cole, 1999.

Forsythe, George, Michael A. Malcolm, and Cleve B. Moler, *Computer Methods for Mathematical Computations,* Englewood Cliffs, NJ: Prentice-Hall, 1977.

   Forsythe is the classic reference for solving systems of linear equations using LU decomposition. It contains a constructive proof that matrix *A* can be factored into matrices *L* and *U,* as well as error analyses of the algorithms. It has program listings in Algol, FORTRAN, and PL/I.

       For more contemporary textbooks that describe Gaussian elimination and LU decomposition, see Chapra and Canale, Sections 9.1–9.4 and 10.1; Cheney and Kincaid, Sections 6.1 and 6.2; Woodford and Phillips, in Chapter 1; Atkinson and Harley, Chapter 4; and Scheid, Chapter 26.

Monahan, John F., *Numerical Methods of Statistics,* Cambridge, UK: Cambridge University Press, 2001.

   Monahan provides advanced coverage of polynomial regression in Chapter 5.

Scheid, Francis, *Numerical Analysis,* New York: McGraw-Hill, 1988.

Woodford, C., and C. Phillips, *Numerical Methods with Worked Examples,* London: Chapman and Hall, 1997.

Woodford and Phillips discuss polynomial regression in Section 3.4.2.

CHAPTER 11

MATRIX INVERSION, DETERMINANTS, AND CONDITION NUMBERS

L U decomposition, as described in Chapter 10, not only allows us to solve a system of linear equations, but the algorithm makes it relatively simple to compute a square matrix's inverse and determinant. In this chapter, we'll also compute the matrix's *condition number,* a scalar value that indicates how well-conditioned (or ill-conditioned) is the system of linear equations represented by the matrix.

A matrix's inverse and its determinant are both used in two traditional algorithms for solving systems of equations. If we have the system $Ax = b$ to solve for x, we can use matrix algebra and multiply both sides of the equation by A^{-1}, the inverse of A, giving us $x = A^{-1}b$. The other algorithm, called *Cramer's rule,* uses determinants to solve for x. These algorithms are now mostly of historical interest only, because LU decomposition followed by forward and back substitution is superior.

Certain engineering and statistical applications do require the computation of a matrix's inverse, so it is still useful to know how to compute it.

11.1 The Determinant

Once a square matrix A has been decomposed into matrices L and U, the determinant of A is the product of the diagonal elements of U. However, each row exchange that we do for partial pivoting during the decomposition flips the sign of the determinant:

$$\det A = (-1)^k \times u_{0,0} \times u_{1,1} \times \ldots \times u_{n,n}$$

In class `LinearSystem` of package `numbercruncher.matrix` (see Listing 10–0 in Chapter 10), variable `exchangeCount` keeps track of the number of row exchanges, and if this value is odd, we need to negate the value of the product of the diagonal elements of `LU`.

Using LU decomposition is a much more efficient way to compute a determinant than the traditional way, especially for larger matrices. The traditional way, expansion by cofactors, is actually a recursive algorithm.

11.2 The Inverse

We can use the LU decomposition algorithm to compute the inverse of square matrix A column by column. Each column j is the solution of the system $Ax = i_j$, where i_j is the jth column of the identity matrix I, since $AA^{-1} = I$.

This is actually an efficient way to compute the inverse. We need to decompose matrix A only once. Then, we can solve each system $Ax = i_j$ using forward substitution and back substitution.

For example, if A is a 3×3 matrix, then the second column of A^{-1} is the solution x of the system

$$Ax = \begin{bmatrix} 0 \\ 1 \\ 0 \end{bmatrix}$$

11.3 The Norm and the Condition Number

How do we measure how well-conditioned or ill-conditioned is a system of linear equations? In Chapter 10, we said that the solution to an ill-conditioned system is very sensitive to changes (perhaps due to roundoff errors) in the values of the coefficients.

The *condition number* of the system's coefficient matrix A is defined to be

$$\text{cond } A = \|A\| \times \|A^{-1}\|$$

where $\|A\|$ is the norm of the matrix A, and $\|A^{-1}\|$ is the norm of its inverse. The Euclidean norm of any square matrix A is the square root of the sum of the squares of all its elements:

$$\|A\| = \sqrt{\sum_i \sum_j a_{i,j}^2}$$

A well-conditioned system has a "small" condition number, and an ill-conditioned matrix has a "large" condition number. This is a somewhat fuzzy measure—there are no hard and fast rules about how small a condition number must be before we can say for sure that a system is well-conditioned, and how large a condition number must be before we can say for sure that a system is ill-conditioned. We can use the number to compare the condition of two similarly sized systems. We'll see some examples of this in the following paragraphs.

For example, the norm of the 3×3 identity matrix I_3 is $\|I_3\| = \sqrt{3}$. Since $I_3^{-1} = I_3$,

$$\text{cond}\, I_3 = \|I_3\| \times \|I_3^{-1}\| = \sqrt{3} \times \sqrt{3} = 3$$

which is considered small, and, indeed, an identity matrix is extremely well-conditioned.

Note that the condition number of a matrix is somewhat expensive to compute, since it requires computing the inverse of the matrix.

11.4 The Invertible Matrix Class

Listing 11–0 shows class `InvertibleMatrix` in package `numbercruncher.matrix`. This is a subclass of `LinearSystem`, and we add methods to compute the inverse of the matrix, its determinant, its norm, and its condition number.

Listing 11–0 Class `InvertibleMatrix`.

```
package numbercruncher.matrix;

import numbercruncher.mathutils.Epsilon;

/**
 * A matrix that can be inverted.  Also, compute its determinant,
 * norm, and condition number.
 */
public class InvertibleMatrix extends LinearSystem
{
    /**
     * Constructor.
     * @param n the number of rows = the number of columns
     */
    public InvertibleMatrix(int n) { super(n); }

    /**
     * Constructor.
     * @param values the array of values
     */
    public InvertibleMatrix(float values[][]) { super(values); }

    /**
     * Compute the inverse of this matrix.
     * @return the inverse matrix
     * @throws matrix.MatrixException if an error occurred
     */
    public InvertibleMatrix inverse() throws MatrixException
    {
        InvertibleMatrix inverse  = new InvertibleMatrix(nRows);
        IdentityMatrix    identity = new IdentityMatrix(nRows);
```

```
        // Compute each column of the inverse matrix
        // using columns of the identity matrix.
        for (int c = 0; c < nCols; ++c) {
            ColumnVector col = solve(identity.getColumn(c), true);
            inverse.setColumn(col, c);

        }

        return inverse;
    }

    /**
     * Compute the determinant.
     * @return the determinant
     * @throws matrix.MatrixException if an error occurred
     */
    public float determinant() throws MatrixException
    {
        decompose();

        // Each row exchange during forward elimination flips the sign
        // of the determinant, so check for an odd number of exchanges.
        float determinant = ((exchangeCount & 1) == 0) ? 1 : -1;

        // Form the product of the diagonal elements of matrix U.
        for (int i = 0; i < nRows; ++i) {
            int pi = permutation[i];        // permuted index
            determinant *= LU.at(pi, i);
        }

        return determinant;
    }

    /**
     * Compute the Euclidean norm of this matrix.
     * @return the norm
     */
    public float norm()
    {
        float sum = 0;

        for (int r = 0; r < nRows; ++r) {
            for (int c = 0; c < nCols; ++c) {
                float v = values[r][c];
                sum += v*v;
            }

        }
```

```
       return (float) Math.sqrt(sum);
   }


   /**
    * Compute the condition number based on the Euclidean norm.
    * @return the condition number
    */
   public float condition() throws MatrixException
   {
       return norm() * inverse().norm();
   }
}
```

Using the algorithm described in Section 11.2 method `inverse()` computes the columns of the matrix inverse. It repeatedly solves the system with the corresponding columns of the appropriate identity matrix as the right-hand side.

Method `determinant()` forms the product of the diagonal elements of LU. It obtains diagonal elements via the permutation vector. If the number of row exchanges during decomposition was odd, it negates the product.

Method `norm()` computes and returns the Euclidean norm of the matrix, and matrix `condition()` computes and returns its condition number.

11.5 Hilbert Matrices

Program 11–1 exercises our ability to compute the inverse of a matrix with a Hilbert matrix. A Hilbert matrix H_n is a square $n \times n$ matrix whose elements are defined as

$$h_{i,j} = \frac{1}{i + j + 1}$$

For example,

$$H_4 = \begin{bmatrix} 1 & \frac{1}{2} & \frac{1}{3} & \frac{1}{4} \\ \frac{1}{2} & \frac{1}{3} & \frac{1}{4} & \frac{1}{5} \\ \frac{1}{3} & \frac{1}{4} & \frac{1}{5} & \frac{1}{6} \\ \frac{1}{4} & \frac{1}{5} & \frac{1}{6} & \frac{1}{7} \end{bmatrix}$$

It turns out that Hilbert matrices are extremely ill-conditioned with very high condition numbers; therefore, they are notoriously difficult to invert accurately. Program 11–1 demonstrates this with the 4 × 4 Hilbert matrix. See Listing 11–1.

Listing 11–1   Demonstrate the matrix inversion algorithm with a Hilbert matrix.

```
package numbercruncher.program11_1;

import numbercruncher.matrix.*;

/**
 * PROGRAM 11-1: Hilbert Matrices
 *
 * Test the matrix inverter with a Hilbert matrix.  Hilbert matrices are
 * ill-conditioned and difficult to invert accurately.
 */
public class HilbertMatrix
{
    private static final int RANK = 4;

    private void run(int rank) throws MatrixException
    {
        System.out.println("Hilbert matrix of rank " + rank);
        InvertibleMatrix H = new InvertibleMatrix(rank);

        // Compute the Hilbert matrix.
        for (int r = 0; r < rank; ++r) {
            for (int c = 0; c < rank; ++c) {
                H.set(r, c, 1.0f/(r + c + 1));
            }
        }
        H.print(15);

        // Invert the Hilbert matrix.
        InvertibleMatrix Hinv = H.inverse();
        System.out.println("\nHilbert matrix inverted");
        Hinv.print(15);

        System.out.println(""\nHilbert matrix condition number = " +
                        H.norm()*Hinv.norm());

        // Invert the inverse.
        InvertibleMatrix HinvInv = Hinv.inverse();
        System.out.println("\nInverse matrix inverted");
        HinvInv.print(15);

        // Multiply P = H*Hinv.
        System.out.println("\nHilbert matrix times its inverse " +
                        "(should be identity)");
        SquareMatrix P = H.multiply(Hinv);
        P.print(15);
```

```
            // Average norm of P's rows.
            float normSum = 0;
            for (int r = 0; r < rank; ++r) {
                normSum += P.getRow(r).norm();
            }
            System.out.println("\nAverage row norm = " + normSum/rank +
                                    " (should be 1)");
        }

        /**
         * Main.
         * @param args the array of arguments
         */
        public static void main(String args[])
        {
            HilbertMatrix test = new HilbertMatrix();

            try {
                test.run(RANK);
            }
            catch(MatrixException ex) {
                System.out.println("*** ERROR: " + ex.getMessage());
                ex.printStackTrace();
            }
        }
    }
```

Output:

```
Hilbert matrix of rank 4
Row   1:            1.0              0.5       0.33333334            0.25
Row   2:            0.5       0.33333334             0.25             0.2
Row   3:     0.33333334             0.25              0.2      0.16666667
Row   4:           0.25              0.2       0.16666667      0.14285715

Hilbert matrix inverted
Row   1:      15.999718        -119.9972        239.99367       -139.99605
Row   2:      -119.9972        1199.9725       -2699.9382        1679.9615
Row   3:      239.99367       -2699.9382         6479.862        -4199.914
Row   4:     -139.99605        1679.9615        -4199.914        2799.9465

Hilbert matrix condition number = 15613.463

Inverse matrix inverted
Row   1:      0.9999907       0.49999347       0.33332846       0.24999614
Row   2:     0.49999347       0.33332878        0.2499966       0.19999732
Row   3:     0.33332846        0.2499966       0.19999747       0.16666469
Row   4:     0.24999614       0.19999732       0.16666469       0.14285558
```

```
Hilbert matrix times its inverse (should be identity)
Row  1:             1.0    3.0517578E-5   1.2207031E-4   -6.1035156E-5
Row  2:   -3.8146973E-6            1.0            0.0    -6.1035156E-5
Row  3:   -3.8146973E-6            0.0            1.0    -3.0517578E-5
Row  4:             0.0    1.5258789E-5   6.1035156E-5      0.99993896

Average row norm = 0.99998474 (should be 1)
```

As we can see from the output, although all the elements of H_4 are less than or equal to 1, the elements of its inverse can be several orders of magnitude larger. The condition number of H_4 is nearly 16,000, indicating that it is very ill-conditioned.

Because of their high condition numbers, we cannot reliably invert Hilbert matrices larger than 6×6 using single-precision arithmetic and LU decomposition.

11.6 Comparing Solution Algorithms

In Program 11–2, we return to our original system of linear equations from the beginning of Chapter 10:

$$3x_1 + x_2 - 5x_3 + 4x_4 = -18$$
$$2x_1 - 3x_2 + 3x_3 - 2x_4 = 19$$
$$5x_1 - 3x_2 + 4x_3 + x_4 = 22$$
$$-2x_1 + 4x_2 - 3x_3 - 3x_4 = -14$$

whose correct solution is $x_1 = 1$, $x_2 = -2$, $x_3 = 3$, and $x_4 = -1$. The program solves this system using LU decomposition followed by forward and back substitution. Then, to compare, it solves the system using the matrix inverse and by using determinants with Cramer's rule. See Listing 11–2.

Listing 11–2 Comparison of algorithms for solving a system of linear equations.

```java
package numbercruncher.program11_2;

import java.util.Random;
import numbercruncher.matrix.*;

/**
 * PROGRAM 11-2: Compare Solution Algorithms
 *
 * Compare algorithms for solving a system of linear equations.
 */
public class CompareSolutions
{
    /**
     * Run the test.
```

```
 * @param A the coefficient matrix
 * @param b the right-hand-side vector
 * @param correct the known correct solution vector
 * @throws matrix.MatrixException if an error occurred
 */
private void run(InvertibleMatrix A, ColumnVector b,
                 ColumnVector correct)
    throws MatrixException
{
    System.out.println("Coefficient matrix A");
    A.print(14);

    System.out.print("\nb =");
    b.print();

    // Solve the system using LU decomposition
    // with iterative improvement.
    ColumnVector x = A.solve(b, true);
    System.out.println("\nLU decomposition:");
    System.out.print("    x =");
    x.print();
    System.out.println("Error vector norm = " +
                       x.subtract(correct).norm());

    InvertibleMatrix Ainv = A.inverse();

    System.out.println("\nA inverse");
    Ainv.print(14);

    float detA  = A.determinant();
    float condA = A.norm()*Ainv.norm();

    // Solve the system by multiplying A-inverse by b.
    x = Ainv.multiply(b);
    System.out.println("\nMultiplication by inverse:");
    System.out.print("    x =");
    x.print();
    System.out.println("Error vector norm = " +
                       x.subtract(correct).norm());

    System.out.println("\n    Determinant of A = " + detA);
    System.out.println("Condition number of A = " + condA);

    int              nRows   = A.rowCount();
    InvertibleMatrix As[]    = new InvertibleMatrix[nRows];
    float            dets[]  = new float[nRows];

    // Loop to create matrices A(i) for Cramer's rule.
    for (int i = 0; i < nRows; ++i) {
```

```
        As[i] = new InvertibleMatrix(A.copyValues2D());
        As[i].setColumn(b, i);
        dets[i] = As[i].determinant();

        System.out.println("\nA[" + (i+1) + "], determinant = " +
                            dets[i]);
        As[i].print(14);
    }

    // Solve the system using Cramer's rule.
    x = new ColumnVector(nRows);
    for (int i = 0; i < nRows; ++i) x.set(i, dets[i]/detA);

    System.out.println("\nCramer's rule:");
    System.out.print("    x =");
    x.print();
    System.out.println("Error vector norm = " +
                        x.subtract(correct).norm());
}

/**
 * Main.
 * @param args the array of arguments
 */
public static void main(String args[])
{
    // Matrix A.
    InvertibleMatrix A = new InvertibleMatrix(new float[][] {
        { 3,  1, -5,  4},
        { 2, -3,  3, -2},
        { 5, -3,  4,  1},
        {-2,  4, -3, -5},
    });

    // Column vector b.
    ColumnVector b =
            new ColumnVector(new float[] {-18, 19, 22, -14});

    // The known correct solution.
    ColumnVector correct =
            new ColumnVector(new float[] {1, -2, 3, -1});

    CompareSolutions compare = new CompareSolutions();

    try {
        compare.run(A, b, correct);
    }
    catch(MatrixException ex) {
        System.out.println("*** ERROR: " + ex.getMessage());
```

```
                    ex.printStackTrace();
            }
        }
}
```

Output:

```
Coefficient matrix A
Row   1:             3.0                1.0             -5.0             4.0
Row   2:             2.0               -3.0              3.0            -2.0
Row   3:             5.0               -3.0              4.0             1.0
Row   4:            -2.0                4.0             -3.0            -5.0

b =   -18.0   19.0   22.0   -14.0

LU decomposition:
   x =   1.0   -2.0   3.0   -1.0
Error vector norm = 0.0

A inverse
Row   1:     0.08121827     -0.02538071      0.20812182      0.11675127
Row   2:    -0.12436548     -0.49238577      0.33756346      0.16497461
Row   3:    -0.19035533     -0.28426397      0.23096447      0.007614213
Row   4:    -0.017766498    -0.21319798      0.04822335     -0.11928934

Multiplication by inverse:
   x =   0.9999999   -1.9999995   2.9999998   -1.0000004
Error vector norm = 6.529362E-7

     Determinant of A = 394.00003
Condition number of A = 11.255114

A[1], determinant = 393.99997
Row   1:            -18.0               1.0             -5.0             4.0
Row   2:             19.0              -3.0              3.0            -2.0
Row   3:             22.0              -3.0              4.0             1.0
Row   4:            -14.0               4.0             -3.0            -5.0

A[2], determinant = -787.99994
Row   1:             3.0               -18.0            -5.0             4.0
Row   2:             2.0                19.0             3.0            -2.0
Row   3:             5.0                22.0             4.0             1.0
Row   4:            -2.0               -14.0            -3.0            -5.0

A[3], determinant = 1182.0
Row   1:             3.0                1.0             -18.0            4.0
Row   2:             2.0               -3.0              19.0           -2.0
Row   3:             5.0               -3.0              22.0            1.0
Row   4:            -2.0                4.0             -14.0           -5.0
```

```
A[4], determinant = -394.00003
Row  1:            3.0            1.0           -5.0          -18.0
Row  2:            2.0           -3.0            3.0           19.0
Row  3:            5.0           -3.0            4.0           22.0
Row  4:           -2.0            4.0           -3.0          -14.0

Cramer's rule:
   x =   0.9999998  -1.9999996  2.9999998  -1.0
Error vector norm = 4.6552717E-7
```

LU decomposition, followed by forward and back substitution, produced the exact solution. Computing $x = A^{-1}b$ introduced some errors, as did Cramer's rule.

Cramer's rule is computationally very expensive. First, we compute det A. Next, we create the matrices $A^{(1)}, A^{(2)}, \ldots, A^{(n)}$, where $A^{(1)}$ is matrix A with its first column replaced by b, $A^{(2)}$ is A with its second column replaced by b and so on. Then, we compute the determinant of each of the matrices $A^{(i)}$, which means we must perform LU decomposition on each of them. Finally, the solution is

$$x_1 = \frac{\det A^{(1)}}{\det A}$$

$$x_2 = \frac{\det A^{(2)}}{\det A}$$

$$\ldots$$

$$x_n = \frac{\det A^{(n)}}{\det A}$$

The output in Listing 11–2 shows that cond A is about 11.3, which means that A is well-conditioned, and so we shouldn't be too surprised that LU decomposition followed by forward and back substitution computes such a good solution. In general, this algorithm will do better than using the matrix inverse or Cramer's rule.

References

Bronson, Richard, *Matrix Operations,* New York: McGraw-Hill, 1989.

Traditional algorithms for computing determinants can be found in most textbooks on elementary linear algebra, such as Bronson in Chapter 5 and Lipschutz and Lipson in Chapter 8. Lipschutz and Lipson also discuss Cramer's rule.

Chapra, Seven C., and Raymond P. Canale, *Numerical Methods for Engineers,* 3rd edition, New York: WCB/McGraw-Hill, 1998.

This book discusses matrix inversion in Section 10.2 and matrix norms and condition numbers in Section 10.3.

Forsythe, George, and Cleve B. Moler, *Computer Solutions of Linear Algebraic Systems,* Englewood Cliffs, NJ: Prentice Hall, 1967.

This text covers matrix norms in Chapter 2, condition numbers in Chapter 8, computation of the determinant in Chapter 14, matrix inversion in Chapter 18, and Hilbert matrices in Chapter 19.

Lipschutz, Seymour, and Marc Lipson, *Linear Algebra,* 3rd edition, New York; McGraw-Hill, 2001.

PART IV

THE JOYS OF COMPUTATION

Numerical computation isn't all work and no play. The final part of this book covers its lighter side. However, "light" doesn't mean "frivolous"—there's useful material in these last chapters, too!

Chapter 12 covers Java's `BigNumber` and `BigDecimal` classes, which support "arbitrary precision" arithmetic—subject to memory constraints, we can have numbers with as many digits as we like. This chapter explores how these classes can be useful. We compute a large prime number with more than 3,000 digits, and we write functions that can compute values such as $\sqrt{2}$ and e^x to an arbitrary number of digits of precision.

Mathematicians over the centuries have created formulas for computing the value of π. Enigmatic Indian mathematician Ramanujan devised several very ingenious ones in the early 20th century. An iterative algorithm supposedly can compute more than 2 billion decimal digits of π. In Chapter 13, we use the big number functions from Chapter 12 to test some of these formulas and algorithms.

Chapter 14 is about random number generation. A well-known algorithm generates uniformly distributed random values. We examine algorithms that generate random normally distributed and exponentially distributed random values. We conclude with a Monte Carlo algorithm that uses random numbers to compute the value of π.

Mathematicians have mulled over prime numbers since nearly prehistoric times. Chapter 15 explores primality testing and investigates formulas that generate prime numbers, and it looks for patterns in the distribution of prime numbers.

The final chapter, Chapter 16, introduces fractals, which are beautiful and intricate shapes that are recursively defined. There are various algorithms for generating different types of fractals, such as Julia sets and the Mandelbrot set. In fact, Newton's algorithm for finding roots, which we saw in Chapter 5, when applied to the complex plane, can generate a fractal.

CHAPTER 12

BIG NUMBERS

In the first three chapters of this book, we looked at the limitations of both integers and floating-point numbers. Of course, one major limitation is their precision—the `long` integer type has 19 digits, and the `double` floating-point type has about 17 significant digits. We also saw how the Java floating-point types only implement the default *round to nearest* rounding mode of the IEEE 754 floating-point standard.

Besides the primitive numeric types, Java implements big number, or *arbitrary-precision,* data types—the `BigInteger` and `BigDecimal` classes in the `java.math` package. These classes represent numbers that have arbitrary numbers of digits of precision, and they have methods to perform the common arithmetic operations on these values. The operations are implemented in software, and so there will be significant performance penalties.

A `BigInteger` object represents an integer value. A `BigDecimal` object represents a decimal value—a value that has a whole part to the left of the decimal point and a fractional part to the right of the point. `BigDecimal` values also allow you to specify how they are rounded during arithmetic operations.

`BigInteger` and `BigDecimal` values are *immutable.* Once you've created such an object and initialized its value, you cannot change the value. Most of the methods that operate on these values create new objects to hold the result values.

This chapter takes a brief look at these two classes. We'll look at `BigInteger` values and prime numbers. (Chapter 15 will have a lot more to say about prime numbers.) We'll also write some `BigDecimal` functions that will enable some interesting computations in the next chapter.

12.1 Big Integers

BigInteger objects are useful when we have values that are larger than what type long can handle. Like the values of the primitive integer types, a BigInteger value is encoded in the two's-complement format (see Chapter 2).

The class includes methods to perform the basic arithmetic operations on BigInteger objects. The result of such an operation is always a new BigInteger object, since the objects are immutable. The arithmetic methods include abs() , add() , divide() , divideAndRemainder() , max() , min() , mod() , multiply() , negate() , pow() , remainder() , and subtract() . Method signum() returns $-1, 0$, or $+1$, depending on whether the value is negative, zero, or positive, respectively.

There are also methods that perform some bitwise operations, such as and() , andNot(), bitLength() , clearBit() , flipBit() , not() , or() , setBit() , shiftLeft() , shiftRight() , testBit() , and xor() .

Method valueOf() is a "factory method"—it creates a new BigInteger object from a long value. Method compareTo() compares a BigInteger value to another and returns $-1, 0$, or $+1$, depending on whether the value is less than, equal to, or greater than the other, respectively.

12.2 A Very Large Prime Number

Program 12–1 is a very simple demonstration of BigInteger values. It computes a very large number, a Mersenne prime.[1] Mersenne primes are of the form

$$M_n = 2^n - 1$$

In this case, we compute $M_{11,213}$, which was the largest known Mersenne prime when it was first discovered in 1963. As shown in Listing 12–1, it has 3,376 digits.

Listing 12–1 Computing the Mersenne prime $M_{11,213}$.

```
package numbercruncher.program12_1;

import java.math.BigInteger;
import java.util.Random;

/**
 * PROGRAM 12-1: Big Prime Number
 *
 * Demonstrate BigInteger by computing
 * the Mersenne prime 2^11213 - 1.
 */
public class BigPrime
```

---

[1]   Marin Mersenne (1588-1648) was a French priest who taught philosophy and investigated formulas that generate prime numbers.

```
{
    private static final int EXPONENT = 11213;

    /** the prime number */     private BigInteger prime;

    /**
     * Compute and print 2^EXPONENT - 1.
     */
    private void compute() throws Exception
    {
        // Compute the value.
        prime = BigInteger.valueOf(1);
        for (int i = 1; i <= EXPONENT; ++i) {
            prime = prime.add(prime);
        }
        prime = prime.subtract(BigInteger.valueOf(1));

        // Print it.
        System.out.println("2^" + EXPONENT + " = ");
        print(prime);
    }

    /**
     * Print the big prime number.
     * @param prime the big prime number
     */
    private void print(BigInteger prime)
    {
        String primeString = prime.toString();
        int length    = primeString.length();
        int groups    = length/3;     // no. of groups of three digits
        int exGroups  = length%3;     // no. of extra-group digits
        int lines     = groups/16;    // no. of lines of 16 groups
        int exLines   = groups%16;    // no. of extra-line groups

        int index     = 0;            // substring index
        int lineWidth = 4*16;

        // Print a right-justified partial line, if any.
        if (exLines > 0) {
            int padding = lineWidth - 4*exLines - exGroups - 1;
            for (int i = 0; i < padding; ++i) System.out.print(" ");

            // Print the extra-group digits.
            System.out.print(primeString.substring(0, exGroups) + ",");
            index = exGroups;

            // Print the extra-line groups.
            for (int i = 0; i < exLines; ++i) {
```

```
            index = printGroup(primeString, index, length);
        }
        System.out.println();
    }

    int count = 0;   // group counter

    // Loop to print whole lines.
    while (index < length) {
        index = printGroup(primeString, index, length);

        // End of line?
        if (++count == 16) {
            System.out.println();
            count = 0;
        }
    }

    // Print statistics.
    System.out.println();
    System.out.println("Number of digits = " + length);
    System.out.println("Number of bits   = " + prime.bitLength());
}

/**
 * Print a group of digits followed by a comma.
 * @param primeString the prime number as a string
 * @param index the substring index
 * @param length the string length
 * @return the new index value
 */
private int printGroup(String primeString, int index, int length)
{
    System.out.print(primeString.substring(index, index += 3));

    // Append a comma unless it's the last group.
    if (index < length) System.out.print(",");

    return index;
}

/**
 * Main.
 * @param args the array of program arguments
 */
public static void main(String args[])
{
    try {
        BigPrime bp = new BigPrime();
```

```
        bp.compute();
    }
    catch(Exception ex) {
        System.out.println("ERROR: " + ex.getMessage());
    }
    }
  }
}
```

Output:

```
2^11213 - 1 =
```

```
                                      2,814,112,013,697,373,
133,393,152,975,842,584,191,818,662,382,013,600,787,892,419,349,
345,515,176,682,276,313,810,715,094,745,633,257,074,198,789,308,
535,071,537,342,445,016,418,881,801,789,390,548,709,414,391,857,
257,571,565,758,706,478,418,356,747,070,674,633,497,188,053,050,
875,416,821,624,325,680,555,826,071,110,691,946,607,460,873,056,
965,360,830,571,590,242,774,934,226,866,183,966,309,185,433,462,
514,537,484,258,655,982,386,235,046,029,227,507,801,410,907,163,
348,439,547,781,093,397,260,096,909,677,091,843,944,555,754,221,
115,477,343,760,206,979,650,067,087,884,993,478,012,977,277,878,
532,807,432,236,554,020,931,571,802,310,429,923,167,588,432,457,
036,104,110,850,960,439,769,038,450,365,514,022,349,625,383,665,
751,207,169,661,697,352,732,236,111,926,846,454,751,701,734,527,
011,379,148,175,107,820,821,297,628,946,795,631,098,960,767,492,
250,494,834,254,073,334,414,121,627,833,939,461,539,212,528,932,
010,726,136,689,293,688,815,665,491,671,395,174,710,452,663,709,
175,753,603,774,156,855,766,515,313,827,613,727,281,696,692,633,
529,666,363,787,286,539,769,941,609,107,777,183,593,336,002,680,
124,517,633,451,490,439,598,324,823,836,457,251,219,406,391,432,
635,639,225,604,556,042,396,004,307,799,361,927,379,900,586,400,
420,763,092,320,813,392,262,492,942,076,312,933,268,033,818,471,
555,255,820,639,308,889,948,665,570,202,403,815,856,313,578,949,
779,767,046,261,845,327,956,725,767,289,205,262,311,752,014,786,
247,813,331,834,015,084,475,386,760,526,612,217,340,579,721,237,
414,485,803,725,355,463,022,009,536,301,008,145,867,524,704,604,
618,862,039,093,555,206,195,328,240,951,895,107,040,793,284,825,
095,462,530,151,872,823,997,171,764,140,663,315,804,309,008,611,
942,578,380,931,064,748,991,594,407,476,328,437,785,848,825,423,
921,170,614,938,294,029,483,257,162,979,299,388,940,695,877,375,
448,948,081,108,345,293,394,327,808,452,729,789,834,135,140,193,
912,419,661,799,488,795,210,328,238,112,742,218,700,634,541,149,
743,657,287,232,843,426,369,348,804,878,993,471,962,403,393,967,
857,676,150,371,600,196,650,252,168,250,117,793,178,488,012,000,
505,422,821,362,550,520,509,209,724,459,895,852,366,827,477,851,
619,190,503,254,853,115,029,403,132,178,989,005,195,751,194,301,
340,277,282,730,390,683,651,120,587,895,060,198,753,121,882,187,
788,657,024,007,291,784,186,518,589,977,788,510,306,743,945,896,
108,645,258,766,415,692,825,664,174,470,616,153,305,144,852,273,
```

```
884,549,635,059,255,410,606,458,427,323,864,109,506,687,636,314,
447,514,269,094,932,953,219,924,212,594,695,157,655,009,158,521,
173,420,923,275,882,063,327,625,408,617,963,032,962,033,572,563,
553,604,056,097,832,111,547,535,908,988,433,816,919,747,615,817,
161,606,620,557,307,000,377,194,730,013,431,815,560,750,159,027,
842,164,901,422,544,571,224,546,936,793,234,970,894,954,668,425,
436,412,347,785,376,194,310,030,139,080,568,383,420,772,628,618,
722,646,109,707,506,566,928,102,800,033,961,704,343,991,962,002,
059,794,565,527,774,913,883,237,756,792,720,065,543,768,640,792,
177,441,559,278,272,350,823,092,843,683,534,396,679,150,229,676,
101,834,243,787,820,420,087,274,028,617,212,684,576,388,733,605,
769,491,224,109,866,592,577,360,666,241,467,280,158,988,605,523,
486,345,880,882,227,855,505,706,309,276,349,415,034,547,677,180,
618,296,352,866,263,005,509,222,254,318,459,768,194,126,727,603,
047,460,344,175,581,029,298,320,171,226,355,234,439,676,816,309,
919,127,574,206,334,807,719,021,875,413,891,580,871,529,049,187,
829,308,412,133,400,910,419,756,313,021,540,478,436,604,178,446,
757,738,998,632,083,586,207,992,234,085,162,634,375,406,771,169,
707,323,213,988,284,943,779,122,171,985,953,605,897,902,291,781,
768,286,548,287,878,180,415,060,635,460,047,164,104,095,483,777,
201,737,468,873,324,068,550,430,695,826,210,304,316,336,385,311,
384,093,490,021,332,372,463,463,373,977,427,405,896,673,827,544,
203,128,574,874,581,960,335,232,005,637,229,319,592,369,288,171,
375,276,702,260,450,911,735,069,504,025,016,667,755,214,932,073,
643,654,199,488,477,010,363,909,372,005,757,899,989,580,775,775,
126,621,113,057,905,717,449,417,222,016,070,530,243,916,116,705,
990,451,304,256,206,318,289,297,738,303,095,152,430,549,772,239,
514,964,821,601,838,628,861,446,301,936,017,710,546,777,503,109,
263,030,994,747,397,618,576,207,373,447,725,441,427,135,362,428,
360,863,669,327,157,635,983,045,447,971,816,718,801,639,869,547,
525,146,305,655,571,843,717,916,875,669,140,320,724,978,568,586,
718,527,586,602,439,602,335,283,513,944,980,064,327,030,278,104,
224,144,971,883,680,541,689,784,796,267,391,476,087,696,392,191

Number of digits = 3376
Number of bits   = 11213
```

Each time the program doubles the BigInteger value with the add() method, it creates a new BigInteger object, and the old object (whose value remains unchanged) becomes available for eventual garbage collection.

Since any value that is one less than a power of two is just a string of 1 bits in the two's-complement format, the program could simply have used the setBit() method to set 11,213 bits. But like the add() operation, each setBit() operation would create a new BigInteger object—the new object's bit length would be one longer than the previous object.

12.3 Big Integers and Cryptography

The `BigInteger` class also contains methods that are useful for cryptography. Although this topic is beyond the scope of this book, it's worth a quick look.

A public key encryption system requires two keys. All message senders know the public key, which they use to encrypt their messages. Only the recipient of the messages knows the private key, which he or she uses to decrypt the messages.

The trick is to be able to give out the public key to multiple senders of secret messages, without making it easy to then figure out the corresponding private key that decrypts the messages. One scheme for generating keys relies on the fact that it is extremely difficult to factor a very large number (50 digits or more) that is the product of two primes.[2]

Class `BigInteger` has a constructor that generates a large, random integer value with a certain level of certainty that it is prime. Arguments to this constructor include the desired bit length of the number and the certainty level. The higher the certainty level, the longer it takes this constructor to create a `BigInteger` object. Method `isProbablePrime()` tests a given `Big-Integer` value to determine, to a given level of certainty, whether or not the value is prime. Like the constructor, the higher the level of certainty, the longer it takes this method to execute. (We'll examine primality testing in Chapter 15.)

Encrypting and decrypting messages involves modulo arithmetic[3] with large integer values, and `BigInteger` includes the methods `modInverse()` and `modPow()`.

12.4 Big Decimal Numbers

`BigDecimal` values are useful for dealing with very large decimal values and when we must have "exact arithmetic." The prototypical example is keeping track of the U.S. national debt down to the last penny.

Like `BigInteger`, class `BigDecimal` values have arbitrary precision. `BigDecimal` values also have a fractional part. The *scale* of a `BigDecimal` value is the number of digits in the fractional part, all of which are considered significant digits.

`BigDecimal` includes methods to perform the basic arithmetic operations, and these methods all create new `BigDecimal` objects. They include `abs()`, `add()`, `divide()`, `max()`, `min()`, `multiply()`, `negate()`, and `subtract()`. The scale of a result object depends on the scale of the operands—it's always large enough so that no digits of precision are lost.

Like the `BigInteger` class, there are also the methods `signum()` and `compareTo()`, as well as the factory method `valueOf()`, which creates a `BigDecimal` value from a double value. Methods `scale()` and `setScale()` get and set the value's scale, respectively, with the latter returning a new object. Methods `movePointLeft()` and `movePointRight()`

---

[2] The *Fundamental Theorem of Arithmetic* states that any integer greater than 2 either is prime or can be factored into a product of primes in a *unique* way.

[3] This is also called *modular arithmetic*. Chapter 15 will explore modulo arithmetic.

return new objects where the decimal point has been moved to the left or right by a specified number of digits.

A unique feature of class BigDecimal is that it allows you to choose how the arithmetic operations, such as division, round the fractional parts of their results to a given scale. There are eight rounding modes, two of which are of interest in this chapter. ROUND_DOWN rounds toward zero. Fractional digits beyond the specified scale are simply dropped. ROUND_HALF_EVEN rounds a value toward its nearest neighbor with the given scale. If the value being rounded is exactly halfway between two neighbors, the chosen value is that of the neighbor whose rightmost digit is even. These rounding constants are passed as arguments, along with the desired scale, to methods such as divide() and setScale().

12.5 Big Decimal Functions

The BigDecimal class does not include methods such as sqrt(), exp(), or ln(), and so we need to write them ourselves. Listing 12–2a shows class BigFunctions in package numbercruncher.mathutils, where we implement several useful functions. (These functions are useful because we need them in the next chapter!) We use some of the algorithms from Chapters 2, 4, and 5.

Listing 12–2a Class BigFunctions, which implements several useful BigDecimal functions.

```
package numbercruncher.mathutils;

import java.math.BigInteger;
import java.math.BigDecimal;

/**
 * Several useful BigDecimal mathematical functions.
 */
public final class BigFunctions
{
    /**
     * Compute x^exponent to a given scale.  Uses the same
     * algorithm as class numbercruncher.mathutils.IntPower.
     * @param x the value x
     * @param exponent the exponent value
     * @param scale the desired scale of the result
     * @return the result value
     */
    public static BigDecimal intPower(BigDecimal x, long exponent,
                                      int scale)
    {
        // If the exponent is negative, compute 1/(x^-exponent).
        if (exponent < 0) {
            return BigDecimal.valueOf(1)
```

```
                        .divide(intPower(x, -exponent, scale), scale,
                               BigDecimal.ROUND_HALF_EVEN);
    }

    BigDecimal power = BigDecimal.valueOf(1);

    // Loop to compute value^exponent.
    while (exponent > 0) {

        // Is the rightmost bit a 1?
        if ((exponent & 1) == 1) {
            power = power.multiply(x)
                       .setScale(scale, BigDecimal.ROUND_HALF_EVEN);
        }

        // Square x and shift exponent 1 bit to the right.
        x = x.multiply(x)
              .setScale(scale, BigDecimal.ROUND_HALF_EVEN);
        exponent >>= 1;

        Thread.yield();
    }

    return power;
}

/**
 * Compute the integral root of x to a given scale, x >= 0.
 * Use Newton's algorithm.
 * @param x the value of x
 * @param index the integral root value
 * @param scale the desired scale of the result
 * @return the result value
 */
public static BigDecimal intRoot(BigDecimal x, long index,
                                 int scale)
{
    // Check that x >= 0.
    if (x.signum() < 0) {
        throw new IllegalArgumentException("x < 0");
    }

    int        sp1 = scale + 1;
    BigDecimal n   = x;
    BigDecimal i   = BigDecimal.valueOf(index);
    BigDecimal im1 = BigDecimal.valueOf(index-1);
    BigDecimal tolerance = BigDecimal.valueOf(5)
                                      .movePointLeft(sp1);
    BigDecimal xPrev;
```

```
    // The initial approximation is x/index.
    x = x.divide(i, scale, BigDecimal.ROUND_HALF_EVEN);

    // Loop until the approximations converge
    // (two successive approximations are equal after rounding).
    do {
        // x^(index-1)
        BigDecimal xToIm1 = intPower(x, index-1, sp1);

        // x^index
        BigDecimal xToI =
                x.multiply(xToIm1)
                    .setScale(sp1, BigDecimal.ROUND_HALF_EVEN);

        // n + (index-1)*(x^index)
        BigDecimal numerator =
                n.add(im1.multiply(xToI))
                    .setScale(sp1, BigDecimal.ROUND_HALF_EVEN);

        // (index*(x^(index-1))
        BigDecimal denominator =
                i.multiply(xToIm1)
                    .setScale(sp1, BigDecimal.ROUND_HALF_EVEN);

        // x = (n + (index-1)*(x^index)) / (index*(x^(index-1)))
        xPrev = x;
        x = numerator
                .divide(denominator, sp1, BigDecimal.ROUND_DOWN);

        Thread.yield();
    } while (x.subtract(xPrev).abs().compareTo(tolerance) > 0);

    return x;
}

/**
 * Compute e^x to a given scale.
 * Break x into its whole and fraction parts and
 * compute (e^(1 + fraction/whole))^whole using Taylor's formula.
 * @param x the value of x
 * @param scale the desired scale of the result
 * @return the result value
 */
public static BigDecimal exp(BigDecimal x, int scale)
{
    // e^0 = 1
    if (x.signum() == 0) {
        return BigDecimal.valueOf(1);
    }
```

```
        // If x is negative, return 1/(e^-x).
        else if (x.signum() == -1) {
            return BigDecimal.valueOf(1)
                        .divide(exp(x.negate(), scale), scale,
                                BigDecimal.ROUND_HALF_EVEN);
        }

        // Compute the whole part of x.
        BigDecimal xWhole = x.setScale(0, BigDecimal.ROUND_DOWN);

        // If there isn't a whole part, compute and return e^x.
        if (xWhole.signum() == 0) return expTaylor(x, scale);

        // Compute the fraction part of x.
        BigDecimal xFraction = x.subtract(xWhole);

        // z = 1 + fraction/whole
        BigDecimal z = BigDecimal.valueOf(1)
                            .add(xFraction.divide(
                                    xWhole, scale,
                                    BigDecimal.ROUND_HALF_EVEN));

        // t = e^z
        BigDecimal t = expTaylor(z, scale);

        BigDecimal maxLong = BigDecimal.valueOf(Long.MAX_VALUE);
        BigDecimal result  = BigDecimal.valueOf(1);

        // Compute and return t^whole using intPower().
        // If whole > Long.MAX_VALUE, then first compute products
        // of e^Long.MAX_VALUE.
        while (xWhole.compareTo(maxLong) >= 0) {
            result = result.multiply(
                                intPower(t, Long.MAX_VALUE, scale))
                        .setScale(scale, BigDecimal.ROUND_HALF_EVEN);
            xWhole = xWhole.subtract(maxLong);

            Thread.yield();
        }
        return result.multiply(intPower(t, xWhole.longValue(), scale))
                        .setScale(scale, BigDecimal.ROUND_HALF_EVEN);
    }

    /**
     * Compute e^x to a given scale by the Taylor series.
     * @param x the value of x
     * @param scale the desired scale of the result
     * @return the result value
```

```
    */
private static BigDecimal expTaylor(BigDecimal x, int scale)
{
    BigDecimal factorial = BigDecimal.valueOf(1);
    BigDecimal xPower    = x;
    BigDecimal sumPrev;

    // 1 + x
    BigDecimal sum  = x.add(BigDecimal.valueOf(1));

    // Loop until the sums converge
    // (two successive sums are equal after rounding).
    int i = 2;
    do {
        // x^i
        xPower = xPower.multiply(x)
                    .setScale(scale, BigDecimal.ROUND_HALF_EVEN);

        // i!
        factorial = factorial.multiply(BigDecimal.valueOf(i));

        // x^i/i!
        BigDecimal term = xPower
                            .divide(factorial, scale,
                                    BigDecimal.ROUND_HALF_EVEN);

        // sum = sum + x^i/i!
        sumPrev = sum;
        sum = sum.add(term);

        ++i;
        Thread.yield();
    } while (sum.compareTo(sumPrev) != 0);

    return sum;
}

/**
 * Compute the natural logarithm of x to a given scale, x > 0.
 */
public static BigDecimal ln(BigDecimal x, int scale)
{
    // Check that x > 0.
    if (x.signum() <= 0) {
        throw new IllegalArgumentException("x <= 0");
    }

    // The number of digits to the left of the decimal point.
    int magnitude = x.toString().length() - x.scale() - 1;
```

```
    if (magnitude < 3) {
        return lnNewton(x, scale);
    }

    // Compute magnitude*ln(x^(1/magnitude)).
    else {

        // x^(1/magnitude)
        BigDecimal root = intRoot(x, magnitude, scale);

        // ln(x^(1/magnitude))
        BigDecimal lnRoot = lnNewton(root, scale);

        // magnitude*ln(x^(1/magnitude))
        return BigDecimal.valueOf(magnitude).multiply(lnRoot)
                    .setScale(scale, BigDecimal.ROUND_HALF_EVEN);
    }
}

/**
 * Compute the natural logarithm of x to a given scale, x > 0.
 * Use Newton's algorithm.
 */
private static BigDecimal lnNewton(BigDecimal x, int scale)
{
    int         sp1 = scale + 1;
    BigDecimal n   = x;
    BigDecimal term;

    // Convergence tolerance = 5*(10^-(scale+1))
    BigDecimal tolerance = BigDecimal.valueOf(5)
                                        .movePointLeft(sp1);

    // Loop until the approximations converge
    // (two successive approximations are within the tolerance).
    do {

        // e^x
        BigDecimal eToX = exp(x, sp1);

        // (e^x - n)/e^x
        term = eToX.subtract(n)
                    .divide(eToX, sp1, BigDecimal.ROUND_DOWN);

        // x - (e^x - n)/e^x
        x = x.subtract(term);

        Thread.yield();
    } while (term.compareTo(tolerance) > 0);
    return x.setScale(scale, BigDecimal.ROUND_HALF_EVEN);
```

```
    }

/**
 * Compute the arctangent of x to a given scale, |x| < 1
 * @param x the value of x
 * @param scale the desired scale of the result
 * @return the result value
 */
public static BigDecimal arctan(BigDecimal x, int scale)
{
    // Check that |x| < 1.
    if (x.abs().compareTo(BigDecimal.valueOf(1)) >= 0) {
        throw new IllegalArgumentException("|x| >= 1");
    }

    // If x is negative, return -arctan(-x).
    if (x.signum() == -1) {
        return arctan(x.negate(), scale).negate();
    }
    else {
        return arctanTaylor(x, scale);
    }
}

/**
 * Compute the arctangent of x to a given scale
 * by the Taylor series, |x| < 1
 * @param x the value of x
 * @param scale the desired scale of the result
 * @return the result value
 */
private static BigDecimal arctanTaylor(BigDecimal x, int scale)
{
    int     sp1     = scale + 1;
    int     i       = 3;
    boolean addFlag = false;

    BigDecimal power = x;
    BigDecimal sum   = x;
    BigDecimal term;

    // Convergence tolerance = 5*(10^-(scale+1))
    BigDecimal tolerance = BigDecimal.valueOf(5)

                                        .movePointLeft(sp1);
    // Loop until the approximations converge
    // (two successive approximations are within the tolerance).
    do {
        // x^i
```

```
            power = power.multiply(x).multiply(x)
                        .setScale(sp1, BigDecimal.ROUND_HALF_EVEN);

            // (x^i)/i
            term = power.divide(BigDecimal.valueOf(i), sp1,
                                BigDecimal.ROUND_HALF_EVEN);

            // sum = sum +- (x^i)/i
            sum = addFlag ? sum.add(term)
                          : sum.subtract(term);

            i += 2;
            addFlag = !addFlag;

            Thread.yield();
        } while (term.compareTo(tolerance) > 0);

        return sum;
    }

    /**
     * Compute the square root of x to a given scale, x >= 0.
     * Use Newton's algorithm.
     * @param x the value of x
     * @param scale the desired scale of the result
     * @return the result value
     */
    public static BigDecimal sqrt(BigDecimal x, int scale)
    {
        // Check that x >= 0.
        if (x.signum() < 0) {
            throw new IllegalArgumentException("x < 0");
        }

        // n = x*(10^(2*scale))
        BigInteger n = x.movePointRight(scale << 1).toBigInteger();

        // The first approximation is the upper half of n.
        int bits = (n.bitLength() + 1) >> 1;
        BigInteger ix = n.shiftRight(bits);
        BigInteger ixPrev;

        // Loop until the approximations converge
        // (two successive approximations are equal after rounding).
        do {
            ixPrev = ix;

            // x = (x + n/x)/2
            ix = ix.add(n.divide(ix)).shiftRight(1);
```

```
            Thread.yield();
        } while (ix.compareTo(ixPrev) != 0);

        return new BigDecimal(ix, scale);
    }
}
```

As we did in our class `numbercruncher.mathutils.IntPower` (see Chapter 2), method `intPower()` partitions the exponent into the sum of powers of 2. Note that, after each multiplication, it resets the scale. Otherwise, the scales of the intermediate results will grow with each iteration. There is also a call to `Thread.yield()` in each iteration.

Method `intRoot()` computes any integral root r of a number using Newton's algorithm:

$$f(x) = x^r - n$$
$$f'(x) = rx^{r-1}$$

where n is the number whose rth root we wish to compute, and

$$x_i = x_{i-1} - \frac{f(x_{i-1})}{f'(x_{i-1})}$$

$$= x_{i-1} - \frac{x_{i-1}^r - n}{rx_{i-1}^{r-1}}$$

$$= \frac{(r-1)x_{i-1}^r + n}{rx_{i-1}^{r-1}}$$

To speed convergence, method `exp()` computes e^x by breaking the exponent into its whole and fractional components and then computing

$$\left[e^{\left(1 + \frac{fraction}{whole}\right)} \right]^{whole}$$

(See Chapter 4.) The method uses the Taylor series for e^x, as implemented by the private method `expTaylor()`. If the value of *whole* is greater than `Long.MAX_VALUE`, then it partitions *whole* into the sum of addends of `Long.MAX_VALUE` and multiplies together the values of each $e^{\text{Long.MAX\_VALUE}}$.

Method `ln()` computes a natural logarithm. The Taylor series is

$$\ln x = 2\left[\left(\frac{x-1}{x+1}\right) + \frac{1}{3}\left(\frac{x-1}{x+1}\right)^3 + \frac{1}{5}\left(\frac{x-1}{x+1}\right)^5 + \cdots\right]$$

for $x > 0$, but since the $\left(\frac{x-1}{x+1}\right)$ terms are close to 1 for large values of x, the series converges very slowly. Instead, the method uses Newton's algorithm:

$$f(x) = e^x - n$$
$$f'(x) = e^x$$

where n is the value whose natural logarithm we want to find and

$$x_i = x_{i-1} - \frac{f(x_{i-1})}{f'(x_{i-1})}$$

$$= x_{i-1} - \frac{e^{x_{i-1}} - n}{e^{x_{i-1}}}$$

This is implemented by the private method `lnNewton()`.

So now how fast we can compute $\ln x$ depends on how fast we can compute e^x. If the value of x is large, method `exp()` will execute slowly. Therefore, method `ln()` employs a simple "strength reduction"—let m be the magnitude (the number of digits to the left of the decimal point) of x. Then, if $m > 3$, instead of computing $\ln x$, the method computes instead

$$\ln x = m \ln(\sqrt[m]{x})$$

This is faster because method `intPower()` uses Newton's algorithm, which converges more rapidly than the Taylor series used by method `expTaylor()`.

Method `arctan()` uses the Taylor series

$$\arctan x = x - \frac{x^3}{3} + \frac{x^5}{5} - \frac{x^7}{7} + \cdots$$

for $|x| < 1$.

Because computing a square root is a common operation, class `BigFunctions` has a special optimized method `sqrt()`. The method first "scales up" to `BigInteger` whole numbers with the equivalent of multiplying by even powers of 10, and then it uses the faster integer arithmetic. It applies Newton's algorithm, and then it "scales down" the result to the appropriate `BigDecimal` value.

The implementation of Newton's algorithm is similar to what we saw in Chapter 5:

$$f(x) = x^2 - n$$
$$f'(x) = 2n$$

where n is the number whose square root we wish to compute, and each approximation x_i is

$$x_i = x_{i-1} - \frac{f(x_{i-1})}{f'(x_{i-1})}$$

$$= x_{i-1} - \frac{x_{i-1}^2 - n}{2x_{i-1}}$$

$$= \frac{x_{i-1}^2 + n}{2x_{i-1}}$$

$$= \frac{1}{2}\left(x_{i-1} + \frac{n}{x_{i-1}}\right)$$

The method goes one step further to avoid the x^2_{i-1} term, which would double the number of digits of precision. (There is no `setScale()` method for `BigInteger` values.) Multiplying by $\frac{1}{2}$ is a simple shift to the right by 1 bit.

Listing 12–2b shows Program 12–2, which tests the methods in class `BigFunctions` by comparing results with those obtained with methods from class `java.lang.Math`.

Listing 12–2b Testing class `BigFunctions`.

```
package numbercruncher.program12_2;

import java.math.BigDecimal;
import numbercruncher.mathutils.BigFunctions;

/**
 * PROGRAM 12-2: Test BigFunctions
 *
 * Test the BigFunctions by comparing results with
 * class java.lang.Math.
 */
public class TestBigFunctions
{
    private static final int SCALE = 40;

    /**
     * Run the test.
```

```
    */
private void run()
{
    System.out.println("2^(-25) = " + Math.pow(2, -25));
    System.out.println("          = " +
        BigFunctions.intPower(BigDecimal.valueOf(2), -25, SCALE));

    System.out.println();
    System.out.println("sqrt 2 = " + Math.sqrt(2));
    System.out.println("         = " +
        BigFunctions.sqrt(BigDecimal.valueOf(2), SCALE));

    System.out.println();
    System.out.println("2^(1/3) = " + Math.exp(Math.log(2)/3));
    System.out.println("          = " +
        BigFunctions.intRoot(BigDecimal.valueOf(2), 3, SCALE));

    System.out.println();
    System.out.println("e^(-19.5) = " + Math.exp(-19.5));
    System.out.println("            = " +
        BigFunctions.exp(new BigDecimal("-19.5"), SCALE));

    System.out.println();
    System.out.println("ln 2 = " + Math.log(2));
    System.out.println("       = " +
        BigFunctions.ln(BigDecimal.valueOf(2), SCALE));

    System.out.println();
    System.out.println("arctan sqrt(3)/3 = " + Math.PI/6);
    System.out.println("                   = " +
        BigFunctions.arctan(
                BigFunctions.sqrt(BigDecimal.valueOf(3), SCALE)
                    .divide(BigDecimal.valueOf(3), SCALE,
                            BigDecimal.ROUND_HALF_EVEN),
                SCALE));
}

/**
 * Main.
 * @param args the array of program arguments
 */
public static void main(String args[])
{
    TestBigFunctions test = new TestBigFunctions();

    try {
        test.run();
    }
    catch(Exception ex) {
```

```
            System.out.println("ERROR: " + ex.getMessage());
        }
    }
}
```

Output:

```
2^(-25) = 2.9802322387695312E-8
        = 0.0000000298023223876953125000000000000000

sqrt 2 = 1.4142135623730951
       = 1.4142135623730950488016887242096980785696

2^(1/3) = 1.2599210498948732
        = 1.2599210498948731647672106072782835057024

e^(-19.5) = 3.398267819495071E-9
          = 0.0000000033982678194950712251407378768109

ln 2 = 0.6931471805599453
     = 0.6931471805599453094172321214581765680755
arctan sqrt(3)/3 = 0.5235987755982988
                 = 0.5235987755982988730771072305465838140328 5
```

Of course, we can write many more `BigFunctions` methods, but these are the ones we'll need for Chapter 13. They can serve as models for any more methods we may choose to write later.

References

The classes `BigInteger` and `BigDecimal` , which are in the `java.math` package, are fully described by the Java documentation supplied by Sun Microsystems, Inc.

Clawson, Calvin C., *Mathematical Mysteries: The Beauty and Magic of Numbers,* New York: Plenum Press, 1996.
Graff, Jon C., *Cryptography and E-Commerce,* New York: John Wiley and Sons, 2001.
Knudsen, Jonathan, *Java Cryptography,* Sebastapol, CA: O'Reilly, 1998.

Clawson contains a brief but good introduction to public key encryption in Chapter 9. Graff and Knudsen are good introductory texts to cryptography; the latter is Java-specific.

CHAPTER 13

COMPUTING π

It is truly amazing that a number so easily described—the ratio of a circle's circumference to its diameter—could have occupied the minds of so many eminent mathematicians over the centuries. The number π is both irrational and transcendental,[1] and people have been attempting to devise formulas and algorithms that compute estimates of its value or that can generate as many of its exact digits as possible.

In this chapter, we'll look at some of these attempts. The `BigFunctions` class we wrote in Chapter 12 will enable us to test some of the formulas and algorithms.

13.1 Estimates of π and Ramanujan's Formulas

Some people claim that the Christian Bible implies that the value of π is 3. Other estimates that were used throughout history include $3\frac{1}{8} = 3.125$ (Babylonians, ca. 2000 B.C.), $\left(\frac{16}{9}\right)^2 \approx 3.16049$ (Egyptians, ca. 2000 B.C.), $\frac{211,875}{67,441} \approx 3.14163$ (Archimedes, 3rd century B.C), $\frac{377}{120} \approx 3.14167$ (Ptolemy, 2nd century A.D.), $\frac{157}{50} = 3.14$ (Liu Hui, A.D. 263), $\frac{355}{113} \approx 3.14159$ (Valentinus Otho, A.D. 1573), and $\left(\frac{39}{22}\right)^2 \approx 3.14256$ (Simon Duchesne, A.D. 1583).

In 1914, Ramanujan[2] published several remarkable formulas that give approximate values for π that are accurate to 15 to 31 decimal places. These formulas are shown in Table 13–1.

---

[1] An *irrational number* is one that cannot be expressed as the ratio of two integers. A *transcendental number* is one that cannot be the root of a polynomial equation with integer coefficients. Another transcendental number is *e*, the base of natural logarithms.

[2] Srinivasa Ramanujan (1887–1920) was one of India's greatest mathematical geniuses. In 1913, when he was but a poor clerk living in Madras, he wrote to famous mathematician G.H. Hardy at Cambridge University in England. Hardy was so impressed by the theorems included in the letter that he had Ramanujan brought to the university. Until he became seriously ill and returned to India in 1919, Ramanujan made major contributions to number theory, elliptic functions, continued fractions, and infinite series.

Table 13–1   Ramanujan's formulas for π.

Decimal Places	Ramanujan's Formulas for π
15	$\pi = \dfrac{12}{\sqrt{130}} \ln\left\{\dfrac{\left(2 + \sqrt{5}\right)\left(3 + \sqrt{13}\right)}{\sqrt{2}}\right\}$
16	$\pi = \dfrac{24}{\sqrt{142}} \ln\left\{\sqrt{\dfrac{10 + 11\sqrt{2}}{4}} + \sqrt{\dfrac{10 + 7\sqrt{2}}{4}}\right\}$
18	$\pi = \dfrac{12}{\sqrt{190}} \ln\left\{\left(2\sqrt{2} + \sqrt{10}\right)\left(3 + \sqrt{10}\right)\right\}$
22	$\pi = \dfrac{12}{\sqrt{130}} \ln\left\{\dfrac{\left(3 + \sqrt{5}\right)\left(2 + \sqrt{2}\right)\left[\left(5 + 2\sqrt{10}\right) + \sqrt{61 + 20\sqrt{10}}\right]}{4}\right\}$
31	$\pi = \dfrac{4}{\sqrt{522}} \ln\left\{\left(\dfrac{5 + \sqrt{29}}{\sqrt{2}}\right)^3 \left(5\sqrt{29} + 11\sqrt{6}\right)\left(\sqrt{\dfrac{9 + 3\sqrt{6}}{4}} + \sqrt{\dfrac{5 + 3\sqrt{6}}{4}}\right)^6\right\}$

Program 13–1 tests these formulas, using the `BigFunctions` class we developed in Chapter 12. See Listing 13–1.

Listing 13–1 Estimates of π computed by Ramanujan's formulas.

```
package numbercruncher.program13_1;

import java.math.BigDecimal;
import numbercruncher.mathutils.BigFunctions;

/**
 * PROGRAM 13-3: Ramanujan's Formulas for pi
 *
 * Compute estimates of pi using Ramanujan's formulas.
 */
public class PiRamanujan
{
    private void compute()
    {
        int digits;       // number of digits
        int scale;
```

```
BigDecimal term, a, b, c, d, e, lnArg, pi;
BigDecimal sqrt2, sqrt5, sqrt6, sqrt10, sqrt13, sqrt29;
BigDecimal sqrt130, sqrt142, sqrt190, sqrt310, sqrt522;

// --- 15 digits ---

digits = 15;
scale  = digits + 2;

sqrt2   = BigFunctions.sqrt(BigDecimal.valueOf(  2), scale);
sqrt5   = BigFunctions.sqrt(BigDecimal.valueOf(  5), scale);
sqrt13  = BigFunctions.sqrt(BigDecimal.valueOf( 13), scale);
sqrt130 = BigFunctions.sqrt(BigDecimal.valueOf(130), scale);

term = BigDecimal.valueOf(12)
            .divide(sqrt130, scale,
                    BigDecimal.ROUND_HALF_EVEN);
a = BigDecimal.valueOf(2).add(sqrt5);
b = BigDecimal.valueOf(3).add(sqrt13);
lnArg = a.multiply(b)
            .divide(sqrt2, BigDecimal.ROUND_HALF_EVEN)
            .setScale(scale, BigDecimal.ROUND_HALF_EVEN);
pi = term.multiply(BigFunctions.ln(lnArg, scale))
            .setScale(digits, BigDecimal.ROUND_HALF_EVEN);
System.out.println(digits + " digits: " + pi);

// --- 16 digits ---

digits = 16;
scale  = digits + 2;

sqrt2   = BigFunctions.sqrt(BigDecimal.valueOf(  2), scale);
sqrt142 = BigFunctions.sqrt(BigDecimal.valueOf(142), scale);

term = BigDecimal.valueOf(24)
            .divide(sqrt142, scale,
                    BigDecimal.ROUND_HALF_EVEN);
a = BigDecimal.valueOf(10)
            .add(BigDecimal.valueOf(11).multiply(sqrt2))
            .divide(BigDecimal.valueOf(4), scale,
                    BigDecimal.ROUND_HALF_EVEN);
b = BigDecimal.valueOf(10)
            .add(BigDecimal.valueOf(7).multiply(sqrt2))
            .divide(BigDecimal.valueOf(4), scale,
                    BigDecimal.ROUND_HALF_EVEN);
lnArg = BigFunctions.sqrt(a, scale)
            .add(BigFunctions.sqrt(b, scale));
pi = term.multiply(BigFunctions.ln(lnArg, scale))
            .setScale(digits, BigDecimal.ROUND_HALF_EVEN);
System.out.println(digits + " digits: " + pi);
```

```
// --- 18 digits ---

digits = 18;
scale  = digits + 2;

sqrt2   = BigFunctions.sqrt(BigDecimal.valueOf(  2), scale);
sqrt10  = BigFunctions.sqrt(BigDecimal.valueOf( 10), scale);
sqrt190 = BigFunctions.sqrt(BigDecimal.valueOf(190), scale);

term = BigDecimal.valueOf(12)
            .divide(sqrt190, scale,
                    BigDecimal.ROUND_HALF_EVEN);
a = BigDecimal.valueOf(2).multiply(sqrt2).add(sqrt10);
b = BigDecimal.valueOf(3).add(sqrt10);
lnArg = a.multiply(b)
            .setScale(scale, BigDecimal.ROUND_HALF_EVEN);
pi = term.multiply(BigFunctions.ln(lnArg, scale))
            .setScale(digits, BigDecimal.ROUND_HALF_EVEN);
System.out.println(digits + " digits: " + pi);

// --- 22 digits ---

digits = 22;
scale  = digits + 2;

sqrt2 =   BigFunctions.sqrt(BigDecimal.valueOf(  2), scale);
sqrt5   = BigFunctions.sqrt(BigDecimal.valueOf(  5), scale);
sqrt10  = BigFunctions.sqrt(BigDecimal.valueOf( 10), scale);
sqrt310 = BigFunctions.sqrt(BigDecimal.valueOf(310), scale);

term = BigDecimal.valueOf(12)
            .divide(sqrt310, scale,
                    BigDecimal.ROUND_HALF_EVEN);
a = BigDecimal.valueOf(3).add(sqrt5);
b = BigDecimal.valueOf(2).add(sqrt2);
c = BigDecimal.valueOf(5)
            .add(BigDecimal.valueOf(2).multiply(sqrt10));
d = BigFunctions.sqrt(BigDecimal.valueOf(61)
                            .add(BigDecimal.valueOf(20)
                                    .multiply(sqrt10)),
                    scale);
e = c.add(d).multiply(a).multiply(b)
            .setScale(scale, BigDecimal.ROUND_HALF_EVEN);
lnArg = e.divide(BigDecimal.valueOf(4), scale,
                    BigDecimal.ROUND_HALF_EVEN);
pi = term.multiply(BigFunctions.ln(lnArg, scale))
            .setScale(digits, BigDecimal.ROUND_HALF_EVEN);
System.out.println(digits + " digits: " + pi);
```

```
    // --- 31 digits ---

    digits = 31;
    scale  = digits + 2;

    sqrt2   = BigFunctions.sqrt(BigDecimal.valueOf(  2), scale);
    sqrt6   = BigFunctions.sqrt(BigDecimal.valueOf(  6), scale);
    sqrt29  = BigFunctions.sqrt(BigDecimal.valueOf( 29), scale);
    sqrt522 = BigFunctions.sqrt(BigDecimal.valueOf(522), scale);

    term = BigDecimal.valueOf(4)
                .divide(sqrt522, scale,
                        BigDecimal.ROUND_HALF_EVEN);
    a = BigDecimal.valueOf(5).add(sqrt29)
                .divide(sqrt2, BigDecimal.ROUND_HALF_EVEN);
    b = BigDecimal.valueOf(5).multiply(sqrt29)
                .add(BigDecimal.valueOf(11).multiply(sqrt6))
                .setScale(scale, BigDecimal.ROUND_HALF_EVEN);
    c = BigDecimal.valueOf(9)
                .add(BigDecimal.valueOf(3).multiply(sqrt6))
                .divide(BigDecimal.valueOf(4), scale,
                        BigDecimal.ROUND_HALF_EVEN);
    d = BigDecimal.valueOf(5)
                .add(BigDecimal.valueOf(3).multiply(sqrt6))
                .divide(BigDecimal.valueOf(4), scale,
                        BigDecimal.ROUND_HALF_EVEN);
    e = BigFunctions.sqrt(c, scale)
                .add(BigFunctions.sqrt(d, scale));
    lnArg = BigFunctions.intPower(a, 3, scale)
                .multiply(b)
                .multiply(BigFunctions.intPower(e, 6, scale))
                .setScale(scale, BigDecimal.ROUND_HALF_EVEN);
    pi = term.multiply(BigFunctions.ln(lnArg, scale))
                .setScale(digits, BigDecimal.ROUND_HALF_EVEN);
    System.out.println(digits + " digits: " + pi);
}

/**
 * Main.
 * @param args the array of program arguments
 */
public static void main(String args[])
{
    PiRamanujan formulas = new PiRamanujan();

    try {
        formulas.compute();
    }
```

```
        catch(Exception ex) {
            System.out.println("ERROR: " + ex.getMessage());
        }
    }
}
```

Output

```
15 digits: 3.141592653589793
16 digits: 3.1415926535897931
18 digits: 3.141592653589793238
22 digits: 3.1415926535897932384626
31 digits: 3.1415926535897932384626433832794
```

To help ensure the accuracy of the last digit of each formula's estimate of π, the program computes with a scale that is greater than the purported number of digits of accuracy. In the output shown in Listing 13–1, the last digit of the 16-digit result and of the 31-digit result is each off by 1 (the digits should be 2 and 5, respectively).

13.2 Arctangent Formulas That Generate π

In 1706, John Machin, a professor of astronomy in London, devised a formula for π using the arctangent function. He relied on the fact that $\tan \frac{\pi}{4} = 1$ and the tangent addition identity

$$\tan (\alpha + \beta) = \frac{\tan \alpha \pm \tan \beta}{1 \mp (\tan \alpha)(\tan \beta)}$$

for any angles α and β. Then, using an angle θ such that $\tan \theta = \frac{1}{5}$,

$$\tan 2\theta = \frac{2 \tan \theta}{1 - \tan^2 \theta} = \frac{\frac{2}{5}}{1 - \frac{1}{25}} = \frac{2}{5} \times \frac{25}{24} = \frac{5}{12}$$

$$\tan 4\theta = \frac{2 \tan 2\theta}{1 - \tan^2 2\theta} = \frac{\frac{10}{12}}{1 - \frac{25}{144}} = \frac{10}{12} \times \frac{144}{119} = \frac{120}{119}$$

Machin's keen observation was that

$$\tan 4\theta = \frac{120}{119} = 1 + \frac{1}{119} = \tan \frac{\pi}{4} + \frac{1}{119}$$

Therefore,

$$\tan 4\theta - \tan \frac{\pi}{4} = \frac{1}{119}$$

And so

$$\tan\left(4\theta - \frac{\pi}{4}\right) = \frac{\tan 4\theta - \tan \frac{\pi}{4}}{1 + (\tan 4\theta)\left(\tan \frac{\pi}{4}\right)} = \frac{\frac{1}{119}}{1 + \left(\frac{120}{119}\right)(1)} = \frac{1}{119} \times \frac{119}{239} = \frac{1}{239}$$

By taking the arctangent of both sides, he got

$$4\theta - \frac{\pi}{4} = \arctan \frac{1}{239}$$

Since he started with $\tan \theta = \frac{1}{5}$, he had $\theta = \arctan \frac{1}{5}$. So finally,

$$\frac{\pi}{4} = 4 \arctan \frac{1}{5} - \arctan \frac{1}{239}$$

This formula means that, if we have a means to compute the arctangent function to an arbitrary precision, we can compute π to the same precision. But that's exactly what our `BigFunctions.arctan()` method does.

In 1949, the ENIAC computer was programmed[3] to compute 2,035 decimal digits of π using this formula. It required 70 hours, including card-handling time.

Since Machin's formula, mathematicians have discovered other formulas for π that use the arctangent function. Several of those formulas, including the original, are shown in Table 13–2.

In Chapter 12, we wrote the `BigFunctions.arctan()` method using the Taylor series for the arctangent function:

$$\arctan x = x - \frac{x^3}{3} + \frac{x^5}{5} - \frac{x^7}{7} + \dots$$

for $|x| < 1$.

Obviously, the smaller the value of x, the sooner the terms will approach zero, and so the faster the series will converge. Therefore, we want to choose the formula with the smallest valued arguments for arctangent.

---

[3] Programming the ENIAC was a tedious, time-consuming, and error-prone process of setting switches and rewiring the machine by plugging and unplugging a myriad of cables.

Table 13–2 Arctangent formulas for π.

$$\frac{\pi}{4} = 4 \arctan \frac{1}{5} - \arctan \frac{1}{239}$$

$$\frac{\pi}{4} = \arctan \frac{1}{2} + \arctan \frac{1}{3}$$

$$\frac{\pi}{4} = 2 \arctan \frac{1}{2} - \arctan \frac{1}{7}$$

$$\frac{\pi}{4} = 2 \arctan \frac{1}{3} + \arctan \frac{1}{7}$$

$$\frac{\pi}{4} = 8 \arctan \frac{1}{10} - 4 \arctan \frac{1}{515} - \arctan \frac{1}{239}$$

$$\frac{\pi}{4} = 3 \arctan \frac{1}{4} + \arctan \frac{1}{20} + \arctan \frac{1}{1985}$$

$$\frac{\pi}{4} = 24 \arctan \frac{1}{8} + 8 \arctan \frac{1}{57} + 4 \arctan \frac{1}{239}$$

Program 13–2 computes π using the original Machin formula and the fifth formula in Table 13–2. Like the old ENIAC program, it computes 2,035 digits with each formula.

Listing 13–2a shows utility class `PiFormula` in package `numbercruncher.piutils`. It contains two methods, `printPi()`, which prints out the computed digits of π, and `timestamp()`, which returns a string containing the current time and the elapsed time period.

Listing 13–2a The utility class `PiFormula`.

```java
package numbercruncher.piutils;

import java.math.BigDecimal;
import java.text.DecimalFormat;
import java.text.SimpleDateFormat;
import java.util.Date;

/**
 * Utility class for programs that compute pi.
 */
public abstract class PiFormula
{
    private static final DecimalFormat DECIMAL_FORMAT =
                                new DecimalFormat("00");
    private static final SimpleDateFormat TIME_FORMAT =
                                new SimpleDateFormat("HH:mm:ss.SSS");

    protected long startTime;
    protected long markTime;
```

```java
/**
 * Print the string containing the digits of pi.
 * @param piString the string containing the digits of pi
 */
protected void printPi(String piString)
{
    System.out.print("\npi = " + piString.substring(0, 2));

    int index  = 2;
    int line   = 0;
    int group  = 0;
    int length = piString.length();

    // Loop for each group of 5 digits
    while (index + 5 < length) {
        System.out.print(piString.substring(index, index+5) +
                            " ");
        index += 5;

        // End of line after 10 groups.
        if (++group == 10) {
            System.out.println();

            // Print a blank line after 10 lines.
            if (++line == 10) {
                System.out.println();
                line = 0;
            }

            System.out.print("        ");
            group = 0;
        }
    }

    // Print the last partial line.
    if (index < length) {
        System.out.println(piString.substring(index));
    }
}

/**
 * Return a timestamp string that contains the elapsed time period.
 * @param time the starting time of the period
 * @return the timestamp string
 */
protected String timestamp(long time)
{
    // Current time in hh:mm:ss.
```

```
        String tString = TIME_FORMAT.format(new Date());

        long    elapsed = (System.currentTimeMillis() - time + 500)
                            /1000;
        long    hours   = elapsed/(60*60);
        long    minutes = (elapsed%(60*60))/60;
        long    seconds = elapsed%60;

        // Current time followed by elapsed time as (hh:mm:ss).
        return tString + " (" + DECIMAL_FORMAT.format(hours) +
                        ":" + DECIMAL_FORMAT.format(minutes) +
                        ":" + DECIMAL_FORMAT.format(seconds) +
                        ")";

    }
}
```

Listing 13–2b shows Program 13–2 and its output. The elapsed time in each timestamp, (hh:mm:ss), is the time required for the computation in the *previous* line. As we expected, method BigFunctions.arctan() executes faster with smaller argument values.[4]

Listing 13–2b Computing π with two arctangent formulas.

```
package numbercruncher.program13_2;

import java.math.BigDecimal;
import java.text.DecimalFormat;
import java.text.SimpleDateFormat;
import java.util.Date;

import numbercruncher.mathutils.BigFunctions;
import numbercruncher.piutils.PiFormula;

/**
 * PROGRAM 13-2: Arctangent Formulas for pi
 *
 * Compute pi with two arctangent formulas.
 */
public class PiArctan extends PiFormula
{
    private static final DecimalFormat DECIMAL_FORMAT =
                            new DecimalFormat("00");
    private static final SimpleDateFormat TIME_FORMAT =
                            new SimpleDateFormat("HH:mm:ss.SSS");

    /**
     * Compute the digits of pi using two arctangent formulas.
```

---

[4] The timings for Programs 13–2 and 13–3 are from running the JDK 1.3.1_01 virtual machine on a 266 MHz Pentium II.

```
 * @param digits the number of digits of pi to compute
 */
private void compute(int digits)
{
    int   scale     = digits + 3;
    long startTime = System.currentTimeMillis();
    long markTime;

    System.out.println("digits = " + digits);
    System.out.println("scale  = " + scale);

    BigDecimal big1 = BigDecimal.valueOf(1);
    BigDecimal big4 = BigDecimal.valueOf(4);
    BigDecimal big8 = BigDecimal.valueOf(8);

    // --- First formula ---

    System.out.println("\n ----- First arctan formula -----\n");
    System.out.println(timestamp(startTime) + " START TIME\n");

    System.out.println(timestamp(startTime) + " Initializing");
    markTime = System.currentTimeMillis();

    BigDecimal r5   = big1.divide(BigDecimal.valueOf(5), scale,
                                  BigDecimal.ROUND_HALF_EVEN);
    BigDecimal r239 = big1.divide(BigDecimal.valueOf(239), scale,
                                  BigDecimal.ROUND_HALF_EVEN);

    System.out.println(timestamp(markTime) +
                       " Computing arctan(1/5)");
    markTime = System.currentTimeMillis();

    BigDecimal arctan5 = BigFunctions.arctan(r5, scale);

    System.out.println(timestamp(markTime) +
                       " Computing arctan(1/239)");
    markTime = System.currentTimeMillis();

    BigDecimal arctan239 = BigFunctions.arctan(r239, scale);

    System.out.println(timestamp(markTime) + " Computing pi");
    markTime = System.currentTimeMillis();

    BigDecimal term = big4.multiply(arctan5)
                          .setScale(scale,
                                    BigDecimal.ROUND_HALF_EVEN)
                          .subtract(arctan239);
    BigDecimal pi = big4.multiply(term)
                        .setScale(digits, BigDecimal.ROUND_DOWN);
```

```
System.out.println(timestamp(markTime) + " pi computed");
printPi(pi.toString());

System.out.println("\n" + timestamp(startTime) +
                   " TOTAL TIME");

// --- Second formula ---

startTime = System.currentTimeMillis();

System.out.println("\n----- Second arctan formula -----\n");

System.out.println(timestamp(startTime) + " START TIME\n");

System.out.println(timestamp(startTime) + " Initializing");
markTime = System.currentTimeMillis();

BigDecimal r10  = big1.divide(BigDecimal.valueOf(10), scale,
                              BigDecimal.ROUND_HALF_EVEN);
BigDecimal r515 = big1.divide(BigDecimal.valueOf(515), scale,
                              BigDecimal.ROUND_HALF_EVEN);
r239 = big1.divide(BigDecimal.valueOf(239), scale,
                   BigDecimal.ROUND_HALF_EVEN):

System.out.println(timestamp(markTime) +
                   " Computing arctan(1/10)");
markTime = System.currentTimeMillis();

BigDecimal arctan10 = BigFunctions.arctan(r10, scale);

System.out.println(timestamp(markTime) +
                   " Computing arctan(1/515)");
markTime = System.currentTimeMillis();

BigDecimal arctan515 = BigFunctions.arctan(r515, scale);

System.out.println(timestamp(markTime) +
                   " Computing arctan(1/239)");
markTime = System.currentTimeMillis();

arctan239 = BigFunctions.arctan(r239, scale);

System.out.println(timestamp(markTime) + " Computing pi");
markTime = System.currentTimeMillis();

term =
    big8.multiply(arctan10)
        .setScale(scale, BigDecimal.ROUND_HALF_EVEN)
        .subtract(big4.multiply(arctan515)
```

```
                          .setScale(scale,
                                    BigDecimal.ROUND_HALF_EVEN))
                    .subtract(arctan239);
            pi = big4.multiply(term)
                    .setScale(digits, BigDecimal.ROUND_DOWN);

            System.out.println(timestamp(markTime) + " pi computed");
            printPi(pi.toString());

            System.out.println("\n" + timestamp(startTime) +
                               " TOTAL TIME");
    }

    /**
     * Main.
     * @param args the array of program arguments
     */
    public static void main(String args[])
    {
        PiArctan pi = new PiArctan();

        try {
            pi.compute(2035);
        }
        catch(Exception ex) {
            System.out.println("ERROR: " + ex.getMessage());
        }
    }
}
```

Output:

```
digits = 2035
scale  = 2038

----- First arctan formula -----

02:16:56.680 (00:00:00) START TIME

02:16:56.680 (00:00:00) Initializing
02:16:57.620 (00:00:01) Computing arctan(1/5)
02:48:19.310 (00:31:22) Computing arctan(1/239)
02:57:35.650 (00:09:16) Computing pi
02:57:35.650 (00:00:00) pi computed

pi = 3.14159 26535 89793 23846 26433 83279 50288 41971 69399 37510
        58209 74944 59230 78164 06286 20899 86280 34825 34211 70679
        82148 08651 32823 06647 09384 46095 50582 23172 53594 08128
        48111 74502 84102 70193 85211 05559 64462 29489 54930 38196
```

```
44288 10975 66593 34461 28475 64823 37867 83165 27120 19091
45648 56692 34603 48610 45432 66482 13393 60726 02491 41273
72458 70066 06315 58817 48815 20920 96282 92540 91715 36436
78925 90360 01133 05305 48820 46652 13841 46951 94151 16094
33057 27036 57595 91953 09218 61173 81932 61179 31051 18548
07446 23799 62749 56735 18857 52724 89122 79381 83011 94912

98336 73362 44065 66430 86021 39494 63952 24737 19070 21798
60943 70277 05392 17176 29317 67523 84674 81846 76694 05132
00056 81271 45263 56082 77857 71342 75778 96091 73637 17872
14684 40901 22495 34301 46549 58537 10507 92279 68925 89235
42019 95611 21290 21960 86403 44181 59813 62977 47713 09960
51870 72113 49999 99837 29780 49951 05973 17328 16096 31859
50244 59455 34690 83026 42522 30825 33446 85035 26193 11881
71010 00313 78387 52886 58753 32083 81420 61717 76691 47303
59825 34904 28755 46873 11595 62863 88235 37875 93751 95778
18577 80532 17122 68066 13001 92787 66111 95909 21642 01989

38095 25720 10654 85863 27886 59361 53381 82796 82303 01952
03530 18529 68995 77362 25994 13891 24972 17752 83479 13151
55748 57242 45415 06959 50829 53311 68617 27855 88907 50983
81754 63746 49393 19255 06040 09277 01671 13900 98488 24012
85836 16035 63707 66010 47101 81942 95559 61989 46767 83744
94482 55379 77472 68471 04047 53464 62080 46684 25906 94912
93313 67702 89891 52104 75216 20569 66024 05803 81501 93511
25338 24300 35587 64024 74964 73263 91419 92726 04269 92279
67823 54781 63600 93417 21641 21992 45863 15030 28618 29745
55706 74983 85054 94588 58692 69956 90927 21079 75093 02955

32116 53449 87202 75596 02364 80665 49911 98818 34797 75356
63698 07426 54252 78625 51818 41757 46728 90977 77279 38000
81647 06001 61452 49192 17321 72147 72350 14144 19735 68548
16136 11573 52552 13347 57418 49468 43852 33239 07394 14333
45477 62416 86251 89835 69485 56209 92192 22184 27255 02542
56887 67179 04946 01653 46680 49886 27232 79178 60857 84383
82796 79766 81454 10095 38837 86360 95068 00642 25125 20511
73929 84896 08412 84886 26945 60424 19652 85022 21066 11863
06744 27862 20391 94945 04712 37137 86960 95636 43719 17287
46776 46575 73962 41389 08658 32645 99581 33904 78027 59009

94657 64078 95126 94683 98352 59570 98258
```

02:57:36.640 (00:40:40) TOTAL TIME

----- Second arctan formula -----

02:57:36.690 (00:00:00) START TIME

02:57:36.690 (00:00:00) Initializing

```
02:57:37.900 (00:00:01) Computing arctan(1/10)
03:19:34.300 (00:21:56) Computing arctan(1/515)
03:27:41.160 (00:08:07) Computing arctan(1/239)
03:36:57.060 (00:09:16) Computing pi
03:36:57.060 (00:00:00) pi computed

pi = 3.14159 26535 89793 23846 26433 83279 50288 41971 69399 37510
              . . .

         94657 64078 95126 94683 98352 59570 98258

03:36:57.940 (00:39:21) TOTAL TIME
```

13.3 Generating Billions of Digits

In 1985, two brothers who are mathematicians, Jonathan Borwein and Peter Borwein, published an algorithm that can generate billions of digits of π—assuming the computer has sufficient memory! Program 13–3 implements this algorithm, which is simple to describe.

Set $a_0 = 6 - 4\sqrt{2}$ and $y_0 = \sqrt{2} - 1$. Then iterate

$$y_i = \frac{1 - \sqrt[4]{1 - y_{i-1}^4}}{1 + \sqrt[4]{1 - y_{i-1}^4}}$$

$$a_i = a_{i-1}(1 + y_i)^4 - 2^{2i+1} y_i(1 + y_i + y_i^2)$$

and the a_i will converge quartically toward $\frac{1}{\pi}$.

Iteration #1 produces 8 correct decimal digits, iteration #2 produces 41 digits, iteration #3 produces 171 digits, iteration #4 produces 694 digits, and each subsequent iteration increases the number of correct digits by more than a factor of 4. Because it needs to test for convergence, the program will do one more iteration than necessary. But it stops partway through the last iteration when it realizes that's the last one.

This program computes the digits of π in several phases, and each phase can consist of several tasks. Table 13–3 shows the phases and tasks.

Listing 13–3a shows class `PiBorweinAlgorithm`, which implements the algorithm.

Listing 13–3a Class `PiBorweinAlgorithm`.

```
package numbercruncher.program13_3;

import java.math.BigDecimal;
import numbercruncher.mathutils.BigFunctions;

/**
 * Implement the Borwein algorithm for pi.
 */
class PiBorweinAlgorithm implements PiBorweinConstants
{
```

Table 13-3 Phases and tasks of the Borwein algorithm for π.

Phase	Task	Computation
Initialization	constants	BigDecimal 1, 2, 4, 6, and $5 \times 10^{-(scale + 1)}$
	sqrt2	$\sqrt{2}$
	y	$y_0 = \sqrt{2} - 1$
	a	$a_0 = 6 - 4\sqrt{2}$
Iteration i	y4	y_{i-1}^4
	yRoot4	$\sqrt[4]{1 - y_{i-1}^4}$
	y	$y_i = \left(1 - \sqrt[4]{1 - y_{i-1}^4}\right) \Big/ \left(1 + \sqrt[4]{1 - y_{i-1}^4}\right)$
	aTerm	$a_{i-1} (1 + y_i)^4$
	power2	2^{2i+1}
	y2	y_i^2
	a	$a_i = a_{i-1} (1 + y_i)^4 - 2^{2i+1} y_i (1 + y_i + y_i^2)$
Inverting		$1/a_i$

```
/** number of pi digits */    private int digits;
/** computation scale */      private int scale;
/** iteration counter */      private int iterations;

/** value of pi */            private BigDecimal     pi;
/** parent object */          private PiBorweinParent parent;

/**
 * Constructor.
 * @param digits the number of digits to compute
 * @param parent the parent object
 */
PiBorweinAlgorithm(int digits, PiBorweinParent parent)
{
    this.digits = digits;
    this.parent = parent;
    this.scale  = Math.max(((int) (1.005f*digits)), (digits + 5));
}

/**
 * Get the number of iterations.
```

```
 * @return the number of iterations
 */
int getIterations() { return iterations; }

/**
 * Get the value of pi as a string.
 * @return the string
 */
String getPi() { return pi.toString(); }

/**
 * Compute the digits of pi.
 * Notify the parent of each phase and task.
 */
void compute()
{
    parent.notifyScale(scale);

    // Initialization phase.
    parent.notifyPhase(INITIALIZING);
    parent.notifyTask("constants");

    BigDecimal big1    = BigDecimal.valueOf(1);
    BigDecimal big2    = BigDecimal.valueOf(2);
    BigDecimal big4    = BigDecimal.valueOf(4);
    BigDecimal big6    = BigDecimal.valueOf(6);
    BigDecimal power2 = big2;

    parent.notifyTask("sqrt2");
    BigDecimal sqrt2 = BigFunctions.sqrt(big2, scale);

    parent.notifyTask("y");
    BigDecimal y = sqrt2.subtract(BigDecimal.valueOf(1));

    parent.notifyTask("a");
    BigDecimal a =
        big6.subtract(
            big4.multiply(sqrt2)
                .setScale(scale, BigDecimal.ROUND_HALF_EVEN));

    BigDecimal y2, y4, yRoot4, yNumerator, yDenominator;
    BigDecimal aTerm4, aTerm;

    // Loop once per iteration.
    for (;;) {
        parent.notifyPhase(++iterations);

        parent.notifyTask("y4");
        y4 = y.multiply(y)
```

```
                          .setScale(scale, BigDecimal.ROUND_HALF_EVEN);
          y4 = y4.multiply(y4)
                          .setScale(scale, BigDecimal.ROUND_HALF_EVEN);

          parent.notifyTask("yRoot4");
          yRoot4 = BigFunctions.sqrt(big1.subtract(y4), scale);
          yRoot4 = BigFunctions.sqrt(yRoot4, scale);

          parent.notifyTask("y");
          yNumerator   = big1.subtract(yRoot4);
          yDenominator = big1.add(yRoot4);
          y = yNumerator.divide(yDenominator, scale,
                                BigDecimal.ROUND_HALF_EVEN);

          if (y.signum() == 0) break;

          parent.notifyTask("aTerm");
          aTerm4 = big1.add(y);
          aTerm4 = aTerm4.multiply(aTerm4)
                          .setScale(scale, BigDecimal.ROUND_HALF_EVEN);
          aTerm4 = aTerm4.multiply(aTerm4)
                          .setScale(scale, BigDecimal.ROUND_HALF_EVEN);
          a = a.multiply(aTerm4)
                          .setScale(scale, BigDecimal.ROUND_HALF_EVEN);

          parent.notifyTask("power2");
          power2 = power2.multiply(big4)
                          .setScale(scale, BigDecimal.ROUND_HALF_EVEN);

          parent.notifyTask("y2");
          y2 = y.multiply(y)
                          .setScale(scale, BigDecimal.ROUND_HALF_EVEN);

          parent.notifyTask("a");
          aTerm = big1.add(y).add(y2);
          aTerm = power2.multiply(y).multiply(aTerm)
                          .setScale(scale, BigDecimal.ROUND_HALF_EVEN);
          a = a.subtract(aTerm)
                          .setScale(scale, BigDecimal.ROUND_HALF_EVEN);
      }

      // Inversion phase.
      parent.notifyPhase(INVERTING);
      pi = big1.divide(a, digits, BigDecimal.ROUND_DOWN);

      parent.notifyPhase(DONE);
    }
}
```

Method `compute()` executes the algorithm. It notifies the parent object of the current phase and task. The parent object must implement interface `PiBorweinParent`, shown in Listing 13–3b.

To ensure the accuracy of the last few computed digits of π, method `compute()` does its computations with a scale that is 0.5% greater than the desired number of digits (at least five digits more).

Listing 13–3b Interface `PiBorweinParent`.

```
package numbercruncher.program13_3;

/**
 * Interface for the parent of a PiBorwein object.
 */
interface PiBorweinParent
{
    /**
     * Scale notification.
     * @param scale the scale being used
     */
    void notifyScale(int scale);

    /**
     * Phase notification.
     * @param phase the current phase
     */
    void notifyPhase(int phase);

    /**
     * Task notification.
     * @param task the current computation task
     */
    void notifyTask(String task);
}
```

Phase notification is done with a set of constants in interface `PiBorweinConstants`, which is shown in Listing 13–3c.

Listing 13–3c Constants for the Borwein algorithm in interface `PiBorweinConstants`.

```
package numbercruncher.program13_3;

/**
 * Constants for the Borwein pi algorithm.
 */
```

```
interface PiBorweinConstants
{
    static final int INITIALIZING = -1;
    static final int INVERTING    = -2;
    static final int DONE         = -3;
    static final int STOPPED      = -4;

    static final String STOPPED_EXCEPTION = "STOPPED";
}
```

Finally, Listing 13–3d shows Program 13–3 and its output. The noninteractive version of the program prints timestamped lines, each of which contains the current phase and task. As in Program 13–2, each timestamp includes the elapsed time (hh:mm:ss) of the previous phase.

Listing 13–3d Program 13–3 and its output.

```
package numbercruncher.program13_3;

import java.math.BigDecimal;

import numbercruncher.mathutils.BigFunctions;
import numbercruncher.piutils.PiFormula;

/**
 * PROGRAM 13-3: The Borwein Pi Algorithm
 *
 * Compute digits of pi by the Borwein algorithm.
 */
public class PiBorwein extends PiFormula
                       implements PiBorweinParent, PiBorweinConstants
{
    /** number of digits to compute */  private int digits;

    /** the Borwein algorithm */
    private PiBorweinAlgorithm algorithm;

    /**
     * Compute the digits of pi using the Borwein algorithm.
     * @param digits the number of digits of pi to compute
     */
    private void compute(int digits)
    {
        this.digits = digits;

        startTime = System.currentTimeMillis();
        System.out.println(timestamp(startTime) + " START TIME\n");
```

```
        algorithm = new PiBorweinAlgorithm(digits, this);
        algorithm.compute();
    }

    /**
     * Main.
     * @param args the array of program arguments
     */
    public static void main(String args[])
    {
        PiBorwein pi = new PiBorwein();

        try {
            int digits = Integer.parseInt(args[0]);
            pi.compute(digits);
        }
        catch(Exception ex) {
            System.out.println("ERROR: " + ex.getMessage());
        }
    }

    //----------------------------------//
    // Implementation of PiBorweinParent //
    //----------------------------------//

    /**
     * Scale notification.
     * @param scale the scale being used
     */
    public void notifyScale(int scale)
    {
        System.out.println("digits = " + digits);
        System.out.println("scale  = " + scale);
    }

    /**
     * Phase notification.
     * @param phase the current phase
     */
    public void notifyPhase(int phase)
    {
        switch (phase) {

            case INITIALIZING: {
                System.out.print("\n" + timestamp(startTime) +
                                 " Initialization:");
                break;
            }
```

```
        case INVERTING: {
            System.out.println("\n" + timestamp(markTime) +
                              " Inverting");
            break;
        }
        case DONE: {
            System.out.println(timestamp(markTime) +
                              " pi computed");

            String totalTime = timestamp(startTime);
            printPi(algorithm.getPi());

            System.out.println("\n" + algorithm.getIterations() +
                              " iterations");
            System.out.println(totalTime + " TOTAL COMPUTE TIME");

            break;
        }

        default: {
            System.out.print("\n" + timestamp(markTime) +
                              " Iteration " + phase + ":");
            break;
        }
    }

    markTime = System.currentTimeMillis();
}

/**
 * Task notification.
 * @param task the current computation task
 */
public void notifyTask(String task)
{
    System.out.print(" " + task);
}
}
```

Output:

```
01:29:30.720 (00:00:00) START TIME

digits = 700
scale  = 705
```

```
01:29:30.720 (00:00:00) Initialization: constants sqrt2 y a
01:29:31.320 (00:00:01) Iteration 1: y4 yRoot4 y aTerm power2 y2 a
01:29:32.370 (00:00:01) Iteration 2: y4 yRoot4 y aTerm power2 y2 a
01:29:33.580 (00:00:01) Iteration 3: y4 yRoot4 y aTerm power2 y2 a
01:29:35.170 (00:00:02) Iteration 4: y4 yRoot4 y aTerm power2 y2 a
01:29:36.870 (00:00:02) Iteration 5: y4 yRoot4 y aTerm power2 y2 a
01:29:38.520 (00:00:02) Iteration 6: y4 yRoot4 y
01:29:39.230 (00:00:01) Inverting
01:29:39.620 (00:00:00) pi computed

pi = 3.14159 26535 89793 23846 26433 83279 50288 41971 69399 37510
        58209 74944 59230 78164 06286 20899 86280 34825 34211 70679
        82148 08651 32823 06647 09384 46095 50582 23172 53594 08128
        48111 74502 84102 70193 85211 05559 64462 29489 54930 38196
        44288 10975 66593 34461 28475 64823 37867 83165 27120 19091
        45648 56692 34603 48610 45432 66482 13393 60726 02491 41273
        72458 70066 06315 58817 48815 20920 96282 92540 91715 36436
        78925 90360 01133 05305 48820 46652 13841 46951 94151 16094
        33057 27036 57595 91953 09218 61173 81932 61179 31051 18548
        07446 23799 62749 56735 18857 52724 89122 79381 83011 94912

        98336 73362 44065 66430 86021 39494 63952 24737 19070 21798
        60943 70277 05392 17176 29317 67523 84674 81846 76694 05132
        00056 81271 45263 56082 77857 71342 75778 96091 73637 17872
        14684 40901 22495 34301 46549 58537 10507 92279 68925 89235

6 iterations
01:29:39.620 (00:00:09) TOTAL COMPUTE TIME
```

Screen 13–3 shows the interactive[5] version of Program 13–3 after it has computed 100,200 digits of π. This applet was run in Microsoft's Internet Explorer version 6.0 (on a 266 MHz Pentium II), which evidently contains a very fast Java virtual machine.

The first 100,200 digits of π were computed in 1961 on an IBM 7090 computer using the arctangent formula

$$\frac{\pi}{4} = 24 \arctan \frac{1}{8} + 8 \arctan \frac{1}{57} + 4 \arctan \frac{1}{239}$$

It required 8 hours and 43 minutes.

---

[5] Each interactive program in this book has two versions, an applet and a standalone application. You can download all the Java source code. See the downloading instructions in the preface of this book.

Screen 13–3 The interactive version of Program 13–3 after it computed 100,200 digits of π.

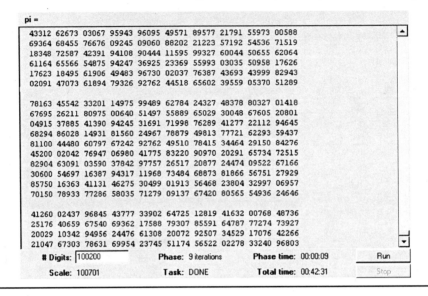

References

Beckmann, Peter, *A History of Pi,* New York: St. Martin's Press, 1971.

This book lists estimates of π through history on pages 196–197. It is a fascinating account of the history of π. Chapter 13 includes the derivation of Machin's arctangent formula.

Berggren, Lennart, Jonathan Borwein, and Peter Borwein, eds. *Pi: A Source Book,* New York: Springer-Verlag, 1997.

This invaluable collection of writings on π ranges from technical and scholarly papers to the quirky and whimsical.

Borwein, Jonathan M., and Peter B. Borwein, "Ramanujan and Pi." In *Pi: A Source Book,* edited by L. Berggren, J. Borwein, and P. Borwein, New York: Springer-Verlag, 1997.

This paper is about Ramanujan's formulas for π, but it also includes the Borweins' algorithm for generating billions of π's digits.

Ramanujan, "Modular Equations and Approximations to π." In *Pi: A Source Book,* edited by L. Berggren, J. Borwein, and P. Borwein, New York: Springer-Verlag, 1997.

In this work, Ramanujan derives his formulas that estimate the value of π to various numbers of decimal digits.

Reitwiesner, "An ENIAC Determination of π and e to 2000 Decimal Places." In *Pi: A Source Book,* edited by L. Berggren, J. Borwein, and P. Borwein, New York: Springer-Verlag, 1997.

Reitwiesner describes using an arctangent formula on the ENIAC to compute the first 2,035 decimal digits of π. This papter is reprinted in Berggren, Borwein, and Borwein, which includes a table of more arctangent formulas on page 687.

Shanks, Daniel, and John W. Wrench, Jr., "Calculation of π to 100,000 Decimals." In *Pi: A Source Book,* edited by L. Berggren, J. Borwein, and P. Borwein, New York: Springer-Verlag, 1997.

Shanks and Wrench describe using an arctangent formula on the IBM 7090 to compute the first 100,200 decimal digits of π.

CHAPTER 14

GENERATING RANDOM NUMBERS

Computers are often used to generate random numbers, which are useful for the simulation of physical phenomena, testing, statistical analysis, and computer games.

In this chapter, we first define what we mean by "random" and ask whether or not an algorithm can truly generate random numbers. We then examine algorithms for generating uniformly distributed, normally distributed, and exponentially distributed random numbers.

Finally, we look at a Monte Carlo algorithm, which uses random numbers to derive a result. The algorithm we'll examine is Buffon's needle, which gives us yet another way to compute the value of π—not as precise as the algorithms in Chapter 13, but certainly intriguing.

14.1 Pseudorandom Numbers

Truly random numbers are unpredictable—you cannot determine the exact value of the next number. However, random values can have certain well-known distributions. When random values are uniformly distributed between a minimum and a maximum value (for example, between 0 and 1), every value has an equal probability of occurring. Random values that are normally distributed have probabilities that are represented by the familiar bell curve.

A random number generator incorporates an algorithm for generating random values. We typically start each algorithm with a given value, called the *seed*. The random number generator uses the seed to generate the first random value, and then it uses the first value to generate the second random value, and so on. But if the algorithm is self-enclosed—it does not incorporate a "live" value from the outside world, such as the level of some electric noise, the least significant bits of the system clock time, or the measured response time of a person—the generator cannot produce unpredictable values.

If such an algorithm is given the same seed value each time, it will always generate the same sequence of values, so we try to compensate by making the initial seed value as random as possible. A common trick is to use the current system clock time (or some of its least significant digits) as the seed. However, although the sequence of generated values will be different for each seed value, the algorithm will precisely determine each "random" value based on the previous value in the sequence.

Therefore, a random number generator can produce values that only *appear* to be random. The best algorithms have long periods—they generate a long sequence of values before the sequence repeats itself. It is common to call the values cranked out by a computer random number generator *pseudorandom numbers*. Though not truly random, these values are still very useful. In the rest of this chapter, we'll drop the prefix *pseudo* when referring to computer-generated random numbers.

14.2 Uniformly Distributed Random Numbers

The most straightforward random numbers to generate are ones that are uniformly distributed between a minimum value and a maximum value. Each value has an equal probability of being anywhere within that range.

A very popular algorithm for generating uniformly distributed random values is the *linear congruential algorithm*. This algorithm generates random integer values that range over all the possible positive and negative values of the integer type. It uses the formula

$$x_{n+1} = (mx_n + a) \bmod d$$

where the x_i are the generated random values, m is a constant multiplier, a is a constant addend, and d is a constant divisor. A seed value kicks off the sequence. The formula relies on the fact that integer arithmetic does not overflow but wraps around. (See Chapter 2.)

The trick is to find the right constants m, a, and d such that the random x values have a long period. The period cannot have more than d different values, and so we want a large value for d. To make the random number generator fast, we can choose d to be 1 less than a power of 2 (and so its binary representation is a string of 1 bits), and then we can perform the modulo operation with a logical *and* operation using the value of d as the mask. We should also choose values of m and d that are relatively prime (they have no factors in common).

In the standard class `java.util.Random`, method `nextInt()` uses the linear congruential algorithm with the constant values $m = 25,214,903,917$, $a = 11$, and $d = 281,474,976,710,655 (= 2^{48} - 1)$.

An algorithm that produces uniformly distributed random integer values can be the basis of other random number generators. For example, method `java.util.Random.nextFloat()` returns a uniformly distributed random float value between 0 and 1 by first generating a random positive 24-bit integer value and then dividing that value by 2^{24}. Uniformly distributed random values can also be used to generate random values with other distributions, as we'll see in the following sections.

14.3 Normally Distributed Random Numbers

Suppose we used a random number generator that produces uniformly distributed `float` values between 0 and 1 to produce n random values at a time, and then we averaged each group of values. How would the averages be distributed?

If we look at a large number of random values that are uniformly distributed between 0 and 1, their overall average should be 0.5. But if we average small groups of these values, say $n = 12$ at a time, then these group averages should "bunch up" around 0.5—some of the averages should be less than 0.5 and others greater, but most of them should be close to 0.5. In fact, the *Central Limit Theorem* of statistics states that these group averages will be normally distributed with a mean of 0.5. In other words, their distribution is the familiar bell curve with its peak at 0.5. So we've managed to derive our first algorithm for generating normally distributed random values.

Other algorithms for generating normally distributed random values are more obscure. We'll investigate two more that also start with uniformly distributed random values.

Method `java.util.Random.nextGaussian()` uses the *polar algorithm*. We begin this algorithm by generating two random values v_1 and v_2 that are uniformly distributed between -1 and $+1$. We then compute the value $s = v_1{}^2 + v_2{}^2$. If $s > 1$, we reject the values of v_1 and v_2 and generate new ones. In other words, if we consider v_1 and v_2 to be the x and y coordinates of a point, we want only uniformly distributed random points that are inside the unit circle.

With two good values of v_1 and v_2, we then compute

$$x_1 = v_1 \sqrt{\frac{-2 \ln s}{s}}$$

and

$$x_2 = v_2 \sqrt{\frac{-2 \ln s}{s}}$$

We won't prove it here—the references at the end of this chapter contain the proofs—but the values of x_1 and x_2 are normally distributed. This algorithm cranks them out two at a time.

Another algorithm is the *ratio algorithm*. Again, we start with two uniformly distributed random values, this time between 0 and 1, and which we'll call u and v. The value of u cannot be 0. We compute the value

$$x = \frac{\left(v - \frac{1}{2}\right)\sqrt{\frac{8}{e}}}{u}$$

Now we subject the value of x to up to three tests:

- **Quick acceptance test:** If $x^2 \leq 5 - 4u \sqrt[4]{e}$ then terminate the algorithm and deliver the value of x.
- **Quick rejection test:** If $x^2 \geq 1.4 + \dfrac{4e^{-1.35}}{u}$ then reject this value of x and compute new values for u and v.
- **Final acceptance test:** If $x^2 \leq -4 \ln u$ then terminate the algorithm and deliver the value of x. Otherwise, reject this value of x and compute new values for u and v.

The values of x that this algorithm delivers are normally distributed. Again, see the references at the end of this chapter for proofs.

Listing 14–1a shows class `RandomNormal` in package `numbercruncher.mathutils`, which implements these three algorithms. Each of the three methods `nextCentral()`, `nextPolar()`, and `nextRatio()` returns the next random value from a normal distribution with a given mean and standard deviation.

Listing 14–1a Class `RandomNormal`, which implements three algorithms for generating normally distributed random values.

```
package numbercruncher.mathutils;

import java.util.Random;

/**
 * Utility class that generates normally-distributed
 * random values using several algorithms.
 */
public class RandomNormal
{
    /** mean */                 private float mean;
    /** standard deviation */   private float stddev;

    /** next random value from
        the polar algorithm   */ private float    nextPolar;
    /** true if the next polar
        value is available   */  private boolean haveNextPolar = false;

    /** generator of uniformly-distributed random values */
    private static Random gen = new Random();

    /**
     * Set the mean and standard deviation.
     * @param mean the mean
     * @param stddev the standard deviation
     */
```

```
public void setParameters(float mean, float stddev)
{
    this.mean   = mean;
    this.stddev = stddev;
}


/**
 * Compute the next random value using the Central Limit Theorem,
 * which states that the averages of sets of uniformly-distributed
 * random values are normally distributed.
 */
public float nextCentral()
{
    // Average 12 uniformly-distributed random values.
    float sum = 0.0f;
    for (int j = 0; j < 12; ++j) sum += gen.nextFloat();

    // Subtract 6 to center about 0.
    return stddev*(sum - 6) + mean;
}


/**
 * Compute the next randomn value using the polar algorithm.
 * Requires two uniformly-distributed random values in [-1, +1).
 * Actually computes two random values and saves the second one
 * for the next invokation.
 */
public float nextPolar()
{
    // If there's a saved value, return it.
    if (haveNextPolar) {
        haveNextPolar = false;
        return nextPolar;
    }

    float u1, u2, r;    // point coordinates and their radius

    do {
        // u1 and u2 will be uniformly-distributed
        // random values in [-1, +1).
        u1 = 2*gen.nextFloat() - 1;
        u2 = 2*gen.nextFloat() - 1;

        // Want radius r inside the unit circle.
        r = u1*u1 + u2*u2;
    } while (r >= 1);

    // Factor incorporates the standard deviation.
    float factor = (float) (stddev*Math.sqrt(-2*Math.log(r)/r));
```

```
        // v1 and v2 are normally-distributed random values.
        float v1 = factor*u1 + mean;
        float v2 = factor*u2 + mean;

        // Save v1 for next time.
        nextPolar      = v1;
        haveNextPolar = true;

        return v2;
    }


    // Constants for the ratio algorithm.
    private static final float C1 = (float) Math.sqrt(8/Math.E);
    private static final float C2 = (float) (4*Math.exp(0.25));
    private static final float C3 = (float) (4*Math.exp(-1.35));


    /**
     * Compute the next random value using the ratio algorithm.
     * Requires two uniformly-distributed random values in [0, 1).
     */
    public float nextRatio()
    {
        float u, v, x, xx;

        do {
            // u and v are two uniformly-distributed random values
            // in [0, 1), and u != 0.
            while ((u = gen.nextFloat()) == 0);   // try again if 0
            v = gen.nextFloat();

            float y = C1*(v - 0.5f);     // y coord of point (u, y)
            x = y/u;                     // ratio of point's coords

            xx = x*x;
        } while (
            (xx > 5f - C2*u)                       // quick acceptance
                &&
            ( (xx >= C3/u + 1.4f) ||               // quick rejection
              (xx > (float) (-4*Math.log(u))) ) // final test
        );

        return stddev*x + mean;
    }
}
```

Program 14–1 demonstrates these algorithms. It generates 100,000 random values with each algorithm and counts how many values fall into each of 32 equal-width intervals. The program prints the results of each algorithm as a bar chart, in which the length of each bar for an interval is determined by that interval's count. The bars form bell curves. See Listing 14–1b.

Listing 14–1b A demonstration of three algorithms for generating normally distributed random values.

```
package numbercruncher.program14_1;

import numbercruncher.mathutils.RandomNormal;
import numbercruncher.randomutils.Buckets;

/**
 * PROGRAM 14-1: Normally-Distributed Random Numbers
 *
 * Demonstrate algorithms for generating normally-distributed
 * random numbers.
 */
public class GenerateRandomNormal
{
    private static final int BUCKET_COUNT = 32;
    private static final int NUMBER_COUNT = 100000;    // 100K

    /** counters of random values that fall within each interval */
    private Buckets buckets = new Buckets(BUCKET_COUNT);

    /** generator of normally-distributed random values */
    private RandomNormal normal;

    /**
     * Test the algorithms with a given mean and standard deviation.
     * @param mean the mean
     * @param stddev the standard deviation
     */
    private void run(float mean, float stddev)
    {
        long startTime;       // starting time of each algorithm

        // Initialize the random number generator
        // and the interval buckets.
        normal = new RandomNormal();
        normal.setParameters(mean, stddev);
        buckets.setLimits(0, BUCKET_COUNT-1);

        // Central limit theorem algorithm.
        startTime = System.currentTimeMillis();
        buckets.clear();
        central();
        print("Central", startTime);
```

```java
    // Polar algorithm.
    startTime = System.currentTimeMillis();
    buckets.clear();
    polar();
    print("Polar", startTime);

    // Ratio algorithm.
    startTime = System.currentTimeMillis();
    buckets.clear();
    ratio();
    print("Ratio", startTime);
}

/**
 * Print the results of an algorithm with its elapsed time.
 * @param label the algorithm label
 * @param startTime the starting time
 */
private void print(String label, long startTime)
{

    long elapsedTime = System.currentTimeMillis() - startTime;

    System.out.println("\n" + label + " (" + elapsedTime +
                       " ms):\n");

    buckets.print();
}

/**
 * Invoke the Central Limit Theorem algorithm.
 */
private void central()
{
    for (int i = 0; i < NUMBER_COUNT; ++i) {
        buckets.put(normal.nextCentral());
    }
}

/**
 * Invoke the polar algorithm.
 */
private void polar()
{
    for (int i = 0; i < NUMBER_COUNT; ++i) {
        buckets.put(normal.nextPolar());
    }
}
```

```
    /**
     * Invoke the ratio algorithm.
     */
    private void ratio()
    {
        for (int i = 0; i < NUMBER_COUNT; ++i ) {
            buckets.put(normal.nextRatio());
        }
    }


    /**
     * Main.
     * @param args the array of program arguments
     */
    public static void main(String args[])
    {
        float mean   = BUCKET_COUNT/2f;
        float stddev = BUCKET_COUNT/6f;

        GenerateRandomNormal test = new GenerateRandomNormal();
        test.run(mean, stddev);
    }
}
```

Output:

```
Central (710 ms):

 0     87: *
 1    164: *
 2    313: **
 3    413: ***
 4    691: *****
 5    994: *******
 6   1430: *********
 7   2005: *************
 8   2572: *****************
 9   3158: *********************
10   3968: **************************
11   4804: ********************************
12   5508: ************************************
13   6241: *****************************************
14   6784: ********************************************
15   7014: **********************************************
16   7068: ***********************************************
17   7028: ***********************************************
18   6791: ********************************************
19   6246: *****************************************
20   5535: ************************************
```

```
21    4840: *******************************
22    3968: **************************
23    3349: ***********************
24    2656: ******************
25    1966: *************
26    1472: *********
27    1042: *******
28     702: *****
29     419: ***
30     283: **
31     172: *


Polar (490 ms):


 0     117: *
 1     190: *
 2     271: **
 3     431: ***
 4     665: *****
 5     929: ******
 6    1432: *********
 7    1989: *************
 8    2478: ****************
 9    3269: *********************
10    3925: *************************
11    4886: *********************************
12    5509: *************************************
13    6212: ******************************************
14    6628: ********************************************
15    7106: ************************************************
16    7261: *************************************************
17    7101: ************************************************
18    6743: *********************************************
19    6339: ******************************************
20    5573: ************************************
21    4816: *******************************
22    3994: *************************
23    3301: *********************
24    2514: ****************
25    1932: ************
26    1391: *********
27     960: *******
28     690: *****
29     443: ***
30     301: **
31     192: *
```

```
Ratio (550 ms):

 0     98: *
 1    183: *
 2    283: **
 3    454: ***
 4    685: *****
 5    995: *******
 6   1428: *********
 7   1933: ************
 8   2497: ****************
 9   3209: ********************
10   4053: **************************
11   4762: ******************************
12   5502: ***********************************
13   6204: ****************************************
14   6758: *******************************************
15   7013: *********************************************
16   7293: ***********************************************
17   7121: **********************************************
18   6838: *******************************************
19   6237: ****************************************
20   5453: ***********************************
21   4802: ******************************
22   3950: *************************
23   3389: *********************
24   2533: ****************
25   2009: *************
26   1342: ********
27   1016: *******
28    673: *****
29    440: ***
30    277: **
31    216: *
```

The program also prints the elapsed time for each algorithm. The algorithm that uses the Central Limit Theorem is the simplest to program and understand, but it's the slowest because it requires the most uniformly distributed random values. The polar algorithm is the fastest of the three, and it is the algorithm used by the method `java.util.Random.nextGaussian()`.

The interval counters used by Program 14–1 are implemented by class `Buckets`, which is shown in Listing 14–1c.

Listing 14–1c Class `Buckets`, which implements the interval counters.

```
package numbercruncher.randomutils;

import numbercruncher.mathutils.AlignRight;
```

```java
/**
 * Counters of random values that fall within each interval.
 */
public class Buckets
{
    private static final int MAX_BAR_SIZE = 50;

    private AlignRight ar = new AlignRight();

    /** number of intervals */        private int n;
    /** counters per interval */       private int counters[];
    /** minimum random value */        private float rMin;
    /** maximum random value */        private float rMax;
    /** from min to max */             private float width;

    /**
     * Constructor.
     * @param n the number of intervals
     */
    public Buckets(int n)
    {
        this.n = n;
        this.counters = new int[n];
        clear();
    }

    /**
     * Return the counter value for interval i.
     * @param i the value of i
     * @return the counter value
     */
    public int get(int i) { return counters[i]; }

    /**
     * Set the minimum and maximum random values.
     * @param rMin the minimum value
     * @param rMax the maximum value
     */
    public void setLimits(float rMin, float rMax)
    {
        this.rMin  = rMin;
        this.rMax  = rMax;
        this.width = (rMax - rMin)/n;
    }

    /**
     * Determine a random value's interval and count it.
     * @param r the random value
```

```
    */
    public void put(float r)
    {
        // Ignore the value if it's out of range.
        if ((r < rMin) || (r > rMax)) return;

        // Determine its interval and count it.
        int i = (int) ((r - rMin)/width);
        ++counters[i];
    }

    /**
     * Clear all the interval counters.
     */
    public void clear()
    {
        for (int i = 0; i < counters.length; ++1) counters (i) =0;
    }

    /**
     * Print the counter values as a horizontal bar chart. Scale the
     * chart so that the longest bar is MAX_BAR_SIZE.
     */
    public void print()
    {
        // Get the longest bar's length.
        int maxCount = 0;
        for (int i = 0; i < n; ++i) {
            maxCount = Math.max(maxCount, counters[i]);
        }

        // Compute the scaling factor.
        float factor = ((float) MAX_BAR_SIZE)/maxCount;
        // Loop to print each bar.
        for (int i = 0; i < n; ++i) {
            int b = counters[i];

            // Interval number.
            ar.print(i, 2);
            ar.print(b, 7);
            System.out.print(": ");

            // Bar.
            int length = Math.round(factor*b);
            for (int j = 0; j < length; ++j) System.out.print("*");
            System.out.println();
        }
    }
}
```

Screen 14–1 A screen shot of the interactive version of Program 14–1.

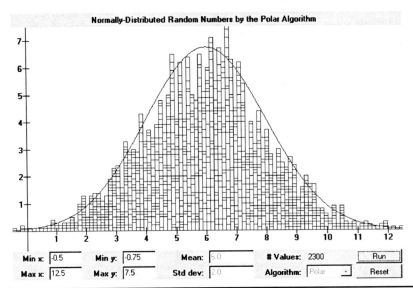

The screen shot in Screen 14–1 shows the interactive[1] version of Program 14–1. With far fewer random values, the bell curve formed by the interval counts is much rougher. The interactive program also plots the bell curve defined by the normal distribution function

$$f(x) = \frac{1}{\sigma\sqrt{2\pi}}e^{\left[-\frac{1}{2}\left(\frac{x-\mu}{\sigma}\right)^2\right]}$$

where μ is the mean of the distribution and σ is its standard deviation.

14.4 Exponentially Distributed Random Numbers

Exponentially distributed random values model service times, component lifetimes, and the elapsed time between two random events. The distribution function is

$$f(x) = \frac{1}{\mu}e^{\left[-\frac{x}{\mu}\right]}$$

where μ is the mean of the distribution.

---

[1]   Each interactive program in this book has two versions, an applet and a standalone application. You can download all the Java source code. See the downloading instructions in the preface of this book.

We'll examine two algorithms for generating exponentially distributed random values. Like the algorithms that generate normally distributed random values, these algorithms also work from uniformly distributed random values. The references at the end of this chapter contain proofs of why they work.

The first algorithm, the *logarithm algorithm,* is simple to program. If values of u are uniformly distributed, then for $u \neq 0$, the values of x defined by

$$x = -\mu \ln u$$

are exponentially distributed.

The second algorithm is the *von Neumann algorithm,* which is named after its discoverer. It is a bit strange:

1. Set $k = 0$.
2. Generate a sequence of uniformly distributed random values $u_1, u_2, \ldots, u_n$ as long as their values are decreasing—that is, until $u_{n+1} > u_n$.
3. If n is even, then deliver the value $x = u_1 + k$. Otherwise, increase k by 1 and go back to the previous step.

The values of x that this algorithm delivers are exponentially distributed.

Listing 14–2a shows class `RandomExponential` in package `numbercruncher.mathutils`, which implements these two algorithms.

Listing 14–2a Class `RandomExponential`, which implements two algorithms for generating exponentially distributed random values.

```
package numbercruncher.mathutils;

import java.util.Random;

/**
 * Utility class that generates exponentially-distributed
 * random values using several algorithms.
 */
public class RandomExponential
{
    private float mean;

    /** generator of uniformly-distributed random values */
    private static Random gen = new Random();

    /**
     * Set the mean.
     * @param mean the mean
     */
    public void setParameters(float mean) { this.mean = mean; }
```

```java
/**
 * Compute the next random value using the logarithm algorithm.
 * Requires a uniformly-distributed random value in [0, 1).
.*/
public float nextLog()
{
    // Generate a non-zero uniformly-distributed random value.
    float u;
    while ((u = gen.nextFloat()) == 0);      // try again if 0

    return (float) (-mean*Math.log(u));
}

/**
 * Compute the next randomn value using the von Neumann algorithm.
 * Requires sequences of uniformly-distributed random values
 * in [0, 1).
 */
public float nextVonNeumann()
{
    int   n;
    int   k = 0;
    float u1;

    // Loop to try sequences of uniformly-distributed
    // random values.
    for (;;) {
        n  = 1;
        u1 = gen.nextFloat();

        float u     = u1;
        float uPrev = Float.NaN;

        // Loop to generate a sequence of ramdom values
        // as long as they are decreasing.
        for (;;) {
            uPrev = u;
            u     = gen.nextFloat();

            // No longer decreasing?
            if (u > uPrev) {

                // n is even.
                if ((n & 1) == 0) {
                    return u1 + k;  // return a random value
                }

                // n is odd.
                else {
```

```
                              ++k;
                              break;              // try another sequence
                        }
                  }
                  ++n;
            }
      }
   }
}
```

Program 14–2 demonstrates both algorithms and, like Program 14–1, prints bar charts with timings. See Listing 14–2b.

Listing 14–2b A demonstration of two algorithms for generating exponentially distributed random values.

```
package numbercruncher.program14_2;

import numbercruncher.mathutils.RandomExponential;
import numbercruncher.randomutils.Buckets;

/**
 * PROGRAM 14-2: Exponentially-Distributed Random Numbers
 *
 * Demonstrate algorithms for generating exponentially-distributed
 * random numbers.
 */
public class GenerateRandomExponential
{
    private static final int NUMBER_COUNT = 100000;     // 100K

    /** counters of random values that fall within each interval */
    private Buckets buckets;

    private RandomExponential exponential;

    private void run(float mean)
    {
        long startTime;     // starting time of each algorithm

        // Initialize the random number generator.
        exponential = new RandomExponential();
        exponential.setParameters(mean);

        // Logarithm algorithm.
        startTime = System.currentTimeMillis();
```

```java
        buckets = new Buckets(32);
        buckets.setLimits(0, 2);
        log();
        print("Logarithm", startTime);

        // von Neumann algorithm.
        startTime = System.currentTimeMillis();
        buckets = new Buckets(13);
        buckets.setLimits(0, 12);
        vonNeumann();
        print("von Neumann", startTime);
    }

    /**
     * Print the results of an algorithm with its elapsed time.
     * @param label the algorithm label
     * @param startTime the starting time
     */
    private void print(String label, long startTime)
    {
        long elapsedTime = System.currentTimeMillis() - startTime;

        System.out.println("\n" + label + " (" + elapsedTime +
                           " ms):\n");
        buckets.print();
    }

    /**
     * Invoke the logarithm algorithm.
     */
    private void log()
    {
        for (int i = 0; i < NUMBER_COUNT; ++i) {
            buckets.put(exponential.nextLog());
        }
    }

    /**
     * Invoke the von Neumann algorithm.
     */
    private void vonNeumann()
    {
        for (int i = 0; i < NUMBER_COUNT; ++i) {
            buckets.put(exponential.nextVonNeumann());
        }
    }

    /**
     * Main.
     */
```

```
     * @param args the array of program arguments
     */
    public static void main(String args[])
    {
        float mean = 0.5f;

        GenerateRandomExponential test =
                            new GenerateRandomExponential();
        test.run(mean);
    }
}
```

Output:

```
Logarithm (330 ms):

 0   11697: **************************************************
 1   10536: *********************************************
 2    9197: ***************************************
 3    8012: ********************************
 4    6986: ***************************
 5    6406: *************************
 6    5447: *********************
 7    4910: ********************
 8    4400: ******************
 9    3894: ****************
10    3332: *************
11    2943: ************
12    2591: ***********
13    2373: **********
14    1973: ********
15    1825: ********
16    1522: *******
17    1400: ******
18    1180: *****
19    1158: *****
20     968: ****
21     845: ****
22     689: ***
23     696: ***
24     595: ***
25     530: **
26     475: **
27     411: **
28     363: **
29     306: *
30     254: *
31     236: *
```

```
von Neumann (550 ms):

 0   31690:  * * * * * * * * * * * * * * * * * * * * * * * * * * * * * * * * * * * * * * * * * * * * * * * * * * * *
 1   22331:  * * * * * * * * * * * * * * * * * * * * * * * * * * * * * * * * * * * *
 2   15291:  * * * * * * * * * * * * * * * * * * * * * * *
 3   10374:  * * * * * * * * * * * * * * * *
 4    6934:  * * * * * * * * * * *
 5    4549:  * * * * * * *
 6    3087:  * * * * *
 7    2009:  * * *
 8    1320:  * *
 9     868:  *
10     527:  *
11     365:  *
12     238:
```

Screen 14–2 shows two screen shots of the interactive version of Program 14–2 in action.

Screen 14–2 Screen shots of the interactive version of Program 14–2, showing the logarithm algorithm and von Neumann's algorithm.

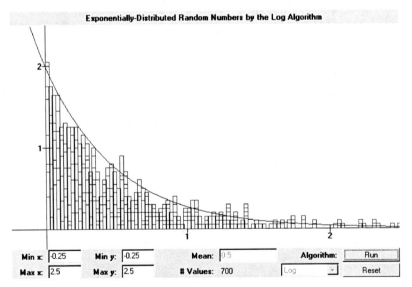

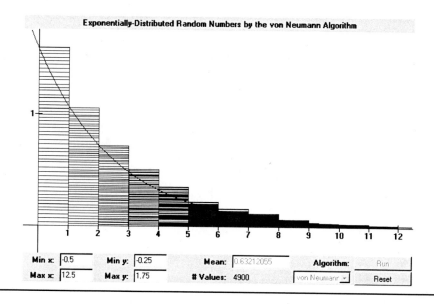

| Min x: | -0.5 | Min y: | -0.25 | Mean: | 0.63212055 | Algorithm: | Run |
| Max x: | 12.5 | Max y: | 1.75 | # Values: | 4900 | von Neumann | Reset |

14.5 Monte Carlo, Buffon's Needle, and π

Besides being the name of a famous European gambling resort, Monte Carlo refers to a type of algorithm that uses random numbers to compute a desired value.[2] Monte Carlo algorithms can succeed when there are no simple computational formulas.

We'll examine a Monte Carlo algorithm for computing the value of π. In Chapter 13, we saw several elegant formulas for π that can compute hundreds of thousands, if not more, digits of π relatively efficiently. Our Monte Carlo algorithm does not do nearly as well, but it is fascinating, nevertheless.

Here is how the algorithm, known as *Buffon's needle,* works.[3] Suppose you dropped needles, each of length 1, at random onto a sheet of paper ruled with parallel lines 1 unit apart. What is the probability that a needle crosses a line?

As shown in Figure 14–1, three uniformly distributed random values represent each needle. The first two random values are the x and y coordinates of the needle's midpoint, from which we measure the perpendicular distance d to the nearest line. The third random value is the needle's angle of rotation θ about its midpoint. We can see that the needle crosses the line whenever $d < \frac{1}{2} \sin \theta$.

---

[2] This bit of naming whimsy is attributed to John von Neumann.

[3] It is named after the person who devised the algorithm, Georges-Louis Leclerc, Comte de Buffon (1707–1788), a French mathematician and scientist.

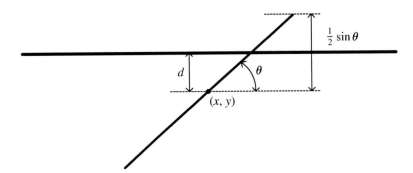

Figure 14–1   A dropped Buffon needle of length 1 that crosses a line. The three uniformly distributed random values are the coordinates *x* and *y* of the needle's midpoint and its angle of rotation θ.

The value of *d* can range from 0 to $\frac{1}{2}$, and the value of θ can range from 0 to π. This is the rectangle in Figure 14–2, and its area is $a_r = \frac{\pi}{2}$. The curve inside the rectangle is the function $f(\theta) = \frac{1}{2} \sin \theta$, and the shaded region under the curve is where $d < \frac{1}{2} \sin \theta$. The area of the shaded region is

$$a_s = \frac{1}{2} \int_0^{\pi} \sin \theta d\theta$$

$$= \frac{1}{2} \big[-\cos \theta \big]_0^{\pi}$$

$$= \frac{1}{2} \big[(-\cos \pi) - (-\cos 0) \big]$$

$$= \frac{1}{2} [1 + 1]$$

$$= 1$$

The probability that a needle crosses a line is the ratio of the shaded area under the curve to the total area of the rectangle:

$$\frac{a_s}{a_r} = \frac{1}{\frac{1}{2}\pi}$$

$$= \frac{2}{\pi}$$

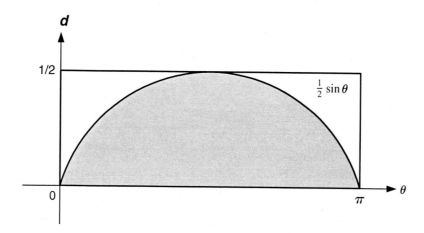

Figure 14–2 The probability that a needle crosses a line is 2/π, the ratio of the shaded area under the curve to the total area of the rectangle.

Therefore, if we continue to drop needles, the ratio of the number of needles that cross a line to the total number of needles approaches $\frac{2}{\pi}$, from which we can compute the value of π.

Listing 14–3a shows class `Needles`, which represents the dropped needles. Method `dropNext()` uses the translation and rotation formulas we saw in Chapter 9.

Listing 14–3a Class `Needles`.

```
package numbercruncher.program14_3;

import java.util.Random;

/**
 * Implementation of Buffon's needles, which are randomly dropped
 * onto a ruled sheet of paper.
 */
class Needles
{
    /** x coord of one end of a needle */        private float x1;
    /** x coord of the other end of a needle */  private float x2;
    /** y coord of one end of a needle */        private float y1;
    /** y coord of the other end of a needle */  private float y2;
    /** angle of rotation about the midpoint */  private float theta;

    /** paper's left edge */    private float xMin;
    /** paper's width */        private float xWidth;
    /** paper's bottom edge */  private float yMin;
    /** paper's height */       private float yHeight;
```

```
/** count of dropped needles */        private int     count;
/** number that cross a line */        private int     crossings;
/** current computed value of pi */    private float   pi;

/** generator of uniformly-distributed random values */
private Random random = new Random(System.currentTimeMillis());

/**
 * Constructor.
 * @param xMin the paper's left edge
 * @param xMax the paper's right edge
 * @param yMin the paper's bottom edge
 * @param yMax the paper's top edge
 */
Needles(float xMin, float xMax, float yMin, float yMax)
{
    this.xMin    = xMin;
    this.xWidth  = xMax - xMin;
    this.yMin    = yMin;
    this.yHeight = yMax - yMin;
}

/**
 * Return the x coordinate of one end of the needle.
 * @return the coordinate
 */
float getX1() { return x1; }

/**
 * Return the x coordinate of one end of the needle.
 * @return the coordinate
 */
float getX2() { return x2; }

/**
 * Return the y coordinate of one end of the needle.
 * @return the coordinate
 */
float getY1() { return y1; }

/**
 * Return the y coordinate of the other end of the needle.
 * @return the coordinate
 */
float getY2() { return y2; }

/**
 * Return the count of all the dropped needles.
 * @return the count
```

```
 */
int getCount() { return count; }

/**
 * Return the number of needles that crossed a line.
 * @return the number of crossings
 */
int getCrossings() { return crossings; }

/**
 * Return the current computed value of pi
 * @return the value
 */
float getPi() { return pi = (2f*count)/crossings; }

/**
 * Return the error of the current computed value of pi
 * @return the error
 */
float getError() { return pi - ((float) Math.PI); }

/**
 * Initialize.
 */
void init()
{
    count = crossings = 0;
}


/**
 * Drop the next needle.
 */
void dropNext()
{
    ++count;

    // Compute random values for the x and y coordinates of the
    // needle's midpoint, and for the needle's angle of rotation.
    float xCenter =  xWidth*random.nextFloat() + xMin;
    float yCenter = yHeight*random.nextFloat() + yMin;
    float theta   = (float) Math.PI*random.nextFloat();

    float sin = (float) Math.sin(theta);
    float cos = (float) Math.cos(theta);

    // Rotate about the origin a 1-unit length needle on
    // the x axis with endpoints at -0.5 and +0.5.
    x1 = -0.5f*cos;
    x2 = +0.5f*cos;
```

```
        y1 = -0.5f*(-sin);
        y2 = +0.5f*(-sin);

        // Translate the needle to its location.
        x1 += xCenter;
        x2 += xCenter;
        y1 += yCenter;
        y2 += yCenter;

        // Does the needle cross a line?
        if (Math.floor(y1) != Math.floor(y2)) ++crossings;
    }
}
```

Program 14–3 demonstrates the Buffon's needle algorithm. See Listing 14–3b. We see from the program's output that this is not really a good way to compute π—it converges very slowly and erratically.

Listing 14–3b A demonstration of Buffon's needle algorithm.

```
package numbercruncher.program14_3;

import numbercruncher.mathutils.AlignRight;

/**
 * PROGRAM 14-3: Buffon's Needle
 *
 * Demonstrate how we can calculate the value of pi using the
 * Monte Carlo technique and Buffon's needle algorithm.
 */
public class Buffon
{
    private static final int MAX_NEEDLES = 10000000;     // 10 million
    private static final int GROUP_SIZE  = MAX_NEEDLES/20;

    /**
      * Main.
      * @param args the array of program arguments
      */
    public static void main(String args[])
    {
        Needles    needles = new Needles(0, 0, 0, 10.5f);
        AlignRight ar      = new AlignRight();
```

```
        ar.print("Needles", 15);   ar.print("Crossings", 15);
        ar.print("Pi", 15);        ar.print("Error", 15);
        ar.underline();

        do {
            // Drop a group of needles.
            for (int i = 0; i < GROUP_SIZE; ++i) needles.dropNext();

            ar.print(needles.getCount(), 15);
            ar.print(needles.getCrossings(), 15);
            ar.print(needles.getPi(), 15);
            ar.print(needles.getError(), 15);
            ar.println();
        } while (needles.getCount() < MAX_NEEDLES);
    }
}
```

Output:

Needles	Crossings	Pi	Error
500000	318282	3.1418679	2.7513504E-4
1000000	636433	3.1425147	9.2196465E-4
1500000	954980	3.141427	-1.6570091E-4
2000000	1273603	3.140696	-8.966923E-4
2500000	1591847	3.1410053	-5.874634E-4
3000000	1910364	3.1407628	-8.299351E-4
3500000	2229064	3.1403315	-0.0012612343
4000000	2547078	3.140854	-7.388592E-4
4500000	2865942	3.1403286	-0.0012640953
5000000	3184564	3.1401472	-0.0014455318
5500000	3502476	3.1406353	-9.57489E-4
6000000	3820892	3.1406279	-9.6488E-4
6500000	4139230	3.1406808	-9.1195107E-4
7000000	4457471	3.1407945	-7.982254E-4
7500000	4775901	3.1407685	-8.24213E-4
8000000	5093656	3.1411622	-4.3058395E-4
8500000	5411821	3.1412716	-3.2114983E-4
9000000	5730361	3.1411633	-4.2939186E-4
9500000	6048652	3.1411958	-3.9696693E-4
10000000	6366532	3.1414278	-1.6498566E-4

Screen 14–3 shows a screen shot of the interactive version of Program 14–3 in action.

Screen 14–3 Buffon's needle algorithm in action.

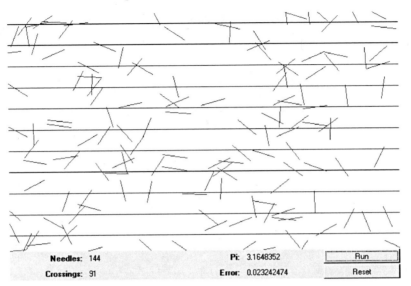

Needles: 144	**Pi:** 3.1648352	Run
Crossings: 91	**Error:** 0.023242474	Reset

References

Beckmann, Peter, *A History of Pi,* New York: St. Martin's Press, 1971.

> Beckmann discusses the Monte Carlo technique and Buffon's needle algorithm in Chapter 15. Both topics are also covered by McCracken.

Knuth, Donald E., *The Art of Computer Programming, Volume 2: Seminumerical Algorithms,* 3rd edition, Reading, MA: Addison-Wesley, 1998.

> The classic reference for random number generation is Chapter 3 of this book. It contains proofs for the polar and ratio algorithms for generating normally distributed random values, as well as for the logarithm algorithm for generating exponentially distributed random values.

McCracken, Daniel D., "The Monte Carlo Method," 1955. In *Computers and Computations,* edited by R. R. Fenichel and J. Weizenbaum, San Francisco: W. H. Freeman and Company, 1971.

Monahan, John F., *Numerical Methods of Statistics,* Cambridge, UK: Cambridge University Press, 2001.

> Section 11.3 of this book proves the ratio algorithm, along with the von Neumann algorithm for generating exponentially distributed random values.

CHAPTER 15

PRIME NUMBERS

Prime numbers have fascinated professional and amateur mathematicians alike since ancient times. It's a simple concept—a *prime* number is any integer greater than 1 that is divisible only by 1 and itself. An integer greater than 1 that is not prime is *composite*. In this chapter, we'll use Java to explore two topics related to prime numbers.

The first topic is *primality testing*. Given a positive integer, how can we tell whether it is prime or composite? Of course, we can systematically try dividing the number by a succession of "trial divisors"—if we find a divisor other than 1 and the number itself that divides evenly into the number (the division leaves no remainder), then the number is composite. If we fail to find such a divisor, then the number must be prime. This algorithm takes far too long, however, if the number we're testing for primality is very large. Are there other ways of testing?

The second topic of this chapter is *prime number generation*. Are there formulas or algorithms that generate prime numbers? A related question is whether or not there are patterns in the distribution of prime numbers.

There are some interesting parallels with Chapter 14, where we explored random number generation. In this chapter, we'll even encounter numbers that are *pseudoprimes*.

Before we get to our two main topics, we need to visit a few key ideas from the branch of mathematics called *number theory*, which is concerned with the properties of numbers, especially the integers.

15.1 The Sieve of Eratosthenes and Factoring

The Sieve of Eratosthenes[1] is a simple way to determine, among the integers 2 through n, which are prime and which are composite. We begin with the integers, 1 through 100, say, arranged in a table:

1	2	3	4	5	6	7	8	9	10
11	12	13	14	15	16	17	18	19	20
21	22	23	24	25	26	27	28	29	30
31	32	33	34	35	36	37	38	39	40
41	42	43	44	45	46	47	48	49	50
51	52	53	54	55	56	57	58	59	60
61	62	63	64	65	66	67	68	69	70
71	72	73	74	75	76	77	78	79	80
81	82	83	84	85	86	87	88	89	90
91	92	93	94	95	96	97	98	99	100

First, we remove the number 1, which is neither prime nor composite. The next number, 2, is the first prime. We leave it alone but remove each subsequent multiple of 2—all even numbers greater than 2 are composite, since they are all divisible by 2.

1	2	3	4	5	6	7	8	9	10
11	12	13	14	15	16	17	18	19	20
21	22	23	24	25	26	27	28	29	30
31	32	33	34	35	36	37	38	39	40
41	42	43	44	45	46	47	48	49	50
51	52	53	54	55	56	57	58	59	60
61	62	63	64	65	66	67	68	69	70
71	72	73	74	75	76	77	78	79	80
81	82	83	84	85	86	87	88	89	90
91	92	93	94	95	96	97	98	99	100

After 2, the next prime is 3, and so we leave 3 alone but remove all of its subsequent multiples. (Many of the numbers will have already been removed.)

---

[1] Eratosthenes (276–194 B.C.) was a Greek mathematician and philosopher who studied prime numbers and who is also known for accurately computing the earth's circumference.

1	2	3	4	5	6	7	8	9	10
11	12	13	14	15	16	17	18	19	20
21	22	23	24	25	26	27	28	29	30
31	32	33	34	35	36	37	38	39	40
41	42	43	44	45	46	47	48	49	50
51	52	53	54	55	56	57	58	59	60
61	62	63	64	65	66	67	68	69	70
71	72	73	74	75	76	77	78	79	80
81	82	83	84	85	86	87	88	89	90
91	92	93	94	95	96	97	98	99	100

We continue similarly with the prime numbers 5, 7, 11, and so on until we've "sieved out" all the primes:

1	2	3	4	5	6	7	8	9	10
11	12	13	14	15	16	17	18	19	20
21	22	23	24	25	26	27	28	29	30
31	32	33	34	35	36	37	38	39	40
41	42	43	44	45	46	47	48	49	50
51	52	53	54	55	56	57	58	59	60
61	62	63	64	65	66	67	68	69	70
71	72	73	74	75	76	77	78	79	80
81	82	83	84	85	86	87	88	89	90
91	92	93	94	95	96	97	98	99	100

Once we have a table of prime numbers, we can use it to compute the *prime factors* of a composite number by repeatedly dividing the composite number by the prime numbers that evenly divide it, until the composite number is reduced to 1.

For example, take the composite number 84:

$$84 / 2 = 42$$
$$42 / 2 = 21$$
$$21 / 3 = 7$$
$$7 / 7 = 1$$

and so the prime factors of 84 are 2, 3, and 7, and $84 = 2^2 \times 3 \times 7$.

Listing 15–0a shows class `PrimeFactors` in package `numbercruncher.mathutils` along with some test output.

Listing 15–0a The Sieve of Eratosthenes and prime factors.

```java
package numbercruncher.mathutils;

import java.util.Vector;
import java.util.Enumeration;

/**
 * Compute the Sieve of Eratosthenes and prime factors.
 */
public class PrimeFactors
{
    /**
     * Compute the Sieve of Eratosthenes.
     * @param n the size of the sieve
     * @return the sieve as a boolean array (each element is true
     *         if the corresponding number is prime, false if the
     *         number is composite)
     */
    public static boolean[] primeSieve(int n)
    {
        int     halfN = (n+1) >> 1;
        boolean sieve[] = new boolean[n+1];

        // Initialize every integer from 2 onwards to prime.
        for (int i = 2; i <= n; ++i) sieve[i] = true;

        int prime = 2;  // first prime number

        // Loop to create the sieve.
        while (prime < halfN) {

            // Mark as composites multiples of the prime.
            for (int composite = prime << 1;
                 composite <= n;
                 composite += prime) sieve[composite] = false;

            // Skip over composites to the next prime.
            while ((++prime < halfN) && (!sieve[prime]));
        }

        return sieve;
    }

    /**
     * Compute the prime factors of an integer value.
     * @param n the value to factor
     * @return an array of distinct prime factors
```

```
     */
    public static int[] factorsOf(int n)
    {
        boolean isPrime[] = primeSieve(n);        // primes <= n
        Vector   v        = new Vector();

        // Loop to try prime divisors.
        for (int factor = 2; n > 1; ++factor) {
            if (isPrime[factor] && (n%factor == 0)) {

                // Prime divisor found.
                v.add(new Integer(factor));

                // Factor out multiples of the divisor.
                do {
                    n /= factor;
                } while (n%factor == 0);
            }
        }

        // Create an array of the distinct prime factors.
        int factors[] = new int[v.size()];
        Enumeration e = v.elements();
        for (int i = 0; e.hasMoreElements(); ++i) {
            factors[i] = ((Integer) e.nextElement()).intValue();
        }

        return factors;
    }

    /**
     * Main for testing.
     * @param args the commandline arguments (ignored)
     */
    public static void main(String args[])
    {
        AlignRight ar = new AlignRight();

        // Test Sieve of Eratosthenes.
        System.out.println("The Sieve of Eratosthenes:\n");
        boolean isPrime[] = primeSieve(100);
        for (int i = 1; i <= 100; ++i) {
            if (isPrime[i]) ar.print(i, 4);
            else            ar.print(".", 4);
            if (i%10 == 0)  ar.println();
        }

        System.out.println();
```

```
    // Test prime factors.
    int k[] = {84, 1409, 3141135, };
    for (int i = 0; i < k.length; ++i) {
        int factors[] = factorsOf(k[i]);
        System.out.print("The prime factors of " +
                        k[i] + " are");
        for (int j = 0; j < factors.length; ++j) {
            System.out.print(" " + factors[j]);
        }
        System.out.println();
    }
  }
}
```

Output:

```
The Sieve of Eratosthenes:

    .   2   3   .   5   .   7   .   .   .
   11   .  13   .   .   .  17   .  19   .
    .   .  23   .   .   .   .   .  29   .
   31   .   .   .   .   .  37   .   .   .
   41   .  43   .   .   .  47   .   .   .
    .   .  53   .   .   .   .   .  59   .
   61   .   .   .   .   .  67   .   .   .
   71   .  73   .   .   .   .   .  79   .
    .   .  83   .   .   .   .   .  89   .
    .   .   .   .   .   .  97   .   .   .

The prime factors of 84 are 2 3 7
The prime factors of 1409 are 1409
The prime factors of 3141135 are 3 5 29 83
```

15.2 Congruences and Modulo Arithmetic

A mathematician would take the boolean Java expression

$$7\%4 == 3$$

and write it

$$7 \equiv 3 \pmod 4$$

which is read "7 is congruent to 3, modulo 4." In this example, the number 4 is the *modulus*.

Modulo arithmetic[2] is key to many primality tests. Like "regular" arithmetic, modulo arithmetic has certain properties. Intuitively, these properties make sense if we think of modulo arithmetic as clock arithmetic, which we first encountered in Chapter 2 when we discussed Java's integer types. Here, if the modulus is m, we can imagine a clock face with the digits from 0 through $m-1$.

One property involves addition. Suppose we wish to compute the value of $a + b$ (mod m), where a, b, and m are integers.[3] One way is first to compute the sum $s = a + b$ using regular addition. Then, starting at 0, we go around the clock face, perhaps several times, counting s digits. The digit where we end up is the value of $a + b$ (mod m).

Another way is to start at 0 and go around the clock face, counting a digits. Where we end up is the value of a (mod m). From that digit, we continue around the clock face by counting b more digits. Where we stop is the value of $a + b$ (mod m)—which is the same digit we arrived at the first way. In other words, we've demonstrated that

$$a + b \ (\text{mod } m) = \lfloor a \ (\text{mod } m) + b \ (\text{mod } m) \rfloor \ (\text{mod } m)$$

On the right-hand side, the final "(mod m)" is necessary to keep the sum inside the square brackets on the clock face, in case the sum exceeds m.

Since multiplication is repeated addition, we also have the multiplication property

$$ab \ (\text{mod } m) = \lfloor a \ (\text{mod } m) \times b \ (\text{mod } m) \rfloor \ (\text{mod } m)$$

Listing 15–0b shows class `ModuloArithmetic` in package `numbercruncher.mathutils`. Its two methods compute ab (mod m) and a^b (mod m).

Listing 15–0b Modulo multiplication and exponentiation.

```
package numbercruncher.mathutils;

/**
 * Perform multiplication and exponentiation modulo arithmetic.
 */
public class ModuloArithmetic
{
    /**
     * Multiply two integer values a and b modulo m.
     * @param a the value of a
     * @param b the value of b
     * @param m the modulus m
     * @return the value of ab (mod m)
     */
```

---

[2] Modulo arithmetic is also called *modular arithmetic.*
[3] Note that the "(mod m)" applies to the entire sum of $a + b$, not just to b.

```java
public static int multiply(int a, int b, int m)
{
    int product = 0;

    // Loop to compute product = (a*b)%m.
    while (a > 0) {

        // Does the rightmost bit of a == 1?
        if ((a & 1) == 1) {
            product += b;
            product %= m;
        }

        // Double b modulo m, and
        // shift a 1 bit to the right.
        b <<= 1;  b %= m;
        a >>= 1;
    }

    return product;
}

/**
 * Raise a to the b power modulo m.
 * @param a the value of a
 * @param b the value of b
 * @param m the modulus m
 * @return the value of a^b (mod m)
 */
public static int raise(int base, int exponent, int m)
{
    int power = 1;

    // Loop to compute power = (base^exponent)%m.
    while (exponent > 0) {

        // Does the rightmost bit of the exponent == 1?
        if ((exponent & 1) == 1) {
            power = multiply(power, base, m);
        }

        // Square the base modulo m and
        // shift the exponent 1 bit to the right.
        base = multiply(base, base, m);
        exponent >>= 1;
    }

    return power;
}
```

```
/**
 * Main for testing.
 * @param args the commandline arguments (ignored)
 */
public static void main(String args[])
{
    int a = 3;
    int b = 13;
    int m = 5;

    // Test modulo multiplication.
    int modProduct = multiply(a, b, m);
    System.out.println(a + "*" + b + " = " + a*b);
    System.out.println(a + "*" + b + " = " + modProduct +
                    " (mod " + m + ")");

    System.out.println();

    // Test modulo exponentiation.
    int modPower = raise(a, b, m);
    System.out.println(a + "^" + b + " = " +
                    IntPower.raise(a, b));
    System.out.println(a + "^" + b + " = " + modPower +
                    " (mod " + m + ")");
}
}
```

Output:

```
3*13 = 39
3*13 = 4 (mod 5)

3^13 = 1594323.0
3^13 = 3 (mod 5)
```

Recall that, in Chapter 2, we wrote the class `IntPower`, which performs exponentiation by partitioning the exponent into the sum of powers of 2. We can similarly compute the value of ab by partitioning the factor b into the sum of powers of 2. For example, if b is 13, we compute $a \times 13$ as

$$a \times 13 = a \times (8 + 4 + 1)$$
$$= (a \times 8) + (a \times 4) + (a \times 1)$$

But $4a$ is $2 \times 2a$, and $8a$ is $2 \times 4a$, so we can just repeatedly double the value of a, and by using the binary representation of 13 (1101), we simply add together the doubled values that correspond to each 1 bit.

Method `ModuloArithmetic.multiply()` uses this algorithm, except that it computes each sum and doubling modulo m, which the addition property allows us to do.

Method `ModuloArithmetic.raise()` is similar to `IntPower.raise()`, except that it invokes `ModuloArithmetic.multiply()` to do each multiplication and squaring. The multiplication property makes that possible.

The test output in Listing 15–0b shows an example result from each method.

With our two new classes, `PrimeFactors` and `ModuloArithmetic`, we're ready to do some primality testing.

15.3 The Lucas Test

In 1640, French mathematician Pierre de Fermat first wrote what is now known as Fermat's Little Theorem.[4] It states

> If p is a prime number, and a is any integer that is *not* divisible
> by p, then $a^{p-1} \equiv 1 \pmod{p}$.

For example, let $p = 5$, and let $a = 7$, which is certainly not divisible by 5. Then $7^{5-1} = 7^4 = 2401 \equiv 1 \pmod{5}$.

By itself, this theorem is not sufficient to prove that p is prime. There are also composite values for p that satisfy $a^p \equiv 1 \pmod{p}$—such composite numbers are called *pseudoprimes*. But based on this theorem, in 1876 Lucas[5] devised a primality test, now known as the Lucas test:

> Let p be a positive integer. If there exists a positive integer a
> such that $a^{p-1} \equiv 1 \pmod{p}$ and, for all prime factors q of $p-1$,
> $a^{(p-1)/q} \not\equiv 1 \pmod{p}$, then p is prime.

For example, let $p = 7$ and $a = 2$. Then $3^{7-1} = 3^6 = 729 \equiv 1 \pmod{7}$, and so 7 passes the first part of the test. The prime factors of $p-1 = 6$ are 2 and 3. We have $3^{(7-1)/2} = 3^3 = 27 \not\equiv 1 \pmod{7}$, and $3^{(7-1)/3} = 3^2 = 9 \not\equiv 1 \pmod{7}$, and so 7 also passes the second part of the test. Therefore, according to the Lucas test, 7 is prime.

This test has two serious drawbacks. First, we need to compute the prime factors of $p-1$. We've written a method to do this, but if p is large, it will take a while, assuming we have sufficient memory. Then there's the matter of finding the integer a. How many integers should we try before we give up and conclude that p is not prime?

---

[4]   This is to distinguish it from the more famous Fermat's Last Theorem, which states that $x^n + y^n = z^n$ has no nonzero integer solutions for x, y, and z when $n > 2$. Fermat (1601–1665) wrote in a math book he was reading at the time that he had discovered a proof for this theorem but that the book's margins were too small to contain it! Actually, the theorem wasn't proved until 1993. Fermat didn't write down a proof for his Little Theorem, either—Euler did it in 1736.

[5]   François-Edouard-Anatole Lucas (1842–1891) was a French mathematics professor.

Listing 15–1a shows our implementation of the Lucas test in class LucasTest in package numbercruncher.primeutils. It tries values of *a* from 2 up to and including *p*. (The values of $a^{(p-1)/q}$ (mod *p*) start to repeat themselves every time the value of *a* reaches a multiple of *p*.)

Listing 15–1a The Lucas test for primality.

```
package numbercruncher.primeutils;

import numbercruncher.mathutils.ModuloArithmetic;
import numbercruncher.mathutils.PrimeFactors;

/**
 * An implemention of the the Lucas test for primality.
 */
public class LucasTest
{
    private static LucasStatus status = new LucasStatus();

    /** number to test for primality */      int p;
    /** prime factors of p-1 */              int q[];
    /** caller of the test */                LucasCaller caller;

    /**
     * Constructor.
     * @param p the number to test for primality
     * @param caller the caller of the test
     */
    public LucasTest(int p, LucasCaller caller)
    {
        this.p      = p;
        this.caller = caller;

        q = PrimeFactors.factorsOf(p-1);
    }

    /**
     * Perform the Lucas test.
     * @return true if p is prime, false if p is composite
     */
    public boolean test()
    {
        // Try integers a from 2 through p.
        for (int a = 2; a <= p; ++a) {
            if (passPart1(a) && passPart2(a)) return true;  // prime
        }

        return false;    // composite
    }
```

```
/**
 * Test if integer a passes the first part of the test.
 * @param a the value of a
 * @return true if [a^(p-1)]%p == 1, else false
 */
private boolean passPart1(int a)
{
    int exponent = p-1;
    int value    = ModuloArithmetic.raise(a, exponent, p);

    // Report status back to the caller.
    if (caller != null) {
        status.a        = a;
        status.q        = 1;
        status.exponent = exponent;
        status.value    = value;
        status.pass     = (value == 1);

        caller.reportStatus(status);
    }

    return (value == 1);    // pass if it's 1
}

/**
 * Test if integer a passes the second part of the test.
 * @param a the value of a
 * @return true if [a^(p-1)/q]%p != 1 for all prime factors q,
 *              else false
 */
private boolean passPart2(int a)
{
    int pm1 = p-1;

    // Loop to try each prime factor.
    for (int i = 0; i < q.length; ++i) {
        int exponent = pm1/q[i];
        int value    = ModuloArithmetic.raise(a, exponent, p);

        // Report status back to the caller.
        if (caller != null) {
            status.a        = a;
            status.q        = q[i];
            status.exponent = exponent;
            status.value    = value;
            status.pass     = (value != 1);

            caller.reportStatus(status);
        }
```

```
                    if (value == 1) return false;    // fail
            }

        return true;     // pass
    }
}
```

The class breaks the test into two parts, methods `passPart1()` and `passPart2()`. It can also report the current status of the test back to the caller. Listing 15–1b shows the class `LucasStatus`.

Listing 15–1b Status of the Lucas test.

```
package numbercruncher.primeutils;

/**
 * The current status of the Lucas test.
 */
public class LucasStatus
{
    /** trial integer a */      int     a;
    /** prime factor */         int     q;
    /** exponent of a */        int     exponent;
    /** modulo value */         int     value;
    /** pass or fail */         boolean pass;

    public int getA()        { return a; }
    public int getQ()        { return q; }
    public int getExponent() { return exponent; }
    public int getValue()    { return value; }
    public boolean didPass() { return pass; }
}
```

In order for the status reporting to work, the caller of the Lucas test must implement the interface `LucasCaller`, shown in Listing 15–1c.

Listing 15–1c Interface `LucasCaller`.

```
package numbercruncher.primeutils;

/**
 * Interface for a caller of the Lucas test.
 */
public interface LucasCaller
{
    /**
```

```
     * Report on the status of the Lucas test.
     * @param status the current status
     */
    void reportStatus(LucasStatus status);
}
```

Finally, Listing 15–1d shows a demonstration program for the Lucas test, as well as its output for three prime numbers and a composite number.

Listing 15–1d Demonstration of the Lucas test.

```
package numbercruncher.program15_1;

import numbercruncher.mathutils.AlignRight;
import numbercruncher.primeutils.LucasTest;
import numbercruncher.primeutils.LucasCaller;
import numbercruncher.primeutils.LucasStatus;

/**
 * PROGRAM 15-1: Lucas Test for Primality
 *
 * Demonstrate the Lucas test for primality.
 */
public class TestLucas implements LucasCaller
{
    private int         prevA = 0;
    private AlignRight ar     = new AlignRight();

    /**
     * Test an integer p for primality.
     * @param p the value of p
     */
    void test(int p)
    {
        System.out.println("\nTESTING " + p + "\n");
        ar.print("a", 5);
        ar.print("q", 10);
        ar.print("exponent", 12);
        ar.print("mod value", 12);
        ar.print("status", 10);
        ar.underline();

        prevA = 0;

        boolean result = (new LucasTest(p, this)).test();

        System.out.println();
        System.out.println(p + " is " +
                          (result ? "prime." : "composite."));
    }
```

```
    /**
     * Report on the test status.
     * @param status the test status
     */
    public void reportStatus(LucasStatus status)
    {
        // Skip a line for a new value of a.
        if ((prevA != 0) && (status.getA() != prevA)) {
            System.out.println();
        }
        prevA = status.getA();

        ar.print(status.getA(), 5);
        ar.print(status.getQ(), 10);
        ar.print(status.getExponent(), 12);
        ar.print(status.getValue(), 12);
        ar.print((status.didPass() ? "pass" : "fail"), 10);
        ar.println();
    }

    /**
     * Main.
     * @param args the commandline arguments (ignored)
     */
    public static void main(String args[])
    {
        TestLucas lucas = new TestLucas();

        // Test various integers.  All but 21 are prime.
        lucas.test(7);
        lucas.test(15787);
        lucas.test(149287);
        lucas.test(21);
    }
}
```

Output:

```
Testing 7
    a        q     exponent   mod value    status
---------------------------------------------------
    2        1        6           1         pass
    2        2        3           1         fail

    3        1        6           1         pass
    3        2        3           6         pass
    3        3        2           2         pass

7 is prime.
```

TESTING 15787

a	q	exponent	mod value	status
2	1	15786	1	pass
2	2	7893	15786	pass
2	3	5262	11258	pass
2	877	18	9552	pass

15787 is prime.

TESTING 149287

a	q	exponent	mod value	status
2	1	149286	1	pass
2	2	74643	1	fail
3	1	149286	1	pass
3	2	74643	149286	pass
3	3	49762	22426	pass
3	139	1074	131616	pass
3	179	834	123639	pass

149287 is prime.

TESTING 21

a	q	exponent	mod value	status
2	1	20	4	fail
3	1	20	9	fail
4	1	20	16	fail
5	1	20	4	fail
6	1	20	15	fail
7	1	20	7	fail
8	1	20	1	pass
8	2	10	1	fail
9	1	20	18	fail
10	1	20	16	fail

```
11          1           20          16          fail

12          1           20          18          fail

13          1           20          1           pass
13          2           10          1           fail

14          1           20          7           fail

15          1           20          15          fail

16          1           20          4           fail

17          1           20          16          fail

18          1           20          9           fail

19          1           20          4           fail

20          1           20          1           pass
20          2           10          1           fail

21          1           20          0           fail

21 is composite.
```

From the program output, it appears that, even for fairly large numbers, *if* the number is prime, it doesn't take too much time or effort to find the integer a that passes the test.

However, if the number is large and composite, the Lucas test can take a long time if we're willing to test all values of a from 2 through p. What we need is a quick way to eliminate composite numbers.

15.4 The Miller-Rabin Test

The Miller-Rabin test[6] is the complement of the Lucas test—it determines quickly whether or not an integer p is composite. It also uses Fermat's Little Theorem, but unlike the Lucas test, it does not require any factoring.

If the Miller-Rabin test decides a number is composite, then the number is definitely composite. However, if the test declares that a number is prime, then the number is *probably* prime. The test is wrong about primality at most 25% of the time. Therefore, the Miller-Rabin test is a *probabilistic* test. (The Lucas test is *deterministic*.)

---

[6]   This test was first proposed in 1976 by Michael Rabin, a computer science professor. He based his work on some previous ideas by mathematician Gary Miller.

To increase the probability that the test's determination of primality for a number is correct, we can rerun the test on the number. Each rerun decreases the probability that the test is wrong by a factor of $\frac{1}{4}$. Thus, after two runs, the probability of error is at most $\left(\frac{1}{4}\right)^2$, or 6.25%. After five runs, the probability of error is less than 0.1%. However, if at any time the test declares that the number is composite, then the number is definitely composite.

The Miller-Rabin test of an integer p involves several steps:

1. Set k to $p-1$.
2. Shift k to the right s bits, until k is odd (its rightmost bit is a 1). Now we have $p - 1 = 2^s k$ and $s \geq 0$.
3. Generate a random integer b such that $1 < b < p$.
4. Set r to $b^k \pmod{p}$.
5. If $r = 1$, then p is probably prime.
6. Do the following three steps at most $s-1$ times, or until the test declares p to be probably prime or definitely composite:

    6.1. If $r = p-1$, then p is probably prime.
    6.2. Otherwise, set r to $r^2 \pmod{p}$.
    6.3. If $r = 1$, then p is definitely composite.

7. After having done the steps 6.1, 6.2, and 6.3 $s-1$ times, p definitely must be composite.

To increase the probability that the test is correct if it states that p is probably prime, we should rerun the test by redoing steps 3 through 7 with a new random value for b. We can continue to rerun the test either until it declares that p is definitely composite or until we're satisfied with the probability that the test is right about p being prime.

Listing 15–2a shows class `MillerRabinTest` in package `numbercruncher. primeutils`, which implements this test. The variable i counts the repetitions of steps 6.1–6.3. The caller specifies how many different random base values b to try.

Listing 15–2a The Miller-Rabin test for primality.

```
package numbercruncher.primeutils;

import java.util.Random;
import numbercruncher.mathutils.ModuloArithmetic;

/**
 * An implementation of the Miller-Rabin test for primality.
 */
public class MillerRabinTest
{
    private static MillerRabinStatus status = new MillerRabinStatus();

    /** number to test for primality */    private int p;
    /** number of times to run the test */ private int iterations;
```

```
/** caller of the test */   private MillerRabinCaller caller;

/**
 * Constructor.
 * @param p the number to test for primality
 * @param iterations the number of times to run the test
 * @param caller the caller of the test
 */
public MillerRabinTest(int p, int iterations,
                       MillerRabinCaller caller)
{
    this.p          = p;
    this.iterations = iterations;
    this.caller     = caller;
}

/**
 * Perform the Miller-Rabin test.
 * @return true if p is probably prime, false if p is composite
 */
public boolean test()
{
    Random random = new Random(0);
    int k = p - 1;
    int s = 0;

    // Shift k to the right s bits to make it odd.
    while ((k & 1) == 0) {
        k >>= 1;
        ++s;
    }

    status.k = k;
    status.s = s;

    // Run the test with different random base values.
    for (int i = 0; i < iterations; ++i) {

        // Generate a random integer base b.
        int    b;
        while ((b = random.nextInt(p)) <= 1);   // want 1 < b < p

        status.b = b;

        // Composite?
        if (!test(k, s, b)) return false;   // definitely composite
    }

    return true;     // most likely prime
}
```

```java
/**
 * Perform the Miller-Rabin test.
 * @param k the value of p-1 shifted right until it is odd
 * @param s the number of right shifts
 * @return true if p is probably prime, false if p is composite
 */
private boolean test(int k, int s, int b)
{
    int pm1 = p-1;
    int sm1 = s-1;

    status.i    = 0;
    status.code = MillerRabinStatus.DONT_KNOW_YET;

    int r = ModuloArithmetic.raise(b, k, p);     // b^k (mod p)
    status.r = r;

    if (r == 1) {
        status.code = MillerRabinStatus.PROBABLY_PRIME;
        reportStatus();

        return true;          // probably prime
    }

    // Loop at most s-1 times.
    int i = 0;
    while (r != pm1) {
        reportStatus();
        status.i = ++i;

        if (i > sm1) {
            status.code = MillerRabinStatus.DEFINITELY_COMPOSITE;
            return false;    // definitely composite
        }

        r = ModuloArithmetic.raise(r, 2, p);     // r^2 (mod p)
        status.r = r;

        if (r == 1) {
            status.code = MillerRabinStatus.DEFINITELY_COMPOSITE;
            reportStatus();

            return false;    // definitely composite
        }
    }

    status.code = MillerRabinStatus.PROBABLY_PRIME;
    reportStatus();
```

```
        return true;                // probably prime
    }

    /**
     * Report the test status back to the caller.
     * @param status the test status
     */
    private void reportStatus()
    {
        if (caller != null) caller.reportStatus(status);
    }
}
```

Like our implementation of the Lucas test, we want the Miller-Rabin test to report its status back to its caller. Listing 15–2b shows class `MillerRabinStatus`.

Listing 15–2b Status of the Miller-Rabin test.

```
package numbercruncher.primeutils;

/**
 * The current status of the Miller-Rabin test.
 */
public class MillerRabinStatus
{
    // Status codes
    public static final int DONT_KNOW_YET        = 0;
    public static final int DEFINITELY_COMPOSITE = 1;
    public static final int PROBABLY_PRIME       = 2;

    /** random base */          int b;
    /** shifted p-1 */          int k;
    /** no. of right shifts */  int s;
    /** counter */              int i;
    /** modulo value */         int r;
    /** status code */          int code;

    public int getB()     { return b; }
    public int getK()     { return k; }
    public int getS()     { return s; }
    public int getIndex() { return i; }
    public int getValue() { return r; }
    public int getCode()  { return code; }
}
```

Listing 15–2c shows the interface `MillerRabinCaller`, which the caller must implement.

Listing 15–2c Interface `MillerRabinCaller`.

```
package numbercruncher.primeutils;

/**
 * Interface for a caller of the Miller-Rabin test.
 */
public interface MillerRabinCaller
{
    /**
     * Report on the status of the Miller-Rabin test.
     * @param status the current status
     */
    void reportStatus(MillerRabinStatus status);
}
```

Finally, Listing 15–2d shows a demonstration program for the Miller-Rabin test, as well as its output for two prime and two composite numbers.

Listing 15–2d Demonstration of the Miller-Rabin test.

```
package numbercruncher.program15_2;

import numbercruncher.mathutils.AlignRight;
import numbercruncher.primeutils.MillerRabinTest;
import numbercruncher.primeutils.MillerRabinCaller;
import numbercruncher.primeutils.MillerRabinStatus;

/**
 * PROGRAM 15-2: Miller-Rabin Test for Primality
 *
 * Demonstrate the Miller-Rabin test for primality.
 */
public class TestMillerRabin implements MillerRabinCaller
{
    private static final int ITERATIONS = 5;

    private static final String CODE_LABELS[] = {
        "???", "composite", "prime?"
    };

    private AlignRight ar = new AlignRight();
```

```java
/**
 * Test an integer p for primality.
 * @param p the value of p
 */
public void test(int p)
{
    System.out.println("\nTESTING " + p + "\n");
    ar.print("b", 10);
    ar.print("k", 10);
    ar.print("s", 5);
    ar.print("i", 5);
    ar.print("r", 10);
    ar.print("status", 12);
    ar.underline();

    MillerRabinTest mrt = new MillerRabinTest(p, ITERATIONS,
                                              this);
    boolean result = mrt.test();

    System.out.println();
    System.out.print(p + " is ");
    System.out.println(result ? "probably prime."
                              : "composite.");
}

/**
 * Report on the test status.
 * @param status the test status
 */
public void reportStatus(MillerRabinStatus status)
{
    ar.print(status.getB(), 10);
    ar.print(status.getK(), 10);
    ar.print(status.getS(), 5);
    ar.print(status.getIndex(), 5);
    ar.print(status.getValue(), 10);

    ar.print(CODE_LABELS[status.getCode()], 12);
    ar.println();
}

/**
 * Main.
 * @param args the commandline arguments (ignored)
 */
public static void main(String args[])
{
    TestMillerRabin millerRabin = new TestMillerRabin();
```

```
        millerRabin.test(21);
        millerRabin.test(8191);
        millerRabin.test(524287);
        millerRabin.test(1604401);
    }
}
```

Output:

Testing 21

b	k	s	i	r	status
12	5	2	0	3	???
12	5	2	1	9	???

21 is composite.

TESTING 8191

b	k	s	i	r	status
1738	4095	1	0	1	prime?
7195	4095	1	0	1	prime?
7187	4095	1	0	8190	prime?
1368	4095	1	0	1	prime?
4550	4095	1	0	8190	prime?

8191 is probably prime.

TESTING 524287

b	k	s	i	r	status
26082	262143	1	0	1	prime?
308713	262143	1	0	1	prime?
125334	262143	1	0	524286	prime?
311826	262143	1	0	524286	prime?
454445	262143	1	0	1	prime?

524287 is probably prime.

TESTING 1604401

b	k	s	i	r	status
637182	100275	4	0	419491	???
637182	100275	4	1	393000	???

```
       637182      100275     4     2     1337735          ???
       637182      100275     4     3     494434           ???

1604401 is composite.
```

15.5 A Combined Primality Tester

We can have a better primality test if we combine the Miller-Rabin and Lucas tests. Since composite numbers are troublesome for the Lucas test, we can first use the Miller-Rabin test to filter out numbers that are definitely composite. The remaining numbers are probably prime, and so we use the Lucas test on them to determine primality for sure.

Listing 15–3a shows class `PrimalityTest` in package `numbercruncher.primeutils`, which combines the two tests.

Listing 15–3a A combined primality tester.

```
package numbercruncher.primeutils;

import numbercruncher.primeutils.MillerRabinTest;
import numbercruncher.primeutils.LucasTest;

/**
 * Primality test that combines the Miller-Rabin and Lucas tests.
 */
public class PrimalityTest
{
    /** number to test for primality */   private int p;
    /** number of times to run the
        Miller-Rabin test */               private int iterations;

    /**
     * Constructor.
     * @param p the number to test for primality
     * @param iterations the number of times to run
     *                   the Miller-Rabin test
     */
    public PrimalityTest(int p, int iterations)
    {
        this.p          = p;
        this.iterations = iterations;
    }

    /**
     * Perform the primality test.
     * @return true if p is prime, false if p is composite
```

```
    */
    public boolean test()
    {
        return (new MillerRabinTest(p, iterations, null)).test()
                && (new LucasTest(p, null)).test();
    }
}
```

Listing 15–3b shows a program that demonstrates this combined primality tester.

Listing 15–3b: Demonstration of the combined primality tester.

```
package numbercruncher.program15_3;

import numbercruncher.primeutils.PrimalityTest;

/**
 * PROGRAM 15-3: Primality Testing
 *
 * Demonstrate the primality test.
 */
public class TestPrimality
{
    public static void main(String args[]).
    {
        // Numbers to test.
        int ps[] = {7, 21, 8191, 15787, 149287, 524287, 1604401};

        // Loop to test each number.
        for (int i = 0; i < ps.length; ++i) {
            int p = ps[i];
            System.out.print(p + " is ");

            System.out.println((new PrimalityTest(p, 5)).test()
                                ? "prime." : "composite.");
        }
    }
}
```

Output:

```
7 is prime.
21 is composite.
8191 is prime.
15787 is prime.
149287 is prime.
524287 is prime.
1604401 is composite.
```

The primality tester in class `numbercruncher.primeutils.PrimalityTest` is similar to the one in class `java.math.BigInteger`. However, in class `BigInteger`, method `isProbablePrime()` uses the more advanced Lucas-Lehmer[7] test instead of the Lucas test. The Lucas-Lehmer test is beyond the scope of this book, but there are references for it at the end of this chapter.

15.6 Generating Prime Numbers

Now that we have a way to test a number for primality, we can also ask, Are there formulas that generate prime numbers? There are such formulas, but mathematicians have yet to find a formula that generates *only* prime numbers.

A well-known formula for primes is the one that generates the so-called Mersenne primes,[8]

$$M_p = 2^p - 1$$

where p itself is prime. For example, $M_2 = 3$, $M_3 = 7$, $M_5 = 31$, $M_7 = 127$ are all prime, but $M_{11} = 2047$ is composite—its factors are 23 and 89. Computer scientists continue to vie for the honor of being the discoverer of the largest known Mersenne prime. As of late 2001, the largest one found is $M_{13,466,917}$ with 4,053,946 digits.

A number of integer-valued quadratic polynomials of the form

$$an^2 + bn + c$$

where a, b, and c are integer constants, generates prime numbers for a limited domain of integer values for the variable n. Perhaps the most famous one was discovered by Euler:

$$n^2 + n + 41$$

which generates only prime numbers for 80 values of n from -40 through 39, each one generated twice. An equivalent polynomial is

$$n^2 - 79n + 1601$$

which simply shifts the range of values for n to 0 through 79 by replacing n with $n + 40$. For the values 0 through 99, the latter polynomial generates 95 prime numbers, 55 of which are distinct. (In fact, about half of the first 2,400 numbers it generates are prime.)

---

[7] Derrick Henry Lehmer (1905–1991), known as the father of computational number theory, taught mathematics at the Berkeley campus of the University of California.

[8] Marin Mersenne (1588–1648) was a French monk who taught philosophy and investigated prime numbers. He first published his formula in 1644.

Another polynomial, published in 1995 by M.L. Greenwood and N. Boston, two amateur mathematicians, is

$$\left| 41n^2 - 4641n + 88007 \right|$$

which generates 90 *distinct* prime numbers for values of *n* from 0 through 99.

Listing 15–4 shows a program that demonstrates these two polynomials. It uses our earlier primality test to check each generated number.

Listing 15–4 Prime-generating quadratic polynomials. Most of the generated numbers are prime for *n* from 0 through 99; composite numbers are marked with a small *c*.

```java
package numbercruncher.program15_4;

import java.util.HashSet;

import numbercruncher.primeutils.PrimalityTest;
import numbercruncher.mathutils.AlignRight;

/**
 * PROGRAM 15-4:   Prime Number Generators
 *
 * Demonstrate two quadratic polynomials that generate prime numbers.
 */
public class PrimeGenerators
{
    private static final String EULER     = "n^2 - 79n + 1601";
    private static final String GREENWOOD = "41n^2 - 4641n + 88007";
    private static final int    WIDTH     = GREENWOOD.length() + 5;

    private static AlignRight ar = new AlignRight();

    public static void main(String args[])
    {
        ar.print("n", 2);
        ar.print(EULER,     WIDTH);
        ar.print(GREENWOOD, WIDTH);
        ar.underline();

        int ePrimeCount = 0;               // count of Euler primes
        int gPrimeCount = 0;               // count of Greenwood primes

        HashSet ePrimes = new HashSet();   // set of Euler primes
        HashSet gPrimes = new HashSet();   // set of Greenwood primes

        String eMark, gMark;     // " " if prime, "c" if composite
```

```
            // Loop to test generated numbers.
            for (int n = 0; n <= 99; ++n) {

                // Prime number generators.
                int ep = n*n - 79*n + 1601;                // Euler
                int gp = Math.abs(41*n*n - 4641*n + 88007); // Greenwood

                // Test for primality.
                boolean epIsPrime = (new PrimalityTest(ep, 5)).test();
                boolean gpIsPrime = (new PrimalityTest(gp, 5)).test();

                ar.print(n, 2);

                if (epIsPrime) {
                    ++ePrimeCount;
                    ePrimes.add(new Integer(ep));
                    eMark = " ";
                }
                else {
                    eMark = "c";
                }

                if (gpIsPrime) {
                    ++gPrimeCount;
                    gPrimes.add(new Integer(gp));
                    gMark = " ";
                }
                else {
                    gMark = "c";
                }

                ar.print(ep + eMark, WIDTH);
                ar.print(gp + gMark, WIDTH);
                ar.println();
            }

        ar.println();

        ar.print(" ", 2);
        ar.print(ePrimeCount + " primes", WIDTH);
        ar.print(gPrimeCount + " primes", WIDTH);
        ar.println();

        ar.print(" ", 2);
        ar.print(ePrimes.size() + " distinct", WIDTH);
        ar.print(gPrimes.size() + " distinct", WIDTH);
        ar.println();
    }
}
```

Output:

n	n^2 - 79n + 1601	41n^2 - 4641n + 88007
0	1601	88007
1	1523	83407
2	1447	78889
3	1373	74453
4	1301	70099
5	1231	65827
6	1163	61637
7	1097	57529
8	1033	53503
9	971	49559
10	911	45697
11	853	41917c
12	797	38219
13	743	34603
14	691	31069
15	641	27617
16	593	24247
17	547	20959
18	503	17753c
19	461	14629
20	421	11587
21	383	8627
22	347	5749
23	313	2953
24	281	239
25	251	2393
26	223	4943
27	197	7411
28	173	9797c
29	151	12101
30	131	14323
31	113	16463c
32	97	18521
33	83	20497c
34	71	22391
35	61	24203
36	53	25933
37	47	27581
38	43	29147
39	41	30631
40	41	32033c
41	43	33353
42	47	34591
43	53	35747
44	61	36821

45	71	37813
46	83	38723
47	97	39551
48	113	40297c
49	131	40961
50	151	41543
51	173	42043
52	197	42461
53	223	42797
54	251	43051
55	281	43223
56	313	43313
57	347	43321
58	383	43247c
59	421	43091c
60	461	42853
61	503	42533
62	547	42131
63	593	41647
64	641	41081
65	691	40433
66	743	39703
67	797	38891
68	853	37997
69	911	37021
70	971	35963
71	1033	34823c
72	1097	33601
73	1163	32297
74	1231	30911
75	1301	29443
76	1373	27893
77	1447	26261
78	1523	24547
79	1601	22751
80	1681c	20873
81	1763c	18913
82	1847	16871
83	1933	14747
84	2021c	12541
85	2111	10253
86	2203	7883
87	2297	5431
88	2393	2897
89	2491c	281
90	2591	2417
91	2693	5197
92	2797	8059

93	2903	11003
94	3011	14029
95	3121	17137
96	3233c	20327
97	3347	23599
98	3463	26953
99	3581	30389

	95 primes	90 primes
	55 distinct	90 distinct

Along with finding the next Mersenne prime, mathematicians also strive to find quadratic polynomials that generate the highest percentage of primes for the largest domain of input values.

15.7 Prime Number Patterns

If there are quadratic polynomials that generate a high percentage of prime numbers, then there is a pattern to the distribution of these generated primes. Can we make this pattern visible?

If we arrange the numbers in a spiral, then the formulas that generate numbers that lie diagonally are quadratic polynomials. In the following example, the numbers 1, 3, 7, 13, 21, and so on are generated by the formula $n^2 + n + 1$ for integer values of $n \geq 0$.

100	99	98	97	96	95	94	93	92	91
65	64	63	62	61	60	59	58	57	90
66	37	36	35	34	33	32	31	56	89
67	38	17	16	15	14	13	30	55	88
68	39	18	5	4	3	12	29	54	87
69	40	19	6	1	2	11	28	53	86
70	41	20	7	8	9	10	27	52	85
71	42	21	22	23	24	25	26	51	84
72	43	44	45	46	47	48	49	50	83
73	74	75	76	77	78	79	80	81	82

Because so many primes are generated by quadratic polynomials, we can see these primes as diagonal "streaks." These streaks are visible even with only 100 numbers. For example, the primes 5, 19, 41, and 71 are generated by the polynomial $4n^2 + 10n + 5$ for $n = 0, 1, 2,$ and 3.

Another way to see these streaks is to arrange the numbers diagonally at right angles to the main diagonal from the upper left to the lower right. However, with 100 numbers, they are less visible than with the spiral arrangement.

1	3	6	10	15	21	28	36	45	55
2	5	9	14	20	27	35	44	54	64
4	8	13	19	26	34	43	53	63	72
7	12	18	25	33	42	52	62	71	79
11	17	24	32	41	51	61	70	78	85
16	23	31	40	50	60	69	77	84	90
22	30	39	49	59	68	76	83	89	94
29	38	48	58	67	75	82	88	93	97
37	47	57	66	74	81	87	92	96	99
46	56	65	73	80	86	91	95	98	100

Screen 15–5a is a screen shot of Program 15–5 displaying a 500 × 500 spiral arrangement.[9] When we start with 41 instead of 1, the prime numbers generated by Euler's original polynomial

Screen 15–5a Prime streaks with the numbers arranged in a spiral. The long diagonal streak from the lower left corner to the upper right corner consists of the primes generated by Euler's quadratic polynomial.

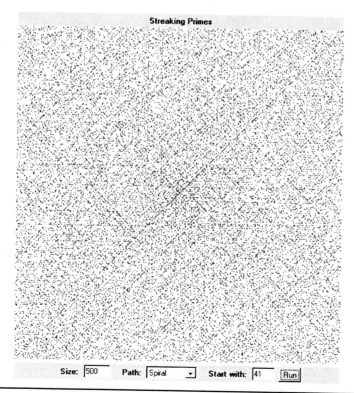

Screen 15–5b Prime streaks with the numbers arranged diagonally across the main diagonal.

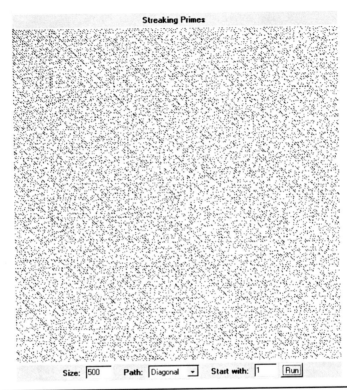

$n^2 + n + 41$ appear dramatically as the long diagonal from the lower left corner to the upper right corner. Other diagonal streaks are visible.

Screen 15–5b is a screen shot of Program 15–5 displaying a 500×500 diagonal arrangement. With more numbers, the prime streaks are more visible. Unlike the spiral arrangement, the streaks here are all parallel to the main diagonal.

References

Congruences, prime numbers, and primality testing are major topics of elementary number theory.

Crandall, Richard, and Carl Pomerance, *Prime Numbers: A Computational Perspective,* New York: Springer-Verlag, 2001.

This book discusses the theoretical and computational aspects of prime numbers. Crandall and Pomerance cover primality testing in Chapter 4.

Gardner, Martin, "The Remarkable Lore of Prime Numbers." In *Mathematics: An Introduction to Its Spirit and Use,* edited by M. Kline, San Francisco: W.H. Freeman and Company, 1979.

This is an article about patterns in prime numbers when numbers are arranged in a spiral.

Herkommer, Mark, *Number Theory: A Programmer's Guide,* New York: McGraw-Hill, 1999.

This book on number theory emphasizes computer programming. Chapter 8 discusses both the Lucas test and the Miller-Rabin test, and it includes programs written in C that implement these tests.

Koshy, Thomas, *Elementary Number Theory with Applications,* San Diego: Harcourt Academic Press, 2002.

This is an excellent introduction to number theory. The textbook covers congruences in Chapter 4, Fermat's Little Theorem in Chapter 7, and primality testing in Chapter 10. Some of the necessary background for understanding the Lucas-Lehmer test is in Chapter 11.

Ribenboim, Paulo, *The New Book of Prime Number Records,* New York: Springer-Verlag, 1996.

This book also discusses the theoretical and computational aspects of prime numbers. Ribenboim covers primality testing in Chapter 2 and prime-generating polynomials in Chapter 3.

The Web is a good place to search for information on primality testing. For example, *http://mathworld.wolfram.com/Lucas-LehmerTest.html* has a good explanation of the Lucas-Lehmer test, and it includes links to related topics.

CHAPTER **16**

FRACTALS

Since the ancient days of Plato and Euclid of classical Greece, mathematicians have worked with "pure" geometric figures and solids, such as circles, rectangles, spheres, cubes, and pyramids. But these are human-made and do not generally occur in nature, which is rough-edged and chaotic. In the 20th century, mathematicians began to study shapes generated by functions that are iterated. In the past 30 years or so, their ideas have come together into a new branch of mathematics called *fractals*. Mathematicians now use fractals to model dynamical systems and to describe shapes and patterns found in nature.

We saw iterated functions in the last part of Chapter 5 when we used fixed-point iteration to find the roots of a function. In this chapter, we'll use that as a starting point, then move on to the generation of fractal images of Julia sets, and finally to the Mandelbrot set.

This chapter can only graze the surface of this new mathematics. Explaining why *iterated* functions generate *recursive* images is beyond the scope of this book, but we can still appreciate the intricacy and beauty of the fractal images.

16.1 Fixed-Point Iteration and Orbits

In Chapter 5, we saw how we can iterate a function by applying it to itself repeatedly. If there is a value that remains unchanged by the iteration, then that value is a *fixed point*, and we are performing *fixed-point iteration*. The function $f(x) = x^2$ has a fixed point at 0, since

$$f(0) = f(f(0)) = f(f(f(0))) = \ldots = f^N(0) = 0$$

and another fixed point at 1.

429

If we perform fixed-point iteration on a function with a starting value x_0, then the values that the iteration generates is the *orbit* of x_0. For $f(x) = x^2$, the orbit of 0.5 is 0.5, 0.25, 0.0625, 0.00390625, . . . and the orbit of 3 is 3, 9, 81, 6561, ...

0 is an attracting fixed point for $f(x) = x^2$, since the orbit of any x in the region $-1 < x < 1$ converges to 0. This region is the fixed point's *basin of attraction*. On the other hand, 1 is a repelling fixed point for the function. If we choose an x value slightly less than 1, its orbit converges to 0, and any x value greater than 1 has an orbit that "escapes" to infinity.

Some orbits neither converge nor escape but are periodic—the orbit values cycle. A simple example is the function $f(x) = \frac{1}{x}$, which has two fixed points, -1 and $+1$, and the orbit of any other value $x \neq 0$ is the cycle $x, \frac{1}{x}, x, \frac{1}{x}, x$, and so on.

16.2 Bifurcation and the Real Function $f(x) = x^2 + c$

For the class of functions of the form $f(x) = x^2 + c$, where c is a constant, let's see what happens under fixed-point iteration. The plot of such a function is a parabola centered about the y axis, and different values of c simply move the parabola up or down the axis.

As shown in Figure 16–0a, when $c > \frac{1}{4}$, the parabola lies above the $x = y$ line, and all orbits escape to $+$infinity.

When $c = \frac{1}{4}$, the parabola touches the $x = y$ line at $x = \frac{1}{2}$, and so that is a fixed point. See Figure 16–0b. It is a repelling point, since all orbits escape to $+$infinity.

Finally, when $c < \frac{1}{4}$, the parabola crosses the $x = y$ line at two different fixed points, x_1 and x_2, where $x_1 < x_2$. See Figure 16–0c. The behavior of the orbit of x depends on where x is in re-

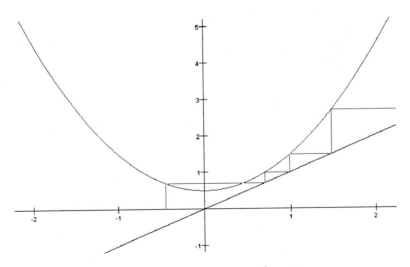

Figure 16–0a   Fixed-point iteration of the function $f(x) = x^2 + 0.5$.

lation to x_1 and x_2. For all $x > x_2$, the orbits escape to $+$infinity. For all x between $-x_2$ and x_2, the orbits eventually become periodic about x_1. Finally, for all $x < -x_2$, the orbits again escape to $+$infinity.

Thus, we see that the different values for c affect the behavior of orbits. Another way to examine this behavior graphically is to plot the orbits of only $x = 0$ for various values of c. For an

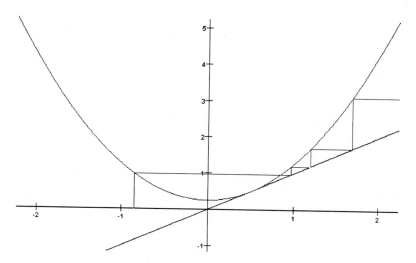

Figure 16–0b   Fixed-point iteration of the function $f(x) = x^2 + 0.25$.

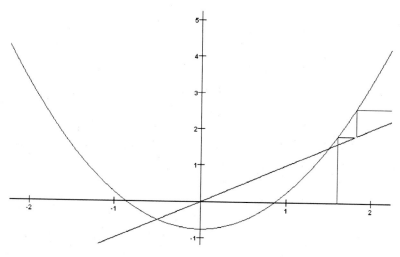

Figure 16–0c   Fixed-point iteration of the function $f(x) = x^2 - 0.75$ with different starting x values.

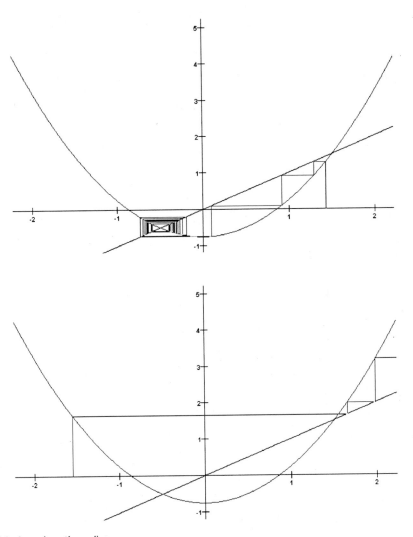

Figure 16–0c   *(continued)*

iterated function, the value 0 is the *critical point,* and its orbit is the *critical orbit.* Program 16–1
plots the critical orbits, and Screen 16–1a shows its output.

In Screen 16–1a, the different values of c from -2 through $+2$ run along the horizontal
axis. Above each value of c, the program plots vertically the values of the orbit of $x = 0$.

Listing 16–1 shows class `PlotThread` of the program.[1] The constant `MAX_ITERS` is 200,
so the program computes only the first 200 values of each orbit. Also, the constant `SKIP_ITERS`

---

[1]   You can download all the Java source code for the programs in this chapter. See the downloading instructions in the
preface of this book.

Screen 16–1a The bifurcation diagram of $f(x) = x^2 + c$ for $-2 < c < +2$ and the orbits of $x = 0$.

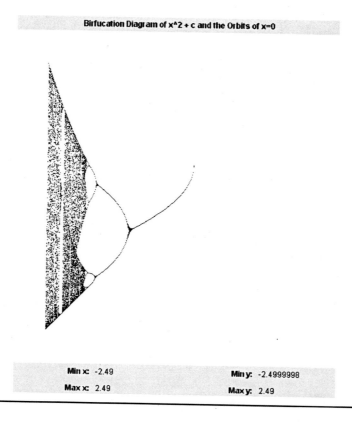

Birfucation Diagram of x^2 + c and the Orbits of x=0

Min x: -2.49	Min y: -2.4999998
Max x: 2.49	Max y: 2.49

is 50. The program does not plot the first 50 values of each orbit—it's interested only in each orbit's eventual behavior.

Listing 16–1 Class `PlotThread` of Program 16–1, which plots the bifurcation diagram of the function $f(x) = x^2 + c$.

```
private static final int SKIP_ITERS =   50;
private static final int MAX_ITERS   = 200;

/**
 * Graph thread class that creates a bifurcation diagram of
 * the function f(x) = x^2 + c.  For each value of c, it plots
```

```
 * the values of the orbit of x=0.
 */
private class PlotThread extends Thread
{
    public void run()
    {
        // Loop over the horizontal axis.
        for (int col = 0; col < w; ++col) {
            float c = xMin + col*delta;
            float x = 0;

            for (int i = 0; i < MAX_ITERS; ++i) {
                x = x*x + c;

                if (i >= SKIP_ITERS) {
                    float y = x;
                    int row = Math.round((yMax - y)/delta);
                    plotPoint(col, row, Color.blue);
                }
            }

            // Draw a row of the graph.
            drawPlot();
            yield();
        }
    }
}
```

The result is a *bifurcation* diagram, so-called because it shows how, for certain values of c, the orbit values split into two camps. "Holes" in the diagram indicate periodic orbits. As the value of c changes from left to right, the orbits change from being chaotic to periodic to stable.

There is order even in the chaotic regions. The diagram is recursive—if we "zoom in" on a rectangular region of the diagram, we see that this region of the graph is similar to the whole graph. This recursive behavior, or "self similarity," is the key characteristic of fractal images.

The screen shots in Screen 16–1b show this. We use the mouse to drag a rectangle around a region of the diagram, and then the program redraws that region at a larger scale.

Theoretically, we can continue zooming into the diagram indefinitely. But in this program, at the zoomed-in "higher resolutions," the single-precision computations will have lost too many significant digits to be accurate.

Screen 16–1b Zooming in on a rectangular region of the bifurcation diagram.

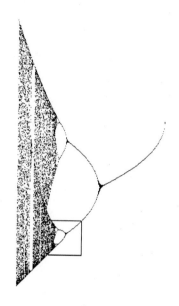

Birfucation Diagram of x^2 + c and the Orbits of x=0

Min x: -1.6	Min y: -1.5199997
Max x: -1.0	Max y: -1.0

16.3 Julia Sets and the Complex Function $f(z) = z^2 + c$

Let's now move to the complex plane and iterate the function $f(z) = z^2 + c$, where z and c are complex numbers. If we let the horizontal axis represent the real parts of the complex numbers and the vertical axis represent their imaginary parts, then we can generate two-dimensional graphs.

We'll need to be able to do some basic complex arithmetic:

$$(a + bi) \pm (c + di) = (a + c) \pm (b + d)i$$
$$(a + bi) \times (c + di) = (ac - bd) + (ad + bc)i$$

$$\frac{a + bi}{c + di} = \frac{ac + bd}{c^2 + d^2} + \left(\frac{bc - ad}{c^2 + d^2}\right)i$$

Screen 16–1b *(continued)*

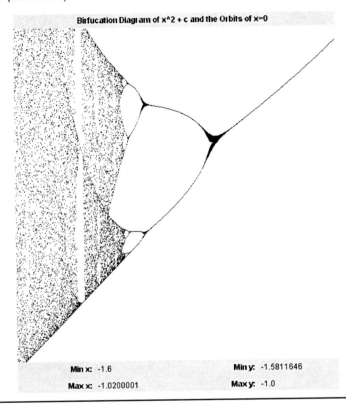

Birfucation Diagram of x^2 + c and the Orbits of x=0

Min x: -1.6		**Min y:** -1.5811646	
Max x: -1.0200001		**Max y:** -1.0	

Also,

$$a + bi = c + di \text{ if and only if } a = c \text{ and } b = d$$

Listing 16–2a shows class `Complex` in package `numbercruncher.mathutils`.

Listing 16–2a Class `Complex`.

```
package numbercruncher.mathutils;

/**
 * Perform basic complex arithmetic.  The complex objects are
 * immutable, and complex operations create new complex objects.
 */
public class Complex
{
    /** the real part */        private float real;
    /** the imaginary part */   private float imaginary;
```

```
    /**
     * Constructor.
     * @param real the real part
     * @param imaginary the imaginary part
     */
    public Complex(float real, float imaginary)
    {
        this.real      = real;
        this.imaginary = imaginary;
    }


    /**
     * Return this complex number's real part.
     * @return the real part
     */
    public float real() { return real; }


    /**
     * Return this complex number's imaginary part.
     * @return the imaginary part
     */
    public float imaginary() { return imaginary; }


    /**
     * Compute this complex number's modulus
     */
    public float modulus()
    {
        return (float) Math.sqrt(real*real + imaginary*imaginary);
    }


    /**
     * Return whether or not this complex number
     * is equal to another one.
     * @param z the other complex number
     * @return true if equal, false if not
     */
    public boolean equal(Complex z)
    {
        return (real == z.real()) && (imaginary == z.imaginary());
    }


    /**
     * Add another complex number to this one.
     * @param a the other complex number
     * @return a new complex number that is the sum
     */
    public Complex add(Complex z)
```

```
{
    return new Complex(real + z.real(),
                       imaginary + z.imaginary());
}


/**
 * Subtract another complex number from this one.
 * @param a the other complex number
 * @return a new complex number that is the difference
 */
public Complex subtract(Complex z)
{
    return new Complex(real - z.real(),
                       imaginary - z.imaginary());
}


/**
 * Multiply this complex number by another one.
 * @param a the other complex number
 * @return a new complex number that is the product
 */
public Complex multiply(Complex z)
{
    return new Complex(real*z.real() - imaginary*z.imaginary(),
                       real*z.imaginary() + imaginary*z.real());
}


/**
 * Divide this complex number by another one.
 * @param a the other complex number
 * @return a new complex number that is the quotient
 */
public Complex divide(Complex z)
{
    float denom = z.real()*z.real() + z.imaginary()*z.imaginary();
    float qr    = (real*z.real() + imaginary*z.imaginary())/denom;
    float qi    = (imaginary*z.real() - real*z.imaginary())/denom;

    return new Complex(qr, qi);
}
/**
 * Return the string representation of this complex number.
 * @return the string representation
 */
public String toString()
{
```

```
        String operator = (imaginary >= 0) ? "+" : "-";
        return real + operator + Math.abs(imaginary) + "i";
    }
}
```

Note that class `Complex` follows the design pattern of classes `java.math.BigDecimal` and `java.math.BigInteger`. Each `Complex` object is immutable, and a `Complex` operation generates a new `Complex` object.

Program 16–2 iterates complex functions of the form $f(z) = z^2 + c$ for various values of c to plot the set of points whose orbits are bounded—they do not escape. This set of points whose orbits either converge or cycle is called the Julia set, and the plot is a fractal image.[2] The program forms a complex value $z = x + yi$ for each point in the xy plane. It can accept a manually entered value for the complex number c, or the program can randomly generate a value. Listing 16–2b shows class `PlotThread` of the program, which performs the iterations and plots the resulting Julia set.

Listing 16–2b Class `PlotThread` of Program 16–2, which plots the Julia set of the complex function $f(z) = z^2 + c$.

```
private static final int MAX_ITERS      = 32;
private static final int ESCAPE_MODULUS =  2;

/**
 * Graph thread class that iterates z^2 + c as z varies over
 * each point in the complex plane bounded by the rectangle
 * xMin, xMax, yMin, yMax.
 */
private class PlotThread extends Thread
{
    public void run()
    {
        // Loop over each graph panel pixel.
        for (int row = 0; row < h; ++row) {
            float y0 = yMax - row*delta;              // row => y0
            for (int col = 0; col < w; ++col) {
                float   x0 = xMin + col*delta;        // col => x0
                Complex z  = new Complex(x0, y0);     // z = x0 + y0i
```

---

[2] French mathematician Gaston Julia (1893–1978) was 25 when he first developed his theories on complex functions whose values stay bounded as the functions are iterated. Unfortunately, his work was mostly forgotten until the 1970s.

```
        if (stopFlag) return;

        boolean escaped = false;
        int     iters   = 0;
        float   x       = x0;
        float   y       = y0;
        float   modulus;

        // Iterate z^2 + c, keeping track of the
        // iteration count.
        do {
            z = z.multiply(z).add(c);
            modulus = z.modulus();
            escaped = modulus > ESCAPE_MODULUS;
        } while ((++iters < MAX_ITERS) && (!escaped));

        // Escaped: Set the shade of gray based on the
        // number of iterations needed to escape.  The
        // more iterations, the darker the shade.
        if (escaped) {
            int k = 255 - (255*iters)/MAX_ITERS;
            k = Math.min(k, 240);
            plotPoint(col, row, new Color(k, k, k));
        }

        // No escape: Set the colors based on the
        // last computed modulus.
        else {
            int m = ((int) (100*modulus))
                                /ESCAPE_MODULUS + 1;
            int r = (307*m)&255;
            int g = (353*m)&255;
            int b = (401*m)&255;
            plotPoint(col, row, new Color(r, g, b));
        }
    }

    // Draw a row of the graph.
    drawPlot();
    yield();
        }
    }
}
```

The values of the orbit of each value of z are complex. To determine whether the orbit escapes or stays bounded, `PlotThread` tests the moduli of the orbit values. If the modulus of any orbit value is greater than `ESCAPE_MODULUS`, then the orbit has escaped. If there is no escape after `MAX_ITERS` number of iterations, then the orbit is bounded.

For each value of z whose orbit escapes, `PlotThread` plots a point in a shade of gray to represent the point's "escape velocity"—the more iterations it took to escape, the darker the shade. If the orbit did not escape, then `PlotThread` plots a point using a color based on the modulus of the last computed orbit value.

As we can see from Listing 16–2b, the programming is very straightforward, yet it produces beautifully intricate images. Screen 16–2a shows screen shots of two examples of the images this program can generate.

Screen 16–2a Screen shots of two fractal images of Julia sets produced by Program 16–2.

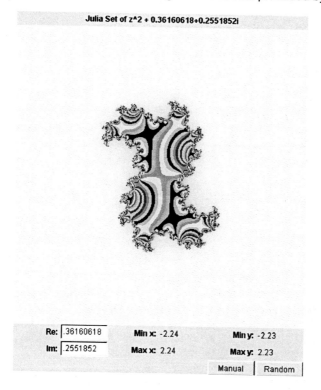

Screen 16–2a *(continued)*

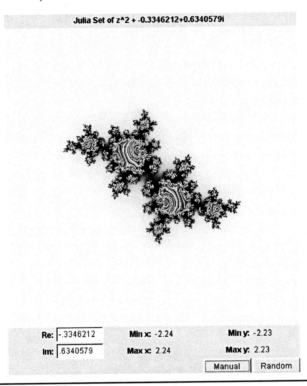

Julia Set of z^2 + -0.3346212+0.6340579i

Re:	-.3346212	Min x: -2.24	Min y: -2.23
Im:	.6340579	Max x: 2.24	Max y: 2.23
			Manual Random

Like the bifurcation diagram, the fractal image of a Julia set is recursive. Screen 16–2b shows using the mouse to select a rectangular region to zoom into. Each region resembles the whole image. At "higher magnifications," we can also see more clearly the different escape velocities. The gray shading is darkest at the border of the fractal image, since that is the boundary between points on one side whose orbits are bounded and points on the other side whose orbits barely escaped at the maximum number of iterations.

16.4 Newton's Algorithm in the Complex Plane

In Chapter 5, we examined Newton's algorithm, where the iteration formula was

$$x - \frac{f(x)}{f'(x)}$$

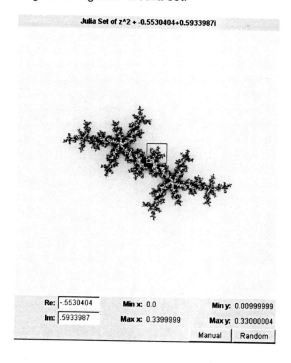

Julia Set of z^2 + -0.5530404+0.5933987i

Re:	-.5530404	Min x:	0.0	Min y:	0.00999999
Im:	.5933987	Max x:	0.3399999	Max y:	0.33000004
				Manual	Random

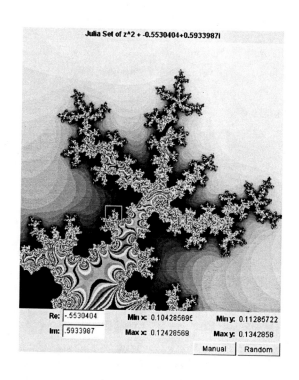

Julia Set of z^2 + -0.5530404+0.5933987i

Re:	-.5530404	Min x:	0.104285695	Min y:	0.11285722
Im:	.5933987	Max x:	0.12428569	Max y:	0.1342858
				Manual	Random

Screen 16–2b *(continued)*

We can also apply this formula in the complex plane. For example, consider the complex function $f(z) = z^3 - 1$, where z is a complex number. This function has three roots: $1, -\frac{1}{2} + \frac{\sqrt{3}}{2}i \, (\approx -0.5 + 0.9i)$, and $-\frac{1}{2} - \frac{\sqrt{3}}{2}i \, (\approx -0.5 - 0.9i)$. If we apply Newton's algorithm, the iteration formula is

$$z - \frac{z^3 - 1}{3z^2}$$

and the three roots are each attracting fixed points.

Of course, for a point z in the complex plane, the number of iterations required to converge to one of the fixed points depends on the point's location. But what is intriguing is that the basins of attraction (the sets of points that converge their corresponding fixed points) do not cleanly separate the plane into three contiguous regions. Instead, their basins are intricately intertwined along their borders.

Program 16–3 plots this behavior by coloring each point in the complex plane red, green, or blue, depending on to which fixed point its orbit converges, and setting the color intensity based on the number of iterations needed to reach the fixed point. The result will be the fractal image of a Julia set. Listing 16–3 shows the program's class `PlotThread`.

Listing 16–3 Class `PlotThread` of Program 16–3, which plots the Julia set from applying Newton's algorithm to the complex function $f(z) = z^3 - 1$.

```java
private static final int      MAX_ITERS = 100;
private static final Complex ONE       = new Complex(1, 0);
private static final Complex THREE     = new Complex(3, 0);

/**
 * Graph thread class that applies Newton's Method to z^3 - 1
 * starting at each point in the complex plane.
 */
private class PlotThread extends Thread
{
    public void run()
    {
        // Loop over each graph panel pixel.
        for (int r = 0; r < h; ++r) {
            for (int c = 0; c < w; ++c) {

                if (stopFlag) return;

                // Convert the pixel coordinates to the
                // initial (x, y) in the complex plane.
                float x = xMin + c*delta;
                float y = yMax - r*delta;

                Complex z = new Complex(x, y);
                Complex zOld;

                // Loop until z converges.
                // Keep track of the number of iterations.
                int iters = 0;
                do {
                    Complex zSquared = z.multiply(z);
                    Complex zCubed   = zSquared.multiply(z);

                    zOld = z;
                    z = z.subtract(zCubed.subtract(ONE)
                            .divide(THREE.multiply(zSquared)));
                } while ((++iters < MAX_ITERS)
                            && (!z.equal(zOld)));

                // Set the color intensity based on
                // the number of iterations.
                int k = 20*(iters%10);

                // Set red, green, or blue according to
                // which root z converged to.
                if (z.real() > 0) {
```

```
                    // 1
                    plotPoint(c, r, new Color(k, k, 255));
                }
                else if (z.imaginary() > 0) {
                    // -0.5+0.8660254i
                    plotPoint(c, r, new Color(k, 255, k));
                }
                else {
                    // -0.5-0.8660254i
                    plotPoint(c, r, new Color(255, k, k));
                }
            }

            // Draw a row of the graph.
            drawPlot();
            yield();
        }
    }
```

Screen 16–3 shows the program's initial output. Because it is a graph of a Julia set, we can repeatedly use the mouse to zoom into any rectangular region. Each zoomed-in region will resemble the larger region it was taken from.

Screen 16–3 The Julia set from applying Newton's algorithm to the complex function $f(z) = z^3 - 1$.

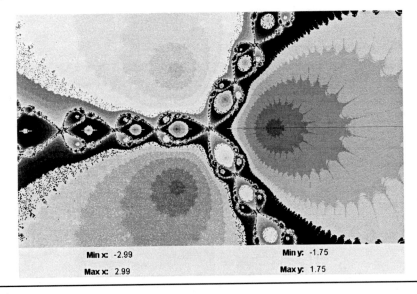

| Min x: -2.99 | Min y: -1.75 |
| Max x: 2.99 | Max y: 1.75 |

16.5 The Mandelbrot Set

Program 16–2 iterated complex functions of the form $f(z) = z^2 + c$ by varying the value of z over the complex plane for any given value of the constant c. The results were graphs of the Julia sets containing those z values whose orbits were bounded.

We can turn this around and vary the value of the constant c over the complex plane and, for each value of c, compute its critical orbit—the orbit that starts with $z_0 = 0 + 0i$. (Compare this with the bifurcation diagram.) The graph we would generate is the Mandelbrot set containing the c values with bounded critical orbits.[3]

Listing 16–4 shows class `PlotThread` of Program 16–4, which plots the Mandelbrot set.

Listing 16–4 Class `PlotThread` of Program 16–4, which plots the Mandelbrot set of the complex function $f(z) = z^2 + c$.

```
private static final int MAX_ITERS      = 32;
private static final int ESCAPE_MODULUS =  2;

/**
 * Graph thread class that iterates z^2 + c as c varies over
 * each point in the complex plane bounded by the rectangle
 * xMin, xMax, yMin, yMax.
 */
private class PlotThread extends Thread
{
    public void run()
    {
        // Loop over each graph panel pixel.
        for (int row = 0; row < h; ++row) {
            float y0 = yMax - row*delta;                // row => y0

            for (int col = 0; col < w; ++col) {
                float    x0 = xMin + col*delta;     // col => x0
                Complex c  = new Complex(x0, y0);   // z = x0 + y0i
                Complex z  = new Complex(0, 0);

                if (stopFlag) return;

                boolean escaped = false;
                int     iters   = 0;
                float   x       = x0;
                float   y       = y0;
                float   modulus;
```

---

3   Benoit Mandelbrot, who was born in Poland in 1924, is currently a mathematics professor at Yale University. In the 1970s, while working as a researcher at IBM, he explored Julia sets and coined the word *fractals*. He is now recognized as the founder of fractal geometry.

```
// Iterate z^2 + c, keeping track of the
// iteration count.
do {
    z = z.multiply(z).add(c);
    modulus = z.modulus();
    escaped = modulus > ESCAPE_MODULUS;
} while ((++iters < MAX_ITERS) && (!escaped));

// Escaped: Set the shade of gray based on the
// number of iterations needed to escape.  The
// more iterations, the darker the shade.
if (escaped) {
    int k = 255 - (255*iters)/MAX_ITERS;
    k = Math.min(k, 240);
    plotPoint(col, row, new Color(k, k, k));
}

// No escape: Set the colors based on the modulus.
else {
    int m = ((int) (100*modulus))
                        /ESCAPE_MODULUS + 1;
    int r = (101*m)&255;
    int g = (149*m)&255;
    int b = (199*m)&255;
    plotPoint(col, row, new Color(r, g, b));
}
}

// Draw a row of the graph.
drawPlot();
yield();
}
}
}
```

As before, we consider a point to be bounded if its modulus does not exceed ESCAPE_MODULUS within MAX_ITERS number of iterations. Like Program 16–2, this program plots in shades of gray the points with escaping critical orbits. It plots in color the points with bounded critical orbits. Screen 16–4a shows the initial plot of the Mandelbrot set.

Like all the other fractal images, the image of the Mandelbrot set is recursive. By using the mouse to zoom into various regions along the "coastline" of the set, we can find images such as those in Screen 16–4b.

One way to look at the Mandelbrot set is that it is a catalogue of Julia sets. Because each point within the Mandelbrot set represents a c value for the function $f(z) = z^2 + c$, we could feed each such c value into Program 16–2 to generate and plot the corresponding Julia set.

Screen 16–4a The initial plot of the Mandelbrot set by Program 16–4.

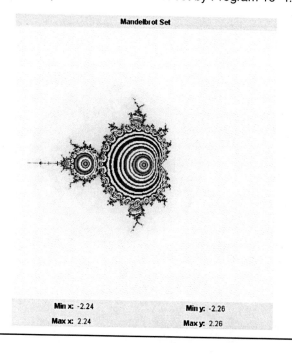

Mandelbrot Set

Min x: -2.24 Min y: -2.26
Max x: 2.24 Max y: 2.26

Screen 16–4b Two zoomed-in regions of the Mandelbrot set.

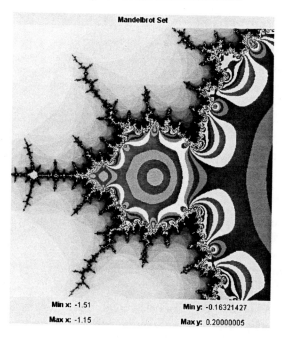

Mandelbrot Set

Min x: -1.51 Min y: -0.16321427
Max x: -1.15 Max y: 0.20000005

Screen 16–4b *(continued)*

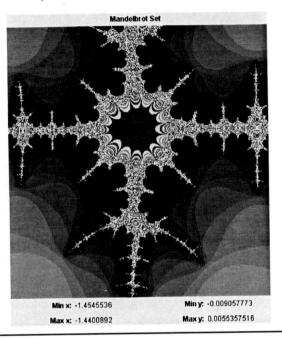

Mandelbrot Set

Min x: -1.4545536   Min y: -0.009057773

Max x: -1.4400892   Max y: 0.0055357516

References

Devaney, Robert L., *Chaos, Fractals, and Dynamics: Computer Experiments in Mathematics,* Menlo Park, CA: Addison-Wesley, 1990.

This is a good introductory book on fractals. It explains the mathematics carefully, and it contains simple programs written in BASIC.

Gleick, James, *Chaos: Making a New Science,* New York: Viking, 1987.

This is an excellent, nonmathematical introduction to chaos.

Mandelbrot, Benoit B., *The Fractal Geometry of Nature,* New York: W. H. Freeman and Company, 1983.

This is the original source material, and it discusses some of the motivations of the author and founder of fractal geometry.

Peitgen, Heinz-Otto, Hartmut Juergens, and Dietmar Saupe, *Chaos and Fractals: New Frontiers of Science,* New York: Springer-Verlag, 1992.

In nearly 1,000 pages, this advanced textbook presents a thorough, yet readable, discussion of fractals and their applications.

Index

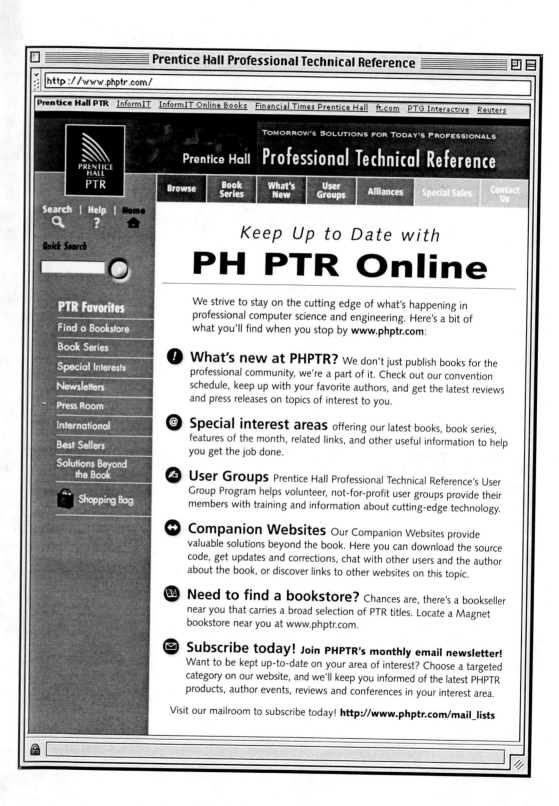

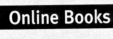